PRAISE FOR "GRADUATE SCHOOL"

"This guidebook takes the guesswork out of the graduate education process. If I had to select one guide as the single most important tool for prospective graduate students or for those working with prospective graduate students, I would recommend your 2nd edition without hesitation. It's like having your own personal advising staff on call. . . . In a word, Magnificent!"

Mary K. Clark, PhD
Program Representative and Director of the Rackham Summer Institute
Office of Student Recruitment and Support
H.H. Rackham School of Graduate Studies, University of Michigan

"Finally, a resource to guide you through the maze of resources about graduate and professional study offered in print and online. This unusually thorough, honest, and complete reference book quickly helps you find and evaluate the information you need . . . a 'must' if you are considering any kind of graduate program."

Paula Zimmer
Director, Employer & Educational Recruiting
Career Development Office, Smith College

"Making the investment in a graduate program is a significant decision of time, money, and effort. This resource will guarantee a very competitive rate of return."

Mary Jean Thornton
Catholic Library Association Journal, February 1999

"The new and expanded edition offers something for everyone, whether they are clearly focused on a specific career path or just weighing their options. Resources like this one are far too rare."

Larry Knopp, PhD, Professor & Head of Geography
University of Minnesota-Duluth

"Graduate School is a thoughtful, detailed selection of strategic tools. Including new media services, such as the World Wide Web, this resource collection is at once extensive and precise."

Andrew Carr, Master of Journalism Candidate
Temple University School of Communication & Theater
Client Relations Manager, Delaware Investments, Philadelphia

"This newly reorganized volume integrates a vast amount of information. Professional advisors and students alike will profit from the insightful and frank reviews of both print and Internet resources. The directory of Helpful Organizations rounds out the offerings, making this book a true 'find.'"

Mary L. Hanneman, PhD, Visiting Assistant Professor & Assistant Director
Pacific Rim Center, University of Washington, Tacoma

GRADUATE SCHOOL

The Best Resources
to
HELP YOU CHOOSE,
GET IN, & PAY

Second Edition

Jane Finkle, MS
Editor

A RESOURCE PATHWAYS GUIDEBOOK

Seattle, Washington

Published by Resource Pathways, Inc.
22525 S.E. 64th Place, Suite 253
Issaquah, WA 98027

Editor: Jane Finkle, MS

Managing Editor:
        Julie Pickering, MA

Researchers:
        Joan Elmenhurst, Jacquelline Cobb Fuller,
        Dana Lynch, Lesley Reed, Lisle Steelsmith

Book Design and Production:
        Sandra Harner and Kelly Rush
        Laing Communications Inc., Redmond, WA

Printing: DeHart Printing, Santa Clara, CA

Publisher's Cataloging-in-Publication

Graduate school : the best resources to help you
        choose, get in, & pay / Jane Finkle, editor. --
        2nd ed.
            p. cm.
        Includes bibliographical references and index.
        LCCN: 99-65819
        ISBN: 1-892148-11-0

        1. Universities and colleges--Graduate work--
Bibliographies. 2. Student aid--United States--
Handbooks, manuals, etc. 3. Graduate students--
Scholarships, fellowships, etc.--United States--
Handbooks, manuals, etc. I. Finkle, Jane.

Z5814.U7G73 2000   016.3712'17
                     QBI99-1429

CONTENTS

I. Introduction   1

Graduate & Professional Schools: Making It Happen!   2

How This Guidebook Is Organized   4

How We Develop Our Reviews & Recommendations   8

II. Resource Reviews   11

Obtaining A Master's Or PhD   12

   General Resources   19

   Arts, Humanities & Social Sciences   50

     General   50

     Education   53

     English & Foreign Languages   55

     Psychology & Social Work   56

     Visual & Performing Arts   65

   Sciences & Engineering   69

   Miscellaneous   79

Choosing, Getting Into, & Excelling In Business School   84

Choosing, Getting Into, & Excelling In Law School   124

**Choosing, Getting Into, & Excelling In Medical School &
Other Health Science Programs**   174

Financing A Graduate Or Professional Degree   226

Scholarship Directories & Search Services   254

**Of General Interest To Prospective Graduate &
Professional Students**   292

III. A Quick Guide To Internet Resources   317

Obtaining A Master's Or PhD   319

Choosing, Getting Into, & Excelling In Business School   319

Choosing, Getting Into, & Excelling In Law School   320

Choosing, Getting Into, & Excelling In Medical School & Other Health Science Programs   321

Financing A Graduate Or Professional Degree   322

Scholarship Directories & Search Services   323

Of General Interest To Prospective Graduate & Professional Students   324

IV. Helpful Organizations   325

Of General Interest   327

Law School   328

Health Sciences   329

Business School   331

Financial Aid & Scholarships   333

Testing Services   335

Professional Associations   335

Arts & Humanities   335

Psychology, Counseling, & Social Work   338

Other Social Sciences   339

Sciences & Engineering   341

University Organizations   343

Counseling & Career Planning Organizations   344

General Advising   344

Career Counseling   344

Prelaw Counseling   346

Prehealth Counseling   347

International Students & Overseas Study   348

V. Indices   349

Title Index   350

Author Index   354

Publisher Index   357

Media Index   362

Subject Index   366

Resources Of Interest To Specific Audiences   **370**

    Persons Of Color   **370**

    Women   **370**

    International Students   **371**

    Disabled Students   **371**

About The Editor   **373**

About The Advisory Council   **374**

I
INTRODUCTION

Graduate & Professional Schools: Making It Happen!

The dream can start early. Many students are determined to become a doctor or lawyer from childhood, and now medical school or law school is just around the corner. And there's the kid who sets her heart on becoming a geneticist after that first fruit fly experiment in middle school.

Others think about graduate or professional school much later in life. They graduate from college and work for a few years—maybe even have a family—then they notice the job market favors degreed candidates, and they decide to add some letters after their name. Or perhaps they discover a new interest or cause that they want to devote their career to.

Early or late, these folks are in good company. Increasing numbers of college graduates—fresh out of school or seasoned by a few years in the marketplace—are applying to a graduate or professional program.

Some are drawn to the intellectual challenge inherent in graduate education. They thrive on the challenge of the quantitative coursework culminating in a PhD in Economics, the satisfaction of responding well to cold calls in a law school course, or the thrill of discovering mind-body connections in a Master's course in Psychobiology.

Many want to cultivate skills that will help them solve research questions, cure diseases, or manage businesses. Others look forward to a career in teaching, helping others achieve their dreams.

A graduate or professional degree may provide the confidence necessary to take bold steps: change a career, become an entrepreneur, or branch out into a new endeavor. There is no denying the cachet that comes with these degrees. On a resume, it can make the difference between getting that interview and being passed over.

A college degree used to be the key to a satisfying career with respect and good pay, but in many fields, expectations are rising. More and more professional positions require a graduate or professional degree.

The financial rewards for completing a graduate or professional degree are just as enticing. Consider this: The average starting salary for a Wharton MBA graduate is $80,000, and many MBA graduates receive an average $20,000 sign-up bonus, so these folks may start out at close to $100,000 a year. Good performance can up the ante with annual bonuses for valued MBA graduates running an average $25,000.

And in traditionally less remunerating fields, such as education, a teacher with a graduate degree usually earns substantially more than does a colleague with similar experience, but no advanced degree.

Prospective graduate and professional students have to keep these benefits, and their own personal goals, clearly in mind as they traverse the rugged terrain to an advanced degree. The costs and challenges are many. In some fields, each year leading up to graduation is designed as a winnowing process to separate the mildly interested from the doggedly intent, the casual student from the gifted scholar.

Consider these eye-opening statistics:

- Only about one in six who begins a PhD program in the humanities or social sciences finishes.

- The national acceptance rate for medical school applicants stands at 43 percent.

- The median registered time needed to complete a PhD in the sciences has stretched to seven years, eight years for PhDs outside the sciences.

- It is not unusual for an MBA or JD to cost close to $100,000 when you add up the cost of tuition, living expenses, books, computer equipment, and forgone income.

The investment of time, emotional energy, and financial resources necessary to complete a graduate or professional degree is substantial. Those who succeed have one thing in common: they do their homework before school starts, taking advantage of the many resources that can help them make informed decisions.

This guidebook is designed to help students, their families, and advisors do the research essential to academic success. We've identified the best resources for background information, insider insights, and practical advice on success in graduate and professional school—everything from choosing a program to making the most of that new degree. The resources reviewed in this book will help students on each leg of their journey to a graduate or professional degree.

How This Guidebook Is Organized

In this guidebook, we have:

- Identified the key issues facing students considering graduate or professional school and their advisors.

- Provided detailed full-page reviews of over 280 readily available resources, print and Internet, so readers can identify those best suited to their needs and interests.

- Created an extensive table of contents and multiple indexes, which serve as clear "pathways" to the most useful resources for each key issue and discipline.

The competition for admission to and success in these programs can be intimidating. This guidebook is designed to help students and their advisors identify the best resources to help them beat the odds.

We have divided the guidebook into five sections. Following this introduction, readers will find:

Resource Reviews

The heart of the book, these full-page reviews of books, websites, and software products are arranged in eight topical sections. Each includes a fact-filled description, an evaluation section, ease-of-use and overall ratings, background on authors, and publishing and purchasing information.

We've reviewed these resources with the potential graduate or professional student and their advisors in mind. We've thought about the questions that students and advisors would ask, and we found plenty of resources answering those questions. Here are just a few addressed in the reviewed resources.

Obtaining A Master's Or PhD

What criteria should be considered when choosing a program? How can students best identify the program that is right for them? What's the best way to contact faculty at programs of interest? What criteria do departments base their admissions decisions on? How can students establish a good working relationship with their advisors? What skills help students succeed in graduate school? What about international students and nontraditional students who have taken time off between college and graduate study?

Choosing, Applying To, & Excelling In Business School

What should a student look for in a business school? How many years of work experience do students need before applying? What is the average GPA for students at specific schools? What about their GMAT scores? How can students make their application stand out in a crowd? How do they best prepare for a successful MBA experience? What are the latest trends in post-MBA employment?

Choosing, Applying To & Excelling In Law School

How can students be sure that they really want to be a lawyer? How do they identify the program that will work for them? What are the most important factors in law school admissions decisions? How are LSAT scores and GPA used in the admissions process? What have successful applicants to Harvard Law said in their personal statements? Which programs offer joint JD-MBAs? Which schools are distinguished by a strong representation of female or minority faculty?

Choosing, Applying To & Excelling In Medical School & Other Health Science Programs

Medical school represents a big commitment—How can students be sure it is the right choice for them, and how do they identify the program that suits their needs and interests? What about other health science programs, such as dentistry, nursing, and veterinary medicine? What is the best way to learn about a particular program? How does the admissions process work for each discipline? What should applicants focus on to hone their competitive edge? Where do students looking for extra preparation go for help? What about future trends in employment? What should students be thinking about now?

Financing A Graduate Or Professional Degree

Graduate and professional schools cost a lot of money. Where can students, and their families, go to learn about federal and state financial aid programs? What is the average loan burden taken on by students pursuing a terminal Master's? What about a PhD or professional degree? What is a FAFSA?

Scholarship Directories & Search Services

What is the best way to research scholarships? How many scholarships are available for graduate and professional study, and where can students and advisors find out about them? How do they find out about opportunities for under-represented groups? Should students pay a scholarship search service to handle the search for them? What is the difference between "portable" and school-specific scholarships?

Of General Interest To Prospective Graduate & Professional Students

What skills do all prospective graduate and professional students need? What's the secret to writing an outstanding personal statement? How can students and their advisors harness the World Wide Web in researching programs, applying to schools, and financing higher education? Are there any general resources that give students an overview of their options?

These full-page reviews are arranged according to Overall Rating (1–4 Stars) within each topical section: the best resources are always listed first. In each section, we also recommend several outstanding resources—approximately 25 percent of the total—to help readers save time and meet their specific requirements.

A Quick Guide To Internet Resources

This listing of Internet Resources is designed for those readers who want to go straight to the World Wide Web for advice and information. It is arranged by Principle Subject, within each Subject by Overall Rating, then alphabetically by title. Included are the title of the resource, its URL, or Internet "address," its Overall Rating, and a reference to the page in this guidebook where readers will find an in-depth review.

Helpful Organizations

This comprehensive directory provides up-to-date contact and background information on 130-plus organizations offering information, support, and services. The directory is organized by the following topical sections.

- Of General Interest
- Law School
- Health Sciences
- Business School
- Financial Aid & Scholarships
- Testing Services
- Professional Associations
  Arts & Humanities
  Psychology, Counseling, & Social Work
  Other Social Sciences
  Sciences & Engineering

- University Organizations
- Counseling & Career Planning Organizations
  General Advising
  Career Counseling
  Prelaw Counseling
  Prehealth Counseling
  International Students & Overseas Study

Indices

To help readers get to the information they need quickly, we've compiled six indexes. The **Title**, **Author**, and **Publisher** indexes are arranged alphabetically. The **Subject** and **Media** indexes are arranged by Overall Rating, and within Rating groups, alphabetically.

We also provide an index of **Resources Of Interest To Specific Audiences**. This index is arranged by Specific Audience, and within these categories by Subject and Overall Rating. Specific Audiences include:

- Persons Of Color
- Women
- International Students
- Disabled Students

This index is designed to make the most of the resources reviewed here. In our research, we encountered several dozen resources that may be of special interest to specific groups of students. For example, we review an excellent scholarship directory, *Financial Aid for the Disabled and Their Families*.

We also encountered resources designed for the general student population, which devote substantial attention to issues of interest to specific groups. One example is *Princeton Review Best Law Schools 2000*. The bulk of this book comprises profiles of law schools; however, the authors devote an entire chapter to "Diversity in Law School: A Progress Check" and another excellent chapter focuses on the present status of women in law school.

Remember: some of these resources are written specifically for one or more of these groups. Others are written for the general student population, but include chapters that may be helpful to these groups. We encourage readers to consider these resources for a more specific perspective on graduate and professional school selection, admissions, and matriculation.

How We Develop Our Reviews & Recommendations

Our editors and researchers have worked hard to identify consumer-oriented resources focused on graduate and professional education, including books and Internet websites.

We have created a concise, one-page review of each resource. These reviews contain information about the resource (author, publisher, and edition), describe its content and focus, evaluate its quality, style, scope, and effectiveness, and summarize our findings in an Overall Rating and an Ease-Of-Use Rating. We also provide prices and "where to find/buy" information.

FOUR STAR RATING SYSTEM
★★★★   Highly recommended—top quality at a fair price!
★★★   Well done; a solid resource
★★   Worth considering—check the description
★   Your time and money are better spent elsewhere.

We have put a great deal of time and effort into reviewing and evaluating these resources. Here is how the process works:

- **Printed Material:** We read the book cover to cover, identify the author's focus, and make a judgment about how the contents are best applied. Our judgment about the relative quality of each book is based upon readability, organization, depth, and style. We make every effort to ensure that we review the latest editions and never include out-of-print resources.

- **Internet Websites & Online Services:** We review all websites and online services that have significant original material related to graduate and professional programs, financial aid, and scholarships. Our reviews consider the site's graphic and navigation design, as well as the usefulness of the material relative to that available in other media. We revisit sites frequently to stay abreast of revisions and improvements.

We include the current "address" (URL) of the home page or a specific page within a website to facilitate direct access on the

Internet. Of course, the World Wide Web is a dynamic place, and many URLs will change over time. If you find that an address is outdated, we recommend that you simply delete the last expression in the address and hit the "Enter" or "Return" key again.

This procedure will point your browser to a file "further up" in the website's file directory. In most cases, you will return to the website's home page (indicated by the phrase ending in ".com," ".edu," ".gov," etc.). From there, you can find your way back to the specific information or page you were looking for.

Because our mission is to help you find your way through this "forest" of information and take control of the issue at hand, we also make carefully considered recommendations on which resources will best serve your needs.

We recommend only 25 percent of the products reviewed. These recommendations are based on each resource's value, relative to alternatives in the same media and against all available sources regardless of media.

We are confident in the service we provide in these reviews. The best resources reviewed here will help students and their advisors make informed decisions for an exciting future. We wish our readers the best of luck as they embark on their journey toward a graduate or professional degree, or work to help others realize their education dreams.

II

RESOURCE
REVIEWS

II. Obtaining A Master's Or PhD

In this chapter, we introduce resources focusing on graduate study in the pursuit of a Master's or doctoral degree. Some students pursue what is called a "terminal" Master's—part of a practical professional program aimed at enhancing students' professional skills or employability, such as a Master's in Education or Social Work. Others are motivated by a desire to broaden their understanding of the world or to help others.

Students on the academic track may start out with a Master's and go on to enter a doctoral program designed to train scholars for independent research and/or teaching, or increasingly, to enhance their marketability in a highly competitive workplace.

The resources reviewed here offer advice on program selection, admissions, study, and job placement for those interested in a Master's or PhD. Some address the broad spectrum of issues facing these prospective students. Others focus on a specific element—in some cases, a particular program; in others, a specific part of the application or study process.

Resource reviews are arranged in the following topical categories, and within each category, by Overall Rating.

- General Resources, covering a broad spectrum of fields and issues
- Arts & Humanities & Social Sciences
  General
  Education
  English & Foreign Languages
  Psychology & Social Work
  Visual & Performing Arts
- Sciences & Engineering
- Miscellaneous resources of interest

Before diving into these resource reviews, we suggest prospective students consider the following steps in the graduate school process.

Making the Decision: Do I Really Want To Go To Graduate School? Should I Pursue A Master's Or PhD?

Those considering obtaining a Master's or PhD often perform an internal analysis of the costs and benefits of graduate school. Many resources reviewed here are designed to help prospective students assess their professional goals and determine which degree, if either, is best suited for their intended career.

These resources also remind students of the benefits associated with each degree. This insight may be particularly beneficial for the growing number of non-traditional students (those who have been out of college for five or more years) seeking an advanced degree, because some of these students have less access to high-quality graduate school advising.

Several of the guides we recommend devote significant attention to the various costs associated with specific programs. One of the factors that prospective students must take into account is the amount of time required to finish a program. The median time spent in a doctoral program is inching close to eight years! Terminal Master's programs generally last two years, although they can take a lot longer if pursued on a part-time basis.

In addition to the time commitment, students should consider the cost of the program, opportunities for research and internships, and the employment outlook upon graduation.

The resources reviewed here will help prospective students make this important decision. We also urge students, and former students, to take advantage of the career planning services at their alma mater and to talk to their professors about grad school decisions. These folks have plenty of professional expertise and can offer practical tips on navigating the graduate school decision. They also can help on program selection, admission, and study processes.

Researching Programs & Creating A Short List

Although some applicants have their heart set on a particular program from the start, most will need help prioritizing the criteria required to research and select the programs to which they'll apply.

Students interested in a terminal Master's program often base their decision on a program's reputation, size, location, academic rigor, facilities, and financial aid resources, as do many students seeking a professional degree in law, business, or medicine.

Prospective doctoral students are more likely to focus on program specifics and potential advisors, because the ultimate success or failure of a PhD often rides on the doctoral advisor and a program's unique focus and strengths.

Many professors and researchers recommend prospective grad students take advantage of professional associations, such as the American Psychological Association or the Association of American Geographers, and these professional associations' printed and online guides. This is a great way to better understand the field.

Advisors at undergraduate career counseling centers also urge prospective applicants to get in touch with professors, current students, and recent graduates who can provide valuable "insider" information about individual programs, department "culture," faculty specialties, and potential advisors. E-mail is the perfect tool for learning about programs through the "grapevine."

Such networking can make the difference between a mediocre educational experience and a truly satisfying one. While the resources reviewed here provide plenty of valuable information, most do not provide the up-to-date details a professor or current grad student can offer.

And remember: Program rankings and descriptions of broad fields, such as Anthropology or Biology, do not reflect all-important differences in narrower specializations, such as linguistic anthropology or plant physiology. Department and program focus and identity can change rapidly, so smart students look to future colleagues for information on specializations within their prospective discipline.

Students should also remember that their undergraduate institution's career counseling center is a great place to get advice and do research. Most centers have their own reading room, stocked with the latest directories and brochures. And the in-house advisors know where to locate information.

Once students have a clear idea of what they are looking for in a program, the next step is consulting resources describing graduate programs in their chosen field. A number of graduate program directories are available. Some are Internet-based searchable databases. Others are hefty paperback guides containing profiles of graduate school departments and programs.

Some graduate school guides present only objective data on schools, such as the cost of tuition, number of students enrolled, admissions standards, and financial aid. Directories that describe the departments themselves in great detail, as opposed to general information on the whole university, are more useful in our view. We recommend guides that include subjective information on a program's reputation or strengths in a particular area. Such resources can help a political science student determine which departments specialize in East Asian nationalism and a philosophy student track down professors researching epistemic agency.

As students narrow down their search, they may look for resources that rank schools based on a predetermined set of criteria. Ranking schools is a controversial practice that critics say produces an unfair hierarchy based on highly subjective opinions. Students seem to place a great deal of confidence in these rankings, however; the number of applications to a particular school can fluctuate significantly on the word of the more popular ranking publications. Whether students choose to consider rankings in their selection process, they should remember that the quality of the department is as important as the overall reputation of the university.

The guides that we recommend here also outline other methods of researching potential programs, such as campus visits, reviews of faculty publications, and interviews with current and recently graduated students.

Applying To Graduate Programs

Applications for graduate school are usually due in December or January. Students should start requesting applications in September. Too often students and recent grads put off this task until spring.

Applicants should apply to several schools, depending on the level of competition in their field. Their qualifications are evaluated by departmental committees made up of professors who will teach and advise those they admit. For some Master's programs, such as Education, Social Work, Public Policy, International Affairs, and Journalism, decisions are made by the admissions office, with participation from a faculty member. Some programs admit large numbers and count on the crushing coursework of the first year to weed out stragglers. Recent trends suggest programs are admitting fewer applicants, however, in part as a way to increase the funding a department can offer students.

The resources recommended here will help students establish an application "To Do" list and calendar. While many resources cover nuts and bolts application information, we recommend those that include practical tips, as well as insider advice and strategies for making a competitive application. Some applications require a résumé, C.V., or curriculum vitae, as it is known in the academic world.

Application requirements vary from field to field, but five factors are always important:

GPA

An applicant's undergraduate GPA, especially in the major field, is heavily weighted. However, students will be relieved to hear that admissions committees are interested in extenuating circumstances that may account for disappointing grades. The resources we recommend offer guidelines for how and when to "explain" an uneven undergraduate record.

The GRE

The GRE (Graduate Record Examination) General Test measures verbal, quantitative, and analytical reasoning skills. It is currently offered as a computer-based test. The traditional paper-based format is only used at international test sites and for subject tests.

Subject Tests are required for some PhD programs. These measure achievement in a specific area and assume an undergraduate major or extensive background in that discipline.

GRE scores are an important factor in admitting students and in selecting fellowship and assistantship recipients. Applicants planning to take the GRE—and most should—must obtain a copy of the GRE Bulletin. This free publication describes the test, provides registration instructions, and features sample test questions.

For more information about the GRE, or to download a copy of the GRE Bulletin, see our full-page review of GRE Online on page 39. Most career planning centers will have copies of the Bulletin on hand.

Contact the Educational Testing Service, which administers the GRE at:

> Graduate Record Examinations
> Educational Testing Service
> P.O. Box 6000
> Princeton, NJ 08541-6000
> email: gre-info@ets.org
> phone: (609) 771-7670

The Miller Analogies Test

The Miller Analogies Test (MAT) is a standardized test of verbal analogies used to assist graduate departments and schools in their admissions process. Some PhD programs in Psychology and Education offer applicants a choice of taking the GRE or the MAT.

The MAT comprises 100 analogies, given in a timed, 50-minute test period. It is given at "Controlled Test Centers," usually on college and university campuses around the United States. For registration information, contact:

> The Psychological Corporation
> Miller Analogies Test
> P.O. Box 96152
> Chicago, IL 60693
> phone: 1-800-622-3231

Letters Of Recommendation

How should students pick professors to write their graduate school recommendations? Is a tepid letter from a big name better than a rousing personal letter from a lesser-known professor? Should applicants provide potential recommenders "talking points," or is this unethical?

Most graduate schools ask for three or four letters of recommendation. Applicants tend to ask professors from their major department to write the recommendations. It may help to solicit recommendations from well-known, or at least senior, faculty, but it is more important to get recommendations from professors who know the applicant well and can personalize the letter, backing up the applicant's commitment to graduate study.

Many career counselors suggest that students and alums open a "credential file" for letters of recommendation at their undergraduate institution. The file is used to hold recommendations and is especially useful for students or recent alums who plan on applying to graduate or professional school at some time in the future. Professors write the best recommendations when the student is still fresh in their mind.

Too often professors' letters fall flat because they don't really know their undergraduates. All the more reason for undergraduates to take a proactive approach to their education. We urge students to get acquainted with the professors by taking advantage of office hours when they can discuss their academic interests. They might even get a job with a professor doing research or helping out with departmental functions. Applicants who have been out of school for a few years might consider volunteer work with a researcher or related public-service organization.

Students should also consider providing a copy of their transcript, a sample of class work, and résumé to the professor, so the professor will have a better idea of what the student has done outside the classroom, in the university community and outside world.

Personal Statement

The "Statement of Purpose" or "Personal Statement" is one of the most important parts of the application. It should be tailored to the type of professional program, centering around the applicant's point of view on key issues, related experiences, and career goals. Also, it should demonstrate the applicant's understanding of the department, the interests of key faculty, new research areas, and the applicant's potential contribution to the department. How do applicants acquire this understanding? Our top ranked guides spell out informal and formal sources of information.

In some programs, such as Psychology or Social Work, applicants may be asked to write an additional essay that is somewhat more autobiographical, or they may be asked to comment on a specific public policy or social issue.

Additional Requirements For Art Students

Applicants to visual and performing arts programs are usually asked to submit, or perform, a sample of their work. This means a portfolio for visual artists, a writing sample for creative writers, a demo tape for film students, and perhaps an audition for drama applicants and musicians. Requirements vary from program to program, but applicants should begin preparing well in advance.

Writing Sample

Time for applicants to dust off that paper from an upper-division undergraduate course—but they should be sure to check it for spelling and grammatical errors.

Writing samples demonstrate applicants' intellectual prowess. A paper on a topic they will be investigating as a doctorate student will bolster the application. This can be an opportunity for a marginal applicant to shine!

Excelling In Graduate School And Preparing For The Job Market

In part because of their duration, doctoral programs have the highest attrition rate of any graduate degree. As we noted in the Introduction, only one in six students in doctoral programs in the humanities or social sciences finishes with a degree.

In this chapter, we recommend several excellent guides that can help students persevere and excel in their graduate program. Several offer insight on essential topics, such as managing time, building a reputation for excellence among colleagues and professors, preparing for qualifying exams, writing a dissertation, speaking with confidence during oral presentations, and preparing for the job market. We have also reviewed resources describing career options open to PhDs outside the tight academic market.

With proper preparation and an understanding of how their graduate program operates, students will excel in, and enjoy, the graduate school experience.

General Resources

THE ACADEMIC'S HANDBOOK

 Recommended For:
Obtaining a Master's or PhD

Description:

This collection of essays by university professors and administrators is designed as a guide for those planning or beginning an academic career. It focuses on the academic institution as a workplace. Part I examines life in "The Academy" and the role and functions of the academician from several perspectives. Included are essays on personal and professional goals, life at a small liberal arts college, the moral responsibilities of a teaching career, and the issues facing women and minorities in academia. Part II looks at a classic problem: the politics of academic life. Also covered are the newer issues of interdisciplinarity, internationalization, and harassment. Responsible academic research is also addressed. Part III focuses on employment: getting a job, analyzing the job market, navigating the tenure system, and understanding how (well) academics are compensated. Part IV looks at teaching and advising with essays on running a lecture course, class discussion, advising, and addressing gender discrimination in class. Part V comprises two articles: one on Federal funding for research; the other on new academics' quests for private funds. Part VI focuses on publishing: how to write scholarly articles, how to publish in science, and how the "networked environment" affects publishing and scholarship. Part VII looks at academic communities and administrations: how institutions are governed, the role of the department in the institution, and the importance of participation in the larger academic community of professional organizations.

Evaluation:

This book grows out a mid-1980s discussion involving 50 faculty and students from around the country. The second edition draws on conversations among students and faculty involved in a project called "Preparing Graduate Students for the Professional Responsibilities of College Teachers," developed by the Association of American Colleges and Universities and supported by a grant from the Fund for the Improvement of Postsecondary Education. The result? A thoughtful discussion of issues of interest to future faculty members and those just considering a career in academia. The essays are consistently well-written and thorough. While many are not conclusive—who can be on such mercurial factors as political correctness or the effect of new technologies on the academic's work?—this insight-packed volume earned our highest recommendation for those considering an academic career. The writers take the would-be professor behind the scenes to a world that many of us didn't full understand in college. It is an enlightening tour.

Where To Find/Buy:

Bookstores and libraries.

Overall Rating
★★★★
The thinking person's guide to an academic career

Design, Ease Of Use
★★★★
Great writing; thoughtfully edited and presented; includes index

1–4 Stars

Author:
A. Leigh DeNeef & Craufurd D. Goodwin (editors)

A. Leigh DeNeef is Professor of English and Associate Dean of the Graduate School at Duke University. Craufurd D. Goodwin is James B. Duke Professor of Economics at Duke University

Publisher:
Duke University

Edition:
2nd (1998)

Price:
$18.95

Pages:
348

ISBN:
0822316730

Media:
Book

Principal Focus:
Obtaining a Master's or PhD

MA/PhD Subtopic:
General Resources

★★★★

Overall Rating
★★★★
A comprehensive guide with valuable information on accreditation

Design, Ease Of Use
★★★★
Excellent indexes make navigation easy

1–4 Stars

Author:
Pat Criscito

Criscito is author of Barron's *Designing the Perfect Resume* and *Resumes in Cyberspace*, and the president and founder of ProType, Ltd., in Colorado Springs.

Publisher:
Barron's Educational Series

Edition:
1999

Price:
$18.95

Pages:
537

ISBN:
0764107259

Media:
Book

Principal Focus:
Obtaining a Master's or PhD

MA/PhD Subtopic:
General Resources

General Resources

BARRON'S GUIDE TO DISTANCE LEARNING
Degrees, Certificates, Courses

 Recommended For:
Obtaining a Master's or PhD

Description:
This guide profiles nearly 800 accredited schools, which offer degrees, certificates, and courses via distance learning. Designed for students at the undergraduate, graduate, and doctoral levels, it first explains and provides a brief history of distance learning. The author describes teaching methods and financing options. She also suggests a personality evaluation to help potential students determine if they have the discipline needed for this approach. She includes student profiles to help readers "see" how other individuals adapt to distance learning. Institution profiles feature contacts, a summary of options, available degrees or certifications, admission requirements, tuition, financial aid options, accreditation information, and a general description of the school. Also included in the guide are numerous Internet resources, such as sites providing financial aid and accreditation information. Seven indexes aid navigation: by state and province; by on-campus requirements; by fields of study (Undergrad, Grad, Doctoral, and Certificate); and by Individual Classes.

Evaluation:
Although the bulk of listings in this guide are aimed at undergraduate students, it offers a significant number for graduate and doctorate programs. This guide is well-organized, clearly written, and navigable by *seven* indexes, making it the best directory to distance learning we've found. We're also impressed by the hefty list of Internet resources included. This guide best serves students who are aren't yet sure what career path they will take, and advisors and employers who need to provide the latest information and resources on distance learning. An added plus: large type and good use of bulleted text. Overall, an excellent tool for students at all levels, their advisors, and employers.

Where To Find/Buy:
Bookstores and libraries.

General Resources

GETTING WHAT YOU CAME FOR
The Smart Student's Guide To Earning A Master's Or Ph.D.

 Recommended For:
Obtaining a Master's or PhD

Description:

Geared to students contemplating graduate school or already there, this guide walks students through choosing whether to attend graduate school, where to go, when, and how to finance it. Later chapters discuss major milestones in the degree earning process: taking qualifying exams, choosing a thesis committee, finding a thesis topic, writing and defending the thesis, giving an oral presentation, and landing the first job. The emphasis is on practical advice, coping strategies and organizational tools to get students through the process with as little confusion as possible. Some chapters primarily dispense information, such as "Financial Aid" which explains the overall process, how schools assess need, types of aid and how to apply. Other chapters primarily offer counseling and insight, such as "Playing Politics: Building a Reputation" which discusses networking, attitude, correspondence and conferences. The book closes with an appendix on "Buying Your Computer and Software," and "Useful Internet Addresses."

Evaluation:

There is no other book of this high caliber addressing the topic of preparing for graduate school and excelling while there. The author weaves stories from his own travails attaining a Ph.D., as well as hundreds of humorous and informative stories from students, faculty and other educational professionals. Each chapter goes beyond generalities to deliver specific advice for the issue at hand. For example, the section on choosing a graduate school correctly emphasizes the pivotal role of a thesis adviser. It includes a nuanced discussion of the "differences between adviser-student relationships in the sciences and humanities." While the overall quality of the book is superb, several chapters stand out as real gems. "Managing Yourself" explains how to set up your office and computer for action, and presents a calendar system to lend structure to your days. "Playing Politics" contains guidance on managing relationships with support staff, your thesis adviser, fellow students, faculty and leaders in your field.

Where To Find/Buy:

Bookstores and libraries.

Overall Rating
★★★★
Insider advice on all the major decisions to make prior to and during graduate school

Design, Ease Of Use
★★★★
Entertaining and informational

1–4 Stars

Author:
Robert L. Peters
Robert Peters received his PhD in biology from Stanford University. A conservation biologist, he lives in Washington D.C.

Publisher:
Noonday

Edition:
1997

Price:
$14.00

Pages:
399

ISBN:
0374524777

Media:
Book

Principal Focus:
Obtaining a Master's or PhD

MA/PhD Subtopic:
General Resources

Of Interest To:
Women
Persons of Color
International Students

★★★★

Overall Rating
★★★★

Essays paint a vivid and honest picture of the academic job hunt

Design, Ease Of Use
★★★★

Each contribution unique in style and scope, and highly readable

1–4 Stars

Author:
Christina Boufis & Victoria C. Olsen

Christina Boufis received her PhD in English literature from the City University of New York, Graduate Center. She is an Affiliated Scholar at the Institute for Research on Women and Gender at Stanford University. Victoria C. Olsen received her PhD in English from Stanford.

Publisher:
Riverhead

Edition:
1997

Price:
$12.95

Pages:
368

ISBN:
1573226262

Media:
Book

Principal Focus:
Obtaining a Master's or PhD

MA/PhD Subtopic:
General Resources

General Resources

ON THE MARKET
Surviving The Academic Job Search

 Recommended For:
Obtaining a Master's or PhD

Description:
A diverse group of PhDs address the subject of academic employment in these essays, telling personal stories of the job search—failures and frustrations as well as hard-won successes. The authors come from many different ethnicities and backgrounds, and from diverse academic fields. Their essays are grouped into eight sections, beginning with "First Words: The Application Process," which includes discussions of how contributors survived the job search process. Part 2, "Cattle Call," contains essays discussing aspects of the academic conference and interview. "The Aftermath and Beyond" offers words of wisdom and experience from academics who survived the job search. In Part 4, essayists consider "identities and politics": affirmative action policies, gender, and sexuality. The next section contains contributions on a more personal note. "Different Paths" and "Alternative Careers" are considered in the next two sets of essays, and the final section takes a look at the future of the "Academy."

Evaluation:
The PhD job search is notoriously difficult. In these engrossing and well-written essays, recent PhDs offer a candid look at the "human side of the job search." Although these essays are not intended as "how-to" manuals for PhDs searching for academic appointments, the reader will nevertheless glean plenty of practical advice from these stories. An incredible amount of information is packed into each essay, yet they read as smooth as any novel or short story. Readers will walk away with a vivid picture of the life in the "Academy," as well as a good sense of how the "personal" fits into the "professional" side of the academic job market. Highly recommended for those looking for a realistic portrait of what awaits them in "the academic trenches."

Where To Find/Buy:
Bookstores and libraries.

General Resources

LIFTING A TON OF FEATHERS
A Woman's Guide To Surviving In The Academic World

 Recommended For:
Obtaining a Master's or PhD

Description:

The Council of Ontario Universities Committee on the Status of Women sponsored this book as a way to provide women with the survival skills and strategic information they need to survive in academia. The book grew out of discussions held in 1990–91 as Canadian academes mourned the murder of 14 women colleagues in Montreal. It is intended as a handbook with background material to help readers understand how academia works and where women stand. Chapter 1 provides an overview of the topic and book structure. Chapter 2 describes what the author sees as an essential male academic environment. Chapter 3 looks at the "unwritten rules" of most colleges and universities. Chapter 4 lists 27 widely accepted myths about women and academia. Chapter 5 looks at some common Catch-22 situations affecting women. Two subsequent chapters look at what women can do. The author offers some general principles and suggestions for specific situations. The final chapter comprises teacher and graduate student checklists for "Woman-positive Institutions." It is designed to help women find a good place to work and study, and to provide suggestions on how they can improve the lot of women at their institutions. Numerous appendices and reference materials follow the text.

Evaluation:

Peppered with citations and backed up by a 36-page bibliography, at first glance this book looks more like a scholarly monograph than a guide to anything practical, but don't be fooled. The author has done her homework and created a remarkably usable handbook for women on the frontlines of academia. No flip answers here—this book identifies the problem(s)—cultural, organizational, and personal—and delivers practical suggestions for very specific situations. Especially helpful are the author's presentation of general principles underlying long-term solutions and her practical suggestions for specific situations. Not all the advice pertains to women only. Everyone will benefit from the advice on identifying potential mentors and developing strong support groups. A gem of a resource with practical layout and plenty of helpful checklists, this book will also help those trying to understand how gender bias works in academia. Included three appendices providing data on gender bias, an article on "The Maleness of the Environment," and suggested guidelines for hiring, promotion, and tenure committees. We recommend this handbook to all women considering a career in academia.

Where To Find/Buy:
Bookstores and libraries.

Overall Rating
★★★★
Great combination of background information and practical suggestions; eye-opener for students

Design, Ease Of Use
★★★
Practical resource handbook for women academes committed to advancement

1–4 Stars

Author:
Paula J. Caplan

Paula Caplan is Professor of Applied Psychology at the Ontario Institute for Studies in Education. She is the author of *Between Women: Lowering the Barriers, The Myth of Women's Masochism*, and *Don't Blame Mother: Mending the Mother-Daughter Relationship*.

Publisher:
University of Toronto

Edition:
1993

Price:
$19.95

Pages:
276

ISBN:
0802074111

Media:
Book

Principal Focus:
Obtaining a Master's or PhD

MA/PhD Subtopic:
General Resources

Of Interest To:
Women

★★★★

Overall Rating
★★★★
Valuable information and advice tailored to working adults

Design, Ease Of Use
★★
Slow beginning, but solid advice and helpful resource lists

1–4 Stars

Author:
Von Pittman

Formerly the Associate Dean of Continuing Education at the University of Iowa, Von Pittman is now Director of the Center for Independent Study at the University of Missouri-Columbia. He has developed and administered degree programs for part-time students at four major state universities.

Publisher:
Sage

Edition:
1997

Price:
$21.00

Pages:
140

ISBN:
0761904409

Media:
Book

Principal Focus:
Obtaining a Master's or PhD

MA/PhD Subtopic:
General Resources

General Resources

SURVIVING GRADUATE SCHOOL PART TIME

Description:

This book, part of Sage Publication's Graduate Survival Skills series, is written primarily for working professionals considering part-time graduate school to acquire more credentials. The book opens with a discussion of the development of part-time graduate programs in the United States and the shift away from an elitist model of graduate education. The author describes the advantages and disadvantages of part-time grad school and suggests ways to overcome bureaucratic barriers. He describes four major factors for selecting schools (accessibility, admissibility, reputation, and cost) and reviews the admissions process. He also describes the various formats available to part-time students, including weekend intensives and distance learning, and financing options. The author gives advice on developing a "plan of attack" for program requirements, curricula, and pacing, and some tips on note-taking. Finally, he addresses the emotional challenges faced by adult students, including stress, procrastination, and family needs.

Evaluation:

Contrary to the author's assertion that he uses an "informal, conversational style," this book begins like a scholarly article with its many references to the likes of Thorstein Veblen and Robert Peters. After slogging through the author's historical account of the elitist view of part-time education in the university system, readers will find that this book is an excellent resource for the huge number of part-time students (over 70 percent of master's students, in fact) whose unique needs are not always recognized by schools. After the slow start, the author tailors his advice to this population—with tips on writing a personal statement demonstrating the strengths of work experience and strategies for holding down costs, such as getting credit for past coursework. According to the author, "Life is an endless series of tradeoffs," and while he doesn't gloss over the difficulties, he does demonstrate that disadvantages can be overcome and a part-time graduate education can be satisfying and productive.

Where To Find/Buy:

Bookstores and libraries, or directly from Sage Publications (http://www.sagepub.com); Phone (805) 499-0721; fax (805) 499-0871; email info@sagepub.com

General Resources

THE AFRICAN AMERICAN STUDENT'S GUIDE TO SURVIVING GRADUATE SCHOOL

 Recommended For:
Obtaining a Master's or PhD

Description:

Written by an African American woman with a PhD, this book offers advice on how African American graduate students can better manage their school lives, survive the stress, and achieve their goals. Since graduate school is a human as well as academic experience, the author repeatedly turns to the challenges that face blacks and encourages them to persevere. She believes graduate school must be approached scientifically. The first crucial step is choosing a school with a "goodness of fit." The author provides specific examples of good choices. She explains how to manage the application process and offers tips for increasing chances of getting in. She also discusses the influence of affirmative action and its reversal in some states. Once in school, students should create a master plan for the graduate school years; the author provides a model format. She also offers advice on getting support and learning self-esteem. She then turns to study skills, with tips on preparing for comprehensive exams, writing a thesis or dissertation, and surviving the defense. The final chapter addresses the problem of racism on campus and answers the question "When and how do we combat racism?"

Evaluation:

In the first chapter, Isaac tells three stories of African American graduate school survivors. The third describes her own hard-luck struggle to complete her Masters and doctorate after an emotional divorce that left her broke. It took tremendous determination to survive the stress and lack of support, but when she finished, her life was changed. It is this experience that shapes the book—the author is determined to provide other African Americans the roadmap she lacked, and she firmly believes the struggle is worth it. In fact, she says that African Americans have an urgent "social and cultural obligation" to get advanced degrees. This book not only provides valuable advice, tailored to the black experience, on getting into and succeeding at graduate school; it also serves as a manifesto for achievement, reminding readers of the importance of self-esteem and commitment to the advancement of all African Americans. The author's "scientific approach" offers readers a detailed plan for managing the organizational and academic parts of graduate school, particularly for those in doctorate programs, and her passion provides readers with the support they will need to get through the emotional stresses.

Where To Find/Buy:

Bookstores and libraries, or directly from Sage Publications (http://www.sagepub.com) Phone (805) 499-0721; fax (805) 499-0871; email info@sagepub.com

---

Overall Rating
★★★
Arms readers with strong organizational techniques and the will to succeed

Design, Ease Of Use
★★★★
Passionately written; lots of subheadings, good index and table of contents

1–4 Stars

Author:
Alicia Isaac

Dr. Alicia Isaac received her Doctorate in Public Administration from the University of Georgia. She was the Director of Masters Admissions for the University of Georgia School of Social Work for five years until becoming an assistant professor.

Publisher:
Sage

Edition:
1998

Price:
$21.00

Pages:
138

ISBN:
0761903828

Media:
Book

Principal Focus:
Obtaining a Master's or PhD

MA/PhD Subtopic:
General Resources

Of Interest To:
Persons of Color

★★★

Overall Rating
★★★
A step-by-step approach to
the academic job search for
new PhDs

Design, Ease Of Use
★★★
Well-written; includes lots of
sample vitas and a great job
search timetable

1–4 Stars

Author:
Mary Morris Heiberger and
Julia Miller Vick

Ms. Heiberger is Associate Director
and Ms. Vick is a Graduate Career
Counselor at the Career Planning
and Placement Service at the
University of Pennsylvania.

Publisher:
University of Pennsylvania

Edition:
2nd (1996)

Price:
$14.95

Pages:
194

ISBN:
0812215958

Media:
Book

Principal Focus:
Obtaining a Master's or PhD

MA/PhD Subtopic:
General Resources

General Resources

THE ACADEMIC JOB SEARCH HANDBOOK

Description:

Part 1, "What You Should Know Before You Start," prepares new
PhDs for their academic job search by examining "the structure of
academic careers" and hiring practices. Part 2 offers suggestions for
"Planning and Timing Your Search." Included is a timetable, which
begins two years before one's dissertation is completed and extends to
six months before a position's "start date." Deciding where and when
to apply is the next step; readers learn what they need to know about
the market, the target institution, their own competitiveness, and
more. The importance of advisors, professional networks, conference
presentations, and letters of recommendation is also discussed,
together with tips for "learning about openings." Part 3 focuses on
written materials, such as vitas and correspondence. Samples are
included, together with guidelines for constructing a personal home
page. Aspects of the job search, such as interviews and negotiating
offers, are detailed in Part 4. Part 5 offers advice for "After You Take
the Job." Included is information on tenure and changing positions.

Evaluation:

New PhDs face a highly competitive job market today, especially
with the "uncapping" of the academic retirement age, which has
reduced turnover, and cutbacks in public funding. More than ever,
it is important for new PhDs to understand the academic job search
and all it entails, including networking, researching positions,
preparing vitas, and more. The authors of this volume are capable,
knowledgeable mentors. Their handbook provides harried graduate
students with the must-know basics: a practical timetable, sample
vitas, and interview strategies. This handbook is designed to apply
to all disciplines; readers should remember to check the specific
conventions of their chosen field. This resource is a valuable
supplement to information provided by faculty in the field and
national professional associations.

Where To Find/Buy:

Bookstores and libraries.

General Resources

EMBARK.COM: GOING TO GRADUATE SCHOOL

Description:

Embark.com's graduate school segment comprises three sections: Choose the Right Grad School, Apply to Grad School, and Finance Your Education. Formatted similarly, each section contains an Introduction, Advice & Information articles, and an interactive forum for joining discussions or posting messages. The sections have unique features, too. Choose the Right Grad School offers a personalized search interface that "matches" users to schools. Once a school is "found," users click to view details, apply online, send an e-mail query, or go to the school's website. Details include a three-page overview of the school, with contact info, program contacts, profiles of both the graduate school and the specified program, admissions requirements, and costs. In the online application section, users can apply to any of the site's partner schools. A list of these schools is supplied; users create a password-protected account for privacy. (Embark will even check the application for errors before submission.) The Financial Aid section describes aid sources, such as loans, work study, grants, and scholarships, as well as a Free Application for Federal Student Aid (FAFSA) calculator.

Evaluation:

At the time of this review, this site was still in development. Though it features a long list of partner schools (including Boston University, Columbia, Georgia State, and Harvard), most of the online applications are "coming soon." Other features, like the scholarship search, are under construction. However, even without complete online application capabilities, Embark.com: Going To Graduate School is a rich resource. The school profiles are among the most detailed on the Internet. They provide overviews of the entire graduate school, plus good introductions to specific programs and stats and facts on admissions, applications, enrollment, faculty, tuition, housing, environment/transportation, and financing. With only 6,000 schools in its data base, this site is smaller than some, but what it lacks in quantity it more than makes up for in quality. Two complaints: the search, which goes through seven pages (with 1–2 questions per page), is slower than it should be; and program categorization can be confusing. It took us a while to figure out where Education fit in, and we never did find Creative Writing. Terrific features include the interactive forums—which are actually being used—the sane financial aid advice, and the online applications. These applications save users time, since data common to all applications is only entered once; they also allow references to complete recommendations electronically.

Where To Find/Buy:

On the Internet at http://www.embark.com/grad

Overall Rating
★★★
An outstanding database of grad schools, plus lots more

Design, Ease Of Use
★★★
The school search is slow; program categories sometimes confusing

1–4 Stars

Publisher:
Embark.com

Embark.com (formerly CollegeEdge) is a California-based company "dedicated to helping people fulfill their life's learning and career aspirations."

Media:
Internet

Principal Focus:
Obtaining a Master's or PhD

MA/PhD Subtopic:
General Resources

II. Obtaining A Master's Or PhD

Overall Rating
★★★
An informed guide to the admissions process and surviving grad school

Design, Ease Of Use
★★★
Very readable with clear advice

1–4 Stars

Author:
Richard Jerrard & Margot Jerrard

Currently a professor of mathematics at the University of Illinois, Richard Jerrard was Director of Graduate Studies for his department for four years and has participated in admissions committees at every level. Margot Jerrard is a professional writer specializing in educational topics. She has written and edited for the University of Illinois.

Publisher:
Perigee (Berkley)

Edition:
1998

Price:
$14.00

Pages:
259

ISBN:
0399524169

Media:
Book

Principal Focus:
Obtaining a Master's or PhD

MA/PhD Subtopic:
General Resources

General Resources

THE GRAD SCHOOL HANDBOOK

Description:
This general guidebook to finding, getting into, and succeeding in graduate school is written by two university employees who describe from their insider's position how decisions are made at universities, what procedures are important to being admitted, and how to get off to a good start in grad school. First, they ask readers to take stock of themselves by responding to evaluation questions. They then explain where to get information about fields and programs on the Internet and elsewhere, what to look for in a program, and what to do on a visit. They break down the application process, with a chapter devoted to each component part. The authors describe the process of decision-making that faculty use to select between applicants and what they are looking for in essays, tests, and reference letters. They include sample essays (good and bad), describe how to turn resume gaps into assets, and explain how to get good references. They also discuss how to deal with test anxiety. The final section of their book looks at aspects of life as a graduate student, including advice on teaching assistantships, choosing a thesis director, and returning to school after time-off.

Evaluation:
This book opens with a sales pitch. Why go to grad school? "An exciting future and a job you love can be yours." While this statement and others in the first chapter might make readers wonder if the authors are working for a promotions office, in reality, these writers deliver on their promises. They go in-depth into every topic they address, from the earliest decision to apply grad school to strategies for handling boring teachers once accepted. They rightly advise would-be grad students to think "first, the faculty" when choosing a program or convincing a program that they're the right candidate. They offer smart ideas for learning more about faculty members and provide a detailed explanation about how faculty members decide which students to admit and offer financial aid. They also wisely remind readers that "you have to repay" those loans and encourage them to manage their finances. The smartest applications to graduate schools start the process early and do their research. This book will be a good guide along the way. And the authors' upbeat attitude is inspiring. Readers should note, however, that this guidebook does not focus on the decision to pursue a graduate degree.

Where To Find/Buy:
Bookstores and libraries.

General Resources

GRADUATE SCHOOL
Winning Strategies For Getting In With Or Without Excellent Grades

Description:

The author overviews the general graduate school application process, urging students to make the most of personal and professional achievements. Drawing on a mix of personal experience, information gathered through interviews, and other resources, he offers tips for getting into graduate school with B grades, using a "hard work ethic." He outlines mistakes, large and small, potential students make during the application process and offers advice for reference letters, such as preparing a "outline" of personal qualities and information so the chosen person can make the letter more personalized and less generic. He also suggests contacting prospective faculty members to "test" possible work relationships. A 40-page resource directory, including suggested print resources and Internet sites, and an index follow the text.

Evaluation:

This book provides some of good basic tips for students who aren't graduate school shoo-ins. For those looking for a basic introduction to the application process, it may be helpful. The author's underlying message is "do it right and do it right with pride." His book will be a wake-up call for students who are not aware of the work it takes to get into graduate school, and it will help those who do not know what major to pursue. The author reminds students that graduate school is a whole new ball game, which requires a professional attitude and determination that college may not have demanded. We like this go-get 'em approach, but we were disappointed with several aspects of this book. We couldn't help question the author's credibility since he doesn't reveal where he served as "faculty member, a graduate supervisor, and as a member of graduate admissions committees," and we noted that many of the suggested resources were out-of-date. We can't complain about the detailed table of contents and index, but overall, this book scores high on concept and low on content.

Where To Find/Buy:

Bookstores and libraries.

Overall Rating
★★★
Thoughtful advice; positive outlook

Design, Ease Of Use
★★★
Detailed table of contents and index ease navigation

1–4 Stars

Author:
David G. Mumby, PhD
The author has served as a faculty member, a graduate supervisor, and as a member of graduate admissions committees.

Publisher:
Proto Press

Edition:
1997

Price:
$19.95

Pages:
251

ISBN:
0968217346

Media:
Book

Principal Focus:
Obtaining a Master's or PhD

MA/PhD Subtopic:
General Resources

Overall Rating
★★★
Links to varied resources for future and current graduate students

Design, Ease Of Use
★★★
Simple format; brief, tantalizing descriptions of links

1–4 Stars

Author:
Dan Horn

Currently a graduate student in the psychology department at the University of Michigan, Dan Horn is working in the area of human-computer interaction and computer-supported cooperative work at the Collaboratory for Research on Electronic Work.

Publisher:
Dan Horn

Media:
Internet

Principal Focus:
Obtaining a Master's or PhD

MA/PhD Subtopic:
General Resources

GRADUATE STUDENT RESOURCES ON THE WEB

Description:

The Graduate Student Resource Page is designed by a graduate student to provide links to relevant resources for current and future graduate students. The table of contents features five subheadings. The "Advice/Student Life" section lists links to websites on applying to and surviving grad school, finishing the dissertation, and finding a job. Two national graduate student associations are listed under "Organizations," and four financial aid sources are listed under "Funding." Unlike these sections—which are composed entirely of links to other websites—"Humor" is all original material, much of it from the author's "Happy Hour Archive," an e-mail newsletter. Twenty different pages poke fun at all aspects of graduate school life, from the "Top Ten Lies Told By Graduate Students" to the e-mail chain letter that magically helps students finish their thesis. The final section of this website lists similar resource pages for graduate students, one of which is particularly useful for women. The Graduate Student Resource page is frequently updated, and contributions from visitors are welcome.

Evaluation:

This website serves as a portal to some excellent resources for prospective graduate students and those already slogging through. While a number of the recommended sites are reviewed in this guidebook, Horn has identified many others, which provide a broad range of points of view and agendas. Variety is the keyword here. For example, the "Getting In" section directs students to the massive *US News & World Reports* student guide, to a paper by a former graduate student on how to apply to graduate school, and to Psi Chi's advice on admissions procedures to psychology programs. "Getting Through" and "Getting Out" offer plenty of advice in the form of articles and websites on survival skills, research and writing, and preparing for the work world. The funding sites are also must-visits. The humor section provides an amusing inside peek at graduate student life. Don't miss "Why God Never Received Tenure." The all-text home page is easy to navigate with multiple opportunities to jump to sites of interest, and each recommended link features a brief and tantalizing description.

Where To Find/Buy:

On the Internet at http://www-personal.umich.edu/~danhorn/graduate.html

General Resources

PETERSONS.COM: THE GRADUATE SCHOOL CHANNEL

Description:

For users interested in obtaining a Master's or PhD, this site's main page offers five areas of interest: Graduate School Search, Distance Learning, International Student Information, Resources on Financing Your Education, and Test Preparation. The first three areas are searchable databases that house details on 35,000 graduate programs. In Graduate School Search, users can search by institution name, location, academic area, or keyword. Search results provide a "Quick Overview" of the school and a direct-link list of the institution's "Areas of Graduate Study." By clicking on the "Area" of interest, users get a 1998–99 "Program Profile": faculty and student demographics, entrance requirements, contact information, and more. In some cases (designated by an envelope icon), users can send an e-mail query to the school. Distance Learning is a database of programs/courses offered by accredited institutions at a distance; International Student Information helps international students search for programs in such fields as Computer Science, Engineering, and Physical Sciences. Loans from Key Bank are discussed in the financial aid section. Test Preparation provides tips on the GRE and TOEFL, plus free GRE test prep software. A discussion forum is also featured.

Evaluation:

While these school/program databases don't feature the elaborate "matchmaking" search capabilities of some sites, they have features that others do not. Most databases offer only statistical overviews of the entire school (student demographics, tuition, etc.); Peterson's offers "Program Profiles" for academic areas. For example, visitors interested in Art History may turn up Brown University in their School Search. By clicking on Art History in Brown's list of "Graduate Areas of Study," they will learn Art History-specific details: number of full-time faculty and students, faculty/student demographics, entrance requirements, department contact information, etc. The contents are brief, as are this site's contents in general, but it's a good place to start. International students can browse the main database too, check out Distance Learning, or get in-depth profiles of "featured" study programs in Computer Science, Computer Engineering, Engineering, International Relations, Hospitality Management, Mathematical Sciences, and Physical Sciences. Some fine articles, such as "Tips from Seasoned Grad Students," are also featured on the main page, and the free test-prep software (for Windows and Macintosh) is worth the download time; just be aware of Peterson's omnipresent advertising. The software is designed to help sell their test-prep products.

Where To Find/Buy:

On the Internet at http://www.petersons.com/graduate

Overall Rating
★★★
Special features for international students and helpful grad program search

Design, Ease Of Use
★★★
Users must backtrack occasionally to get to the main contents page

1–4 Stars

Publisher:
Peterson's

Peterson's is a publisher of education guides and a producer of test preparation materials and courses. It is part of the Lifelong Learning Group within Thomson Learning.

Media:
Internet

Principal Focus:
Obtaining a Master's or PhD

MA/PhD Subtopic:
General Resources

Of Interest To:
International Students

Overall Rating
★★★

School rankings, admissions advice, and lots of bonuses for some fields of study

Design, Ease Of Use
★★★

Easy to use; some segments (Engineering, Education) better developed than others

1–4 Stars

Publisher:
U.S. News and World Report

Online U.S. News is the Internet home of the print publication, *U.S. News & World Reports*.

Media:
Internet

Principal Focus:
Obtaining a Master's or PhD

MA/PhD Subtopic:
General Resources

General Resources

U.S. NEWS ONLINE: GRADUATE SCHOOL

Description:

In the middle of U.S. News Online: Graduate School's main page are links to all disciplines covered: Education, Health, The Arts, Public Affairs, Library Science, Engineering, and PhDs. Each discipline has its own page, where users browse rankings for overall "Top Schools" or for specialties within a field. With the exception of PhDs, these discipline-specific pages feature articles as well. For example, the Education page provides access to Top Schools for Education (general), rankings for such specialties as "Elementary Teacher" or "Counseling," and articles on such subjects as "Career Outlook" and school reform. Similarly, Health features Top School rankings for such fields as "Nurse Practitioner-Family" and "Midwifery," rankings for specialties like "Social Work" and "Speech Pathology," and an article on "Nursing: Getting In." The Engineering and Education segments have an additional feature: a personalized "school search" interface. Search results provide vital stats on the chosen school, including contact addresses, demographics, and deadlines. The site also features general articles on choosing a school and returning to school after age 30, plus frequently asked questions on Admissions, a scholarship search, and "expert" advice on financial aid.

Evaluation:

Produced by the magazine famous for ranking schools, rankings are a primary focus here. But they are not the sole focus. In fact, some of the articles and special features, such as the expert financial aid advice forums, the frequently asked questions on Admissions, and "bonuses," like the list of "Best Hospitals" to work at (in Health), are excellent. However, if it is rankings you're after, this is the place to go. One problem: the value of this site depends on the user's area of interest. The best segments are Engineering and Education, both of which include the personalized search feature for finding schools. Other segments are less well-developed. Health, Public Affairs, Library Science, and The Arts are acceptable; PhDs is inexcusably puny. It features only Top School/specialty rankings—no articles, no searchable school stats. Plus, PhDs covers only 11 fields: Biology, Chemistry, Computer Science, Economics, English, Geology, History, Mathematics, Physics, Political Science, and Psychology. Users whose area of study is "none of the above" will have to try the site's advice forums for specific tips. Engineering and education students will benefit most from this terrific introductory site.

Where To Find/Buy:

On the Internet at http://www.usnews.com/usnews/edu/beyond/bchome.htm

General Resources

U.S. NEWS & WORLD REPORT: BEST GRADUATE SCHOOLS

Description:

Every year *U.S. News & World Report* publishes this guide to graduate schools as a separate supplement; it is not one of the magazine's weekly issues. (It is available at newsstands throughout the year.) Contents are divided into eight sections: Introduction, Business, Law, Medicine & Health, Education, Engineering, Library Science, and PhDs. The Introduction features articles on "The Value of an Advanced Degree" and when (or if) one should go to grad school, plus an explanation of *U.S. News & World Report*'s school ranking system. Each topical section features pertinent articles as well as rankings of "top schools" and specialties. For example, "Business" includes an article on Duke University's successful online executive MBA program, ranks the top 50 business schools, then ranks top 10 schools for such specialties as Accounting, Marketing, and International Management. "Education," "Engineering," and "Library Science" are similarly formatted. "Law" offers rankings of the top 50 schools, plus second-, third-, and fourth-tier schools. "Medicine & Health" includes rankings for health disciplines, such as Audiology, Nursing, and Physician Assistant, as well as for medical schools. "PhDs" covers the sciences, social sciences, humanities, and Masters of Arts.

Evaluation:

This magazine-style guide features much of the information offered on the U.S. News Online websites, where users can browse the articles and school rankings for free. Like the websites, this guide offers an index/directory of graduate schools in a variety of fields. The directory presents "vital statistics" on each school, such as requirements and deadlines, and is organized alphabetically by state. Online, users can search these directories by school name; in this print version, they must flip through a dense, small-print list. U.S. News Online also offers an array of additional interactive tools. For example, the site has a "Q & A" segment for asking experts questions, a financial aid section, and links to related sites. The magazine version offers none of these features. Our conclusion: go to the website if you have Internet access. (See the reviews of "U.S. News Online: Graduate School" page 32; "U.S. News Online: Business" page 97; "U.S. News Online: Law" page 144; and "U.S. News Online: Medicine" page 188.)

Where To Find/Buy:

Bookstores and libraries. On the Internet at http://www.usnews.com/usnews/edu/beyond/

Overall Rating
★★★
Rankings for various types of grad schools, plus related articles

Design, Ease Of Use
★★★
Magazine-style format fine for the rankings, articles; directory hard to use

1–4 Stars

Publisher:
U.S. News and World Report
U.S. News and World Report is a weekly news magazine distributed nationally.

Edition:
1999

Price:
$7.95

Pages:
204

Media:
Magazine

Principal Focus:
Obtaining a Master's or PhD

MA/PhD Subtopic:
General Resources

II. Obtaining
A Master's Or PhD

Overall Rating
★★★

A good general introduction to the trials, tribulations, and rewards of graduate study

Design, Ease Of Use
★★★

Quite readable, with a dose of humor

1–4 Stars

Author:
Lesli Mitchell

The author received an MA in English from Georgia State University, and is currently pursuing her PhD at the University of Virginia. She has served as regional director of the MLA Graduate Student Caucus, and as editor of the *GSC Newsletter.*

Publisher:
Peterson's

Edition:
1996

Price:
$14.95

Pages:
209

ISBN:
1560795808

Media:
Book

Principal Focus:
Obtaining a Master's or PhD

MA/PhD Subtopic:
General Resources

General Resources

THE ULTIMATE GRAD SCHOOL SURVIVAL GUIDE

 Recommended For:
Obtaining a Master's or PhD

Description:
Written by an experienced grad school student, this book focuses on general issues related to graduate school, providing an overview of the experience along with tips and advice for success. The first four chapters cover the admissions process, from researching schools to preparing an application timeline, and orienting oneself to a school upon arrival. Successive chapters discuss topics students will likely face while in grad school: coursework and exams, teaching and research, and writing a thesis or dissertation. Conferences and publishing are also covered, with tips on how to find conferences to attend, prepare an abstract, and get financial aid, as well as how and when to start submitting work to journals and other publishers. The last chapter discusses getting a job, with a realistic look at the availability of jobs within academia, and a plug for considering and obtaining employment in nonacademic industries. A section listing additional grad school-related resources is included.

Evaluation:
For students considering applying to grad school, this "survival guide" should open their eyes to the realities and rewards of graduate study. The author guides students toward the right school, and to grad school itself—with plenty of helpful hints and straight talk along the way. The book deals knowledgeably with issues often unknown to those outside academia, such as the importance of networking; the reality of grade inflation ("In most cases, a 'B' in a class indicates that something went wrong"); the necessity of balancing coursework with teaching responsibilities, and avoiding departmental gossip; and, sadly, the bleak reality of the academic job market. The book is genuinely helpful in such matters, but, by nature, is still somewhat general—survival issues are obviously quite different in the fields of, say, art history and chemistry, and this book may also be less useful for professional grad students who don't plan a career in academia, and thus face a very different grad school scene.

Where To Find/Buy:
Bookstores and libraries.

General Resources

THE GAY, LESBIAN, & BISEXUAL STUDENTS' GUIDE TO COLLEGES, UNIVERSITIES, AND GRADUATE SCHOOLS

Description:

Some 6,000 gay, lesbian, and bisexual students from colleges and universities around the country were surveyed for this guidebook. The students ranged in age from 17 to 47; 20 percent were in graduate or professional programs, and all said homophobia was a problem in their schools. In the profiles of the 189 colleges and universities covered in this book, the authors sum up the students' opinions about the atmosphere for gays and lesbians, what services are offered them, and official and unofficial university responses. In particular, each profile describes the institution's position on gay issues and sexual orientation as part of the affirmative action policy. The authors note the percentage of students who have been victims of harassment or who know others who have, whether the school acts in response to harassment, how supportive security forces are, and whether students feel safe on campus. They also describe gay student group activities and curricula addressing gay cultural contributions or issues.

Evaluation:

This book opens with a condemnation of the American education system, which the authors say prefers a silent and invisible gay and lesbian minority, despite surveys indicating that one in six college students is "sexually diverse." The college profiles that follow reinforce this observation: at school after school, students say they have been victimized or know others who have. Forty percent don't feel safe on their campuses, and the same percent say they would have chosen a different program if they had known more about the school environment. This guidebook provides this information. While the authors indicate that homophobia is a problem in all schools, some are clearly better than others. School safety and a climate of hate or tolerance are critical factors for gays and lesbians. A couple of downsides to this book: Only those schools with gay and lesbian student groups on the National Gay and Lesbian Talk Force mailing list are included; and information is beginning to show its age. The survey used by the authors is included in the appendix and can be used to gather information from schools not included or to update those that are.

Where To Find/Buy:

Bookstores and libraries.

Overall Rating
★★★
Critical information for gays and lesbians concerned about safety and curriculum; does not cover all schools

Design, Ease Of Use
★★
Straightforward writing, somewhat dated

1–4 Stars

Author:
Jan-Mitchell Sherrill & Craig A. Hardesty

Jan-Mitchell Sherrill was the founding director of the National Campus Violence Prevention Center at Towson State University and is now the Assistant Dean of Students at The George Washington University. Craig Hardesty is the Director of Student Judicial Services at The George Washington University.

Publisher:
New York University

Edition:
1994

Price:
$17.50

Pages:
279

ISBN:
0814779859

Media:
Book

Principal Focus:
Obtaining a Master's or PhD

MA/PhD Subtopic:
General Resources

Overall Rating
★★★
Good advice for women considering a return to school

Design, Ease Of Use
★★
Lots of subheadings for easy navigation, but writing is uneven

1–4 Stars

Author:
Barbara Rittner & Patricia Trudeau

Barbara Rittner is Associate Professor of Social Work at the University of Georgia and serves on the Admissions Committee in the School of Social Work. Patricia Trudeau is an instructor at the School of Social Work at the State University of New York at Buffalo, and a counselor and instructor at Conestoga College in Kitchner, Ontario.

Publisher:
Sage

Edition:
1997

Price:
$21.00

Pages:
154

ISBN:
0761903909

Media:
Book

Principal Focus:
Obtaining a Master's or PhD

MA/PhD Subtopic:
General Resources

Of Interest To:
Women

General Resources

THE WOMEN'S GUIDE TO SURVIVING GRADUATE SCHOOL

Description:

This book, part of Sage Publication's Graduate Survival Skills series, offers advice to women considering graduate programs, particularly those at the master's level. It is organized around basic decisions faced in the application process and the first weeks of graduate school, beginning with the decision to pursue a graduate degree. Four women with different goals and life circumstances serve as models to demonstrate the issues to be considered. After offering advice on selecting schools, the authors go step-by-step through the application process. A chapter on financing comprise 11 steps to assess personal finances and explains how to find resources on-line. The authors then offer advice on how to get focused and create a structure early in the program. They also offer tips on how to determine which courses and professors are worth taking. They stress the value of networking, rather than competing with other women, and briefly discuss sexual harassment. Finally, they give advice on how to study, read, and write papers efficiently, and what to do if you find yourself falling behind.

Evaluation:

While this book offers enough nuts and bolts information to be useful to women still in college, it is most applicable to those who have taken time off and acquired jobs and families. It addresses the challenges these women face in a number of circumstances and provides the sort of guidance that students usually receive from professors and academic advisors. In particular, it describes women's complex and contradictory dreams and needs as they consider grad school; it helps them to clarify their goals and shows them how to face financial realities. The chapter on financing graduate school is particularly good, with its emphasis on finding hidden expenses and its discussion of the experiences of working graduate women. The authors urge readers to be realistic and remind them that a "good enough" school is often better than the best. They also have some creative ideas for how women can help each other survive boring professors and clinker classes. Unfortunately, their advice on selecting schools is limited, and the writing is uneven.

Where To Find/Buy:

Bookstores and libraries, or directly from Sage Publications (http://www.sagepub.com) Phone (805) 499-0721; fax (805) 499-0871; email info@sagepub.com

General Resources

KAPLAN ONLINE: GRAD SCHOOL

Description:

Kaplan's "Grad School" is a part of the larger Kaplan site, yet it functions as its own entity. The main page offers a side menu of all its section areas: GRE, GRE CAT, Subject Tests, Schools & Programs, Admissions, Financial Aid, First-Year Success, and Careers. The GRE and GRE CAT sections feature articles and tools dedicated to introducing and explaining the exam. Also included is information on test registration and scoring, "Top 10 GRE Facts," and "Top 33 CAT Facts." Three "Focus" pages explore the exam's Math, Verbal, and Analytical portions, and provide practice questions. Users can download free test-preparation software as well; the "Analogies Payoff" and "Sentence Completion Payoff" games (for Macintosh only) are among the available choices. Users will also find an overview of the GRE's Subject Tests, which includes specifics on GRE Psych and English Lit. In Schools & Programs, essays help students differentiate between MA and PhD programs, and decide where to apply. Admissions offers strategies for applying, creating a statement of purpose, and getting recommendations. Financial Aid details options, timelines, and "KapLoan." First-Year Success and Careers sections contain tips from students and links.

Evaluation:

There's only one reason to come this site: for the valuable information it provides on the GRE. The GRE, GRE CAT, and Subject Tests sections offer an effective introduction to the exam and its various components. Scoring methods, test registration, and test-taking tips are presented clearly and efficiently. You can even take "mini-CATs" on such subjects as "'70s Sitcoms," to get an idea of how CAT works and how it generates your score. If you haven't seen the GRE yet, the "Focus" sections, which explain what types of questions are asked in the Math (Quantitative Reasoning, Problem Solving), Verbal, and Analytical areas—and include practice questions—are particularly useful "first looks." The discussion of GRE Subject Tests is a rare but welcome inclusion. The free test-prep software is worth a look, but Kaplan's commercial agenda (they sell test-prep materials) is more evident here than elsewhere; and they save the "more comprehensive software" for their online store. In contrast, not much can be said in favor of the other sections. Schools & Programs is laughably rudimentary, as is Admissions. Financial Aid is worth browsing; it does hit on a few "need to know" basics. Skip the rest altogether. Stick with the GRE-related segments and you'll get the most out of this site.

Where To Find/Buy:

On the Internet at http://www1.kaplan.com/view/article/1,1898,3740,00.html

---

Overall Rating

★★

Visit for the helpful introduction to the GRE, but skip the rest

Design, Ease Of Use

★★★★

Every page includes detailed sidebar menus

1–4 Stars

Publisher:

Kaplan Educational Centers

Kaplan, a subsidiary of The Washington Post Company, is a leading producer of test preparation materials. Their products include prep courses, books, and software.

Media:

Internet

Principal Focus:

Obtaining a Master's or PhD

MA/PhD Subtopic:

General Resources

★★

Overall Rating
★★
Important tips for doing dissertation research

Design, Ease Of Use
★★★
Simple, text-only format

1–4 Stars

Author:
Wanda Pratt

Wanda Pratt is Assistant Professor of Information and Computer Science at the University of California at Irvine.

Media:
Internet

Principal Focus:
Obtaining a Master's or PhD

MA/PhD Subtopic:
General Resources

General Resources

GRADUATE STUDENT ADVICE & RESEARCH SURVIVAL GUIDE

Description:
This website is written by a former graduate student at Stanford University. It draws on her experiences and readings, and her discussions with other Stanford students, faculty, and stuff. The site focuses on the doctorate research process, with specific advice on finding and working with research advisors, making progress on research, finding a thesis topic, and avoiding the research blues. The all-text site has a short table of contents on top, followed by topic titles in bold and tips highlighted by bullets and bold print. Under "Getting the most out of what you read," for example, are five basic guidelines, each followed by specific pointers. To "Be efficient," Pratt gives three pointers on what students need to read and what can be skipped or skimmed. Her advice for working with advisors emphasizes avoiding misunderstandings and structuring the relationship, while her tips on making consistent progress include ideas for avoiding procrastination and overcoming fears. The site also features links to related websites and groups, and information on recommended books.

Evaluation:
This page is relevant only to those who have already embarked on the PhD path, for the advice is specific to researching and working with an advisor. Written in an outline form, it is easy to read and follow, and the guidelines are practical and logical. Students can click on a topic in the table of contents, but the page is so short (five printed pages), it is worth reading through in its entirety. In fact, print it out and keep a copy of it handy; these guidelines could prove invaluable. The list of characteristics of a good advisor (or mentor or committee member) and advice on how to get the most out of the student-advisor relationship are well-rounded and create a positive and responsible structure for communication and support. The tips for research focus not only on making the most of valuable time, but also on staying motivated, on track, and balanced—concise advice to keep in mind. The site was last updated in 1997 and is unlikely to change now that Pratt is a professor.

Where To Find/Buy:
On the Internet at http://www-smi.stanford.edu/people/pratt/smi/advice.html

General Resources

GRE ONLINE

Description:

The Graduate Record Examinations (better known as the GRE) include the GRE General Test, which measures verbal, quantitative, and analytical reasoning skills, and the GRE Subject Tests, which measure achievement in 16 different fields of study. This website answers basic questions prospective test-takers may have: how, when and where to register; how much it costs; how to register for a the test and find the test center closest to home; and how to prepare. Links to an online store filled with GRE prep books and software abound. Also included is information for test-takers with disabilities and details on the fee-waiver program. Students can familiarize themselves with the type of questions asked by taking the interactive GRE General Test Sample Questions. After inputting answers, the button turns red (incorrect) or green (correct). A "Rationale" button appears for certain questions providing an explanation of the answer. Loan and savings calculators are also available.

Evaluation:

Pre-test jitters? Confused about paper-based and computer-based options? Explore this well-designed site for answers to your questions and tips for the test. The site includes "GRE at glance," a good first stop to scope out the site, and a site search function. A nice feature is the quick update on last minute additions to computer-based and paper-based test dates and sites (http://www.gre.org/newannc.html). The interactive test questions are helpful, as are the explanations of key concepts that you should have learned in high school ("An odd integer power of a negative number is negative, and an even integer power is positive"), though most students will want to be more thorough in their test preparation. This site makes great use of the Internet. For example, students can register for the test, add schools to their score report list, and view their scores online (instead of waiting 4–6 weeks as is standard after taking the paper-based test).

Where To Find/Buy:

On the Internet at http://www.gre.org/, or call (800) GRE-CALL to register for the test or to receive the latest test dates. Fax (609) 771-7906, or email gre-info@ets.org/.

Overall Rating
★★
Good source of basic info on the GRE, including test dates

Design, Ease Of Use
★★★
An interactive practice exam is included

1–4 Stars

Publisher:
Educational Testing Service

Educational Testing Service (ETS) is a private, nonprofit organization that develops and administers millions of achievement and admissions tests each year in the U.S. and 180 other countries, including the TOEFL. Their website, http://www.ETS.org, was launched in 1996.

Media:
Internet

Principal Focus:
Obtaining a Master's or PhD

MA/PhD Subtopic:
General Resources

Overall Rating
★★
Upbeat look at nontraditional study

Design, Ease Of Use
★★★
Concise; easy-to-read

1–4 Stars

Author:
Vicky Phillips and Cindy Yager
The authors are partners in the adult education consulting firm, Lifelong Learning.

Publisher:
Princeton Review
(Random House)

Edition:
1998

Price:
$20.00

Pages:
322

ISBN:
0679769307

Media:
Book

Principal Focus:
Obtaining a Master's or PhD

MA/PhD Subtopic:
General Resources

General Resources

PRINCETON REVIEW BEST DISTANCE LEARNING GRADUATE SCHOOLS
Earning Your Degree Without Leaving Home

Description:

This guide introduces 195 accredited institutions offering graduate degrees via distance learning programs. Geared toward individuals looking for an alternative to traditional campus graduate study, this guide explains how students can find the program best suited to their needs. The guide comprises ten brief chapters followed by more than 200 pages of school profiles. The authors use case examples in the first two chapters to describe how returning students' experiences with distance learning. In Chapters Three through Five, the authors explain the admissions process and address some common myths about getting into such programs. Chapters Six through Ten look at options for studying abroad, financial aid, and program choices. Here the authors explain how to design an individualized degree. The college profiles, the bulk of the book, list contact and program information, campus visit and admission requirements, tuition and fee numbers, and a brief history of the institution. The books closes with a bibliography and indexes.

Evaluation:

Although this guide features 195 program profiles, its strengths are in the first ten chapters. The authors paint a positive picture of long-distance learning and provide several examples of "real" people who have benefited from this type of graduate study. The author explain the different teaching methods, such as video tapes, e-mail tests, group discussion online, and guide readers to the one best suits their needs. The question-and-answer format used for the section on admission gives readers a good feel for what they need to do, and each chapter, though brief, is well-organized and clearly written. As with most guides "profiling" numerous programs, the information on individual programs is relatively thin, but the authors provide detailed contact information, including e-mail addresses, which make accessing additional information easy. This book is best suited for individuals who need flexibility in pursuit of a business administration or other common degrees. Those looking for more for more obscure programs, such as music or theater, will be disappointed. There simply isn't much out there.

Where To Find/Buy:

Bookstores, libraries, or by order direct from (800) 733-3000.

General Resources

ASSOCIATION FOR SUPPORT OF GRADUATE STUDENTS

Description:

The Association for Support of Graduate Students (ASGS) is a service organization of graduate students, graduate student organizations, and graduate schools. It publishes *Thesis News*, a quarterly 24-page "news and reference bulletin" for graduate students writing their master's level thesis or doctoral dissertation. The site includes a complete listing of past issues and contents, and several sample articles. (Copies of *Thesis News* are distributed free to ASGS members, membership is $28 per year. The site plans to publish *Thesis News* in an electronic format to be "downloaded at will" in Fall 1999.) Another feature of the site is "Doc Talk," a free, moderated email discussion list for grad students from around the world. "Doc Talk" features information on surviving the thesis-writing process. The list provides extracts and reprints of articles of interest, as well as reviews of resources and answers to students' questions pertaining to their theses. ASGS conducts surveys on the "experiences and perceptions" of grad students working on their theses and presents the results on a regular basis.

Evaluation:

"Misery loves company" and students struggling through the cash-strapped, deadline-driven grad school days are often encouraged and inspired by sharing stories with fellow students. ASGS provides a forum for formal, academic reading and discussion, as well as the informal, interpersonal fellowship that many grad students find revitalizing. "Doc Talk" employs two procedural devices that make it a welcome addition to your email inbox. First, it is "moderated," meaning they pay someone to screen out unwanted electronic traffic (no get-rich-while-working-at-home schemes). Second, it is sent only once a week. If you want to get the flavor of the listserv without formally signing on, click "The Best of Doc-Talk" for an archive of past message strings. Other convenient features at the site include a list of referrals to thesis consultants, including contact numbers for editorial, statistical, and motivational consultants.

Where To Find/Buy:

On the Internet at http://www.asgs.org

Overall Rating

★★

Stop by for a pep-talk if you're suffering from thesis blues

Design, Ease Of Use

★★

Thin content beyond listserv dialogue; quick-loading

1–4 Stars

Publisher:

Association For Support Of Graduate Students

The Association for Support of Graduate Students (ASGS) is a service organization of graduate students, grad-student organizations, and graduate degree-granting institutions. Its services and products are designed to help students complete their theses and obtain their degrees.

Media:

Internet

Principal Focus:
Obtaining a Master's or PhD

MA/PhD Subtopic:
General Resources

Overall Rating

★★

Convincing argument for distance learning with good advice on negotiating inherent difficulties

Design, Ease Of Use

★★

Heavily anecdotal

1–4 Stars

Author:

Darrel L. Hammon & Steven K. Albiston

Darrel Hammon is the Associate Vice-President for Extended Programs and Community Development at Lewis-Clark State College in Lewiston, Idaho. Steven Albiston is the Dean of Students at Eastern Idaho Technical College.

Publisher:

Sage

Edition:

1998

Price:

$21.00

Pages:

104

ISBN:

0761904867

Media:

Book

Principal Focus:

Obtaining a Master's or PhD

MA/PhD Subtopic:

General Resources

General Resources

COMPLETING GRADUATE SCHOOL LONG DISTANCE

Description:

Long distance education has opened the way for those with careers and families to earn graduate degrees without uprooting themselves. This resource, written by two men who completed their doctorate degrees hundreds of miles from their university's main campus, describes the process of selecting and taking long distance programs. It is based on their experience and those of a number of people they surveyed. The authors define the different forms of distance learning—off-campus classes, on-line instruction, independent study, interactive TV—and the pros and cons of each. They mention essentials to look for in programs and review the application process, emphasizing the importance of making contact with staff. Four chapters focus on aspects of graduate work that are more difficult with distance learning—negotiating time, selecting graduate committees and maintaining relationships with faculty, developing cohort groups, and finding literature. The requirements of doctorate programs are also discussed. The book closes with questions and answers from professors of distance learning. Appendices list graduate-level distance programs.

Evaluation:

Like other titles in Sage Publications' Graduate Survival Skills series, this book reflects the approach and experiences of its authors. These authors say they used an "applied, emotive approach." Their emphasis is less on helping readers find or get into graduate distance programs, and more on sharing the personal experiences of the authors and survey respondents. The approach has its pros and cons. Reading about these experiences helps create a warts-and-all portrait of distance learning. The virtues of distance learning are extolled as the wave of the future, making it seem a bright and practical alternative. Also, each chapter opens with a list of questions for readers to consider and ends with points to remember—the former are excellent starting points for readers when researching their needs and programs, and the latter are valuable tips. The downside of this approach is that some chapters are highly anecdotal and less grounded in fact and advice. These authors offer little solid advice for choosing and applying to distance learning programs, for example, but they provide plenty of tips for navigating a program once accepted. A good resource for those wondering if long distance learning will work for them.

Where To Find/Buy:

Bookstores and libraries, or directly from Sage Publications (http://www.sagepub.com) Phone (805) 499-0721; fax (805) 499-0871; email info@sagepub.com

General Resources

GRADSCHOOLS.COM

Description:

The site is arranged in a directory format with listings by curriculum, and, where necessary, subdivided by geography. Users select their desired program, such as biochemistry, political science or finance, from a drop-down menu. To narrow a search that results in too many matches, users choose from a variety of regional restrictions. The search produces a list of schools offering the program. Each listing includes the school name and address, as well as phone and fax numbers. Email addresses and the school's homepage are linked when available. Some entries contain a few lines of description and may mention degrees offered and research areas. The site also features links to financial aid resources on the Web, information about the publisher of the site, and links to some of the site's advertisers.

Evaluation:

On this site, a banner boasts "The Most Comprehensive Online Source of Graduate School Information," and with almost 30,000 program listings, it may be just that. The site is a giant step ahead of other online graduate school directories because its underlying architecture is tailored to the nature of graduate school selection. Whereas most college search sites are geared to high school seniors choosing a college, emphasizing factors, such as school size, location, and tuition, GradSchool.com is arranged around the criteria most important to prospective graduate students: field of study. In order to be genuinely useful, the graduate program menu must operate at a high enough level of detail that someone interested in studying Educational Administration does not have to wade through programs in Early Childhood Development. In most cases, the program selection is adequately specific. The heading "Biology," for example, contains nine subheadings to choose from.

Where To Find/Buy:

On the Internet at http://www.gradschools.com/

Overall Rating
★★
A good basic tool for the first step—identifying schools that offer specific programs

Design, Ease Of Use
★★
Quick and straightforward; nothing fancy or deep

1–4 Stars

Publisher:
Liberty City Promotions, Inc.
Liberty City Promotions, Inc. is an online service provider.

Media:
Internet

Principal Focus:
Obtaining a Master's or PhD

MA/PhD Subtopic:
General Resources

Overall Rating
★★

Very general introduction to programs and the admissions process; good advice for special populations

Design, Ease Of Use
★★

Lots of subheadings, but no index; some useful worksheets

1–4 Stars

Author:
Tim Haft, Dianne Lake, and others

Dianne Lake has developed and taught courses and software for Kaplan. She co-wrote *Getting Into Graduate School*, on which this book is based. Tim Haft, who revised and updated the bulk of the book, has been an academic and career counselor for over 10 years.

Publisher:
Kaplan Educational Centers and Simon & Schuster

Edition:
1999

Price:
$20.00

Pages:
274

ISBN:
0684859556

Media:
Book

Principal Focus:
Obtaining a Master's or PhD

MA/PhD Subtopic:
General Resources

Of Interest To:
Women
Disabled
International Students
Persons of Color

KAPLAN/NEWSWEEK GRADUATE SCHOOL ADMISSIONS ADVISER 2000

Description:
This guidebook was produced by Kaplan, the test preparation service. Part One introduces a variety of graduate programs, including social work, education, psychology, nursing, humanities and social sciences, engineering, computer science, and the sciences. Each program overview describes the current employment picture, types of programs, entrance requirements, tips on what to focus on in the personal statement, and the availability of financial assistance. Textboxes spotlight such things as percentage of men, women, and ethnic groups, and "what's hot" in the field. Part Two provides advice on what to look for in programs and what questions to ask. It also tells how to read a program catalog and includes a "Program Investigation Worksheet." The section on admissions goes over each admission requirement, with an emphasis on the personal statement, and includes sample statements with critiques by two admissions officers. The chapters in Part Four ("Special Considerations") are written by university counselors and focus on the needs and concerns of to re-entry students, African-Americans, people with disabilities, and international students. Part Five addresses finances; the appendix lists schools with graduate programs, including contact numbers, addresses, and URLs.

Evaluation:
This guidebook is an odd mix of general advice of limited use and in-depth discussions, which are truly enlightening. The descriptions of different fields of study include some valuable insights into the employment picture and tips under "Words to the Wise," but in general, they only skim the surface. The chapters on the admissions process are also surprisingly incomplete, except for the one on the personal statement, which includes excellent advice from real-life admissions officers. We question the value of the 50-page appendix since there is no indication of what type of graduate programs each school offers. On the other hand, "Selecting a Program" covers ground that others books miss, detailing "must-know" information and listing essential quality of life considerations, such as family needs (from good schools to spouse employment), the makeup of the population, and the cost of living. Finally, every chapter in the "Special Considerations" section is highly recommended. The authors write in lively prose and delve right to the heart of the issues affecting each population. Too bad the rest of the book doesn't live up to their standards.

Where To Find/Buy:
Bookstores and libraries.

General Resources

MS. MENTOR'S IMPECCABLE ADVICE FOR WOMEN IN ACADEMIA

Description:

In this question-and-answer volume, Ms. Mentor, a feisty feminist curmudgeon born of the imagination of Emily Toth, a professor of English and women's studies, offers practical advice on issues affecting women (and men) in the world of academia. Ms. Mentor's wisdom is dispensed in topical chapters, each beginning with a brief introduction describing the issue at hand. Included are chapters on graduate school, the job hunt, behavior at conferences and professional gatherings, the first year on the job, the "perils and pleasures of teaching," race and gender issues, sexual harassment, tenure, and life after tenure, and retirement. An extensive bibliography of women in academia follows the text, together with a brief index. The book is based on a series of advice columns aimed at women professors and graduate students, which ran in *Concerns*, the journal of the Women's Caucus for the Modern Languages.

Evaluation:

This book is funny, clever, and right on the mark when it comes to most issues affecting women in the academic workplace and graduate school. Ms. Mentor (Toth) is one professor of English who knows how to write and what women really encounter on campus and at conferences. The questions—drawn from columns and letters from Ms. Mentor's fans—are painfully frank. Some seem too wacky to be true, but our friends around campus assure us that these things do happen! Ms. Mentor's answers are generally hilarious and usually helpful. She clearly knows what is going on and has strategies for dealing with most situations. At times, her answers can be glib. We were disappointed in her responses to questions from an overweight academe and from gay and lesbian writers. Too often she recommends laying low until after tenure. We'd like a more sincere approach to personal identity. We were also surprised at the short answer to a female PhD stranded on the "wife track" (also known as the "mommy track") after following her husband to a new job at a research university. This serious problem affects hundreds of female academes with families. Ms. Mentor offered few practical suggestions or encouragement. Overall, however, this book gives the studious woman a good idea of what lies ahead in the academic world.

Where To Find/Buy:

Bookstores and libraries.

Overall Rating

★★

Intelligent and very funny; plenty of practical advice and insights amidst the barbs

Design, Ease Of Use

★★

Q & A format makes for difficult navigation; read by the chapter—it's fun

1–4 Stars

Author:
Emily Toth

Emily Toth is Professor of English and Women's Studies at Louisiana State University, author of *Unveiling Kate Chopin*, and co-author of *The Curse: A Cultural History of Menstruation*.

Publisher:
University of Pennsylvania

Edition:
1997

Price:
$15.95

Pages:
222

ISBN:
0812215664

Media:
Book

Principal Focus:
Obtaining a Master's or PhD

MA/PhD Subtopic:
General Resources

Of Interest To:
Women

Overall Rating

★★

Comprehensive information on graduate schools but little on individual departments

Design, Ease Of Use

★

Just the facts, little explanation, qualitative data, or navigation help

1–4 Stars

Author:

Harold R. Doughty

Mr. Doughty is a management and educational consultant. He is the former Executive Vice President and COO at American Commonwealth University, VP for Admissions, Financial Aid and Enrollment at U.S. International University, as well other administrative posts. He is also author of *The Penguin Guide To American Law Schools* and *The Penguin Guide To American Medical And Dental Schools*.

Publisher:

Penguin

Edition:

8th (1997)

Price:

$24.95

Pages:

635

ISBN:

0140469869

Media:

Book

Principal Focus:

Obtaining a Master's or PhD

MA/PhD Subtopic:

General Resources

General Resources

GUIDE TO AMERICAN GRADUATE SCHOOLS

Description:

This directory describes over 1,200 institutions offering post-baccalaureate study. After a brief introductory section discussing graduate and professional school selection, admission, financing and structure, the author lists graduate institutions alphabetically. Entries present background information on the school (size, tuition, location, library statistics, Web address, average housing costs). These entries are followed by brief paragraphs on each graduate degree program or school within the university. For example, under Adelphi University, readers find the Graduate School of Arts and Sciences, and the Schools of Business and Management, Education, Nursing and Social Work described in separate sections. These sections include information on tuition; enrollment; admission requirements, standards and deadlines; financial aid opportunities and deadlines; degree requirements; and fields of study. Indexes list institutions by state and fields of study.

Evaluation:

Though comprehensive in its coverage of a wide range of post-baccalaureate degree programs, the usefulness of this directory is hindered by its organization. Students interested in a graduate degree in Architecture, for example, must turn to the Fields of Study index to look up which institutions offer the degree. Here one finds a befuddling list of 82 institutions, with no indication of their relative strength or weakness. Students must then look up each program in the directory of institutions to learn more about the program; a slow and maddening process. This organization will work best for students interested in a graduate program offered by a small number of institutions (such as Bacteriology offered by four universities) or for students at the first stage of research who are interested in which schools offer their degree program and basic information on those programs. Other resources must be tapped to learn the reputation of programs, their particular assets, and details, such as minority enrollment figures.

Where To Find/Buy:

Bookstores and libraries.

General Resources

PRINCETON REVIEW ONLINE: GRADUATE

Description:

Princeton Review Online has dedicated a portion of its larger site to meet the needs of graduate school applicants (MAs/PhDs). From the main page of "Grad School," users can access all of topical sections and Special Features of this site-within-a-site. The topical sections are titled School Search, The Transition, and GRE. School Search offers articles on choosing a school, weighing a Master's degree vs. doctoral work, and finding sympathetic professors. Another article details the "practicalities" students should consider in their school search: costs and funding, type of facilities, campus location, teaching loads, etc. The Transition section features articles on such subjects as stress management, procrastination, and the "Pros and Cons of Grad School." In GRE, users will find strategies for maximizing scores and for taking the GRE CAT, as well as an explanation of GRE scoring. Accessible from every page are the site's Special Features. These include a practice GRE, a "Birkman Career Style" guide/quiz, and a searchable database designed to match students with tutors. An essay written especially for engineering applicants is highlighted on the main page; an online discussion forum is also provided.

Evaluation:

It is pity that the Princeton Review Online's "Graduate" segment isn't as developed or as helpful as its segments dedicated to Medicine, Law, and Business. The "professional" school segments feature searchable databases of schools, school "rankings," and valuable articles. "Graduate," on the other hand, has a last-minute, thrown-together feel, as if the Princeton Review people felt obligated, but not motivated, to provide something for the nonprofessional crowd. This section is slapdash, offering only the most obvious and basic tips in its articles on choosing a school and making the transition. Example: The essay on "Choosing A Grad School" basically says choose your school wisely because no one can afford to send out mass applications. To "size up" a school, users are advised to look at the academic quality of the program, their chances of getting in, and practical considerations like the weather. Duh! This site has little to teach those considering advanced degrees. The only section of value is the GRE page, which offers tips on taking the GRE, maximizing scores, and understanding the GRE CAT. Unfortunately, that page is primarily focused on selling Princeton Review's GRE preparation products. All in all, students are advised to look elsewhere.

Where To Find/Buy:

On the Internet at http://www.review.com/Graduate

Overall Rating

★

A few good pointers on the GRE and GRE CAT, but little else

Design, Ease Of Use

★★★

Easy to navigate, because there's not much here

1–4 Stars

Publisher:

Princeton Review

The Princeton Review is a leading test preparation organization; it produces preparation classes, books, and educational software.

A portion of the larger Princeton Review Online, this site-within-a-site focuses on business schools. Sections include a business school search feature, tips on getting in and interviewing, and advice on making the transition. Also included is information on registering and preparing for the GMAT, and for finding scholarships and financial aid. An online discussion forum is also featured.

Media:

Internet

Principal Focus:

Obtaining a Master's or PhD

MA/PhD Subtopic:

General Resources

Overall Rating

★

Folksy and practical, but would benefit from updating

Design, Ease Of Use

★★

A simple site to navigate

1–4 Stars

Author:

David Burrell

Mr. Burrell is currently a graduate student in American history at Ohio State University concentrating on early U.S. science and religion. A 1991 graduate of Holy Cross College, his background includes posts as Smithsonian researcher and high school teacher.

Media:

Internet

Principal Focus:

Obtaining a Master's or PhD

MA/PhD Subtopic:

General Resources

General Resources

GETTING IN: AN APPLICANT'S GUIDE TO GRADUATE SCHOOL ADMISSIONS

Description:

The text of this online guide was written in 1995 by a current graduate student in history. After four years of updates and free distribution via the Internet, the book is now being published in a paper version. Thus the site now contains excerpts from the book but not the entire text. A very detailed Table of Contents describes the chapters and sections of the book. Seven sections are available online; to read the others, you must now purchase the book. The online chapters include the Introduction plus: Deciding Where to Apply, Contacting Faculty Members, Visiting Schools, Commando Tactics While Waiting, and a Final Note. The emphasis throughout the guide is on the less well-known aspects of graduate school admissions, beyond grades, scores, and letters of recommendation. The site includes a fairly comprehensive set of links and a page on graduate student humor, with creative writing and jokes about graduate school life.

Evaluation:

As the Internet becomes more commercial and "professional," pages like this one created and maintained by a real graduate student will become less common. Too bad. The author wrote the guide out of his own frustrating experience applying to, and being rejected by three graduate programs. The next year, after a great deal of soul searching and learning about strategies for successfully navigating the admissions process, he was admitted to six quality programs. He wrote his guide to "illuminate a path through the confusion" for other students. He mixes down-in-the-trenches practicality ("Most students apply to far too few programs their first time around") with encouraging words and motivational stories. His tips are at times unconventional; his view is that most application guides are too conservative. Both his online guide and his website are filled with folksy wisdom and humor. Check out "Grad Student Humor and Life" and chuckle at the "You just might be a graduate student if . . ." series.

Where To Find/Buy:

On the Internet at http://www.h-net.msu.edu/~burrell/guide0.html. The entire text can be purchased by contacting: The Graduate Group, P.O. Box 370351, West Hartford, CT 06137-0351; (860) 233-2330

General Resources

PETERSON'S GUIDE TO DISTANCE LEARNING PROGRAMS 1999

Description:
With 850 listings of institutions offering distance learning programs, this guide is designed to help students and employers take advantage of electronic learning opportunities. The introduction includes student profiles to show readers what kind of people are using this nontraditional form of education. Peterson's also answers questions about what distance learning is and how it works, both technically and conceptually. The guide addresses trends in education and attempts to help students select an institution and program, paying special attention to schools that have certain geographical restrictions or limited learning opportunities. This guide also covers academic advising, explaining how credits are applied. It offers study tips as well. Financial options are briefly addressed to give prospective students a general idea of what is available. These comments are followed by a glossary comprised largely of technical definitions. The school profiles feature institution background, course delivery sites, media usage, geographic restrictions, available services, tuition, registration, and contact information. The profiles are followed by approximately 80 "in-depth" school profiles from institutions that provided additional details. Program, Individual Course, and Geographic Indexes follow the text.

Evaluation:
Peterson's educational guides are generally excellent research tools, but this one doesn't make the grade. The duplicate school profiles serve no good purpose and only force readers to flip back and forth, wondering what they have missed. Why not consolidate this information in one profile, using larger type for all entries? We sense that Peterson's felt pressured to compete with the other distance learning guides, but they should have taken the time to make a more usable product. The information is in here somewhere—it's just hard to find. An online database or CD-ROM would be more useful. And the introductory comments on selecting a program and financing a degree don't make up for the organizational problems. Look to other directories for a better product. *Barron's Guide To Distance Learning* offers similar profiles in a more usable format and provides excellent advice.

Where To Find/Buy:
Bookstores and libraries.

Overall Rating
★
Adequate

Design, Ease Of Use
★★
Duplicates some information; navigation confusing

1–4 Stars

Publisher:
Peterson's

Edition:
3rd (1998)

Price:
$26.95

Pages:
698

ISBN:
0768901294

Media:
Book

Principal Focus:
Obtaining a Master's or PhD

MA/PhD Subtopic:
General Resources

Arts, Humanities & Social Sciences—General

★★★★

Overall Rating
★★★★
Detailed and subjective analysis of 23 disciplines and programs

Design, Ease Of Use
★★★★
Comprehensive; a delight to read

1–4 Stars

Author:
Robert Clark & John Palattella

Clark and Palattella are the editors of the award-winning *Linguafranca* magazine.

Publisher:
Linguafranca

Edition:
1997

Price:
$24.95

Pages:
524

ISBN:
0963023802

Media:
Book

Principal Focus:
Obtaining a Master's or PhD

MA/PhD Subtopic:
Arts, Humanities & Social Sciences

Art & Humanities Subtopic:
General

REAL GUIDE TO GRAD SCHOOL
What You Better Know Before You Choose Humanities & Social Sciences

 Recommended For:
Obtaining a Master's or PhD

Description:

The editors of Linguafranca, a magazine on academia, have conducted interviews with hundreds of professors, graduate students, and administrators to produce this guide. Part One describes "the rise of the research scholar" and the admissions and financing process. The rest of this hefty, guide is devoted to an analysis of 23 disciplines and the departments who teach them. The chapter on English, for example, begins with "Why English," and moves into "How English Has Taken Shape," a section examining the recent history of the discipline and a description of prominent subfields. "What's Next" recommends schools to consider for various academic focuses, and "The Job Market" speaks to the current supply and demand for PhDs. Throughout the book, the editors intersperse snippets about the daily life of the grad student: teaching, professional networking, intra-program personality conflicts; competition; and jockeying for position among colleagues.

Evaluation:

This book begins with: "There are hundreds of good reasons to go to graduate school—but let's get real . . . to decide to get a PhD in the humanities or social sciences in the late 1990s takes guts." Thus opens a book that affirms the call to scale the intellectual heights of a PhD program, while challenging would-be grad students with sobering statistics and details of what life in grad school and beyond is really like. The editors write in a frank, from-the-hip style that belies the serious scholarship undergirding the book's information and advice. The nuts and bolts of the application process are covered, but their hip and sophisticated prose focuses on the all-important tertiary issues that prospective students must consider: departmental interpersonal dynamics; funding priorities; and the like. Their emphasis on the department, rather than the school as a whole, is right on target. Their in-depth and comprehensive evaluations of 23 disciplines are invaluable for prospective grad students.

Where To Find/Buy:

Bookstores and libraries.

Arts, Humanities & Social Sciences—General

PETERSON'S GRADUATE STUDIES IN ARTS, HUMANITIES, & ARCHAEOLOGY 1998

Description:

Designed as a directory and guidance tool for those pursuing a graduate program in the arts, humanities, or archaeology, this guide provides more than 5,200 listings of programs in a hefty print volume and includes a companion CD-ROM (for Windows or Mac), which describes 134 programs in-depth. The first section of the book provides general information, academic direction, and school selection and financial advice. Included is "The Insider's Guide to Graduate School," written by Kevin Boyer, Executive Director of the National Association of Graduate-Professional Students, in which Boyer notes issues to consider when making educational and career decisions. A brief description of the application process, including a timetable and specifics on essay writing, interviews, and auditions follows. The financial section describes loans, grants, fellowships, and other available aid, including an estimated debt management repayment schedule. Two brief sections on graduate admission test requirements and school accreditation information round out the introduction. The profiles are arranged by study area. Each profile provides basic program details, such as number of faculty and students, degree and entrance requirements, tuition, financial aid, and contact information. A school index, noting programs offered, follows the profiles.

Evaluation:

Like most Peterson's guides, this resource is professional in presentation, content, and organization. The book is big—two-inches thick—and has tiny print, but it is navigable. A CD icon next to program listings in the book indicates a program is covered in more depth on the companion CD-ROM. A nice feature—too bad only 134 programs, out of 5,200, get this in-depth treatment. The CD is easy to install and simple to use. The profiles in the print volume are basic, covering only a few features for each program. The advice and information offered in the beginning of the book are brief and generic. These introductions are found in all of Peterson's "Compact Guides." Without more detailed information on specific issues of interest to those considering graduate work in these fields (e.g., job prospects, identification of effective mentors/advisors, etc.), this resource is best used as a very preliminary guide to available programs.

Where To Find/Buy:

Bookstores and libraries.

Overall Rating
★★
Broad coverage of programs, but generic advice on admissions and aid

Design, Ease Of Use
★★★
Well-indexed with consistent information; tiny print; useful CD-ROM companion

---

1–4 Stars

Publisher:
Peterson's

Edition:
1998

Price:
$24.95

Pages:
852

ISBN:
0768900042

Media:
Book + CD-ROM

Principal Focus:
Obtaining a Master's or PhD

MA/PhD Subtopic:
Arts, Humanities & Social Sciences

Art & Humanities Subtopic:
General

Arts, Humanities & Social Sciences—General

PRINCETON REVIEW BEST GRADUATE PROGRAMS: HUMANITIES & SOCIAL SCIENCES

Overall Rating
★★
Good descriptions of the overall atmosphere of each school, but little in-depth information on specific programs

Design, Ease Of Use
★★
Lively writing, extensive cross-referencing; good tips on researching programs

1–4 Stars

Author:
Jonathan Spaihts

The author is a researcher and freelance writer in New York City. A graduate of Princeton University, he has worked for *Princeton Review* as a teacher, writer, researcher, and course developer. He is also author of *The Best Graduate Programs: Physical & Biological Sciences.*

Publisher:
Princeton Review
(Random House)

Edition:
2nd (1998)

Price:
$25.00

Pages:
578

ISBN:
037575203X

Media:
Book

Principal Focus:
Obtaining a Master's or PhD

MA/PhD Subtopic:
Arts, Humanities & Social Sciences

Art & Humanities Subtopic:
General

Description:

This hefty guide by The Princeton Review profiles 56 of the best graduate schools in the humanities and social sciences. Schools were deemed "the best" based on research by the National Research Council and the Council for Graduate Schools, admissions selectivity, faculty reputation, class sizes, library and computer facilities, and the opinions of graduate students themselves. The book opens with six chapters of information and advice on deciding to go to graduate school, choosing, applying to, financing, and surviving a grad school education. Each school is profiled in a two-page spread with a sidebar listing vital statistics (including most noteworthy programs). Profiles include an overview of the school's history, reputation, and academic quality; students opinions of their school, professors, and peers; admissions deadlines and information about minority and transfer policies; and a description of campus life and the surrounding area. The statistics on individual departments are then given in bar form. These include a profile of students, admissions requirements, average GRE scores, and financial facts (number of students funded and amount).

Evaluation:

The Princeton Review takes on an enormous task in this "buyer's guide" and does a good introductory job. Because of the broad scope of the subject matter, they do not profile the individual Master's/PhD programs in any detail. Rather, they focus on the schools themselves and then give readers advice on researching the departments themselves. A chapter on using professional societies as resources explains how to tap into these organizations to learn more about the field; it includes contacts and descriptions for 17 societies. The author wisely stresses finding professors who share your research interests and offers advice on how to seek them out. The writing is engaging (rare for a factual guide like this) and the inclusion of student opinions (based on surveys of thousands of graduate students) gives the school descriptions a more honest flavor than official school literature. You'll learn which are the up-and-coming programs, the strengths and weaknesses of each school, and which issues students consistently complain about. You'll also get a good feel for the environment, the social scene, and the cost of living. A good place to start your graduate school search, this guide will frustrate those who want to in-depth information on competing programs.

Where To Find/Buy:

Bookstores and libraries.

Arts, Humanities & Social Sciences—Education

PETERSON'S COMPACT GUIDES: GRADUATE STUDIES IN EDUCATION

Description:

More than 7,850 accredited graduate programs in education are profiled in this Peterson's guide. Schools are arranged first in alphabetical order under General Education. The individual programs are then listed under their particular focus—administration, instruction, and theory; instructional levels from early childhood to adult education; and 16 subject areas. A separate section describes graduate and professional programs in physical education, including recreation, kinesiology, and sports administration. The profiles are capsule summaries of basic information—student body, degrees awarded, entrance and degree requirements, expenses, financial aid awards, and areas of faculty research. Seventy-four programs submitted more in-depth descriptions, which are presented in a CD-ROM provided with the book. Also in the book are short introductory chapters about factors to consider when choosing schools, applications and the dos and don'ts of personal essays. Tips on finding financial aid and handling loan debts are also provided.

Evaluation:

This is a massive book, but the program profiles it provides are extremely short, giving only vital statistics. The format is generally consistent, making it easy to compare programs. However, we found that information is missing from some entries and tuition costs are presented in a variety of ways, some of which are not terribly helpful (for example, hourly costs with no clue as to how many hours a program requires). It is unfortunate that so few programs opted to provide the longer descriptions, which give more detailed information about research facilities, school location, and faculty members. Nevertheless, this book covers many more programs than its main competitor, the Allyn & Bacon guide (reviewed on page 53). Peterson's version is a better reference for those considering a graduate program in education. What's more, arranging the book by program focus, instead of parent institution, makes this book easier to use; readers can turn directly to their area of interest. This guide is only a first stepping stone in the research process, however. As for the introductory chapters, Peterson's recycles this material from guidebook to guidebook. Because it is so generally written, it is of little practical use to readers, except as an introduction to the application process.

Where To Find/Buy:

Bookstores and libraries.

Overall Rating

★★

Capsule summaries of a huge number of programs; little detail

Design, Ease Of Use

★★★

Good classification system; recycled introductory chapters

1–4 Stars

Publisher:
Peterson's

Edition:
1998

Price:
$24.95

Pages:
1163

ISBN:
078900026

Media:
Book + CD-ROM

Principal Focus:
Obtaining a Master's or PhD

MA/PhD Subtopic:
Arts, Humanities & Social Sciences

Art & Humanities Subtopic:
Education

Overall Rating

★

Statistics on 300 education programs, nothing more

Design, Ease Of Use

★★★

Easy-to-use format with good indexing system

1–4 Stars

Author:

Mark J. Drozdowski & Patrick Cullen

Mark Drozdowski is an education consultant, university administrator, freelance writer, and a doctoral candidate at Harvard University's Graduate School of Education. Patrick Cullen is a freelance writer. Both authors received their Master's Degrees in higher education from Harvard.

Publisher:

Allyn & Bacon

Edition:

1997

Price:

$19.95

Pages:

175

ISBN:

0205195113

Media:

Book

Principal Focus:

Obtaining a Master's or PhD

MA/PhD Subtopic:

Arts, Humanities & Social Sciences

Art & Humanities Subtopic:

Education

Arts, Humanities & Social Sciences—Education

INSIDER'S GUIDE TO GRADUATE PROGRAMS IN EDUCATION

Description:

The authors, both graduates of education programs, surveyed over 1,000 deans and faculty members to develop profiles of almost 300 colleges and universities. Each profile comprises a one-column table of statistics. Information includes available programs, research areas, the number of faculty in each, research institutes and centers, student body demographics, tuition and housing costs, number of applicants versus those accepted and those enrolled, and required tests and scores. Programs are arranged by state and indexed under 22 program headings, from adult education to special education. In a brief introduction, the authors provide guidelines for deciding whether graduate school is the right choice, and advice on the application process. They also discuss the "peculiar nature of ed schools," which have highly diversified programs and student populations, address the challenges of education today, and describe three innovative reform initiatives.

Evaluation:

The title of this resource—"Insider's Guide"—is misleading. While this is one of very few full-length guides devoted to graduate programs in education that we found, the authors provide little more than the bare statistical bones for 300 (out of more than 1,200) education schools and departments in the U.S. (They chose the most prestigious and highly attended schools). Information is gleaned from deans and faculty—insiders to be sure—but we get no description of curricula, programs, or school environment. The authors did not gather any information from students, and so they are unprepared to address the strengths and weaknesses of each program from the consumer's point of view. The introductory chapter is also short on advice and information. The best feature of this resource is the indexing system, which allows readers to identify which schools have programs in their interest area and whether there is a critical mass of faculty teaching and researching the subject. Otherwise, this resource is merely a starting point, helping readers find out whether they have the finances and the scores necessary for admission to specific schools. They will need to do a lot more research after that.

Where To Find/Buy:

Bookstores and libraries.

English & Foreign Languages

THE MLA GUIDE TO THE JOB SEARCH
A Handbook For Departments & For PhDs & PhD Candidates In English & Foreign Languages

 Recommended For:
Obtaining a Master's or PhD

Description:

This book opens with chapters devoted to "general advice" for the academic job hunt, discussing how to begin the search early, while still in school, and ways to make oneself more "marketable." The authors also address such practicalities as preparing for the cost of the job search, making up a vita, writing a letter of application, and preparing for the interview. Chapters 2–3 are directed to the job seeker and the various departments, respectively, offering advice and information for those involved in both ends of the hiring process. Chapter 4 discusses opportunities in the nonacademic job market, and offers tips on translating academic skills into skills valued in the workplace. This chapter also contains advice about how to research employment fields and tailor a resume to fit a nonacademic job. Chapter 5 looks at general employment prospects in the professional labor market. The last two chapters discuss the academic labor market and "job training" in graduate programs. Appendices include official MLA statements on hiring and adjunct faculty, and employment and salary statistics for PhDs.

Evaluation:

At $10.00, *The MLA Guide To The Job Search* gives PhD candidates a lot of bang for their buck. The academic job search is, as the preface points out, a stressful process, especially for candidates in English and foreign languages who find themselves competing for a relatively small number of positions. This little handbook lays out the nuts and bolts of the process and clearly describes opportunities in nonacademic job markets. PhD candidates will find this book opens up their eyes to the postgraduate school unknown; it offers a valuable set of practical tools and a good sense of what's out there (and what isn't) for humanists. However, readers should be aware that this book represents the "official" MLA view of the system. They may want to consider additional resources that provide different perspectives on the academic job hunt.

Where To Find/Buy:

Bookstores and libraries.

Overall Rating
★★★★
Practical tips combined with excellent discussions of academic and professional job markets

Design, Ease Of Use
★★★★
Clear, concise treatment of complex topics

1–4 Stars

Author:
English Showalter, Howard Figler, Lori G. Kletzer, Jack H. Schuster, & Seth R. Katz

Showalter is professor of French at Rutgers University. Figler is a career consultant. Kletzer is assistant professor of economics at the University of California, Santa Cruz. Schuster is professor of education and public policy at the Claremont Graduate School. Katz is assistant professor of English at Bradley University.

Publisher:
Modern Language Association Of America

Edition:
2nd (1996)

Price:
$10.00

Pages:
156

ISBN:
0873526821

Media:
Book

Principal Focus:
Obtaining a Master's or PhD

MA/PhD Subtopic:
Arts, Humanities & Social Sciences

Art & Humanities Subtopic:
English & Foreign Languages

Arts, Humanities & Social Sciences—Psychology & Social Work

★★★★

Overall Rating
★★★★
The best kind of hand-holding: directions, insights, details, special tips

Design, Ease Of Use
★★★★
Written in a question-and-answer format; includes a detailed table of contents

1–4 Stars

Author:
Patricia Keith-Spiegel, PhD

Dr. Keith-Spiegel has been the Graduate School Counselor in the psychology department at California State University in Northridge for more than 20 years. She has published four books and over 50 articles.

Publisher:
Lawrence Erlbaum Associates

Edition:
1991

Price:
$22.50

Pages:
373

ISBN:
0805806385

Media:
Book

Principal Focus:
Obtaining a Master's or PhD

MA/PhD Subtopic:
Arts, Humanities & Social Sciences

Art & Humanities Subtopic:
Psychology & Social Work

THE COMPLETE GUIDE TO GRADUATE SCHOOL ADMISSION
Psychology & Related Fields

 Recommended For:
Obtaining a Master's or PhD

Description:

Dr. Keith-Spiegel's guide to the graduate school application process is designed to be a comprehensive resource for students interested in psychology or a related field. The text is divided into five parts. Part I, "Overview of the Pursuit of Graduate Study in Psychology and Related Fields," features application timetables and checklists, "specialized hints" for "categories" of students, such as non-psychology majors, and a description of what schools look for in an applicant. Part II offers strategies for "Enhancing Your Chances" of acceptance. Chapters discuss academic factors, attracting support, research/field experience, and performing well on the GRE. In Part III, "Making Your Choices," the chapters focus on school and program selection: finding a "good match," considering finances and aid, and researching schools. Part IV covers "The Application Process." It includes chapters on recommendations, including advice on who, when, and how to ask for a recommendation, as well as chapters on filling out forms and preparing statements of purpose and essays. Preparing for the preselection interview, accepting offers, and handling rejection are among the topics addressed in Part V, "The Post-Application Period."

Evaluation:

The author has served as a graduate school counselor for more than 20 years and has carefully researched graduate school application and selection procedures. Her thorough knowledge of the subject shows in this excellent guide for students pursuing graduate degrees in psychology and related fields. She walks the reader through the entire application process one step at a time, providing detailed directions, concrete ideas, and insightful advice along the way. For example, she tells readers how to best "market" their undergraduate school, even if they aren't well known or are religious. (She warns readers of potential prejudices on the part of the selection committee.) She also offers specialized tips to particular groups of students, including psychology majors and non-psychology majors, MAs applying to doctoral programs, graduate students transferring from other fields, as well as to women, ethnic minorities, gays and lesbians, physically disabled persons, and foreign-born or international students. A detailed table of contents directs readers to sections of interest (No index!); the text, written in a question-and-answer format, is concise and easy-to-read. This resource is "how-to-apply" hand-holding at its best. Take advantage!

Where To Find/Buy:
Bookstores and libraries.

Arts, Humanities & Social Sciences—Psychology & Social Work

GETTING IN
A Step-By-Step Plan For Gaining Admission To Graduate School In Psychology

 Recommended For:
Obtaining a Master's or PhD

Description:

This book describes five major phases for applying to graduate programs in psychology and offers a step-by-step plan for each. To help potential applicants decide whether grad school in psychology is for them, the authors explain how to identify one's motivation, interests, skills, and qualifications. They also examine the criteria that selection committees look at and offer advice for improving qualifications. To help readers narrow their field, they describe types of degrees, specialties, areas of concentration, and three models for psych training. Also discussed are seven steps for choosing programs to apply to, worksheets to summarize applicants' needs and qualifications, and data on each program of interest. (The book does not include program descriptions—readers are referred to the American Psychological Association's *Graduate Study in Psychology* reviewed by us on page 57). The authors then offer advice on procuring letters of reference, writing the essay, preparing for an interview, and other parts of the application process. Appendices include a resource list, a guide to the American Psychological Association divisions, and information on the Minority Fellowship Program.

Evaluation:

The American Psychological Association created this book to help qualified candidates find their way through the fiercely competitive admissions process for grad programs in psychology. For those lacking insider knowledge or a clear application strategy, the process can be discouraging. This comprehensive resource is easy-to-read and concise, and addresses the needs of specific populations, such as minorities, gays, and people with disabilities, always in context. The systematic approach demystifies the process and makes it manageable. The background discussion on concentrations, degrees, and models of study is detailed and informative. The worksheets and checklists are excellent, and the advice on getting letters of reference, writing essays (complete with techniques for overcoming writer's block), and preparing for interviews will help any reader prepare for the application process. Readers should note that they will need an additional guide for specific programs, but this book's detailed, "insider" information and step-by-step approach make it an excellent choice for those looking at graduate school in psychology.

Where To Find/Buy:

Bookstores and libraries.

Overall Rating
★★★★
Great strategies for learning about programs and the application process

Design, Ease Of Use
★★★★
Step-by-step approach with useful worksheets and checklists

1–4 Stars

Publisher:
American Psychological Association

Located in Washington, D.C., the American Psychological Association (APA) is the largest scientific and professional organization representing psychology in the United States.

Edition:
1997

Price:
$14.95

Pages:
221

ISBN:
1557982198

Media:
Book

Principal Focus:
Obtaining a Master's or PhD

MA/PhD Subtopic:
Arts, Humanities & Social Sciences

Art & Humanities Subtopic:
Psychology & Social Work

★★★★

Overall Rating
★★★★
Insightful and systematic suggestions for finding the "best fit"

Design, Ease Of Use
★★★
Detailed plan with worksheets and chart; no index to find specific programs

1–4 Stars

Author:
Michael A. Sayette, Tracy J. Mayne, & John C. Norcross

Michael Sayette is Associate Professor of Psychology at the University of Pittsburgh, with a secondary appointment as Associate Professor of Psychiatry at the Western Psychiatric Institute and Clinic, University of Pittsburgh School of Medicine. Tracy Mayne is an Adjunct Assistant Professor at New York University and a principal investigator at Gay Men's Health Crisis. John Norcross is Professor and former Chair of Psychology at the University of Scranton and a coeditor of the APA Psychotherapy Videotape Series.

Publisher:
Guilford

Edition:
1998/1999

Price:
$21.95

Pages:
322

ISBN:
1572302747

Media:
Book

Principal Focus:
Obtaining a Master's or PhD

MA/PhD Subtopic:
Arts, Humanities & Social Sciences

Art & Humanities Subtopic:
Psychology & Social Work

Arts, Humanities & Social Sciences—Psychology & Social Work

INSIDER'S GUIDE TO GRADUATE PROGRAMS IN CLINICAL & COUNSELING PSYCHOLOGY (1998–1999)

 Recommended For:
Obtaining a Master's or PhD

Description:

This revised and updated guidebook presents a systematic approach to selecting a graduate program in psychology. This newest edition includes several newly accredited programs, expanded coverage of financial aid, and websites. Seven chapters explain how to create an individualized plan that simultaneously markets applicants and makes them wise consumers, choosing the program that best suits their goals. The authors describe the differences between counseling and clinical programs, and the practice-oriented PsyD and the research-oriented PhD. They go over five grad school selection criteria and explain how to increase applicant marketability in terms of research skills, course work, clinical experience, and entrance exams. They then present a process for selecting schools based on research interests, clinical opportunities, and theoretical orientation. Advice is also given on mastering the application process and the interview. Included are one-column reports on over 300 schools, comprised of information gleaned from admissions office responses about faculty orientation, research areas, entrance requirements, and applicant admissions.

Evaluation:

This resource for future psychologists leans heavily on the authors' process for selecting and applying to schools, but offers less substantive program descriptions than the American Psychological Association guidebook to graduate programs in psychology. The authors' step-by-step process is detailed and shows readers how to find the programs that meet their interests and objectives. It is a time-consuming process that require filling out worksheets and cross-referencing charts, but we think the approach will dramatically increase applicants' chances of finding and gaining admission to a program that excites them. The worksheets and charts—which are in the form of appendices—are well-designed. One invaluable chart lists the research areas provided by each school, the number of faculty involved and grants received, in order to show how intensively the school pursues particular areas of interest. This documentation is unique to this guidebook and is perhaps what makes it an "insider's guide." Another useful worksheet helps applicants rate how well they meet a school's requirements. An excellent choice for understanding training models, choosing the appropriate degree and emphasis, finding the school that fits, and then selling yourself. Check the website for updates (http://www.guilford.com/gradpsych)

Where To Find/Buy:
Bookstores and libraries.

Arts, Humanities & Social Sciences—Psychology & Social Work

GRADUATE STUDY IN PSYCHOLOGY 1998–1999
With 1999 Addendum

Description:

This annual guidebook, with a 75-page addendum updating 1998's text, lists information about over 500 graduate-level programs in psychology in the United States, from degrees in human sexuality to traditional PhDs in clinical psychology. All the information was self-reported by the institutions in response to questionnaires sent out by the association. The first ten pages are composed of background text and include American Psychological Association (APA) policies regarding graduate education, rules for acceptance of offers for admission and financial aid, and some general information about applying to graduate school, such as suggestions for selecting the right program and submitting an application. The next section, the 75-page addendum, contains specific changes to the text paginated separately. The next 500 pages are profiles of programs arranged by state. Each one gives statistics on programs and degrees offered, the number of applicants who applied, were accepted, and enrolled in each program, degree and admission requirements, and tuition. Descriptions are also given of the orientation, objectives and emphasis of the department, available internships and practica, as well as special facilities and resources such as clinics, hospitals and other practicum sites, computers, and study populations. An index lists programs by area of study offered.

Evaluation:

The editor of this hefty resource recommends that readers use it in conjunction with the APA's *Getting In: A Step-By-Step Plan For Gaining Admission to Graduate School in Psychology* reviewed on page 59 and for good reason. While it provides extensive information about a huge number and variety of graduate level psychology programs, it offers next-to-no advice on how to choose between schools or gain admission. It does, however, provide important statistics on a vast array of specialties, acceptance rates, and prerequisites for admission. Unfortunately, the information on program orientation, objectives, and emphasis is quite general, so applicants must do their own research on faculty specializations and grants. The information on internships, practica, and associated facilities and resources gives a good sense of program orientations and research possibilities. Be forewarned: this book was not designed with readers' eyes in mind—print is tiny and statistics are listed in paragraph form, rather than in a more readable table format, and readers must match the updated information in the addendum to the existing content, which may prove frustrating. Still, there is no better resource describing the variety of the psychology and counseling disciplines.

Where To Find/Buy:

Bookstores and libraries.

Overall Rating
★★★★
Valuable information about over 500 psychology programs

Design, Ease Of Use
★★
Very small print; poor formatting of statistics

1–4 Stars

Publisher:
American Psychological Association

Located in Washington, D.C., the American Psychological Association (APA) is the largest scientific and professional organization representing psychology in the United States.

Edition:
(32nd) 1998

Price:
$21.95

Pages:
545 + 75-page addendum

ISBN:
1557985898

Media:
Book

Principal Focus:
Obtaining a Master's or PhD

MA/PhD Subtopic:
Arts, Humanities & Social Sciences

Art & Humanities Subtopic:
Psychology & Social Work

★★★

Overall Rating
★★★
Inspiring information on career possibilities and funding

Design, Ease Of Use
★★
Trails of links, some broken; quickest loading site in town!

1–4 Stars

Publisher:
American Psychological Association

Located in Washington, D.C., the American Psychological Association (APA) is the largest scientific and professional organization representing psychology in the United States.

Media:
Internet

Principal Focus:
Obtaining a Master's or PhD

MA/PhD Subtopic:
Arts, Humanities & Social Sciences

Art & Humanities Subtopic:
Psychology & Social Work

Arts, Humanities & Social Sciences—Psychology & Social Work

AMERICAN PSYCHOLOGICAL ASSOCIATION: STUDENT INFORMATION/EDUCATION PROGRAMS

Description:

Within the American Psychological Association's vast website are two pages of use to students and others considering a higher degree in psychology. The APA Student Information home page (http://www.apa.org/students/) comprises seven sites, each containing a list of links to further information about its particular topic. The "Career Information" site links to articles, websites, and videos describing the breadth of career options in psychology. Included is a link to the APA's 52 specialized areas of interest within the field. The "Undergraduate Information" page features a map to other sites answering frequently asked questions, and links to a list of accredited graduate programs. Links to funding sources provide information on grants, fellowships and scholarships, as well as specific information for students of color. The APA Education Programs home page (http://www.apa.org/ed/) features a similar financial aid page. "Information for Students" links to openings in graduate schools, related books and pamphlets, an APA article listing the steps to getting into graduate school, rules for acceptance of offers for admission and financial aid, and information on respecialization training.

Evaluation:

While these APA websites offer plenty of valuable information, finding it can be difficult. The home pages are attractively designed and quick to load, but to access information, visitors must travel through maze-like lists, and more lists, of links. The "Answers to Frequently Asked Questions" page is particularly misleading, as no questions or answers are given. Instead, the page is subdivided by category, such as Areas of Interest, Careers, and Graduate Education and Training. These categories lead to links to sources of information on the topic (usually written by the APA). A number of these links are broken, and the graduate and postgraduate links are limited in number. The two sections most deserving of attention are the articles on psychology careers (at http://www.apa.org/students/), which describe a wide and sometimes unusual variety of career possibilities, and the funding information found at both sites. The funding sources differ on each page, so students are advised to explore both. Also check out the 52 areas of interest for more inspiring ideas on career direction (http://www.apa.org/about/division.html). The APA article on steps to getting into graduate school is also useful, if rather basic.

Where To Find/Buy:

On the Internet at http://www.apa.org/students/ and http://www.apa.org/ed/

Arts, Humanities & Social Sciences—Psychology & Social Work

GUIDE TO SELECTING & APPLYING TO MASTER OF SOCIAL WORK PROGRAMS (1999)

Description:

The author of this book draws on personal and professional experience in social work to show readers how to find a school that best meets their individual needs. In this third edition, he adds a summary of "dos and don'ts" after each chapter, and provides additional worksheets to help readers with applications and personal statements. In Part I, he explains what prospective students should look for in programs and how to find the optimum field work site. He also offers advice balancing academic challenges and field work, and explains license qualifications and potential. In Part II, the author describes what school officials look for in applicants: for example, a solid biographical statement, strong academic background, and related experience. He explains what steps students should take when accepted and suggests blocking out some "free time" before school begins. Part III of the guide comprises sources to guide readers with specific needs. This section also includes a chart comparing several leading graduate programs. A two-page index rounds out the book.

Evaluation:

This up-to-date, well-organized tool gives those interested in a Masters of Social Work an inside look into program policies and issues, along with the author's practical advice. This advice can be basic at times, but readers will appreciate his interesting personal perspectives and balanced presentation. Of special note is the author's fine comparison of academic programs. Applicants unclear about the nuances of the clinical and policy/administration aspects of social work practice will learn from this discussion. The author's experience as assistant dean, educator, and counselor lends credibility to the book, and his straightforward prose style make reading more enjoyable, compared to the many "selecting and applying" books. Especially helpful is the chart comparing leading graduate programs. It gives applicants a quick understanding of each program's offerings and requirements. A good resource for those considering advanced study in social work, this small, quick-read would be even more appealing if it cost less.

Where To Find/Buy:

Bookstores and libraries.

Overall Rating
★★
Basic and practical advice; encouraging

Design, Ease Of Use
★★★
Clearly written and well-organized; user-friendly layout

1–4 Stars

Author:
Jesus Reyes, AM, ACSW

The author is Director of Parents and Children Services with the Office of the Chief Judge of the Circuit Court of Cook County, IL. His social work experience includes work in health care, academics, and private practice.

Publisher:
White Hat Communications

Edition:
3rd (1999)

Price:
$19.95

Pages:
221

ISBN:
0965365336

Media:
Book

Principal Focus:
Obtaining a Master's or PhD

MA/PhD Subtopic:
Arts, Humanities & Social Sciences

Art & Humanities Subtopic:
Psychology & Social Work

II. Obtaining A Master's Or PhD

Arts, Humanities & Social Sciences—Psychology & Social Work

Overall Rating
★★
Comprehensive coverage of programs, but generic advice on admissions and aid

Design, Ease Of Use
★★★
Well-indexed with consistent information; tiny print; useful companion CD-ROM

1–4 Stars

Publisher:
Peterson's

Edition:
1998

Price:
$24.95

Pages:
810

ISBN:
0768900034

Media:
Book + CD-ROM

Principal Focus:
Obtaining a Master's or PhD

MA/PhD Subtopic:
Arts, Humanities & Social Sciences

Art & Humanities Subtopic:
Psychology & Social Work

PETERSON'S GRADUATE STUDIES IN SOCIAL SCIENCES & SOCIAL WORK 1998

Description:

Written for those considering a graduate degree in the social sciences or social work, this guide comprises more than 4,850 program listings in a thick print volume and includes a companion CD-ROM (for Windows and Mac), which profiles 225 programs in-depth. The first section of the book contains general information, academic direction, and school selection and financial advice. Included is "The Insider's Guide to Graduate School," written by Kevin Boyer, Executive Director of the National Association of Graduate-Professional Students, in which Boyer notes issues to consider when making educational and career decisions. A separate section is devoted to the application process, including a timetable and specifics on essay writing, interviews, and auditions. The financial section describes assistance alternatives, from loans to grants to fellowships, and includes an estimated debt management repayment schedule. These introductory sections are found in all of Peterson's "Compact Guides." Profiles are arranged by study area. Each profile provides basic program details, such as number of faculty and students, degree and entrance requirements, tuition, financial aid, and contact information. A school index, noting programs offered, follows the profiles.

Evaluation:

This guide is comparable to most Peterson's guides—professional in presentation, content, and organization. It is two-inches thick and has tiny print, but in general, it is navigable. Especially useful are the in-depth descriptions of 225 programs provided on the companion CD-ROM. These detailed profiles are a real bonus with plenty of faculty background information. Too bad there aren't more of them. The CD is easy to install and simple to use—as easy as one or two clicks. The profiles in the print volume are basic with only a handful of factors noted for each program. Students will appreciate the mention of distance learning options, which increases the usability and target audience for this book. However, the advice and information offered in the beginning of the book are brief and generic. The special concerns and interests of those considering social work or the social sciences are not addressed. Without more detailed information on specific issues of interest to this audience, this resource is best used as a very preliminary guide to available programs.

Where To Find/Buy:

Bookstores and libraries.

Arts, Humanities & Social Sciences—Psychology & Social Work

ALLYN & BACON GUIDE TO MASTER'S PROGRAMS IN PSYCHOLOGY & COUNSELING PSYCHOLOGY

Description:

This resource describes the admission criteria, degree requirements, tuition costs, and assistantship possibilities at over 300 master's programs in psychology in the United States, U.S. Territories, and Canada. The authors asked program directors to complete a 55-item survey; the answers are presented in a standardized form. The book opens with two indexes, one which lists schools by state and the other by program type. Next, a five-page glossary defines terms used in the application process. One-page descriptions of the programs form the bulk of the book. These descriptions list basic information, such as addresses and websites, number of openings, application deadlines and requirements, and minimum required GPA and GRE scores. They also indicate the relative weight given to scores, letter of intent, research experience, and the like, and the acceptance rates for 1996–97. No advice is given on the application process.

Evaluation:

This book fills a previously unfilled niche. Other guidebooks for graduate programs in psychology focus on doctorate-level programs since the higher degree is generally considered necessary for employment and is regarded as the terminal level. However, many students apply to master's level programs for a variety of reasons—to improve their chances of getting into a doctorate program, as a backup in case they're not admitted to a doctorate program, or because a terminal master's degree is their primary goal. This reference book provides basic information about master's programs. The best listings include comments from program directors, who expand on a program's curricula, emphasis, or student body. Those programs that did not supply this detailed information are indistinguishable. This unevenness is a problem, as is the book's layout: the type is tiny, and the page numbering is infuriating. School profiles are arranged by region with page numbers grouped accordingly (for example, Mountain Pacific Region schools cover pages MP1-MP44). The dual indexes ease navigation to a certain extent, but this page numbering system is sure to frustrate readers.

Where To Find/Buy:

Bookstores and libraries.

Overall Rating

★★

Focus on terminal masters; good for a preliminary look at programs

Design, Ease Of Use

★★

Unnecessarily small print; annoying page numbering

I–4 Stars

Author:

William Buskist & Amy Mixon

William Buskist and Amy Mixon are professors in the Department of Psychology at Auburn University in Alabama.

Publisher:

Allyn & Bacon

Edition:

1998

Price:

$21.95

Pages:

250

ISBN:

0205274366

Media:

Book

Principal Focus:

Obtaining a Master's or PhD

MA/PhD Subtopic:

Arts, Humanities & Social Sciences

Art & Humanities Subtopic:

Psychology & Social Work

Overall Rating

★

Important advice on strengthening a psych application, but thin compared to other resources

Design, Ease Of Use

★★

Question-and-answer format with many valuable worksheets and sample forms

1–4 Stars

Author:

William Buskist & Thomas R. Sherburne

William Buskist and Thomas Sherburne are both professors in the psychology department at Auburn University in Alabama.

Publisher:

Allyn & Bacon

Edition:

1996

Price:

$14.95

Pages:

108

ISBN:

0205198589

Media:

Book

Principal Focus:
Obtaining a Master's or PhD

MA/PhD Subtopic:
Arts, Humanities & Social Sciences

Art & Humanities Subtopic:
Psychology & Social Work

Arts, Humanities & Social Sciences—Psychology & Social Work

PREPARING FOR GRADUATE STUDY IN PSYCHOLOGY
101 Questions And Answers

Description:

This book answers the many questions that these two authors have been asked by their undergraduate students over the course of their years as professors of psychology. Questions and answers form the first half of the book, which is divided into eight topical chapters, while the second half is composed of a series of appendices of charts and sample writings to help students through the application process. Questions range from explanations of how psychology programs are organized and function to a suggested course of action if the applicant is not accepted to any school. The authors discuss what to look for in psychology programs, how to prepare for the GRE, what makes letters of intent and recommendation effective, and how to make the right impression in an application and interview. The appendices include a timetable for preparing for and applying to graduate schools, brief descriptions of psychology concentrations, sample vita and letters of intent, a worksheet for comparing graduate programs, and a rating sheet used by faculty to evaluate applicants. Also included are suggested readings and a glossary.

Evaluation:

This book takes only a couple of hours to read and provides precise answers to the most important questions posed by psychology applicants. The authors emphasize that graduate psychology programs are very competitive. Their ultimate purpose is to help readers strengthen their applications. While the book offers valuable tips to those people embarking on the application process—with, for example, its discussion and samples of how to write effective vita and letters of intent, and advice on how to research and compare programs—it's more useful for undergraduate students planning ahead. In fact, the timetable for preparing for a graduate program begins with the freshman year (complete the admonition to earn "As" in psychology classes), and marks out such dates as when to join Psi Chi, become a research assistant, and prepare a vita. This little guide may also be helpful later in the first year of graduate school. It includes a lengthy discussion of what to look for in a major professor or advisor. We hope the authors provide an index next time out. Without one, it is difficult to find the answers to specific questions. In general, this resource is thin on content, compared to others on psychology programs.

Where To Find/Buy:

Bookstores and libraries.

Arts, Humanities & Social Sciences—Visual & Performing Arts

FILM SCHOOL CONFIDENTIAL
The Insider's Guide To Film Schools

 Recommended For:
Obtaining a Master's or PhD

Description:

This guidebook presents objective and subjective information about film schools to give readers an inside look at what really happens there. The objective information comes from the admissions offices of the 26 programs discussed here; the bulk of the evaluative text draws on interviews with students, graduates, and faculty members. The book opens with a description of the erratic history of the film industry and film schools, and describes the current career outlook for graduates. In "Before You Go," the authors describe what students should plan to get out of film school, share the pros and cons of mainstream, independent, and experimental film schools, and discuss new film technology. The bulk of the book is the program evaluations, which average five pages each of mostly descriptive text. Included is information on program focus, length of program, graduation requirements, etc. The authors also give a rough estimate of the actual costs and "nitty-gritty information," such as comments, advice, complaints, recommendations, and information about the schools' equipment and facilities. Closing chapters discuss life after film school and jobs. Includes a glossary and examples of thesis films.

Evaluation:

In the film school world, there is a huge gap between what film schools tell prospective students and what really goes on, at least according to these two authors. If only half of their warnings are true, this book is a must-read for anyone contemplating film school. The authors give the lowdown on what students must get out of film school if they want to make it in the highly competitive film industry (e.g., you have to make a film), and they identify the programs that support students in their goals. According to the authors, many programs take much longer to complete than advertised. Production costs often aren't mentioned when students apply, and many students don't have access to the equipment they need to make a film. This invaluable information should influence a student's choice of school and help cut costs. The authors clearly have a beef with the film industry and film schools, who they say exploit students, and they are not shy about sharing their criticisms. Their book is cynical and sometimes depressing, but would-be film students will be grateful for the upfront approach. An "insider's guide" that lives up to its name.

Where To Find/Buy:
Bookstores and libraries.

Overall Rating
★★★★
Inside scoop on what film schools really offer

Design, Ease Of Use
★★★
Lively text and extensive program descriptions

1–4 Stars

Author:
Karin Kelly & Tom Edgar

The authors are graduates of the NYU/Tisch School of the Arts graduate film program. Karin Kelly works in television and writes screenplays, while Tom Edgar is a writer, filmmaker, and website creator.

Publisher:
Perigee (Berkley)

Edition:
1997

Price:
$13.95

Pages:
260

ISBN:
0399523391

Media:
Book

Principal Focus:
Obtaining a Master's or PhD

MA/PhD Subtopic:
Arts, Humanities & Social Sciences

Art & Humanities Subtopic:
Visual & Performing Arts

★★★★

Overall Rating
★★★★
Comprehensive resource for aspiring performers

Design, Ease Of Use
★★★
Schools for all disciplines lumped together alphabetically; indexed by state/country

1–4 Stars

Author:
Carole J. Everett

Ms. Everett is a graduate of Barnard College and a renowned mezzo-soprano. She also holds advanced degrees from the Universita in Siena, Italy. For seven years, she served as the director of admissions at the Juilliard School in New York.

Publisher:
IDG Books Worldwide

Edition:
3rd (1998)

Price:
$19.95

Pages:
310

ISBN:
0028619137

Media:
Book

Principal Focus:
Obtaining a Master's or PhD

MA/PhD Subtopic:
Arts, Humanities & Social Sciences

Art & Humanities Subtopic:
Visual & Performing Arts

Arts, Humanities & Social Sciences—Visual & Performing Arts

THE PERFORMING ARTS MAJOR'S COLLEGE GUIDE

 Recommended For:
Obtaining a Master's or PhD

Description:

This guidebook, written by the former Director of Admissions for The Juilliard School, provides information on 300-plus colleges, universities, and conservatories worldwide with a focus on performance in dance, drama, and music. The first half of this guidebook outlines the process of applying to and auditioning for programs in these disciplines. Each discipline is covered in its own chapter with the music section further divided by instrument. The chapters cover advanced study and how to handle auditions (including what to wear and what not to do), and include an admissions checklist. The author provides program rankings in Part 5, based on surveys and interviews with performers, faculty, and students. Part 6 contains institution profiles arranged alphabetically; the information here is also survey-based. The profiles range in length from one paragraph to two pages; the amount of information given depends on how thoroughly the institution filled out the survey. Each profile includes the usual statistics as well as deadline information, information for international students, and an author comment.

Evaluation:

The main strength of this book is the author's in-depth experience with applications and auditions. She has "seen it all" and wants to make sure that her readers benefit from her experiences. Although the various chapters on music, dance, and drama cover the same general points, each contains specific tips and details to help students in those disciplines get into the program of their choice. The weakest part of this book is the section describing the many programs and institutions. It is not nearly as comprehensive as the first half of the book; clearly, the author is more interested in getting people in, not helping them decide where to go. She does not provide definitive program descriptions, but readers will get a general feel for each program and can contact the programs for more information. Despite the thin program profiles, this resource is recommended as a first-tier tool for students who wish to pursue a career in the performing arts.

Where To Find/Buy:

Bookstores and libraries.

Arts, Humanities & Social Sciences—Visual & Performing Arts

PETERSON'S PROFESSIONAL DEGREE PROGRAMS IN THE VISUAL & PERFORMING ARTS

Description:

This general overview to professional degree programs in the visual and performing arts comprises four main parts: a quick-reference chart of programs, program descriptions, an appendix, and an index of schools. The quick-reference chart (about 25 pages) is organized geographically and provides basic information about schools described in the book (name of school and location, degrees offered, enrollment, tuition and fees). The program descriptions comprise the bulk of the book and are subdivided into four sections: art, dance, music, and theater. Within each section, schools are listed alphabetically. At the beginning of each section, a brief introduction discusses choosing the right program, the application process, and aspects specific to that discipline. Schools' descriptions include school type and enrollment, degrees offered and majors within each degree, profiles of students and faculty, student life, expenses including financial aid information, application information, and contact information. The appendix lists all U.S. and Canadian four-year colleges and universities that offer undergraduate degrees in the visual and performing arts. The index is organized alphabetically by school.

Evaluation:

Peterson's book is exactly what it claims to be: "a first step when identifying potential programs." Although the book profiles many school programs (1,000), valuable details and nuances are missing. Information was supplied by the schools themselves; no philosophy or mission statements are included. Students need this information. They also need to hear from current students or graduate students about the quality of the programs. Also lacking is a discussion of how each program is perceived in the professional visual and performing arts fields. And no mention of the quality or availability of facilities is made. Finally, a listing of professional alumni who have graduated from the various programs would be helpful for students. Some useful information is provided, however. It's nice to know where graduate students serve as instructors, where awards and financial aid are available for specific programs, and what kind of clubs and performance groups are open to new students. This guide is best for a general overview; check elsewhere for more in-depth and pertinent information.

Where To Find/Buy:

Bookstores and libraries.

Overall Rating
★★
An all-inclusive guide based upon information submitted by schools

Design, Ease Of Use
★★★
Arranged alphabetically within each program type; small print

1–4 Stars

Publisher:
Peterson's

Edition:
5th (1998)

Price:
$26.95

Pages:
591

ISBN:
076890112X

Media:
Book

Principal Focus:
Obtaining a Master's or PhD

MA/PhD Subtopic:
Arts, Humanities & Social Sciences

Art & Humanities Subtopic:
Visual & Performing Arts

Overall Rating

★

Good introduction to the field, but dated

Design, Ease Of Use

★★

Organized alphabetically by state only

1–4 Stars

Author:

Ernest Pintoff

Mr. Pintoff is a professor of film at the University of Southern California and a former animator and film director in motion pictures and television. He won an Academy Award for *The Critic*.

Publisher:

Penguin

Edition:

1994

Price:

$16.95

Pages:

510

ISBN:

0140172262

Media:

Book

Principal Focus:

Obtaining a Master's or PhD

MA/PhD Subtopic:

Arts, Humanities & Social Sciences

Art & Humanities Subtopic:

Visual & Performing Arts

Arts, Humanities & Social Sciences—Visual & Performing Arts

THE COMPLETE GUIDE TO AMERICAN FILM SCHOOLS

Description:

The author has compiled a state-by-state listing of American schools for those seeking a career in television, the cinema, or video. The author himself has been involved in animation, television and film directing, and writing; he currently is a professor of film at the University of Southern California. Each school listing in his book includes the location of the school (rural, suburban, urban), the number of students, the academic calendar (quarter, semester), entrance requirements, degrees offered, curricular emphasis, special activities, facilities and equipment that are available to students, names of well-known alumni, and a "Guide POV" (point of view). The POV is a subjective overview of each program based on input from departments, catalogs, and students. At the end of each state section is an anecdote from a student, graduate, and professional reflecting on their own experiences and offering advice to those contemplating a career in these fields. Two glossaries defining academic and technical terms and an index follow the text.

Evaluation:

This guide addresses many of the key points influencing students' decisions to go into this industry and their choice of school. Each school's important features are highlighted. As a result, comparing schools is easy, though we wish tuition figures were included. Pintoff does a fine job distinguishing various types of schools, both two and four-year institutions. Although the "Guide POV" reads like an advertisement for some schools, this feature and the lists of distinguished alumni add interest and a personal feel to the book. Pintoff and many of the anecdotes reflect upon the importance of gaining "a broad-based background"; they advise readers not to overlook the humanities. While this guide will be helpful in identifying film school options, students should seek information from professionals in the field and others to find out how these schools are perceived in the industry.

Where To Find/Buy:

Libraries and bookstores.

Sciences & Engineering

A PH.D. IS NOT ENOUGH!
A Guide To Survival In Science

 Recommended For:
Obtaining a Master's or PhD

Description:

Peter J. Feibelman, a physicist at Sandia National Laboratories, has put together a "pocket mentor" for the aspiring scientist. He believes that young scientists lacking career survival skills run the risk of myriad pitfalls. He focuses on what it takes to succeed, from graduate school through the post-doc years to employment. The first four chapters discuss issues pertinent to science students, including choosing a thesis adviser and giving an effective oral presentation. Chapter 4 discusses the important of publishing scholarly articles. The next two chapters focus on job-specific issues: the relative benefits and drawbacks of positions in academia, government, and industrial labs, and the job interview. Chapter 7 is devoted to the quest for grant money and the elements of a successful proposal. Finally, Chapter 8 focuses on how to establish a research program, and the importance of "problem" vs. "technique" orientation when building a research program.

Evaluation:

For students considering life as a scientist or struggling to begin their careers, this is an important book. For novices, it offers a highly realistic look at what a career in science entails; for scientists, it offers excellent advice about establishing oneself in the field. The writing throughout is excellent—concise and to the point—just right for busy scientists. The author sums up his advice in a nutshell: young scientists must be taught career survival skills if they are to avoid moving "from graduate study to scientific retirement without passing through a career." Readers will find this book is chockfull of choice tidbits, from how to choose projects and why to find an older, established scientist for an advisor, to the benefits and pitfalls of careers in academia and in industry. It is rare to find a book that balances such expert knowledge with excellent writing. A highly valuable resource.

Where To Find/Buy:

Bookstores and libraries.

Overall Rating
★★★
A thorough look at careers in science

Design, Ease Of Use
★★★★
Excellent, from-the-hip writing throughout; compact size

1–4 Stars

Author:
Peter J. Feibelman
The author is a solid state physicist at Sandia National Laboratories in New Mexico.

Publisher:
Addison-Wesley

Edition:
1993

Price:
$12.95

Pages:
109

ISBN:
0201626632

Media:
Book

Principal Focus:
Obtaining a Master's or PhD

MA/PhD Subtopic:
Sciences & Engineering

II. Obtaining
A Master's Or PhD

★★★

Overall Rating
★★★
Concise; encouraging advice

Design, Ease Of Use
★★★
User-friendly; great table of contents and "Action Points"; no index

1–4 Stars

Publisher:
National Academy Press

National Academy Press publishes reports issued by the National Academy of Sciences, National Academy of Engineering, Istitute of Medicine, and National Research Council.

Edition:
1996

Price:
$11.95

Pages:
134

ISBN:
0309053935

Media:
Book

Principal Focus:
Obtaining a Master's or PhD

MA/PhD Subtopic:
Sciences & Engineering

Sciences & Engineering

CAREERS IN SCIENCE AND ENGINEERING
A Student Planning Guide To Grad School And Beyond

Description:

Designed as an educational and career guide for undergraduate and graduate science and engineering students, this book provides insights about the fields and tips on making career and educational choices. It also aims to help students find their best attributes and use them to succeed in their chosen careers. "Action Points," a bulleted summary, follow each chapter. Readers gain perspective from profiles of scientists and engineers making various career moves and from scenarios describing common dilemmas found in each chapter. Further discussion on these scenarios is found in the appendix. This guide, which is also designed with advisors in mind, is available free of charge on the Internet at http://www.nap.edu/readingroom/books/careers.

Evaluation:

This small book provides a thorough introduction to science and engineering education and careers. The career profiles are eye-catching—light green pages with photographs—and to the point; readers get a real feel for life in the sciences. This book paints an exciting portrait of the sciences and engineering by highlighting nontraditional fields, such as patent lawyers and education consultants. It also encourages students to be involved in every aspect of their education, suggesting they take an active approach to their advisors and get a new advisor if they aren't getting enough guidance. The advice on skill enhancement is practical. For example, those who have excellent research skills but poor communication or professional etiquette are advised to join Toastmasters, civic groups, or professional groups to balance and enhance their qualities. Some points are commonsense, but we like the thoughtful and organized personation. Students will appreciate the many scenarios and profiles, and the clear organization. A good resource for college students considering career directions.

Where To Find/Buy:

Bookstores and libraries, and free of charge on the Internet at http://www.nap.edu/readingroom/books/careers

Sciences & Engineering

PETERSON'S COMPUTER SCIENCE & ELECTRICAL ENGINEERING PROGRAMS

Description:

Peterson's collected data on the 700-plus computer science schools profiled in this book by sending out surveys to the schools themselves. Each school returned a list of basic information regarding student enrollment, graduate faculty (broken down by sex and sometimes race), tuition and housing costs, and students services and facilities. Detailed information was also provided on the relevant programs, which include artificial intelligence, computer engineering, computer science, electrical engineering, information science, medical informatics, software engineering, and systems science. For each of these areas of study, the guide features additional data about faculty research areas and expenditures, entrance and degree requirements, and financial aid. In addition, about 400 programs submitted longer, paragraph-style profiles, which provide more detail, along with a list of the faculty and their research. The book opens with articles describing the high tech field, tips on selecting and applying to schools, and a list of sources of financial aid. The programs are indexed by school and type of program.

Evaluation:

This guide follows usual Peterson's format—print so tiny you need a magnifying glass, and information based solely on what the universities chose to submit, rather than any research by Peterson's itself. To be fair, this book covers a huge number of programs and effectively outlines the fundamentals. Readers interested in the wide variety of programs that fall under the computer science and electrical engineering headings will learn at a glance—how much a program costs and whether there is enough research in their area of interest to make a program attractive. While the in-depth profiles simply mirror the information that universities send out to potential applicants, it is useful to have all this information in one place and make comparisons amongst programs. The opening chapter, "Designing the 21st Century: Computer Science and Electrical Engineering Graduate Students Take on the Future," describes an exciting and dynamic career, including the employment and income potentials of the various fields and degrees. The chapters on applying and financial aid, however, are standard Peterson's boilerplate with references to completely unrelated fields (including advice on giving auditions for acting school!).

Where To Find/Buy:

Bookstores and libraries.

Overall Rating
★★★
Essential information on program cost and research areas

Design, Ease Of Use
★★★
Tiny print, but easy-to-use format

1–4 Stars

Publisher:
Peterson's

Edition:
1999

Price:
$26.95

Pages:
788

ISBN:
0768901472

Media:
Book

Principal Focus:
Obtaining a Master's or PhD

MA/PhD Subtopic:
Sciences & Engineering

★★★

Overall Rating
★★★
Thorough with practical advice; professional presentation

Design, Ease Of Use
★★★
Well-indexed; clearly written; tiny print

1–4 Stars

Publisher:
Peterson's

Edition:
1998

Price:
$24.95

Pages:
1,125

ISBN:
076890000X

Media:
Book + CD-ROM

Principal Focus:
Obtaining a Master's or PhD

MA/PhD Subtopic:
Sciences & Engineering

Sciences & Engineering

PETERSON'S GRADUATE STUDIES IN BIOLOGY, HEALTH, & AGRICULTURAL SCIENCES

Description:

This large print directory briefly profiles more than 6,700 programs offered by accredited colleges; it comes with a companion CD-ROM (for Windows and Mac), which features in-depth profiles of 1,180 of these programs. The book begins with several introductory essays offering general information on grad school, academic direction, and school selection and financial advice. An excerpt from *Graduate School and You: A Guide for Prospective Graduate Students* and advice from the executive director of the National Association of Graduate-Professional Students focus on important educational decisions. Also discussed are the application process; a timetable is included, together with tips on essay writing, interviews, and auditions. The finance section describes loan, grant, and fellowship options and includes an estimated debt management repayment schedule. A three-page list of abbreviations used in the book follows. Each print profile includes basic details about the program: number of faculty and students, degree and entrance requirements, tuition, financial aid, and contact information. In-depth profiles on the CD-ROM provide additional contacts and faculty names and background. A school index follows the print profiles.

Evaluation:

The introductions in this book follow verbatim from Peterson's other "Compact Guides," but there is no denying the breadth of its coverage. More than 6,700 programs—that should help students get started. Especially useful are the in-depth descriptions of 1,180 programs included on the companion CD-ROM, a much higher percentage than other "Compact Guides." CD installation and navigation are easy; the only drawback is searching five separate alphabetical files for programs. The profiles in the print volume are basic at best: just the facts, ma'am, with no interpretation or local flavor. The contact numbers are current, however, so students can follow up for details. The brief introductions at the beginning of the book are practical, though generic; students are encouraged to examine their personal qualities and needs when searching for programs. The financial aid coverage is thin, but it serves as a good preliminary checklist, and the debt repayment schedule gives students a glimpse at what they can expect after graduation. Loan and grant options are clearly defined, and additional Internet sources help students jump-start the search for grant money. An adequate tool for those beginning the grad school search in these fields.

Where To Find/Buy:

Bookstores and libraries.

Sciences & Engineering

THE PH.D. PROCESS
A Student's Guide To Graduate School In The Sciences

Description:

This book focuses on the academic side of graduate school in the sciences. The authors aim to provide students with insights to help them make the most of the graduate school years and prepare for life beyond grad school. They draw on their own knowledge and experience and offer quotes, advice, and anecdotes from other professors, scientists, grad students, and postdoctoral fellows. Covered here are many aspects of graduate school not addressed elsewhere, such as selecting an advisor and the unique structure of science graduate programs. Divided into 17 chapters, the book describes daily graduate school experiences and the clubs, projects, seminars, classes, research, and other elements necessary to survive. The authors also guide readers through the main stages of graduate programs in the sciences and advise them on identifying potential mentors, participating in groups, scoring on research opportunities, and more. They also address stress, insecurity, and the unique circumstances of foreign students. Rounding out the text are discussions of the dissertation, oral exams, and career opportunities. References, suggested readings and an index close the book.

Evaluation:

The authors provide an honest but sometimes negative look at how students and professionals feel about their school experiences. Interestingly, many of the anecdotes quoted here put a discouraging spin on higher eduction in the sciences. Readers simply considering a career in the sciences may be put off, but those committed to such a career will appreciate this book's clear-eyed view of the graduate school "experience." For prospective students who haven't had a chance to talk to those already in these graduate programs or to recent graduates, this book offers valuable insights, in a very usable format. The mix of anecdotes and tips is a winner. The authors note the potential isolation of students and the importance of networking and identifying an effective mentor. They also offer valuable advice and anecdotes to students coming from abroad. For those headed to graduate school in the sciences, we recommend putting this book at the top of the reading list.

Where To Find/Buy:

Bookstores and libraries.

Overall Rating
★★★
A evenhanded but sometimes gloomy look at graduate school in the sciences

Design, Ease Of Use
★★★
Clearly written and organized

1–4 Stars

Author:
Dale F. Bloom, Jonathan D. Karp, & Nicholas Cohen

Bloom performed her doctoral studies in Psychology at UCLA and is a full-time author. Karp is an assistant professor of biology at Rider University. Cohen is a professor of microbiology and immunology at the University of Rochester Medical Center.

Publisher:
Oxford University

Edition:
1998

Price:
$16.95

Pages:
209

ISBN:
0195119002

Media:
Book

Principal Focus:
Obtaining a Master's or PhD

MA/PhD Subtopic:
Sciences & Engineering

Of Interest To:
International Students

★★★

Overall Rating
★★★
Nice balance of advice,
information, and statistics

Design, Ease Of Use
★★★
Clear format

1–4 Stars

Publisher:
Princeton Review
(Random House)

Edition:
2nd (1998)

Price:
$21.00

Pages:
438

ISBN:
0375752056

Media:
Book

Principal Focus:
Obtaining a Master's or PhD

MA/PhD Subtopic:
Sciences & Engineering

Sciences & Engineering

PRINCETON REVIEW BEST GRADUATE PROGRAMS: ENGINEERING

Description:

This guidebook from the Princeton Review profiles 131 engineering schools offering master's and doctoral level programs. It is based on information from The American Society for Engineering Education (a nonprofit organization which, in part, collects and publishes data on engineering institutions) and responses to surveys of 4,500 students. Four chapters of background information and advice open the book. The authors describe the current state of engineering, shifts in curriculum, and the impact of new technology. They focus on three factors when considering programs—academic quality, chances of admittance, and practical considerations, such as cost and location. A chapter on applying to schools describes the process and suggests ways to increase one's admission chances. The final chapter presents a range of funding possibilities. School profiles include one column of factual information in small print—admission and degree requirements, financial facts, and selected research areas—followed by text describing academics, student life, admissions, and financial aid. Additional statistical information for each engineering department follows.

Evaluation:

This guidebook makes good use of factual information and student feedback to profile engineering programs. Important statistics—such as lists of research areas and degree requirements—are set apart in smaller print and columns, while school descriptions combine information with student opinions and occasional quotes, providing numerous insights in a small space. Information on individual departments is minimal, but profiles of faculty and students and annual research expenditures are provided. The program profiles are well-written and lively, though they are generally shorter and less detailed than some other Princeton Review guides, which offer richer detail about campus life and the area around the university. The introductions are helpful. We especially liked the advice on narrowing down the field of school choices: the authors stress the value of talking to professors and matching research interests and funding. And for the application process, they provide good strategies for boosting GRE scores and tips on distinguishing oneself from other applicants. Readers should note that much of the introductory material appears in all volumes in Princeton Review's "Best Graduate Programs" series. We noted a cut-and-paste feel to many of the introductions.

Where To Find/Buy:

Bookstores and libraries.

Sciences & Engineering

PRINCETON REVIEW BEST GRADUATE PROGRAMS: PHYSICAL & BIOLOGICAL SCIENCES

Description:

This book contains 63 school profiles with a total of 600 graduate programs in the physical and biological sciences. Princeton Review surveyed graduate students, professors, admission faculty, and financial aid officers to compile the general school profiles. Schools were selected on the basis of data supplied by the National Research Council and the Council of Graduate Schools. In the six introductory chapters preceding the school profiles, readers will find advice on selecting schools and programs, helpful resources for funding and information, and tips on how to survive the graduate school experience. This guide aims to help students focus on and attain their academic goals. Each of the 63 school profiles includes a two-page general description of the institution with basic enrollment figures, costs, and admission requirements. These descriptions are followed by complete listing of the graduate programs in the physical and biological sciences. Listings contain contact information, joint degrees and concentrations, student statistics, and application and degree statistics. Following the profiles are ratings data for each school, an alphabetical index, and a departmental index.

Evaluation:

This Princeton Review guide is an excellent preliminary tool packed with insights on the graduate school process. Combining a serious approach with occasional humor, the author provides readers the information they will need to start the graduate school search. He is realistic about graduate school life, never sugarcoating or dismissing the experience. He tells students upfront what they can expect and provides tips for making life easier. For example, he directs students to professional societies that students can contact for more detailed guidance. He also examines each aspect of the graduate school decision as well as life inside the programs he describes. Because of the broad scope of the subject matter, the author does not profile the individual Master's/PhD programs in any detail—only stats here, but we found the inclusion of e-mail addresses and program URLs a big plus. These connections, combined with a little networking, will make identifying the right program a lot easier.

Where To Find/Buy:

Bookstores and libraries.

Overall Rating
★★★
Comprehensive and upbeat

Design, Ease Of Use
★★★
Clearly written and user friendly; well-organized

1–4 Stars

Author:
Jonathan Spaihts

The author is a researcher and freelance writer in New York City. A graduate of Princeton University, he has worked for Princeton Review as a teacher, writer, researcher, and course developer. He is also author of *The Best Graduate Programs: Humanities & Social Sciences*.

Publisher:
Princeton Review
(Random House)

Edition:
2nd (1998)

Price:
$25.00

Pages:
523

ISBN:
0375752048

Media:
Book

Principal Focus:
Obtaining a Master's or PhD

MA/PhD Subtopic:
Sciences & Engineering

Overall Rating
★★★
Thorough presentation of science and engineering career development

Design, Ease Of Use
★★★
Clearly written with helpful diagrams and appendices

1–4 Stars

Author:
Richard M. Reis

The author is the executive director of the Stanford Integrated Manufacturing Association and associate director of Global Learning Partnerships for the Stanford University Learning Laboratory. He has held numerous faculty positions and was editor of the astronomy magazine, *Mercury*, prior to going to Stanford.

Publisher:
IEEE

Edition:
1997

Price:
$44.95

Pages:
416

ISBN:
0780311361

Media:
Book

Principal Focus:
Obtaining a Master's or PhD

MA/PhD Subtopic:
Sciences & Engineering

Sciences & Engineering

TOMORROW'S PROFESSOR
Preparing For Academic Careers In Science & Engineering

Description:

Written for graduate and postdoctorate students considering a teaching career in science and engineering, this book helps with academic preparation and the selection process. The author draws on personal experience and the experiences of faculty, graduate students, and post-docs from 20 institutions. In Part I, he explores and compares the differences between institutions and their various disciplines, using seven schools as examples. In Part II, he helps students prepare for an academic career focusing on strategies and potential teaching assignments. Vignettes, which are used throughout the book, portray various student perspectives on teaching and school experiences. Part III helps those in the last year of graduate study prepare for the next step in career management, explaining what opportunities are available and how to approach each type, how to negotiate contracts, and how to properly accept offers. Part IV addresses how those currently in early-stage teaching positions can work toward future research projects and set the groundwork for their career. Here the author looks more specifically at teaching styles and methods, and what it takes to be an effective professor. Part V comprises seven appendices. An index rounds out the book.

Evaluation:

The author's professional and teaching experience, clear writing, and lively vignettes provide a well-balanced look at the world of teaching in the sciences and engineering. Especially helpful to younger students is Part II in which the author provides practical advice on the realities of academic career choices. Without dismissing the importance of research and hard work, he stresses the importance of networking. He reminds students that "what" they know should be reinforced by "who" they know. In his view, networking will inevitably enhance their chances of finding a good job. He also reminds students how hard work in school will help ease the transition into academia. The author holds the reader's attention and effectively demonstrates his points with vignettes, illustrating how scientists at each stage in their career handle their work. Appendices include numerous professional society contacts, questions to ask when considering programs or job offers, and proposal considerations. This book, though expensive, is a worthwhile investment for students at each step in their career development.

Where To Find/Buy:

Bookstores and libraries.

Sciences & Engineering

PETERSON'S COMPACT GUIDES: GRADUATE STUDIES IN ENGINEERING, COMPUTER SCIENCE & INFORMATION STUDIES 1998

Description:

More than 3,400 accredited graduate programs in computer science, engineering, and information studies are listed in this resource. The information is based on surveys that Peterson's sent out to universities. The results are short profiles, listing basic information—student body figures, entrance and degree requirements, expenses, and contacts. Some 618 schools provided more in-depth descriptions featured on the CD-ROM. These profiles are written in paragraph form and describe the programs of study, research facilities, costs, school history and location, and the student body. They also include a list of faculty members, their degrees, and areas of expertise. Brief introductory chapters offer advice on selecting and applying for schools. These are written by various authorities and explain the difference between professional, Masters, and PhD degrees; note issues to consider when choosing a field and school; and describe the elements of the application process. The chapter on paying for graduate school suggests putting together a financial plan, lists funding sources, and explains how to use the World Wide Web as a resource.

Evaluation:

Get out your magnifying glass for this mammoth listing of every engineering, computer science, and information studies-related programs in America. Better yet, skip the book and go straight to the CD-ROM. The book itself is nothing more than a starting point. The introductory chapters provide only basic information about selecting and applying to programs and are reproduced verbatim from Peterson's other "Compact Guides." The introductions provide no information specific to these particular programs, and occasionally mention unrelated fields, a hint that they've been cut and pasted. The program profiles presented in the book are capsule summaries, listing only the briefest information. Skim them to see where the programs are, then turn to the CD-ROM for the real thing. Unfortunately, the CD-ROM lists universities alphabetically, rather than by program as the book does. This means users must consult the book to make an initial list of target schools. The CD-ROM profiles provide valuable descriptions of programs, research facilities, and the faculty. They also describe how well students have fared after graduation. However, with so few schools submitting these more detailed reports for the CD-ROM, this product is of limited value.

Where To Find/Buy:

Bookstores and libraries.

Overall Rating
★★
Detailed descriptions in CD-ROM; book text minimal

Design, Ease Of Use
★★
Good school index, but tiny print and thin content

1–4 Stars

Publisher:
Peterson's

Edition:
1998

Price:
$24.95

Pages:
649

ISBN:
0768900050

Media:
Book + CD-ROM

Principal Focus:
Obtaining a Master's or PhD

MA/PhD Subtopic:
Sciences & Engineering

II. Obtaining A Master's Or PhD

Overall Rating

★

The most basic school information

Design, Ease Of Use

★

Small print and thin pages make reading a chore

1–4 Stars

Publisher:

Educational Testing Service

Educational Testing Service (ETS) is a private, nonprofit organization that develops and administers millions of achievement and admissions tests each year in the U.S. and 180 other countries, including the TOEFL.

Edition:

16th (1997)

Price:

$24.99

Pages:

415

ISBN:

0446396222

Media:

Book

Principal Focus:

Obtaining a Master's or PhD

MA/PhD Subtopic:

Sciences & Engineering

Sciences & Engineering

THE OFFICIAL GRE/CGS DIRECTORY OF GRADUATE PROGRAMS

Volume B: Engineering, Business

Description:

This directory to business programs and engineering schools presents data on 865 schools in the U.S. and Canada. Section 1 includes tables with specific program information, such as admissions and degree requirements; GRE score range; number of completed applications received; degrees awarded; financial aid available; and part-time and evening study options. Section 2 includes summaries of general information on the schools, listed alphabetically by state, with such information as academic calendar; geographic setting; enrollment and faculty statistics; percent of students receiving financial assistance; tuition and housing costs; and student services. The third section is composed of narratives on the schools, with "brief summaries on such topics as research affiliations and cooperative programs, library holdings, computer facilities, and institutional resources." The last section contains addresses and phone numbers. An Index of programs follows.

Evaluation:

This book is not easy to use. Not only is information presented in tiny print with relatively little breathing space, but it is divided into four separate sections that force readers to flip back and forth for complete information on any single program. Another drawback: engineering programs share space with business programs, and neither gets the attention or detail they deserve. For example, what use is GRE score data to students considering an MBA? Worse yet, some excellent programs are not even listed. All in all, this directory leaves one wondering at the mysterious ways of the Educational Testing Service.

Where To Find/Buy:

Bookstores and libraries.

Miscellaneous

EDUCATION FOR ACTION: UNDERGRADUATE & GRADUATE PROGRAMS THAT FOCUS ON SOCIAL CHANGE

 Recommended For:
Obtaining a Master's or PhD

Description:

Food First, the publisher, is a nonprofit "research and education center empowering citizens to address the root causes of hunger, poverty, and environmental decline." This book is designed to raise awareness of "socially responsible" undergraduate and graduate programs. Under 20 fields of study, the guide profiles leading "progressive" departments and programs. For example, under the field Geography, the guide describes six departments within U.S. and international colleges and universities. A reader learns that Clark University "has a reputation as a progressive school with a strong international focus;" that some of the courses offered include "Gender Resources and Development" and "Landscapes of the Middle East," and one of their key faculty has an expertise in urban social and economic geography. Reading the other entries under Geography, readers will discover programs geared toward industrial and economic geography, or cultural geography. Each listing includes all pertinent contact information including fax and email addresses where appropriate. Indexes list featured schools, courses, and faculty.

Evaluation:

Bravo to the creators of this niche publication, an invaluable tool for those interested in an education geared toward the principles of sustainable, democratically controlled development. The programs selected for inclusion in this book share a commitment to social change and are the training and education centers that produce many of today's social activists. The editors have done a commendable job of researching programs to provide the level of detail prospective students need to make informed choices about where they pursue their studies. Many books contain lists of all colleges with Geography departments; a handful attempt to highlight particularly strong departments for various topics within Geography; this book alone highlights the strongest "progressive" departments with insights on the star faculty who drive the programs. Rather than attempting a rating system (often an exercise in subjective futility), the creators have made the wise decision to provide evaluative descriptions of departments along with key information on courses offered and the background of key faculty. This latter component is crucial for graduate students whose careers may depend on an adviser-mentor.

Where To Find/Buy:

Bookstores and libraries.

Overall Rating
★★★★
An in-depth guide to the best "progressive" programs and the faculty who run them

Design, Ease Of Use
★★★
Well indexed by school name and key faculty; an invaluable find, but note publication date

1–4 Stars

Author:
Sean Brooks & Alison Knowles
The authors write for *Food First*, a nonprofit research and education-for-action center, which focuses on the causes of hunger and poverty in the United States and around the world.

Publisher:
Food First

Edition:
3rd (1995)

Price:
$8.95

Pages:
131

ISBN:
0935028641

Media:
Book

Principal Focus:
Obtaining a Master's or PhD

MA/PhD Subtopic:
Miscellaneous

Overall Rating
★★★★
A must-read for students considering an environmental career

Design, Ease Of Use
★★★
Well-written and presented with photos and graphics; somewhat dated

1–4 Stars

Publisher:
Peterson's

Edition:
2nd (1995)

Price:
$14.95

Pages:
319

ISBN:
1560794070

Media:
Book

Principal Focus:
Obtaining a Master's or PhD

MA/PhD Subtopic:
Miscellaneous

Miscellaneous

EDUCATION FOR THE EARTH: THE COLLEGE GUIDE FOR CAREERS IN THE ENVIRONMENT

 Recommended For:
Obtaining a Master's or PhD

Description:

The first 50-plus pages of this guide present career information. Six Career Area Overviews present background information on environmental engineering, environmental health, environmental science, environmental studies, natural resource management, and environmental technology. Professional profiles of working environmentalists accompany the essays. An additional section lists pre-baccalaureate programs in environmental technology. The heart of the book is comprised of profiles of 200 programs in environmental fields of study offered at four-year colleges in the U.S. and Canada. Information for these profiles came primarily from information gathered in a survey taken during the Spring of 1994, although this data was supplemented by input from a variety of environmental organizations. Each listing contains facts about the school (enrollment, costs, admissions) and a paragraph about the program itself (enrollment, faculty, degrees). "The Program," "Special Features," and "Career Paths" provide information on course components, fieldwork opportunities, special programs and facilities, and "outcomes—graduate study and employment."

Evaluation:

Students intending to major in the environmental field will benefit tremendously by having a guide to all (or most of) the environmental programs available at American (and a smaller number of Canadian) colleges. Until this book was created, a student researching a specific field, such as environmental policy, had to make due with guides that merely list colleges who offer the major. This book describes college programs and majors in the depth needed to determine which programs are the best fit. Peterson's doesn't evaluate the programs, but the information included here goes beyond the statistical data found in most "objective" college guides. The "Special Features" and "Career Paths" sections of the profile provide important insights and pithy details, the kind that are hard to track down in other guides. The indexes are another great feature, and the profiles of professionals in the field offer the real-life "this is what my day looks like . . ." details that students considering the field really need.

Where To Find/Buy:

Bookstores and libraries.

Miscellaneous

THE GUIDE TO GRADUATE ENVIRONMENTAL PROGRAMS

Description:

This guidebook provides individuals with pertinent information on roughly 160 schools offering graduate programs in environmental studies. It is designed to help readers navigate the application process and compare graduate schools according to their specific needs. Part I focuses on researching institutions with career opportunities in mind; it overviews the various specialties to consider when applying to programs offering graduate study. Part II, the core of the book, profiles institutions; included are program and contact information and areas of specialization. A brief history of the school, tuition rates, enrollment figures, and other statistics are also featured. Profiles are based on surveys conducted in late 1994. Part III contains appendices with additional programs not profiled in this guide, a sample survey form used to gather profile information, and a brief list of resources. The guide concludes with two indexes: one by state and the other by program specialization.

Evaluation:

This book works for us because it focuses on graduate programs in a broad range of environmental fields: biology, energy studies, marine science, land use and regional planning, and many more that students may not be aware of. The Student Conservation Association (SCA) offers practical and thoughtful advice for students contemplating graduate or professional school. The tips on writing personal essays and surviving interviews will boost their chances of being accepted in this increasingly popular field. The program profiles are among the best we've seen—clearly written and complete with phone numbers, URLs, and faculty contacts (no e-mail addresses, though). Too bad they're based on 1994 survey responses and don't cover more programs. Nevertheless, for those hoping to attend environmental graduate school, this guide will be a welcome preliminary tool.

Where To Find/Buy:

Bookstores and libraries.

Overall Rating
★★★
Encouraging advice; based on 1994 survey

Design, Ease Of Use
★★★★
Organized and easy-to-use; indexed by state and program specialization

1–4 Stars

Author:
Student Conservation Association

SCA is a nonprofit organization, conducting educational and vocational programs since 1957. It offers opportunities for education, leadership, and personal and career development.

Publisher:
Island

Edition:
1997

Price:
$16.95

Pages:
447

ISBN:
1559633409

Media:
Book

Principal Focus:
Obtaining a Master's or PhD

MA/PhD Subtopic:
Miscellaneous

II. Obtaining A Master's Or PhD

Overall Rating
★★
Little specific material on graduate-level studies, but introductory text offers good perspectives on alternative fields

Design, Ease Of Use
★★
Listed alphabetically by school, state index; some material incomplete

1–4 Stars

Author:
Miriam Weinstein

Ms. Weinstein has been active in environmental and social causes since her teenage years. Former director of the Eco Design & Builders Guild, she promotes ecological and healthy building practices and recycling.

Publisher:
Sageworks

Edition:
4th (1995)

Price:
$16.00

Pages:
295

ISBN:
0963461834

Media:
Book

Principal Focus:
Obtaining a Master's or PhD

MA/PhD Subtopic:
Miscellaneous

Miscellaneous

MAKING A DIFFERENCE COLLEGE GUIDE

Description:

Weinstein, an environmental and social activist, highlights colleges with innovative programs that offer hands-on experiences for students who are concerned with social and environmental responsibility. Several essays written by students, graduates, professors, and environmentalists outline serious questions facing today's students. Two of the essays address concerns a worried parent may have regarding their child's choice of these programs. Two additional essays discuss college choices for a quality education. The chapter entitled "What is education for?" sums up Weinstein's approach to rethinking education. The second section lists, in alphabetical order, colleges and field programs that offer "relevant, values-based education"; an index lists all of these colleges and programs alphabetically by state. Within each college's description, students will find the number of students attending, the degree of selectivity, a description of the educational atmosphere and the community, and the college's philosophy. Also included is a list of "making a difference studies," programs that address a progressive agenda. Statistics included list student and faculty profiles, tuition costs, and a condensed version of the school's attributes.

Evaluation:

Weinstein's book is of particular use to students and parents seeking an alternative education. Prospective graduate students looking for a progressive approach will also appreciate the spotlight on career-oriented studies and hands-on training for future jobs, though there is little material focused specifically on graduate studies. Weinstein successfully addresses the questions many students—on all levels—have in this era of social and environmental awareness. The essays in the first half of her book are useful for those parents and students who have not quite decided if an innovative program will suit their needs; these narratives serve to convince readers of the need to offer alternatives to traditional educational courses. What remains unclear in the guide is whether the lists of studies are one-time courses or entire programs and whether there are degree options for future study. Weinstein notes that the schools defined their own degree of selectivity and asks readers to consider this in their application choices.

Where To Find/Buy:

Bookstores and libraries.

Miscellaneous

COUNCIL OF GRADUATE SCHOOLS: STUDENT PAGE

Non-Rated Resource

Description:
The Council of Graduate Schools (CGS) hosts this page offering articles as well as links to sites of interest to graduate students. Notable features include a timetable for applying to graduate school and a series of statistics on who's getting what degrees, how long it takes to get a master's or PhD, what the costs are, where the money comes from, and what the employment opportunities look like for new graduates.

Publisher:
Council Of Graduate Schools

CGS is the largest national association specifically dedicated to the improvement and advancement of graduate education. Its 400-plus member organizations comprise colleges and universities in the U.S. and Canada.

Media:
Internet

Principal Focus:
Obtaining a Master's or PhD

Where To Find/Buy:
On the Internet at http://www.cgsnet.org/student/student.htm

II. Choosing, Getting Into, & Excelling In Business School

The Master's in Business Administration is the second most popular graduate degree in America. Each year 90,000-plus students receive an MBA, and approximately 275,000 students are enrolled in MBA programs.

Many of these students are attracted to business school by the promise of a lucrative career. Starting salaries for those with at least three years of work experience and an MBA can average as much as $30,000 a year more than for those with only a bachelor's degree. And an MBA can open doors to more and better career options.

Money isn't everything, however. Many students pursue an MBA because they love the field. They are born entrepreneurs and want to build on their natural assets. Others are motivated by a great idea but realize that they need entrepreneurial and managerial skills to transform that idea into a reality. And, of course, there are those determined to become leaders of corporate America. In fact, the pool of MBA applicants is much more diverse than most people think.

Whatever their motivation, potential MBA students must consider the huge investment of time, emotional energy, and money required by the two-year program. Tuition alone can cost $40,000 or more for two years. Add in living expenses, books, and computer hardware and software required by the program, and the price tag is even higher.

Any undergraduate business major can tell you that prospective business school students need to consider the opportunity cost represented by two years of forgone income and benefits. Because more and more schools are requiring at least two years of work experience of their applicants, the value of that forgone salary may be substantial. The sacrifice is even greater when applying to some of the top schools where three-quarters of admitted students have five or more years of experience.

Making The Decision: Do I Really Want To Go To Business School?

As you read our descriptions of resources, you'll note that some are geared toward helping prospective business school students take a self-inventory to see if they have what it takes to complete the program.

Many resources provide a glimpse into the daily life of an MBA student. A reality check is a good idea for prospective business school students, and anyone considering the investment of so much time, energy, and money in a graduate education. Graduate business school isn't all dreamy strolls down oak-lined paths pondering econometric models. There is time for contemplation and fun, but prospective MBA students will benefit from the realistic descriptions of business school life portrayed in some of our recommended resources.

Other resources offer a clear view about what business school graduates can expect when they enter (or re-enter) the working world. They discuss the range of positions available after graduation and typical starting salaries in specialty fields.

We urge prospective students to draw on these recommended resources to test their resolve and expectations. We also urge them to take advantage of the career planning services at their alma mater and to talk to their professors about business school decisions. These professionals can offer practical tips about education and career choices, and they can help on program selection, admission, and study processes.

Researching Schools And Narrowing Choices

Although some applicants have their heart set on a particular school, most will need help researching schools to choose the six or so where they'll apply. These six should include a couple of "reach" schools, where their record and all-around profile place them in the possible, but not likely, category of admission. The bulk of their applications should go to schools where the applicant has a reasonably good chance of admission, and the final one or two should be "safety" schools where the applicant is fairly confident of gaining admission.

We recommend prospective students use one of the many large directories of business schools for their first round of research. These directories are good for developing a list of potential programs. Some are Internet-based searchable databases, which may contain photos of schools, program information, course descriptions, and more. Others are weighty paperback guides containing relatively compact profiles of the 700-plus accredited business programs in the U.S.

Many of these large directories stick to objective statistics, providing only the cost of tuition, number of students enrolled, average GMAT score, and average starting salaries. Others include subjective information on the schools' reputation, or strengths in particular areas, such as management.

Today's MBA-ers have many different programs to choose from: full-time, part-time, modular, or distance learning programs to name a few. Though many schools have responded to market demand for more "generalist" business graduates, specialized programs, such as marketing, international business, and E-commerce, within traditional full-time programs, are still popular.

There are many new admissions options as well. Some schools offer one-year MBA programs. Others offer deferred admissions for undergraduates, guaranteeing accepted undergrads admissions if they work for two years before matriculating.

The resources we recommend will help potential applicants select the programs best suited to their needs. These recommended resources not only describe business schools, but also help students formulate criteria for comparing programs.

As students narrow their search, they may look for resources that rank schools according to a predetermined set of criteria. As we have already noted, school rankings are controversial. However, students and advisors often look to them for direction. We have reviewed many resources, which rank MBA programs, because they are so influential, but we urge students and advisors to consider other factors, such as program fit, in selection decisions.

We also remind students and graduates that their alma mater's career planning center can help with the research and application process. Many schools employ advisors who can help students and alums narrow down their list of target schools and prepare their applications. Most career planning centers also house libraries of reference materials, as well as plenty of helpful brochures and registration materials.

Applying To Business School

Competition for acceptance to business school is tight at the top and decidedly more relaxed down the ladder. Top-tier programs, such as Wharton, Kellogg, Sloan, Tuck, and Harvard, typically accept only one in six applicants.

On the other extreme, some programs accept virtually all applicants. However, the value of an MBA depends heavily on the quality of the institution conferring the degree. Graduates of top schools earn salaries, which, on average, are double what graduates from lesser schools can expect to earn.

To help applicants gain a competitive advantage when applying to competitive programs, several of the resources we recommend in this chapter offer insider tips on how to build a strong application.

Unlike their friends applying to law school or medical school, business school applicants do not have access to a centralized service that consolidates basic application data and forwards it to the schools they select. Advance planning is a must to ensure adequate time for completing each application. We suggest applicants allow three hours for each application—That's for filling in the blanks, ordering transcripts, and other basic chores. And they shouldn't forget about the time it takes to write essays, secure letters of recommendation, and prepare for the GMAT. Some schools accept online applications.

We also urge students to apply early. Many programs having rolling admissions, and some begin their first evaluation cycle as early as November.

The GMAT

The Graduate Management Admission Test, or GMAT, is a standardized test designed to help business schools assess the qualifications of applicants for advanced study in business. About 850 schools require GMAT scores.

As with the LSAT, GRE, and MCAT, many applicants spend a lot of time and energy preparing for this test; some choose to enroll in GMAT preparation courses.

The GMAT is administered as a computer-adaptive test (CAT) throughout North America and in many countries throughout the world. The paper-based GMAT is also available twice a year where the network of computer-based testing sites is not yet available.

In 1999–2000, basic registration for the GMAT (including 5 score reports) cost $165 in the U.S., U.S. territories, and Puerto Rico. The fee is $210 in all other locations. Each additional report costs $25.

The GMAT Information Bulletin contains a complete set of instructions, as well as sample questions. Most career planning centers will have plenty of copies of the Bulletin, and web surfers can download the Bulletin at http://www.gmat.org/. For more information, see our review of the GMAT *Online: MBA Explorer* website on page 113, or contact the Educational Testing Service, which administers the test at:

GMAT
Distribution and Receiving Center
225 Phillips Boulevard
Ewing, NJ 08628-7435
phone: (609) 771-7330
fax: (609) 883-4349
email: gmat@ets.org

GPA/Rank In Class

An applicant's undergraduate GPA or class ranking is an important element of the application, though each programs weights this element differently. Applicants and advisors should research individual programs to determine where they stand.

Most graduate business programs do not require undergraduate courses in business or management, but they often look for courses in math, calculus, and statistics. Some require some economics background.

Essays

Business school applications usually include several essay questions, ranging from the personal to the straightforward. Applicant responses weigh heavily in the admission process. Applicants should allocate several hours for brainstorming, drafting, writing, editing, proofreading, and spell checking! It is often a good idea to run essays past a friend, counselor, or professor for feedback.

Letters Of Recommendation

As with all graduate and professional schools, letters of recommendation are an important factor in admissions. Applicants should spend some time thinking about who will write an effective letter. While a big name is often a good idea, applicants should be sure that their references can, and will, write a personalized and favorable recommendation. Most graduate schools ask for three or four letters of recommendation, and many prefer employers' letters over those from professors, though some request at least one letter from a professor.

Personal Interviews

Some schools require interviews, and these interviews have a major impact on the final decision. Many MBA programs train alumni to interviews candidates in their geographic area, so candidates don't need to worry about travel expenses.

If an interview is required, applicants should make every effort to participate, and we recommend scheduling an interview, even if it is optional. Applicants should use the interview as an opportunity to distinguish themselves. They should come prepared. An interview is no time for asking basic questions about programs and schedules. Prospective students should do their research and go to their interviews armed with a detailed understanding of program specifics, their own skills and abilities, and their career goals.

Excelling In Business School And Landing A Great Job

After the elation of opening letters of acceptance fades, prospective students should turn their attention to preparing for the challenging two years ahead. What can they expect?

We review several resources designed to give a taste of daily life in business school. The title of one hints at the tenor of these resources: *Snapshots From Hell: The Making of an MBA*. These resources describe the pace of coursework and the relational dynamics among students, who are at times partners and at time competitors.

These resources also offer study strategies, coping tips, and insider advice. Several devote considerable coverage to positioning oneself for a great job after graduation.

In this section, we review nearly three dozen resources on applying to and excelling in business school. The ones we rate highly go a step beyond the nuts and bolts how-to approach; they provide practical tips and insider advice. These resources can help applicants establish an application to-do list and a series of deadlines to ease the application process. Many explain what to do when accepted, wait-listed, or rejected. Others serve as roadmaps through the business school years and beyond. We invite students and their advisors to read these reviews and select those resources that best serve their needs.

Overall Rating
★★★★

Business Week's reporters present the kind of information prospective students seek

Design, Ease Of Use
★★★★

Interviews updated twice a week; articles are current as well

1–4 Stars

Publisher:
Business Week

Business Week is a weekly news magazine focusing on business issues.

Media:
Internet

Principal Focus:
Business School

BUSINESS WEEK ONLINE'S BUSINESS SCHOOLS

 Recommended For:

Business School

Description:

Business Week magazine publishes biennially a ranking of the top business schools in America. The central feature of this site is an online version of the October 1998 cover story on business school rankings. The "Top 25" schools are profiled; each school profile includes lists of key contacts, *Business Week* rating data, strategies for applicants, teaching methods, information on job placements, and contact addresses and phone numbers. *Business Week* bases its rankings, in part, on input from recent graduates and corporate recruiters from surveys sponsored by the magazine. Comments from students about the program they recently completed are included in each profile. Another section presents Q & As with admissions officers from some of the top MBA programs. "Business school News" presents business school stories that have appeared in *Business Week*, as well as online-only original coverage of such topics as curriculum trends, innovative programming, and business school hirings and firings. Also included are links to over 100 business school websites, and recommended reading for the business school applicant.

Evaluation:

Prospective business school students should bookmark this site and visit it often as they develop a list of schools to which they'd like to apply. Although the "ranking" of schools is controversial, the value of this site lies in its in-depth profiles of each school and in its direct links to school websites. The comments from recent graduates are insightful, offering a peek at school personality. Other sections are useful as well, particularly the Q & As with admission officers. *Business Week* presents the transcript of a Q & A with an admission officer from a different top-50 school about twice a week. Readers receive answers to general questions, such as: "How do you best prepare for business school?" and "On what basis do admissions officers judge you?" as well as answers about the officer's school in particular. For example, "What recent changes have occurred in the school's faculty?" or "What is distinctive about the learning environment at your school?" Readers can even email admissions-related questions to Business Week's online reporter.

Where To Find/Buy:

On the Internet at http://www.businessweek.com/tocs/bschools.htm

BUSINESS WEEK'S GUIDE TO THE BEST BUSINESS SCHOOLS

 Recommended For:
Business School

Description:

Written by a senior writer at *Business Week* who also writes the magazine's biennial cover stories on the top schools, this book guides readers to the "top 25" business schools and the "runners-up," using surveys of graduate and corporate recruiters. The first two chapters discuss why one would get an MBA, and how to get into a top program. Chapter 3 includes a table with *Business Week*'s "Top 25 Business Schools," and the next chapter provides statistics for the business schools in such categories as GMAT scores, selectivity, international/women/minority enrollments, pre- and post-MBA annual pay, and outstanding MBA loans. Chapters 5–6 give detailed profiles on the top 25 schools and the "runners-up," with such information as corporate ranking, teaching methods, recent program innovations and changes, placement details, outstanding faculty, application tips, and student life. Profiles also include firsthand accounts from graduates. The last chapter provides information on "the best business schools outside the United States."

Evaluation:

It's amazing how rankings influence and sometimes drive a business school's reputation. In a businesslike business school, reputation is everything (or at least it counts a lot). This book is in many ways an extension of *Business Week*'s ranking of the "best" business schools. It purports to be a "tell-it-like-it-is scouting report on the best of the bunch," a claim the author backs up with reams of research. The rankings are subject to many of the criticisms leveled at similar efforts. However, business school applicants don't seem to mind, as these rankings continue to be very popular. The profiles of the schools are generally thorough, with an emphasis on recent changes in the programs. This guide prominently features both GPA and GMAT scores and also provides a range of scores, which can be immensely encouraging and helpful to applicants. We also like the fact that they list the name of the Director of Admissions and the address of the school in a box on the first page of the description. Applicants will want to contact the schools for more information.

Where To Find/Buy:

Bookstores and libraries.

Overall Rating
★★★★
A useful and thorough guide to the top business school programs

Design, Ease Of Use
★★★★
The writing style is quick and savvy

1–4 Stars

Author:
John A. Byrne

The author is a senior writer at *Business Week*. He has written the magazine's "biennial cover stories surveying the top schools" since the magazine launched its rankings in 1988.

Publisher:
McGraw-Hill

Edition:
5th (1997)

Price:
$16.95

ISBN:
0070094721

Media:
Book

Principal Focus:
Business School

II. Business School

★★★★

Overall Rating
★★★★
A thorough guide to admissions to the "top" MBA programs

Design, Ease Of Use
★★★★
Attractive format; easy navigation with detailed table of contents and index

1–4 Stars

Author:
Richard Montauk

Richard Montauk received an MS in Finance and a JD from Stanford University. Currently, he is the Managing Director of Education USA, a firm that helps applicants get into the world's top business schools.

Publisher:
Prentice Hall

Edition:
1997

Price:
$19.95

Pages:
453

ISBN:
0132463237

Media:
Book

Principal Focus:
Business School

HOW TO GET INTO THE TOP MBA PROGRAMS

 Recommended For:
Business School

Description:

This book was written by a Stanford graduate, who currently runs a firm that helps applicants get into the world's top business schools. The author covers all aspects of the application process, from selecting target schools to responding to acceptance, wait list, or rejection notices. Its 16 chapters cover four major areas: Part I "provides a context for your decisions" with chapters covering such topics as why to get an MBA; types of programs; the rankings and how to use them; and how to "assess and upgrade your own credentials," with a guide to the entire application process. Part II, the "core of the book," helps applicants develop a "marketing strategy" and make the most of essays, recommendations, and interviews. Part III discusses how to respond to wait-listing and rejections, and how to make the most out of business school. An appendix includes 115 examples of successful essays on numerous topics and questions.

Evaluation:

As the author points out, nearly 99 percent of the students who enroll in business school eventually obtain their degrees—the hard part is getting in! Given the daunting statistics, what should applicants determined to get into a top MBA program do? The author knows, and he covers all the bases with this fine treatment of applicant "marketing" based on the best "bang-up application" MBA wannabes can create. Few books are as thorough, nor do they benefit from this experienced author's insightful understanding of the application process. This book also shines because of the author's solid organization of material and excellent navigation tools. The table of contents is detailed and clearly organized; each chapter begins with a brief executive summary; and the three-level index guarantees readers will find what they are looking for. Highly recommended.

Where To Find/Buy:
Bookstores and libraries.

MARKETING YOURSELF TO THE TOP TEN BUSINESS SCHOOLS

 Recommended For:
Business School

Description:

Written by two Harvard Business School grads who were also successful applicants to 11 other top MBA programs, this book is a guide to the successful "marketing" of applicants to top business schools. The first four chapters discuss "market research" on the programs, managing the "grunt work" of the application process, and GMAT tips. Chapters 5–6 discuss "personal positioning," a marketing term that means "the unique space a person, a company, or a product is able to secure in the mind of a target audience," and the importance of diversity for minority and female applicants. The next two chapters focus on the essay portion of the application, including examples of essay answers to common application questions, and analyses of those essays. Chapters 9–10 focus on the interview, and the final "packaging" of the application. Chapter 11 discusses admissions, rejections, wait lists, and deferrals, and the last chapter includes responses to general admissions questions by three top admissions directors.

Evaluation:

This book takes an original and insightful approach to the business school admissions process: it is a game of sales, just like the real business world. However, in this case, the applicant is being marketed, and the choosy buyer is a top MBA program. The two authors build an entire book on the premise that applicants can handle the entire admissions process as they would any marketing campaign, following the tenets of successful sales: "Consider the Competition," "Know Your Target Market," "Pick Your Positioning," and "Develop Your Marketing Messages." Some chapters are less valuable than others: for example, the tips on the GMAT, the application itself, and the interview are fairly basic. However, we liked the helpful series of responses from admissions officers on what they like and don't like in an interview, and the discussion of admission essays. The "winning marketing strategy" approach makes this book well worth the investment.

Where To Find/Buy:

Bookstores and libraries.

Overall Rating
★★★★
An original and insightful guide to "marketing yourself" to business schools

Design, Ease Of Use
★★★★
Clear and helpful format

1–4 Stars

Author:
Phil & Carol Carpenter

Phil and Carol Carpenter both received their MBA degrees from the Harvard Business School in 1994. Currently, Phil works as a high-tech marketing consultant for Regis McKenna, Inc., and Carol is a product marketing manager at Apple Computer.

Publisher:
John Wiley & Sons

Edition:
1995

Price:
$15.95

ISBN:
0471118176

Media:
Book

Principal Focus:
Business School

II. Business School

II. Business School

Overall Rating
★★★★
A superb resource offering
both scope and depth

Design, Ease Of Use
★★★★
Loads of information arranged
clearly and succinctly

1–4 Stars

Publisher:
Peterson's

Edition:
5th (1999)

Price:
$26.95

Pages:
1,272

ISBN:
0768900468

Media:
Book

Principal Focus:
Business School

PETERSON'S GUIDE TO MBA PROGRAMS 1999
A Comprehensive Directory Of Graduate Business Education At U.S., Canadian, & Select International Business Schools

 Recommended For:
Business School

Description:
This hefty guide to "2,900 MBA and master's-level business programs at more than 900 institutions" in the U.S., Canada, and abroad offers a comprehensive listing of programs as well as detailed information on each school and its offerings. The first section discusses today's MBA program as well as future trends in the field, admissions and financial aid, and studying abroad. "MBA Programs At-A-Glance" follows, with a reference chart that provides an overview of programs, helping the reader compare programs in terms of location, accreditation, tuition, financial aid, and more. The bulk of the book is devoted to program profiles, which provide data on program admissions and academics, finances and facilities, placement, and contact information. In-depth two-page descriptions of individual MBA programs follow in the last section; these profiles are prepared by the dean or director of each individual program and arranged alphabetically by institution name. Two separate indexes are included.

Evaluation:
Peterson's has put together an exceptionally useful resource. While dense by necessity, this directory proves remarkably easy to use, with the added value of extreme thoroughness. The user need not worry that a program of interest has been overlooked—in all, more than 900 institutions are profiled here. A wide variety of programs are included, such as part-time and distance learning programs. While other guides may limit the numbers of programs they profile in different ways for different reasons, Peterson's guide offers a full directory of both domestic and foreign programs as well as lesser-known programs, which may be of interest to many applicants. The discussion about MBA programs, which opens the book, is both perceptive and forward-thinking—it avoids run-of-the-mill advice and offers an exciting glimpse at MBA programs today and in the future. MBA applicants cannot afford to overlook this resource.

Where To Find/Buy:
Bookstores and libraries.

EMBARK.COM: GOING TO BUSINESS SCHOOL

 Recommended For:
Business School

Description:

The business school segment of Embark.com features three topical sections: Choose the Right B-School, Apply to B-School, and Finance Your Education. Each section contains an Introduction, Advice & Information articles, and a discussion forum, as well as its own unique feature, such as GMAT tips. Choose the Right B-School offers a career section, which includes a career search, career interest/aptitude test, and links, a free "Recruiter" service that students can use to attract schools, and an MBA Search. The MBA Search lets users search a database of business schools by location, cost, admissions statistics (e.g., average GPA), school statistics (e.g., percentage of women), and/or teaching methods. Search results produce a list of schools. Users then opt to view the school profile, apply online, send an inquiry via e-mail, or go to the school's website. The profiles provide contact info as well as statistics on curriculum, faculty, job placement, and student demographics. In the online application feature, users apply to Embark's partner schools. (A list of partners is provided.) Finance Your Education covers finance sources—loans, work-study, grants, etc.—and a Free Application for Federal Student Aid (FAFSA) calculator.

Evaluation:

Embark.com's business segment is a site future MBAs will want to visit again and again. In the early stages of research, visitors can use the MBA Search to find solid introductory information on business schools. While the school profiles are generally statistical in nature, they include lots of atypical details. For example, these profiles offer stats on percentage of applicants interviewed in person, room & board costs (in addition to the usual tuition costs), and a breakdown of teaching methods, e.g., "50 percent Lecture, 45 percent Case Study, 5 percent Other." The career information is a valuable inclusion, especially for users who aren't sure if an MBA is right for them. Finance Your Education provides a clear explanation of financial air sources, plus helpful expert advice. The "Recruiter" is worth checking out, too; just don't expect miracles: it's designed to helps students attract business schools' attention. The weakest section focuses on the GMAT; skip it. After the research is complete, users can return to this site to see if their schools offer online applications. With an online application, students can pay the application fee using secure check submission, and recommendations can be completed electronically. It saves time, since data required on all applications is entered only; Embark will even check the application for errors before submission.

Where To Find/Buy:

On the Internet at http://www.embark.com/mba

Overall Rating
★★★★
Includes a school search and online applications, plus other valuable tools

Design, Ease Of Use
★★★
Without menus on every page, some backtracking is required

1–4 Stars

Publisher:
Embark.com

Embark.com (formerly CollegeEdge) is a California-based company "dedicated to helping people fulfill their life's learning and career aspirations."

Media:
Internet

Principal Focus:
Business School

II. Business School

Overall Rating
★★★★
A terrific first step in research, especially for international students

Design, Ease Of Use
★★★
Generally well-formatted, but navigating requires some backtracking

1–4 Stars

Publisher:
Peterson's

Peterson's is a publisher of education guides and a producer of test preparation materials and courses. It is part of the Lifelong Learning Group within Thomson Learning.

Media:
Internet

Principal Focus:
Business School

Of Interest To:
International Students

PETERSONS.COM: THE MBA CHANNEL

 Recommended For:
Business School

Description:

All of The MBA Channel's featured articles and content areas are accessible from its main page. The articles discuss such issues as "Your MBA Application Essay" and "A Minority MBA Student Abroad." The content areas include MBA Search, GMAT Test Preparation, and Resources on Financing Your Education. In MBA Search, users can search a database of 900-plus business schools by school name or by performing an "Advanced MBA Program Search." The Advanced search includes program concentrations, location, 1997 average GMAT scores, and 1997 program enrollment. All searches result in "matching" school listings of "Program Profiles." The two-page Profiles provide data on student demographics, tuition, and applications, as well as requirements for various degrees (e.g., MBA, MBA/MA, MBA/MS). A "Description" gives additional information on program and curricular focus, career placement resources, and anticipated costs. In the GMAT section, users can download free test-prep software (for Windows and Mac), get "hot tips," and view an overview of the entire exam. Resources on Financing explores loan options in conjunction with the Access Group.

Evaluation:

The MBA Search feature is an outstanding first stop for business school research. Not only are the 900-plus "Program Profiles" much, much more informative than the profiles found at other sites, most of the schools come with additional "In-Depth Descriptions." The Profiles contain lots of useful and unusual information, such as how many credits are required to attain a specific degree (i.e., MBA with a Concentration in Health Care Management), and how long a DBA takes. Most Descriptions feature a link to the school's website and a "send e-mail" feature. International students will find plenty of help, too: TOEFL minimum score, facilities available, International Student Contact name and address, etc. International students also have the option of browsing "featured" programs from the MBA Search page; there's a database of distance learning programs as well. (For a complete list of all business programs for international students, go to http://www.petersons.com/graduate/agsus). The featured articles are also worth browsing, particularly "Why an MBA? Future Trends and Opportunities." The test-prep software is helpful as well; just keep in mind that it is designed to promote Peterson's products.

Where To Find/Buy:

On the Internet at http://www.petersons.com/mba

U.S. NEWS ONLINE: BUSINESS

 Recommended For:
Business School

Description:

Although technically a part of U.S. News Online's "Graduate School" segment, this "Business" section functions as its own site. The main page works like a descriptive table of contents. It features six major subsections: Find Your Business School, Compare Business Schools, Rankings, Specialties, Web-exclusive Rankings, and Articles. In Find Your Business School, users search for schools by name or conduct a personalized search based on such criteria as location, GMAT scores, and specialties. Search results provide an overview of the "found" school: contact addresses and statistics on admissions, costs, academics, and student demographics. In Compare Business Schools, users enter the names of up to four schools to get a side-by-side comparisons of over 30 criteria (e.g., acceptance rate, costs, percentage of graduates employed within three months). Rankings, Specialties, and Web-exclusive Rankings offer lists of school rankings for such areas as Top Schools, Accounting, and Highest Placement Rates. Articles address entrepreneurship, getting in, and niche programs. Other features include links to "hot jobs" and online application information, plus internal links to "Graduate School's" general-interest articles and advice pages.

Evaluation:

If numbers—rankings, costs, or demographics—play a major role in a student's school choices, this site will seem like a dream come true. The best, and most enjoyable, features of this page are the searches and rankings, both of which are numbers-based. Students can find the school for them by searching by GMAT scores, starting salaries, or zip code (which computes distance from home); the search results in a by-the-numbers overview of the "found" school, detailing demographics, tuition costs, etc. Compare Business Schools (an unusual feature and doubtless a big draw), lets students see the numbers side-by-side. With this feature, they can determine which choices have the most minority students, highest employment rates, or lowest GMAT scores. In the Rankings, students can identify which school is "Number 1" overall, or in Entrepreneurship or student age. Of course, there is more to this site than number-crunching. The articles are well-written and timely, especially the look at such "hot" niche programs as E-commerce and "brand management." Plus, the site provides access to U.S. News Online's advice forums on graduate schools. Numbers rule, however, and number seekers will be most gratified at this site. It's a good starting point for first-time researchers, too.

Where To Find/Buy:

On the Internet at http://www.usnews.com/usnews/edu/beyond/bcbiz.htm

---

Overall Rating
★★★
A fun introduction to business schools; primary emphasis on rankings and stats

Design, Ease Of Use
★★★★
Includes a personalized search mechanism for finding schools

1–4 Stars

Publisher:
U.S. News and World Report

Online U.S. News is the Internet home of the print publication, *U.S. News & World Reports*.

Although technically a part of U.S. News Online's "Graduate School" segment, the "Business" section functions as its own site. Offerings include a personalized search for "Finding your business school" and a "Compare Business Schools" feature that provides side-by-side summaries of four schools. School rankings, articles, and advice are also included.

Media:
Internet

Principal Focus:
Business School

II. Business School

Overall Rating
★★★
A good compilation of successful essays

Design, Ease Of Use
★★★
Essay classifications helpful

1–4 Stars

Author:
Boykin Curry & Brian Kasbar

The authors grew up together in Summit, New Jersey and graduated from Yale in 1988. They are also the authors of *Essays That Worked* for college applicants.

Publisher:
Fawcett Columbine (Ballantine)

Edition:
1987

Price:
$10.00

ISBN:
0449905160

Media:
Book

Principal Focus:
Business School

ESSAYS THAT WORKED FOR BUSINESS SCHOOLS
35 Essays From Successful Applications To The Nation's Top Business Schools

 Recommended For:
Business School

Description:

This book was written by two Yale graduates, the authors of another book on successful essays for college applicants. In all, this book contains 35 business school admissions essays "that worked." The book opens with a brief introduction, an interview with an admissions officer about successful (and unsuccessful) essay techniques and strategies, and some sample questions from various business school applications. The essays themselves are divided into seven groups: "Essays That Discuss Strengths and Weaknesses," "Ethical Essays," "Essays About Work Experiences," "Essays About the MBA," "Essays About Accomplishments," "Extracurricular Essays," and "Off-Beat Essays." A short introduction begins each section, with comments and advice from the authors and admissions officers. The authors' comments are short and directive; the bulk of the book is taken up by the essays themselves.

Evaluation:

Although these essays were first compiled in 1987, this book is still valuable for business school applicants today. Other people's essays can spark new ideas. Although today's applicants may be writing about working for nonprofits or in international business, the basic essay models remain essentially the same. Advice from the authors is minimal, with just an interview with an admissions officer on likes and dislikes of admissions committees, and brief, but worthwhile, introductions to each section on specific essay themes. The essays are as varied and impressive as a business school first-year class, each displaying unique writing styles, experiences, and strengths. We think the book would be even more helpful if the authors offered ideas and techniques for developing good essays, in addition to providing examples.

Where To Find/Buy:

Bookstores and libraries.

SNAPSHOTS FROM HELL
The Making Of An MBA

 Recommended For:
Business School

Description:

This account of one person's journey through an MBA program at Stanford was written by a former White House speechwriter who left Washington to pursue his dream of business. As the author notes, a prospective student often has questions such as, "What will the other students be like? Number-crunchers? Hustlers? What about the professors? The workload? The cost? Can you have a social life?" This book is the author's attempt to answer these questions from his own experiences. He describes this book as "a simple act of decency, like going back to the last calm bend in the river and nailing up a sign that reads, 'Waterfall Ahead.'" The book, focusing on the first year, begins with "Inferno" and "Inferno, Cont'd," describing the fall and winter terms' trials and tribulations. "Purgatorio" tells of spring term's joys and challenges, and finally "Paradiso (Sort Of)" takes a look at the author's and fellow students' work experiences and lives in the real world.

Evaluation:

The author, clearly an experienced hand at enlivening any subject matter, weaves a gripping tale that holds the reader's attention to the last page. His account is at once funny and hair-raising. The stories he tells—struggling with linear equations at Stanford's pre-term "camp" for "poets" (students with weak quantitative skills), slogging through final exams, striving for grades while struggling to maintain a social life, surviving the MBA classroom and the stress of recruiting—come horribly alive for the reader. For potential MBA-ers, this book could serve as a wake-up call to the realities of business school. It is a critical, but honest, look at what business school is and is not. The author asks a professor at one point, "So what is business school . . . Business, or school?" And the professor answers, "That's the problem . . . it's both." At the end, the author looks back on his whole MBA experience: losses, gains, and lessons learned.

Where To Find/Buy:

Bookstores and libraries.

Overall Rating
★★★
A fiercely realistic and eye-opening foray into the world of business school

Design, Ease Of Use
★★★
Fast-paced and funny

1–4 Stars

Author:
Peter Robinson

The author was a speechwriter for former President Ronald Reagan. He attended Stanford University Graduate School of Business, graduating in 1990. After a stint working for the Murdoch empire, he lives and writes in California.

Publisher:
Warner

Edition:
1994

Price:
$11.99

Pages:
286

ISBN:
0446671177

Media:
Book

Principal Focus:
Business School

Overall Rating

★★★

A good "conservative" approach to applying to business school

Design, Ease Of Use

★★★

Well-written and to-the-point

1–4 Stars

Author:

Thomas H. Martinson & David P. Waldherr

Thomas H. Martinson and David P. Waldherr are both GMAT coaches.

Publisher:

Arco (Macmillan)

Edition:

1996

Price:

$12.95

Pages:

149

ISBN:

0028606205

Media:

Book

Principal Focus:

Business School

ARCO'S GETTING INTO GRADUATE BUSINESS SCHOOL TODAY

Description:

As the preface points out, "the quality of programs offered by business schools runs the gamut from poor to acceptable to good to outstanding." This book was written for the applicant applying to schools with regional and national reputations, as it gives information on those parts of an application that could "make the difference between rejection and acceptance" at the most competitive schools. The first chapter introduces the reader to graduate education in business management. The following two chapters take an in-depth look at how admissions officers rate and evaluate an application, and how an applicant can rate and evaluate business schools. Chapter 4 outlines the different parts of an application. Effective and ineffective methods of writing personal statement, as well as examples of "five personal statements that worked," follow. The last chapter discusses the GMAT, with examples from sections of the test. An appendix lists accredited schools of business by state.

Evaluation:

This book is well-written, even humorous in parts, and offers good advice on applying to business school. It takes a fairly conservative approach to the admissions process, giving very specific tables and criteria by which applicants can "guesstimate" how schools may evaluate their application. It pays little attention to less tangible aspects of an application that can sometimes make the difference between an acceptance and a rejection. For applicants looking to tread the straight and narrow, this could be a good thing. Less traditional and less academically-qualified applicants may find this approach a little off-putting. Readers will want to look at two helpful chapters on the personal statement, which stress the importance of this part of the application, while making it clear that a good statement alone cannot save an application. The critiques on style, grammar, and content of various essays are excellent, showing how a personal statement moves from a draft to a final polished version.

Where To Find/Buy:

Bookstores and libraries.

II. Business School

BARRON'S GUIDE TO GRADUATE BUSINESS SCHOOLS

Description:

Composed of three major parts, this "in-depth" guide begins with a description of the admissions process: why go to business school; how to choose a school; the application; financing the degree; and employment outlook. Part II, "The School Scene in a Nutshell," presents in table form information on graduate business programs in the U.S. and Canada, including requirements, concentrations offered, enrollment and student body statistics, faculty, admissions data, and tuition. Part III offers profiles of the business schools, arranged by state, with more detailed information. These profiles provide general background on the schools, as well as information about student body composition, faculty data, programs, admissions, library, research, and computer facilities, and placement data. An index of schools is also provided.

Evaluation:

One of the best things a guidebook of this sort can offer, beyond simply gathering data on hundreds of schools, is a clear, functional layout that makes finding information relatively easy. Barron's guidebook offers clear, concise profiles of U.S. and Canadian business schools. After a brief, but thoughtful discussion about considering, choosing, and applying to business schools, the book goes on to present in table form vital information on graduate business programs. This information helps applicants compare and contrast target schools. The profiles, which make up the largest part of the book, provide more detailed information on each school. Profiles are arranged by state, so it's easy to find what you're looking for. The schools aren't ranked or evaluated; information is provided by the institutions, so don't expect anything critical. Still, this general guide will be a good preliminary tool for business school applicants.

Where To Find/Buy:

Bookstores and libraries.

Overall Rating
★★★
A comprehensive overview of business schools in the U.S. and Canada

Design, Ease Of Use
★★★
Clear, user-friendly layout; school index follows text

1–4 Stars

Author:
Eugene Miller
The author is Executive-in-Residence and Professor at Florida Atlantic University. Formerly, he was Vice Chairman of the USG Corporation, and Senior Vice President of the New York Stock Exchange.

Publisher:
Barron's Educational Series

Edition:
11th (1999)

Price:
$16.95

Pages:
736

ISBN:
0764108468

Media:
Book

Principal Focus:
Business School

Overall Rating
★★★

A general management MBA in book form; a refresher for managers, a companion for students

Design, Ease Of Use
★★★

Dense, sophisticated business theory and practice; arranged in "modules"

1–4 Stars

Author:

This book is a collaborative effort of 97 contributors, including 50 professors from IMD International in Lausanne, Switzerland, The Wharton School of the University of Pennsylvania, and London Business School.

Publisher:
Financial Times Management

Edition:
1997

Price:
$39.95

Pages:
678

ISBN:
0273627295

Media:
Book

Principal Focus:
Business School

THE COMPLETE MBA COMPANION

Description:

In 1994, *The Financial Times* asked three international business schools—IMD International, The Wharton School, and London Business School—to cooperate in the production of a 20-part series on management. The goal of the series (originally titled *FT Mastering Management*) was to share the knowledge and ideas of professors at "top" business schools, and to create an "ideal tester for, companion to, and refresher after an MBA." This book offers the complete, updated text of the entire series; it covers the academic areas studied in a general management MBA. Modeled on the "core" curriculum of a typical MBA degree, the book groups the core management disciplines into 18 main "modules." An introductory module, which explores the history and philosophy of general management, and a concluding module are also included. The modules progress much as courses in an MBA program would: beginning with Accounting, Finance, and Marketing, and ending with Strategic Management and Implementation, Sociopolitical Context and the Business Environment. Diagrams, tables, and summaries, together with case studies, are used to demonstrate points.

Evaluation:

Let's clarify: This book is not a guide to MBA programs in the conventional sense. It contains no information on applications, GMATs, choosing a programs, or financial aid. It is not a resource for finding schools or getting admissions advice. So what is it? It is a general management MBA in a book. The modules "teach" readers about accounting, finance, etc., just as an actual MBA program would. Modules are authored by contributors from three of the world's "top" business schools, so the information is current and representative of "en vogue" management thinking and schooling. The benefits of this text to those considering an MBA are innumerable. Readers will learn exactly what general management MBA involves, whether such study appeals to them, and whether they really need such knowledge. After reading this book, readers may feel they've learned what they need to know and decide not to pursue a management degree. One thing is certain: this resource is a fine litmus test for prospective MBAs. No one will walk away from it uncertain about what an MBA entails; it is not for the feint-hearted.

Where To Find/Buy:
Bookstores and libraries.

GUIDE TO GRADUATE MANAGEMENT PROGRAMS IN THE USA, 1999

Description:

As management education in the U.S. evolves, many prospective students may be confused about which master's-level program is right for them. To help, the editors of this volume have compiled detailed descriptions of a wide range of management programs. Readers search the program profiles using a map of the U.S., which shows school locations and names, and a series of tables presenting "quick facts" about each school. The three-page, individual Program Profiles follow an introductory section; they are arranged alphabetically by school name. Profiles include a program overview, plus information on admissions requirements, expenses, international student support, career placement opportunities, and study demographics. Contact addresses and phone numbers are also provided. Though the bulk of this guide is dedicated to the profiles, the introductory section presents short articles on global trends in management education, educational options, and application tips, with special attention paid to the needs of international students. Also included is a list of accredited management schools. Appendices contain listings for additional resources and a glossary of terms and acronyms.

Evaluation:

For international students considering a management degree in the United States, this guide is a welcome preliminary tool. It is easy to use and read, and offers plenty of information about "International Student Support." Few guides for international students cover as much material in such a user-friendly format. We wonder about the content of the profiles, however. They cover all the vital stats on admission requirements and the like, but they read like advertisements for the schools. The editors note that "all information is verified by program managers and academic deans." We wonder if that means the profiles came straight from the schools. Readers will find no critical information here. That's the norm for most of these omnibus guides, however. This one works as a preliminary resource, especially for international students; it gives readers the opportunity to familiarize themselves with 85 program choices—a reasonable starting point for people interested in master's-level management education. However, as the editors say, there are myriad management education options; readers will need many more specifics before they make a choice about where to apply.

Where To Find/Buy:

Bookstores and libraries.

Overall Rating
★★★
Relatively detailed descriptions of 85 management programs

Design, Ease Of Use
★★★
Textboxes highlight unique features; relatively easy to use

1–4 Stars

Publisher:
EI Education International

Edition:
1999

Price:
$21.95

Pages:
361

ISBN:
1894122232

Media:
Book

Principal Focus:
Business School

Of Interest To:
International Students

II. Business School

Overall Rating
★★★
Accurate, knowledgeable, "insider's" look at getting into business school

Design, Ease Of Use
★★★
Personable tone

1–4 Stars

Author:
James L. Strachan, PhD, CMA

James L. Strachan, PhD, is a member of the admissions committee of the Weatherhead School of Management, Case Western Reserve University, where he also serves as a Senior Lecturer, and as assistant Dean of undergraduate management programs.

Publisher:
VGM Career Horizons
(NTC Publishing Group)

Edition:
1996

Price:
$14.95

Pages:
162

ISBN:
0844281956

Media:
Book

Principal Focus:
Business School

HOW TO GET INTO THE RIGHT BUSINESS SCHOOL

Description:

This book aims to be a guide and mentor for the complex, and sometimes misunderstood, business school application process. As the author notes in his introduction, this book will take away some of the "mystique" surrounding the application process and help readers show their unique characteristics, downplaying their weaknesses and marketing their strengths. The first three chapters discuss recent changes in MBA programs and how to choose the right program. Chapters 4 and 5 look at the inner workings of the admissions committee, and the criteria by which they evaluate applications. The next two chapters discuss how to best present oneself in the essay. Also considered are the types of questions asked on applications and how to answer them. The GMAT is covered in the next two chapters. The last chapters focus on the interview, and "responding to the schools' responses."

Evaluation:

The author's considerable experience with admissions committees is evident in the quality of the information presented in this book. He is fully cognizant of the diverse interests of such committees, which far from relying solely on GPAs and MCAT scores, reach beyond basic statistics to search for an applicant's true worth: "strong communication skills, strong leadership skills, high motivation, the ability to think creatively, and particularly combinations of these qualities." The author' believes "there is a MBA for you," if you believe in yourself and take the initiative to create a strong application. This book provides innumerable opportunities and strategies, from understanding what an admissions committee is looking for to conveying one's own uniqueness and best qualities in the essay. Reading this book may ease some application jitters.

Where To Find/Buy:

Bookstores and libraries.

MBA INFO
The MBA Program Information Site

Description:

For visitors researching MBA programs worldwide, MBA Info offers two sections of interest: The MBA Program Database and MBA Advice Pages. The former is the site's "unique" collection of data on over 2,000 MBA programs from 1,000 universities, business schools, and management colleges in 125 countries. To search the database, users choose any or all of the following criteria: institution name, program structure (e.g., distance, full-time), focus (e.g., entrepreneurship), location, program duration, and start date. A search results in a list of school matches. Users click for more details on a particular school. Details include contact info, program duration, start dates, entry requirements, application deadlines, and enrollment stats. The MBA Advice Pages contain an Introduction to the degree, plus articles on selecting a program and applying. There is also a Glossary, which defines MBA-related terms and acronyms, such as AMBA (The U.K.'s Association of MBAs) and accreditation. Another section reports program and school rankings from publications worldwide. Entries from Hong Kong's *World Executive Digest* and Holland's *Intermediair* are among the Top 10 and Top 25 lists provided.

Evaluation:

There are lots of nice touches at this internationally-flavored site. The Glossary is a terrific tool for familiarizing oneself with terms and acronyms. Defining the acronyms is especially helpful, since new researchers may not be familiar with notations like "AACSB accredited," which pop up all the time. (The AACSB is the main accrediting organization for American MBAs.) The glossary also gives U.S. residents help with foreign associations, such as ASFOR, the Italian Society for Management Training, an accrediting agent for Italian schools. Plus, there are direct links to every organization cited. (The only problem: the Glossary isn't searchable; users must browse alphabetical listings.) The program rankings are great fun as well. With Top 10 and Top 25 lists from publications around the world, researchers get a global perspective on business programs. For example, according the U.K.'s *Financial Times*, which ranked the Top 50 full-time MBA programs, Harvard is Number One, London Business School was 24th, and Georgetown was 35th. As for the school database, it doesn't provide in-depth information, but—considering how many countries it covers—it can be used as a starting point for research. For students interested in studying abroad, this resource is worth visiting.

Where To Find/Buy:

On the Internet at http://www.mbainfo.com

Overall Rating
★★★
An MBA site with a "global bent"; includes an international database and rankings

Design, Ease Of Use
★★★
Straightforward format; users must return to home page to visit new sections

1–4 Stars

Publisher:
WebInfoCo

Founded by two business school graduates, WebInfoCo was established in 1998 to develop, launch, and support this website.

Media:
Internet

Principal Focus:
Business School

Overall Rating
★★★
Recruiter interviews a unique plus for students concerned about job placement

Design, Ease Of Use
★★★
Simple design; users must return to home page to navigate

1–4 Stars

Publisher:
VNU Business Publications

VNU Business Publications is one of the largest publishing and information companies in Europe. Based in The Netherlands, VNU has branches in fifteen European countries, the U.S., Puerto Rico, India, and South Africa.

Media:
Internet

Principal Focus:
Business School

MBA PLAZA

Description:

From the Plaza's home page—which doubles as a table of contents—visitors have access to all of the site's features. These include a worldwide MBA School Program Database, which users can search by keyword or by completing a questionnaire. The questionnaire searches by location, language, concentration, type of MBA course (e.g., distance, full-time), program duration, and accreditations (e.g., AMBA, AACSB). Search results provide contact addresses and, in some cases, additional information about the school. Another feature, Starting an MBA, includes an Introduction to the MBA as well as tips for applying and securing financial aid. Under Editorials (on the home page), users will find a report on the GMAT CAT, plus a search engine for locating the nearest test center. In the Interviews segment, students and MBA school officials discuss studying and working outside the U.S. Included is an interview with two students in an executive MBA course in Slovenia; in another interview, three Canadian students debate the pros and cons of distance learning by computer. The site also features a career guide to management consulting and an interactive discussion forum.

Evaluation:

Developed by VNU Business Publications, one of the largest publishing companies in Europe, this site is international in orientation. The Management Consultancy as a Career guide was originally published in the U.K. The editorials include a discussion with the MBA director at the IEDC in Slovenia about hiring "young talent" vs. "senior talent," using the Eastern European situation as a backdrop. The database, though skimpy on school details, provides contact information for schools and programs around the world. Some U.S. sections are included, such as the GMAT CAT report and test center search, but this site will be most beneficial to students who want to study abroad. For users who fall into that category, the Interviews are a rare treat; they present an enticing look at foreign study. Included are interviews with students at schools in the U.K., the Netherlands, and South Africa, and school officials discuss AACSB accreditation in other countries. (AACSB is the main accrediting agency for American MBAs.) The database at the similarly international "MBA Info" site is better (see our review on page 105), so we suggest using the two sites together: go to "MBA Info" (http://www.mbainfo.com) for initial school research; come here for the insightful interviews and editorials.

Where To Find/Buy:

On the Internet at http://www.mbaplaza.com

PRINCETON REVIEW BEST 75 BUSINESS SCHOOLS
The Buyer's Guide To Business Schools—1999

Description:

The first section, "All About business school," discusses how to choose a school, what an MBA can (and cannot) offer, and what business school "is really like." The second section, "How to Get In," covers the basics of the application process, with an extensive chapter on the essay and sample successful essays from top schools. A mini, semi-humorous ranking based on student polls lists schools in such categories as "Quant Jocks" and "Poets," "Shiny, Happy MBAs," and "School of the Living Dead." The second half of the book focuses entirely on two-page profiles of the programs themselves, with vital stats listed in sidebars: student body demographics; program strengths; prominent alumni; financial facts; recent grad employment data; and the Gourman Report ranking. The main text offers in-depth discussions of academics, placement and recruiting, student and campus life, and admissions. Commentary—criticisms and praise—from current students and recent grads is interspersed throughout. Two indexes are included.

Evaluation:

Although criteria for ranking any school's programs can be vague or even suspect, this book has the advantage of evaluative commentary on the programs from a relatively reliable source—the students themselves. The best part of this book is the savvy, thoughtful, and often humorous comments from students in the programs. One tends to trust their remarks, and, short of contacting the students personally, this approach offers a very real and effective means of evaluating program strengths and weaknesses. Although the book's author professes not to believe in numerical rankings, she includes the Gourman Report rating, which we find unreliable (See page 313 for review) in the profiles. Application information is fairly basic, with the exception of the excellent section on essays. Overall this book will appeal to prospective students who seek input from current students. The student critiques and commentary bring an added dimension to the program profiles.

Where To Find/Buy:

Bookstores and libraries.

Overall Rating
★★★
A useful source of information and student commentary on 75 top programs

Design, Ease Of Use
★★★
Very readable; student comments are entertaining and informative

1–4 Stars

Author:
Nedda Gilbert

Nedda Gilbert graduated from the University of Pennsylvania and received a master's degree from Columbia University. She has been working for The Princeton Review since 1985 and is the creator of their corporate test preparation service.

Publisher:
Princeton Review
(Random House)

Edition:
1998

Price:
$20.00

Pages:
296

ISBN:
0375752005

Media:
Book

Principal Focus:
Business School

II. Business School

Overall Rating
★★★
International focus helpful to students considering overseas MBA programs

Design, Ease Of Use
★★★
Insightful, straightforward program profiles

1–4 Stars

Author:
George Bickerstaffe

Publisher:
Financial Times Management/
Economist Intelligence Unit

Edition:
10th (1999)

Price:
$50.00

Pages:
544

ISBN:
027363710X

Media:
Book

Principal Focus:
Business School

Of Interest To:
International Students

WHICH MBA?
A Critical Guide To The World's Best Programmes

Description:

This thick book covers business school programs in the U.K. and Europe, as well as Asia, Australia, and South Africa. After 10 chapters discussing why and how to get an MBA, including such issues as choosing a program, getting into the school of your choice, financing the MBA degree, and the "MBA Experience," the bulk of the book comprises school profiles, grouped by geographical area: U.K., Europe, North America, and the rest of the world. Profiles include general program information, such as admissions requirements, addresses and telephone numbers, and student demographics (women, foreign, country of origin). General and evaluative comments follow, with a look at the school's history, reputation, location and facilities, and recent program changes. The structure and content of the coursework is described next, together with lists of courses and a description of program emphases and strengths.

Evaluation:

This book reflects and speaks to the growing internationalism in business. For the applicant considering schools in the U.S. and abroad, this book offers detailed, comprehensive information on schools in the U.K. and Europe, including Asia, Australia, and South Africa. The profiles are well-written, focusing mainly on the essentials of location, history, reputation, facilities, and structure and content of the program. Individual classes are also listed, giving applicants a feel for each program. As the first chapter points out, although U.S. schools lead the pack in terms of GMAT scores, they "fall badly behind their European counterparts in the numbers of foreign students they enroll." Thus, some applicants may be looking abroad to acquire the international focus they desire. Although this book does not discuss specific guidelines for applying abroad or the pros and cons of doing so, it offers essential, critical insights into foreign programs.

Where To Find/Buy:

Bookstores and libraries.

ARCO'S BEST GRADUATE BUSINESS SCHOOLS

Description:

This third-edition guide to the "top" 50 business school programs describes and ranks schools on the basis of "standard indices of quality" for admissions stats and student demographics, academic strengths and weaknesses, career services, salary statistics for grads, and quality of student life. Five introductory chapters discuss such issues as MBA programs today, the current job market, and the admissions process. The "heart" of the book consists of program profiles, ranging from "Outstanding Programs" to "Distinguished Programs" to "Recommended Programs." School information is presented in index card-like text boxes. A key is provided to explain rankings. Much of the data is provided by the schools themselves. The ratings of individual concentrations within each curriculum are also provided by the schools.

Evaluation:

Some books offer a detailed compilation of data on schools. Others try to provide a selective evaluation. This book attempts to be both an information source and a ranking system, helping applicants view and evaluate their options. Although the rationale behind this book's ranking system is never made fully clear (the 50 programs were selected "for a variety of reasons, including the standard indices of quality," such as GPA/GMAT scores, faculty reputation, and starting salaries), information is up-to-date. It suffers, however, from the lack of navigation tools. Without an index, there is no way to look up a specific school. That's a problem for the majority of applicants who will be looking for regional or specialty favorites. We'd like to see the use of topical headings as well—then readers would know they were in the "Outstanding" section, without having to flip back to the beginning of the chapter. This book will, of course, be most useful for applicants planning to apply to top schools, and less useful for applicants applying to regional programs or those lower on the totem pole. All in all, this book is a good evaluative tool for applicants applying to the "top" business schools.

Where To Find/Buy:

Bookstores and libraries.

Overall Rating
★★★
An informative guide evaluating the "top" 50 business programs

Design, Ease Of Use
★★
Index-card graphics help readers compare programs, but without an index, it's hard to find anything!

1–4 Stars

Author:
Thomas Bachhuber, EdD
The author is a "career management consultant who has guided thousands of business school applicants."

Publisher:
Arco (Macmillan)

Edition:
3rd (1999)

Price:
$18.95

Pages:
370

ISBN:
002862503X

Media:
Book

Principal Focus:
Business School

II. Business School

Overall Rating
★★★

Original, readable content; includes a business school search feature

Design, Ease Of Use
★★

Clear, direct format; users must "log on" to get school search results

1–4 Stars

Publisher:
Princeton Review

The Princeton Review is a leading test preparation organization; it produces preparation classes, books, and educational software.

A portion of the larger Princeton Review Online, this site-within-a-site focuses on business schools. Sections include a business school search feature, tips on getting in and interviewing, and advice on making the transition. Also included is information on registering and preparing for the GMAT, and for finding scholarships and financial aid. An online discussion forum is also featured.

Media:
Internet

Principal Focus:
Business School

PRINCETON REVIEW ONLINE: BUSINESS

Description:

As part of the larger Princeton Review Online, this site-within-a-site is all about business schools. The main page hosts a sidebar menu that outlines the primary features: School Search, Get Into School, GMAT, The Transition, Scholarships & Aid. School Search houses a database of business schools. Users can search by name or by criteria, such as location, average GMAT, or tuition. Search results provide an overview of the school, detailing academics, demographics, and contact info. Also included are lists of the top-ranked schools by categories, such as Academic, Facilities, Pressure, and Social Life. (Rankings are based on the results of a survey of 18,500 business school students.) Get Into School offers articles on how admissions criteria are weighted, interview "dos and don'ts," and tips on the application process. In the GMAT section, users will find strategies for taking the GMAT CAT, as well as details on GMAT registration and a practice GMAT. Advice on stress management, exam preparation, and an "11-Step Guide to Transferring" are included in The Transition section. Scholarship & Aid examines trends in student financing and provides links to government loan sites and resources. An online discussion forum for business students is also featured.

Evaluation:

Unlike many commercial sites, the Princeton Review offers many original essays and interesting facts and figures. The company definitely pitches its GMAT preparation course, but in a relatively low-key manner. The biggest complaint we have with this site is that School Search—an otherwise fine tool for finding quick, basic information on business schools—requires users to "log on" and give their e-mail address before results are delivered. The search is free, but those leery of giving out their e-mail address may want to find another directory. Users can access the "top rankings" without logging on, however. These rankings aren't the serious, number-crunching variety published by other groups, but they're definitely worth a peek since they're based on student opinion. Other valuable features include the explanation of and strategies for taking the GMAT CAT, the interview and admissions tips, and articles on such topics as "Leadership and the MBA Applicant." The discussion forum is worth checking out too, if only for the novelty. This site is fine starting point for those considering the business school route.

Where To Find/Buy:
On the Internet at http://www.review.com/business/

KAPLAN ONLINE: BUSINESS

Description:

From the first page of Kaplan's "Business" segment, users can access all of this site-within-a-site's main features: GMAT CAT, Schools & Programs, Admissions, Financial Aid, First-Year Success, and Careers in Business. GMAT CAT works as an introduction to the exam. Included are test dates and registration info, explanations of scoring, and a "breakdown" of the exam's components. Three "Focus" pages look at the GMAT's Verbal, Math, and Essay sections; practice questions for each section follow. "Top 40 CAT Facts" and "Cat Strategies" are also provided. In Schools & Programs, users will find advice on choosing a school or program, as well as a direct-link directory of business school home pages (in "Business School Virtual Tours"). Admissions offers guidance on preparing an application, including tips on essays, resumes, recommendations, and interviews, along with a "business school Timetable" for applying. Financial Aid focuses on a student's options and financial aid timeline. Essays on First-Year Success tackle such issues as "What's First Year Really Like?" and what skills an MBA needs to develop. A discussion of starting salaries and a link to Kaplan's "Career Center" comprise the final feature, Careers in Business.

Evaluation:

As is often the case at Kaplan's sites, the test-related pages are the best elements here. The other "Business" features simply can't compare. Schools & Programs addresses valuable topics, such as part-time vs. full-time attendance or "MBA Abroad," but the instructional essays are brief and superficial; they read like brochure-copy. Admissions suffers from a similar handicap. It too covers important territory—the application process and its components—but the advice is just too obvious (e.g., "Sell yourself.") The insights from current students redeem First-Year Success, barely; otherwise, it's a "fluff" piece. The only truly informative section is the GMAT CAT, where terrific features abound. The online "mini-CATs" demonstrate how the CAT works and how it generates scores, and the practice questions for the Verbal, Reading, Data Sufficiency, Math, and Essay areas of the exam provide hands-on exercise. Of particular interest is the article on computer-graded essays, a trend in GMAT scoring that many students may not be aware of. The article explains the process and presents strategies for handling this new development. For students who know little about the GMAT CAT, this site is a fine place to start. It's one of the better introductions.

Where To Find/Buy:

On the Internet at http://www1.kaplan.com/view/zine/1,1899,3,00.html

Overall Rating
★★
A good introduction to the GMAT CAT; other content of little use

Design, Ease Of Use
★★★★
Exceptionally easy to navigate; sidebar menus appear on every page

1–4 Stars

Publisher:
Kaplan Educational Centers

Kaplan, a subsidiary of The Washington Post Company, is a leading producer of test preparation materials. Their products include prep courses, books, and software.

Media:
Internet

Principal Focus:
Business School

II. Business School

Overall Rating
★★
Focused with practical advice

Design, Ease Of Use
★★★
Concise; larger print than most guides

1–4 Stars

Publisher:
Peterson's

Edition:
1999

Price:
$18.95

Pages:
259

ISBN:
0768901251

Media:
Book

Principal Focus:
Business School

PETERSON'S 1999 MBA DISTANCE LEARNING PROGRAMS

Description:

This guide profiles 100 institutions offering graduate business and management degrees via long distance learning. A first edition, it provides students and those considering a business or management degree a general overview of the programs, including course delivery sites, media courses, geographic restrictions, available services, credit-earning options, tuition, application and registration requirements, contact information, and course subjects. The first 50-some pages describe trends and opportunities in the business world. The guide also provides information on a new online application service, *GradAdvantage* (reviewed on page 121), which allows students to apply to an unlimited number of schools using the basic application data with the Graduate Management Admission Test (GMAT) attached. The guide also explains what employers are looking for, so those seeking an MBA can focus their studies on bankable skills. Also addressed are financial aid opportunities and a brief explanation of debt management and loan repayment schedules. A two-page geographical index follows the profiles.

Evaluation:

For those interested in earning a graduate business or management degree via distance learning, this book will help narrow the program choices. We liked the limited focus on business and management programs. It saves readers time digging through more general guides. Also worth mentioning is the use of larger type than other school profile guides. The editors of this volume provide students solid employment advice, suggesting they focus their studies to make themselves more marketable. For example, they notes that employers prefer a business degree with a specialty in taxes over a general masters in marketing. We hope that future editions of this guide provide more profiles and greater detail. Readers also need to be aware that not all distant education programs deliver instruction to homes or workplaces; some are administered to study sites where groups of students come together to learn. Overall, this guide will give prospective students a general idea about what is available. For in-depth information, they will need to contact the schools and talk to alumni and prospective employers.

Where To Find/Buy:

Bookstores and libraries.

GMAT ONLINE: MBA EXPLORER

Description:

The Graduate Management Admission Council (GMAC) site features three topical sections of interest to prospective MBAs: GMAT (Graduate Management Admission Test), MBA Programs, and MBA Financing. Each of these sections, along with all of the site's contents, are outlined in the site index. In GMAT, users will find an introduction to the exam, an explanation of how graduate business schools use the GMAT, registration information, and sample test questions. The sample questions cover the verbal, quantitative, and analytical writing portions of the test. MBA Programs features a database of 500 programs, which users can search by school name, location, program type/length, or concentration. A search results in a list of matching schools, plus links to their respective home pages. Also included are a calendar of MBA forums and information about special GMAC programs, such as Destination MBA, a seminar for minorities. MBA Financing addresses general financial considerations, financial aid options, and financing available to international students. Other sections of the site offer tips on admissions and choosing the right program, as well as profiles of MBA-related careers. The site also features an "MBA Store," offering test preparation products.

Evaluation:

So many areas of this site are not accessible from the home page, the best—and only—way to navigate is via the site index. From the index, users can take full advantage of all the GMAC has to offer: admission tips, financing suggestions, and GMAT advice. "Get Ready For an MBA" features advice on all admission standards: work experience, the essay, letter of recommendation, and the interview. The MBA Financing section contains basic but solid information on the various sources of financial aid available to business school students. The core feature of the site, the GMAT portion, is well-executed; prospective students looking for an introduction to this all-important test will find what they're looking for here. Users can familiarize themselves with the test by reading the instructions and sample questions for each test area, plus there's registration information for both U.S. residents and international students. (The GMAC pays particular attention to international students with a section on financing for international students, as well as instructions on what to do if the GMAT isn't given in one's home country.) Better MBA program databases are available, so users can skip this one. For a first look at the GMAT, however, this is a fine resource.

Where To Find/Buy:

On the Internet at http://www.gmat.org/

Overall Rating
★★
A good place for information on the GMAT; includes useful advice

Design, Ease Of Use
★★
Navigate via the site index

1–4 Stars

Publisher:
GMAC

The Graduate Management Admission Council is a nonprofit organization of graduate business schools worldwide; their products include the Graduate Management Admission Test (GMAT).

Media:
Internet

Principal Focus:
Business School

Of Interest To:
International Students

II. Business School

Overall Rating
★★
Basic overview of the application process, with brief profiles of U.S. schools

Design, Ease Of Use
★★
Readable and down-to-earth, though shallow in parts

1–4 Stars

Author:
Alice Murphey & Shari Holmer Lewis

Alice Murphey is the Assistant Director of Financial Aid for Systems Management at the City University of New York. Shari Holmer Lewis is Assistant Dean for Graduate Business Programs at the University of Illinois at Chicago.

Publisher:
Kaplan (Simon & Schuster)

Edition:
1998

Price:
$20.00

Pages:
320

ISBN:
0684849763

Media:
Book

Principal Focus:
Business School

KAPLAN'S GETTING INTO BUSINESS SCHOOL (1999 EDITION)

Description:

This guide to the business school admissions process consists of six major parts. The first section looks at new directions in business schools. Part 2, "Selecting a Program," discusses the search process itself, and how to choose a suitable program, keeping in mind such factors as location, individual program strengths, teaching methods, and workload. The third section, "Admissions," focuses on the admissions process: how committees evaluate applications, and preparing a successful application. Financial aid (scholarships, loans, grants, and fellowships) is covered in Part 4. A fifth section spotlights special considerations, such as the needs of students fresh out of college, those with disabilities, women, minorities, and international students. Part 6 contains brief profiles of U.S. business schools, with such information as student body demographics, academics, financial aid and tuition, admissions requirements and selectivity, and graduate placement/salary statistics. An appendix includes firsthand "advice and comments from students" on various issues related to business school.

Evaluation:

This resource offers clear and accurate information and advice on the business school admissions process. It takes a "personalized and direct approach," with the added benefit of school responses on selected topics. Particularly helpful sections include the table of "Business School Admissions Stereotypes," which lists the perceived weaknesses and strengths that admissions committees can attribute on the basis of an applicant's background (e.g., "Financial Analysts: Good quantitative skills. . . . Limited management experience; many qualified applicants to top schools with similar experience").

The book then suggests ways to counteract these stereotypes in the application. Other sections, such as those on the essay, interview, and letters of recommendation, are very basic and lack the depth of other books on this subject. In general, this resource skims the surface of many topics and so is less valuable than it could be—applicants want (and need) an "expert" voice and opinion.

Where To Find/Buy:

Bookstores and libraries.

THE MBA PAGE

Description:

Produced and maintained by students at the Max M. Fisher College of Business at Ohio State University, this online web guide details links for prospective and current business students. Links are arranged into nine categories: Neat New Stuff; Sites to Start With; MBA Survival; Books & Periodicals; Business Connections; Fun Stuff; Job; Finding the Right School; and Class Materials. Sites to Start With, MBA Survival, and Finding the Right School are of greatest interest to prospective students. Sites to Start With comprises links to business schools' websites, ratings of business school web pages, plus general links about the Internet and places to go (for new web users). MBA Survival includes links to specific articles as well as sites on MBA trends, analyzing cases, speaking and presenting, and achieving academic excellence. Also included are links to school-produced "survival guides," such as the "Sloan MBA Survival Guide" and Stanford's "The SkyDeck." Finding the Right School offers links to program rankings and advice-oriented sites, such as GMAC, Princeton Review, Kaplan, and Peterson's. Brief descriptions of content accompany each link.

Evaluation:

For future MBAs just beginning their online research who hate using web browsers or search engines, this little guide is a great place to start. It's also a good tool for users new to cyberspace; the "Sites to Start With" category provides instructional links for Net beginners. While the site doesn't boast thousands of links, it does offer cover a wide array of subjects. Links include all of the introductory basics: business school publications, business school websites, "survival guides," advice sites, and MBA-related articles. For fun, users can check out the links in "Neat New Stuff," which range from online MBA communities and entrepreneurial articles to student loan sites. This guide has a sense of humor, which is particularly refreshing in the often sterile, no-nonsense world of MBA research, but it is practical, too. The Books & Periodicals page lists several useful MBA-related magazines, business school alumni magazines, and business school journals. MBA Survival provides links for developing such skills as problem solving, time management, making presentations, and writing, all of which can be used when applying to and attending an MBA program. A good beginning bookmark, but be forewarned: we found several broken links. Time for an update!

Where To Find/Buy:

On the Internet at http://www.cob.ohio-state.edu/dept/fin/oldmba.html

---

Overall Rating
★★
Small but useful web guide for prospective MBAs

Design, Ease Of Use
★★
Compact organization and quick loading; no internal search engine; many broken links

1–4 Stars

Author:
Roman Khlupin

Mr. Khlupin, who designed this page, is an MBA student at Max M. Fisher College of Business at Ohio State University.

Publisher:
Ohio State University

Media:
Internet

Principal Focus:
Business School

II. Business School

Overall Rating
★★
Basic data on diverse business school programs

Design, Ease Of Use
★★
Information arranged in clear categories; profiles cramped

1–4 Stars

Publisher:
Peterson's

Edition:
33rd (1999)

Price:
$34.95

Pages:
1,989

ISBN:
1560799862

Media:
Book

Principal Focus:
Business School

PETERSON'S GRADUATE PROGRAMS IN BUSINESS, EDUCATION, HEALTH, INFORMATION STUDIES, LAW & SOCIAL WORK

Description:

This enormous resource includes information on a wide variety of graduate and professional programs in the fields of business, education, health, information studies, law, and social work. After an introductory section entitled "The Graduate Adviser," which includes advice and information about applying to and financing grad school, the book is divided by field of study, with several individual sections for each field. For example, the business section contains 18 individual sections, such as programs in Business Administration and Management, Entrepreneurship, Human Resources, International Business, Marketing, and Nonprofit Management, to name just a few. Each individual section is then broken down into a "directory," containing basic information about each program (degrees awarded, student demographics; tuition, admissions requirements, contact info., etc.), cross-discipline and other announcements, and full-page, in-depth entries submitted by some schools.

Evaluation:

Considering the vast amount of information gathered in this book, it is relatively easy to use. Readers may need a magnifying glass to read the program profiles, but they will be rewarded with a host of valuable information for whatever branch of business they are interested in. Peterson's is a well-regarded reference publisher, and one can rely on the accuracy of their information. This particular resource strives to cover a lot of ground—nearly 2,000 pages adds up to a hefty tome. As a reference, applicants to the business school programs will find very basic information, helpfully classified by program type. It may be particularly useful for applicants who have no idea what kind of business program they would like to apply to. The book offers a bird's eye view of the different academic and professional programs in business. Eventually, however, most readers will need to find a resource that offers a closer, more detailed look at the individual programs.

Where To Find/Buy:

Bookstores and libraries.

II. Business School

THE PRINCETON REVIEW BUSINESS SCHOOL COMPANION
The Ultimate Guide To Excelling In Business School And Launching Your Career

Description:

This book, put out by The Princeton Review and written by two Wharton School graduates, is intended as a "companion" along the road to the MBA, with information and advice on everything students need to know about business school—from social life to the recruiting process. The first two chapters provide a general introduction to business school, explaining how to prepare before arriving on campus (i.e., finding housing, buying computer hardware and software, brushing up on basic quantitative skills). A discussion of social life and academics follows. Chapters 5–6 describe "Team Projects" and "Case Analysis," both widely integrated into business school curricula; the authors also explain how to learn and profit from these experiences. Key concepts in everything from marketing to accounting follow in the next seven chapters. The final chapter deals with the recruiting process—explaining how to take advantage of it while avoiding common pitfalls, and keeping the job search "as pleasant and rewarding as possible."

Evaluation:

One of the benefits of books written by real MBA grads is the "insider's" advice from people who have really been there. In this small book, readers will find much handy information for success and satisfaction in business school, including advice that incoming students may need to hear, such as keeping grades in perspective, making the "teamwork" aspect of the MBA experience as enriching as possible, and dealing successfully with the recruiting process. The sections covering the basics of marketing, statistics, and such, while perhaps beneficial for the liberal arts grad, are less useful overall—students will eventually need a more in-depth resource on these subjects. Since these chapters form the bulk of the book (56 pages), readers may find it is not worth their pocket money. There is, however, plenty of good advice here—much of which students will eventually learn the hard way. New students may find that this book eases them into the MBA experience.

Where To Find/Buy:
Bookstores and libraries.

Overall Rating
★★
A useful overview of the business school experience from an "insider's" perspective

Design, Ease Of Use
★★
Highly readable, down-to-earth writing style

1–4 Stars

Author:
H.S. Hamadeh & Andy Richard
The authors studied finance and entrepreneurial management at the Wharton School.

Publisher:
Princeton Review
(Random House)

Edition:
1995

Price:
$15.00

Pages:
119

ISBN:
0679764631

Media:
Book

Principal Focus:
Business School

Overall Rating
★★

An informative and generally entertaining look at the MBA experience

Design, Ease Of Use
★★

Narrative slowed by excessive detail

1–4 Stars

Author:
Robert Reid

Robert Reid received an MBA with Distinction from Harvard Business School in 1994. Currently, he lives in Northern California and works in the digital media industry.

Publisher:
Avon (William Morrow)

Edition:
1994

Price:
$11.00

Pages:
331

ISBN:
0380725592

Media:
Book

Principal Focus:
Business School

YEAR ONE
An Intimate Look Inside Harvard Business School

Description:

This narrative takes us on the author's journey from working as a consultant in Warsaw, helping the Polish government privatize its economy, through the trials and tribulations of Harvard Business School back in Cambridge, Massachusetts. A single year in his life as a business school student is recounted in narrative detail, moving chronologically from orientation, meeting fellow students, and surviving the MBA classroom, through final exams, the recruiting and interviewing process, and landing a summer job. Each of the 19 chapters revolves around a single issue or theme in the MBA experience, telling the story of the author's own experiences and insights as well as those of his fellow students. The author touches up such issues as student diversity, the classroom experience (the "case" teaching method; the all-important seating; "cold-calling"), grades, professors, workload, social life (or lack thereof), study groups, romance, money, and hopes and dreams for the future.

Evaluation:

For the prospective MBA student, this book definitely provides what its subtitle promises: "an intimate look inside Harvard Business School." Anecdotes and experiences relevant to the MBA experience in general and to the Harvard MBA in particular are recounted here in great detail, including the necessity for classroom participation and the "shark-like" atmosphere this breeds in the classroom, "chip-shots," "cold-calling," and the case method. The author is honest in his insights, helping us see exactly what works and what doesn't at Harvard and the injustices, and the rewards, of the MBA experience in general. Readers looking for a slice of MBA life will find it here. However, they may also find it heavy-going; frequently the narrative gets bogged down in excessive detail, making this book most interesting for business school hopefuls eager to hear it all or Harvard alums longing to revisit the old days.

Where To Find/Buy:

Bookstores and libraries.

KAPLAN'S INSIDER'S BOOK OF BUSINESS SCHOOL LISTS

Description:

As the introduction points out, "There's more to life than going to class." This book aims at helping prospective business school students discover those little extras not included in every business school curriculum, such as "surfing, shopping, and rock-and-roll." The first chapter, "Getting In and Staying In," lists schools by such categories as "Big Fish, Small Pond," "Purely for Pencil Necks," "For the Very Greedy," and "The Name is Bond, James Stocks-and-Bond." The second chapter groups schools by lifestyle factors, such as "Most Eligible Men/Women," "Schools in the Sticks," and "Most Annual Precipitation." The third chapter, "Entertainment Value," details schools "Near Great Roller coasters," "Near Great Microbreweries," "Near Great Horse Racing," and "Near the Best Alternative Rock Scenes." Finally, Chapter 4 gets serious with categories pertaining to "Your Future:" "Highest Average Student Loan Debt," "Captains of Industry," and "Near the Jobs."

Evaluation:

Applying to and matriculating at a business school program are serious steps for most. Potential MBAs probably won't consider such factors as whether a program is "On the Lollapalooza Tour," but this book offers the stats, just in case. The author is quick to point out that some of the lists are "seriously silly, and a few are strictly for laughs." Some serious lists here may be genuinely helpful, such as schools with the least and most expensive tuition, schools with the greatest cultural diversity, the highest rate of job placement, and schools "where the living is easy" (i.e., where the cost of living is relatively inexpensive). Although students probably won't choose an MBA program by the local availability of legalized gambling, who knows when such information may come in handy! (Perhaps one day you'll own a casino). All in all, this book offers some laughs but few genuinely useful facts on MBA programs.

Where To Find/Buy:

Bookstores and libraries.

Overall Rating
★
Entertaining, but not a serious reference tool

Design, Ease Of Use
★★
Easy to flip through

1–4 Stars

Author:
Mark Baker

Mark Baker is the author of several other nonfiction books, of which two are bestsellers: *Nam: The Vietnam War in the Words of the Men and Women Who Fought There* and *Cops: Their Lives in Their Own Words.*

Publisher:
Kaplan (Simon & Schuster)

Edition:
1997

Price:
$12.00

Pages:
181

ISBN:
0684841797

Media:
Book

Principal Focus:
Business School

II. Business School

Overall Rating
★
Offers the most basic school information

Design, Ease Of Use
★
Small print and thin pages make reading a chore

1–4 Stars

Publisher:
Educational Testing Service

Educational Testing Service (ETS) is a private, nonprofit organization that develops and administers millions of achievement and admissions tests each year in the U.S. and 180 other countries, including the TOEFL.

Edition:
16th (1997)

Price:
$24.99

Pages:
415

ISBN:
0446396222

Media:
Book

Principal Focus:
Business School

THE OFFICIAL GRE/CGS DIRECTORY OF GRADUATE PROGRAMS
Volume B: Engineering, Business

Description:
This directory to business programs and engineering schools presents data on 865 schools in the U.S. and Canada. Section 1 includes tables with specific program information, such as admissions and degree requirements; GRE score range; number of completed applications received; degrees awarded; financial aid available; and part-time and evening study options. Section 2 includes summaries of general information on the schools, listed alphabetically by state, with such information as academic calendar; geographic setting; enrollment and faculty statistics; percent of students receiving financial assistance; tuition and housing costs; and student services. The third section is composed of narratives on the schools, with "brief summaries on such topics as research affiliations and cooperative programs, library holdings, computer facilities, and institutional resources." The last section contains addresses and phone numbers. An index of programs follows.

Evaluation:
This book is not easy to use. Not only is information presented in tiny print with relatively little white space, but it is divided into four separate sections that force readers to flip back and forth for complete information on any single program. Another drawback: business school programs share space with engineering programs, and neither gets the attention or detail they deserve. For example, what use is GRE score data to students considering an MBA? Worse yet, some excellent business programs, such as the University of Washington and Harvard, are not even listed. All in all, this directory leaves one wondering at the mysterious ways of the Educational Testing Service.

Where To Find/Buy:
Bookstores and libraries.

BSCHOOL.COM

Non-Rated Resource

Description:
Still under construction at the time of our review, Bschool.com offers only a few resources in each of its topical sections: Best Business Schools, Bschool Directory, Bschools in the News, and FAQ. The site's goal is to provide links to and information about every graduate and executive education business program website.

Author:
Hal Kirkwood & Wayne Marr

Mr. Kirkwood completed his Master's in Library and Information Services at University of South Carolina; he is currently Assistant Management & Economics Librarian at Purdue University. Professor Marr is formerly the Vice President of Social Science Electronic Publishing, Inc.

Publisher:
Bschool.com

Media:
Internet

Principal Focus:
Business School

Where To Find/Buy:
On the Internet at http://www.bschool.com

FINAID: BUSINESS SCHOOL RESOURCES

Non-Rated Resource

Description:
This site is part of the larger "FinAid Smart Student Guide To Financial Aid" website. "Admissions Guides" offers a link to the MBA Explorer, a site about business school admissions and testing compiled by the Graduate Management Admission Council. "Award Programs" links to the Consortium for Graduate Study in Management. "Loans" describes and links to six lenders that offer loans to students in business school.

Author:
Mark Kantrowitz

Mr. Kantrowitz is a Research Scientist at Just Research, the US software laboratory for Justsystem Corporation of Japan. He is the author of three books, including one on financial aid, and has created several popular websites.

Publisher:
FinAid Page, L.L.C.

Media:
Internet

Principal Focus:
Business School

Where To Find/Buy:
On the Internet at http://www.finaid.org/otheraid/business.phtml

GRADADVANTAGE

Non-Rated Resource

Description:
Students searching for online applications to graduate schools or MBA programs will find what they're looking for at this nonprofit site. Still in development, the site offers a limited number of graduate school applications at the time of this review; however, an array of MBA choices is provided. Schools are arranged alphabetically, by name.

Publisher:
ETS and Peterson's

Educational Testing Service (ETS) is a private, nonprofit organization that develops and administers millions of achievement and admissions tests each year in the U.S. and 180 other countries, including the TOEFL. Peterson's is a publisher of education guides and a producer of test preparation materials and courses. It is part of the Lifelong Learning Group within Thomson Learning.

Media:
Internet

Principal Focus:
Business School

Where To Find/Buy:
On the Internet at http://www.gradadvantage.org

TOP TEN

Non-Rated Resource

Description:
Prospective business students who love rankings can browse four categories of "top" business schools and MBA programs here. Included are lists of the "Top 10" U.S. schools/programs, "Top 10" European schools/programs, plus "Top 50" lists for both the U.S. and Europe. A list of "Top Jobs" is also included.

Publisher:
Business Education Commission

The B.E.C. is a nonprofit organization dedicated to promoting high quality international business education; it has offices in Brussels and Washington.

Media:
Internet

Principal Focus:
Business School

Where To Find/Buy:
On the Internet at http://www.top10.org

II. Choosing, Getting Into, & Excelling In Law School

Every year more than 40,000 adults—students and graduates—apply to law school. A law degree takes three years to complete, if the student is attending full-time, and those who attend part-time need to budget additional semesters or years. Most part-time programs take four years.

Like business school and graduate programs aimed at a Master's or PhD, law school demands an enormous commitment of time, energy, and money. In this chapter, we review resources designed to ease the burden. Some look at the admissions process: How do you get in? Others look at life in law school: How do you survive and excel? And still others consider the law as a career: Is law the right choice for you?

Making The Decision: Do I Really Want To Go To Law School And Become A Lawyer?

As you read our descriptions of resources, you'll note that some are geared toward helping prospective law students get a feel for law school coursework. These resources may also discuss character traits commonly found in successful lawyers, and the range of positions most often taken by law school grads.

Other resources remind prospective applicants about the costs of a law school education, financially and psychologically. They urge applicants to estimate total costs for all three years.

Most law students take out substantial loans. A law school education can mean an investment of $100–120,000 and three years. Applicants should ask themselves what they want to achieve, what kind of work they want to do when they graduate, and how debt will influence their choices after law school. Too often idealistic young lawyers find their commitment to public interest work shaken by the weight of hefty student loans.

Applicants should also ask themselves how three years of law school will affect their personal lives. As many of the reviewed resources note, law school can take a heavy toll on relationships and young families.

Once students have answered these questions for themselves, they are ready to move on to researching law schools.

Researching Schools And Narrowing Choices

Although some applicants are determined to get into a particular school, most will need help researching alternatives so they can choose the six or so where they will apply.

These six should include a couple of "reach" schools, where their LSAT/GPA index and all-around profile place them in the possible, but not likely, admission category. The bulk of their target schools should be those where the applicant has a reasonably good chance of admission, and the final two or three are "safety" schools where the applicant is fairly confident of gaining admission.

We have found numerous directories to help students and advisors with the first round of research when developing a list of target law schools. Some are Internet-based searchable databases. Others are large paperback guides filled with law school profiles. Many offer only basic school statistics, such as the cost of tuition, number of students enrolled, average LSAT scores, and average starting salaries for graduates. Others include subjective information on the school's reputation or strengths in a particular area, such as legal writing.

As students narrow their search, they may look for resources that rank law schools. As we have already noted, school rankings are controversial, but students and advisors still look to them for guidance. Though we review numerous resources that "rank" law schools, we urge students and advisors to also pay careful attention to other factors, such as student body and faculty, expenses, program strengths, and career placement, and bar passage rates.

We also remind students and graduates of the services provided at their alma mater's career planning center. Many schools employ prelaw advisors who can help students and alums narrow down their list of target schools and prepare their applications. Most career planning centers also have a good supply of reference books and brochures to help students with their research.

Applying To Law School

Most law schools accept applications on a rolling basis, meaning that students have a slightly better shot at getting in if they apply early. While competition for law school admission is tough, the 1990s have seen an easing in the cutthroat competition of earlier years. In 1997–98, 78 percent of all senior applicants were admitted to at least one school. Careful research is the key to admission success.

Of the 40-plus resources we review here, many describe how to apply to law school. They can help students write an outstanding personal statement, select people to write letters of recommendation, and modify their résumé for use with their application. Many resources also include advice on what to do when accepted, wait-listed, or rejected.

The resources we rate highly go beyond the basic how-tos and provide their users with practical tips and an insider's view of the admissions process. Prospective law students should use these resources to create an application to-do list and a series of deadlines for accomplishing tasks along the way. Again, prelaw advisors can offer plenty of helpful advice here.

The LSDAS

Subscribing to the Law School Data Assembly Service (LSDAS) is one of the first steps in applying to law school. The LSDAS acts as a clearinghouse for the law schools, and it saves applicants lots of paperwork by forwarding undergraduate and graduate transcripts, letters of recommendation, LSAT scores, and an undergraduate academic summary to target schools.

Most law schools require an LSDAS subscription. A 12-month subscription, which includes reporting to one law school, costs $93. Reports to additional schools cost $9 each at the time of the initial subscription. When ordered later, they cost $11 each.

Students can subscribe to the LSDAS via the Internet at Law School Admission Council Online (http://www.lsac.org, reviewed on page 156 of this guidebook), or by contacting the LSAC at (215) 968-1001.

They can also subscribe by filling out the registration form found in the LSAT & LSDAS Registration and Information Book, available at career planning centers, or write directly to:

Law School Admission Council
Box 2000
Newtown, PA 18940-0998

The LSAT

About 100,000 law school hopefuls take the Law School Admission Test (LSAT) every year. It is offered four times a year (June, October, December, and February) at designated centers throughout the world, and is required by all 182 ABA-Accredited law schools.

Many law schools require that the LSAT be taken by December for admission the following fall. However, many prelaw advisors suggest applicants take the test earlier, in June or October. Students should realize that many law schools average multiple scores. This approach is different than in undergraduate applications where institutions consider only the highest score. Applicants may take the LSAT no more than three times in a two-year period.

The LSAT score is a central piece of the law school application. Some of the resources we review contain sample LSATs to help students practice their test-taking skills. Many students opt for LSAT preparation courses, of which there are many.

For more information or to register, visit Law School Admission Council Online (http://www.lsac.org) or contact the LSAC.

The LSACD

Many applicants are taking advantage of new technology to research and apply to law school. The LSACD is a searchable, electronic version of the widely used *The Official Guide to U.S. Law Schools* (reviewed on page 135) It helps applicants target schools, and consolidates and stores application information for submission to law schools.

LSACD 2000 is available on CD-ROM for Windows for $59. LSACD is also available on the Internet (http://www.lsac.org/) for $49 (unlimited access for a one-year admission cycle).

GPA

An applicant's undergraduate GPA is another important element of the law school application, but law schools don't simply look at numbers. They also consider how challenging an applicant's coursework was and if the applicant took honors classes.

Nevertheless, the sheer volume of applications received by most law schools necessitates some kind of preliminary sorting mechanism, and many schools use "indexing" to presort applications into "A," "B," and "C" groups.

The index is a number created by a mathematical formula, which combines an applicant's LSAT score and undergraduate GPA (Graduate school grades are not factored in.). The number is artificial, of course, but it serves as a tool to help law school admission officers organize the many applications.

The use of indexing does not mean that admissions committees throw out the "C" applications. Every application gets read, so it makes sense for applicants to take a careful look at their test scores and undergraduate careers. If necessary, they should include a short addendum to their application explaining any inconsistencies in grades.

The Personal Statement

Few law schools require personal interviews, but the personal statement is a must. Applicants and advisors must recognize that the personal statement can make or break an application for competitive applicants.

We urge applicants to take their time with these essays. Leave plenty of time for brainstorming about personal or professional experiences.

The personal statement is not an essay on "Why I Want To Go to Law School." Rather, it is a chance for applicants to distinguish themselves by writing about an experience that was maturing, that influenced their choices or changed their view of a particular issue.

We also recommend thinking carefully about presentation and tone. And, as with all application materials, remember that proofreading and spell checking are essential!

Letters Of Recommendation

The letter of recommendation is another important tool in law school admissions. Undergraduates will want to ask a trusted professor or teaching assistant who knows them well. Law school applicants who have been out in the workplace for a few years (or more) should ask employers or other professionals who can write with confidence about their professional abilities and personal character.

We also recommend that students request letters of recommendations before graduation, even if they do not plan to apply to law school right away. Most schools allow students and alums to open a "credential file" for letters of recommendation at their undergraduate institution. The file is used to hold recommendations and is especially useful for those who plan on applying to graduate or professional school at some time in the future. Professors write the best recommendations when the student is still fresh in their mind.

As with business school and graduate programs, well-known professors or professional figures lend a certain quality to an application, but a vague or poorly written recommendation from a big shot is of little value. Applicants should strive for personalized and favorable recommendations. Recommendations are submitted through the LSDAS letter of recommendation service.

Excelling In Law School And Landing A Plum Job

Getting into law school can be tough, but most students will agree that the first year of school is the intellectual equivalent of Ranger training, with professors wielding the Socratic method like a Drill

Master's whistle. During the second and third years, the crushing course load eases to make time for new challenges, such as interviews for the all-important summer internship and, for the selected few, Law Review.

Life in law school and the search for the perfect job are important issues for prospective students. We review several books designed to help law students excel in school, and by so doing, position themselves for satisfying post-graduation employment. Many of the resources we've reviewed offer study strategies, time management coaching, and encouragement for the weary 1L. We also recommend resources offering advice on interviewing, choosing career paths, and landing a good job.

Lawyer jokes notwithstanding, most Americans hold the legal profession in high esteem, and for good reason. Lawyers often command impressive salaries, but more importantly, they are responsible for some of civilized society's most significant tasks. We hope that the resources reviewed here will help students make informed decisions that lead to satisfying careers.

★★★★

Overall Rating
★★★★
Many helpful features

Design, Ease Of Use
★★★★
Deft use of frames speeds
site navigation

1–4 Stars

Publisher:
Boston College Board Of
Trustees

The Boston College Online Law
School Locator was developed by
Dom DeLeo, Associate Director of
Career Services at Boston College.
It is based on the Law School
Locator compiled by J. Joseph Burns.

Media:
Internet

Principal Focus:
Law School

BOSTON COLLEGE ONLINE LAW SCHOOL LOCATOR

 Recommended For:
Law School

Description:

Law school applicants are often advised to apply to several "reach" schools, several schools where they stand a good chance of being admitted, and a few "safety" schools. But how are students supposed to know where they stand relative to the competition? This "locator" is designed to help students locate schools where the first-year class has median LSAT scores and median GPAs similar to their own. After identifying the correct range of GPA and LSAT, students click to a list of schools with home pages linked to the site. The site sponsor, Boston College's Career Center, is quick to point out that scores and grades provide an indication of how competitive the admission process is at each school, but "these numbers and the relative position of each school on the chart do not and cannot indicate the educational quality of a school or its suitability for any individual." For another view of the schools, applicants should check out "Locator 25" at the same site to research the 25 percentile LSAT scores and GPA ranges of first-year classes.

Evaluation:

Bravo to Boston College's Career Center for sponsoring a tool that is genuinely helpful to law school applicants. This site is the fastest (and cheapest!) way we've uncovered for law school applicants in the first stage of research to find a list of reach, good-chance, and safety schools. The Locator is based on data from 1998—the most recent admissions statistics. It can help applicants identify schools where their scores and grades are most competitive for admission and gauge their chance of admission at a particular school; however, it is not designed to be the only resource for formulating a short list of target schools. To research particular schools, applicants will want to look at some of the other resources we recommend in the law school section. In addition to the Locator, check out this site's Law School Application Schedule, and the advice on writing a personal statement (http://careercenter.bc.edu/case.html).

Where To Find/Buy:

On the Internet at http://www.bc.edu:80/bc_org/svp/carct/matrix.html

FINDLAW

Recommended For:
Law School

Description:

FindLaw is primarily an online, direct-link guide to law-related web resources. Formatted Yahoo!-style, its home page divides links into 14 categories, including categories for Law Schools, Legal Organizations, Directories, U.S. Federal Resources, U.S. State Resources, and News & References. Each category has its own menu of subtopics. Law Schools features seven subtopics: Law School Information (school websites, admissions help); Law Reviews; Employment; The Bar (test prep, state bar home pages); Outlines & Exams (constitutional, property, etc.); Course Pages (ethics, environmental, etc.); Law Student Resources; and Pre-Law Resources (financing, preparation). With the exception of Law Student Resources, all topical pages within Law Schools comprise direct-links to web resources; most links are annotated. Law Student Resources, under the heading Study Skills, provides original content: excerpts from the books and workshops of author Carolyn Nygrem. Excerpts provide tips and advice to prelaw students, current law students, bar candidates, and foreign lawyers and students. The site also features LawCrawler, a tool for searching the "Alta Vista Search" web database for legal information.

Evaluation:

For users interested in law schools, this web guide is an excellent research tool. Although it lacks a site search feature (for searching by keyword or subject), the simple organization makes browsing fairly efficient. On the home page, a brief description accompanies each category, so users know what they're getting when they click on a heading; the menu of subtopics helps narrow the search. The links in Law Schools' subtopics of Admissions Information, Financing, and Preparation are relatively few in number, but they cover the basics: LSAT info, Free Application for Federal Student Aid (FAFSA) on the Web, application services, etc. Even better (and rarer) are the links found in Outlines & Exams, Law Reviews, and Course Pages. While these sections are ostensibly directed at current law students, prospective students can use them to learn about the types of courses, exams, and other academic matters they will encounter in school. In fact, students can use many of the site's features to research what it's like to be a lawyer. They can read up on news and trends in the legal community, try their hand at searching legal code and case law databases (via the LawCrawler), or visit the websites of individual lawyers and law firms. FindLaw is a perfect bookmark for before, during, and after law school.

Where To Find/Buy:
On the Internet at http://www.findlaw.com

Overall Rating
★★★★
A perfect bookmark for anyone interested in studying law!

Design, Ease Of Use
★★★★
Well-organized link guide; LawCrawler is a bonus

1–4 Stars

Publisher:
Find Law

FindLaw was launched in 1995 as a list of Internet resources compiled by engineer and attorney Timothy Stanley and attorney Stacy Stern. Today, FindLaw is a growing portal site focused on law and government.

Media:
Internet

Principal Focus:
Law School

II. Law School

★★★★

Overall Rating
★★★★

An informed and practical guide to surviving the law school and career-launching process

Design, Ease Of Use
★★★★

Clear, straightforward writing style

1–4 Stars

Author:
J. Robert Arnett II, Arthur Coon, & Michael DiGeronimo

Arnett, a 1986 grad of the UCLA School of Law, currently practices at the firm of Bickel & Brewer in Dallas. Coon earned his JD in 1986 from the University of California at Davis and is now with the firm of Miller, Starr & Regalia in Oakland, CA. DiGeronimo graduated from the UCLA School of Law in 1986 and is a shareholder with the firm of Miller, Starr & Regalia.

Publisher:
Professional Publications

Edition:
1993

Price:
$19.95

Pages:
211

ISBN:
0912045531

Media:
Book

Principal Focus:
Law School

FROM HERE TO ATTORNEY
The Ultimate Guide To Excelling In Law School & Launching Your Legal Career

 Recommended For:
Law School

Description:
Written by three recent law school graduates, this guide to "law school and beyond" takes readers through the whole process—from choosing a law school, three years of classes, the bar exam, to the job hunt. Part One deals with the application process: how to choose and get into the right school. Part Two discusses the characteristics of all three years of law school, including the "dos and don'ts" of study aids and strategies for preparing for and taking law school exams (creating briefs, course outlines, and exam essay skills). Extracurricular activities are surveyed in Part Three; these include law review, law journals, and moot court. The fourth section deals with job hunting in today's legal job market, with a look at first- and second-year summer jobs, part-time jobs during school, and clerkships. Part Five discusses how to study for and take the bar exam. This book includes six appendices with examples of a formal brief, course outline and mini-outline, class flow chart, and two sample law school exams.

Evaluation:
This book focuses mainly on surviving law school and landing a good job. The first section on applying to law school, while useful, is more fully covered in other books. As a "law school companion," however, this resource is a particularly useful guide—it helps students see exactly what they're getting into and helps soothe fears by detailing excellent success strategies for all three years of law school and the job-hunting days (and months). The tone is down-to-earth and realistic: the authors are recent, successful law school grads and are thus able to provide insights into the experience that "outsiders" may not have. New and experienced law students at any point in their career will find much useful information here, such as which study aids are really worth the money, tips on study skills reinforced with firsthand samples of course outlines and briefs, and a helpful "debunking of myths" about such things as first-year horrors and law review.

Where To Find/Buy:
Bookstores and libraries.

HOW TO GET INTO THE RIGHT LAW SCHOOL

 Recommended For:
Law School

Description:

With more than 20 years experience as a prelaw advisor at a private university, the author of this guide knows how to help students choose a law school and put together a competitive application. Each chapter provides insight into a particular step in the process. "Education Outside the Classroom" offers tips on choosing extracurricular activities. Chapters on the LSAT and the LSCAS Law School Data Assembly Service address relevant questions. A series of chapters address "Making Your List" of target schools, including how to get information on prospective schools, setting priorities, and calculating admission chances. "Filling Out Law School Applications," "Personal Statements," "Letters of Recommendation," and "Interviews" provide information and advice. "Minorities" discusses protected categories, including women and the disabled. The book ends with a chapter all students would rather avoid, "If You Don't Get In," and an appendix entitled "One Big Checklist of Virtually Everything You Have to Do."

Evaluation:

This guide begins with a couple of chapters for younger students hoping to position themselves for law school admissions: "Your College Education" and "Education Outside the Classroom." The rest of the book guides applicants through the admission hoops. It is a good supplement to the hefty tomes describing the nation's accredited law schools. Some of the information is basic, but the focused approach on admissions offers some valuable insights. For example, the author provides a thorough discussion of how students can calculate their odds of admission at a particular school based on GPA and LSAT scores. This will help applicants put together a realistic list of prospective schools, with an appropriate balance of "long shots" and "safety schools." The author also offers plenty of good advice on what to include—and not to include—in law school applications. Applicants will appreciate the level of detail in the chapters on crafting a personal statement and drafting essays. Overall, a good to-the-point primer for law school admissions.

Where To Find/Buy:

Bookstores and libraries.

Overall Rating
★★★★
A practical guide with information and advice on the application process

Design, Ease Of Use
★★★★
An easy-to-follow writing style with plenty of examples and advice

1–4 Stars

Author:
Paul Lermack, PhD

Dr. Lermack is a professor of political science and a prelaw advisor at Bradley University in Illinois. His work focuses on public law, American government, and political theory.

Publisher:
VGM Career Horizons (NTC Publishing Group)

Edition:
2nd (1997)

Price:
$14.95

Pages:
225

ISBN:
084424127X

Media:
Book

Principal Focus:
Law School

Of Interest To:
Women
Persons of Color
Disabled

II. Law School

Overall Rating
★★★★
Authoritative, stimulating collection of essays

Design, Ease Of Use
★★★★
Consistently well-written; provides valuable resource and reading lists

1–4 Stars

Author:
Stephen Gillers (editor)

Stephen Gillers is Professor of Law at New York University School of Law, a nationally recognized expert on legal ethics, and the author of *Regulation of Lawyers: Problems of Law and Ethics.*

Publisher:
Meridian (Penguin)

Edition:
4th (1997)

Price:
$14.95

Pages:
376

ISBN:
0452011787

Media:
Book

Principal Focus:
Law School

Of Interest To:
Women
Persons of Color

LOOKING AT LAW SCHOOL
A Student Guide From The Society Of American Law Teachers

 Recommended For:
Law School

Description:

Twenty-three professors of law from institutions around the country and retired Supreme Court Justice William J. Brennan, Jr. contributed essays to this guide for prospective law students. Its principle goals are to explain what law school is all about and to encourage readers to consider seriously whether law school is right for them. Part I addresses this second issue in essays that distinguish between what lawyers actually do and how they are portrayed in popular media; essays debunk myths, explain the application process, and detail the true costs of paying for law school as well as sources of financial aid. The essays in Part II look at different aspects of the law school experience, from the silence of students in the classroom (with techniques to break it) to advice for women, parents, lesbians and gays, and people of color. Part III explains the contents of first-year courses and advises students on such topics as reading a case. The authors in Part IV look at legal education from a broader perspective with essays on legal ethics, clinical studies, and the application of economics to law. Many chapters end with lists of recommended readings and notes.

Evaluation:

This book is essential reading for those about to enter law school and those considering a career in law. The writers in this "Who's Who" of law professors cover all the essentials—choosing and getting into law school, financial aid, first-year courses—from their perspective as insiders. No one knows torts better than the professor who has taught it for decades and written a dozen books on tort law. Each topic is addressed by experts who are knowledgeable, articulate, and engaging. What makes this book stand out further is that it covers aspects of law school not addressed in other books of this kind, essays that challenge the legal education system itself. These include Sylvia Law's essay on the disparities of wealth and power in America and how legal education reinforces it, and Stephanie Wildman's discussion of the silence of women and minority students. The chapter offering advice to lesbians and gay men, written by two "out" activist lawyers, is particularly useful. If your law professors are as intellectually stimulating as the ones who contributed to this book, you'll have a fascinating and challenging three years.

Where To Find/Buy:

Bookstores and libraries.

THE OFFICIAL GUIDE TO U.S. LAW SCHOOLS 2000

 Recommended For:
Law School

Description:

Published by the Law School Admission Council (LSAC; the folks who produce the LSAT), the bulk of this guide is devoted to two-page profiles of American Bar Association (ABA) accredited law schools. These pages contain information on enrollment and student body; faculty; library; curriculum; special programs; admissions; expenses and financial aid; career services; and student activities. The first 50 pages comprise chapters titled "Preparing for Law School," "Choosing a Law School," and "Financing Your Legal Education." These introductory chapters offer a brief response to questions frequently on the minds of those considering law school: "What are the trends in post-law school employment?" "What criteria should I consider in evaluating a law school?" and "What are the two ABA approved schools in Arizona?" A visual geographic display of law schools in the U.S. helps prospective students research schools in a geographic region of interest.

Evaluation:

We prefer this book to its ABA-sponsored competitor (American Bar Association Approved Law Schools, reviewed on page 172); the LSAC presents its material in prose format—an approach that really works for describing certain features, such as special programs, student activities, and career services. The ABA directory presents all material in a table format. A matter of taste perhaps, but we found the LSAC version more user-friendly. The admission profile grid is a valuable tool for determining the apply/admit ratio for a given LSAT/GPA profile, and the extensive chapter on "Opportunities in Law for Minority Men and Women" includes a table displaying the number and percentage of minority students broken down into racial categories (for example, African-American). This table also presents the number and percentage of full-time minority faculty, as well as scholarship data. We recommend this guide over its competitors because it presents information in the most readable, accessible manner.

Where To Find/Buy:

Bookstores and libraries.

Overall Rating
★★★★
Presents all the basic information students need as they research law schools

Design, Ease Of Use
★★★★
A readable, accessible product

1–4 Stars

Author:
Law School Admissions Council

The Law School Admissions Council is a nonprofit corporation that provides services to the legal education community. Its members are 194 law schools in the U.S. and Canada.

Publisher:
Time (Random)

Edition:
1999

Price:
$20.00

Pages:
442

ISBN:
0812990463

Media:
Book

Principal Focus:
Law School

Of Interest To:
Persons of Color

II. Law School

★★★★

Overall Rating
★★★★
Like sitting down with an experienced prelaw counselor

Design, Ease Of Use
★★★★
Frank, fair, and full of seasoned advice

1–4 Stars

Author:
Ron Coleman

Mr. Coleman is a commercial litigator, author and adjunct professor at Seton Hall University School of Law. He is the author of the *American Bar Association Guide to Consumer Law*.

Publisher:
Princeton Review
(Random House)

Edition:
1996

Price:
$15.00

Pages:
162

ISBN:
067977372X

Media:
Book

Principal Focus:
Law School

THE PRINCETON REVIEW PRELAW COMPANION
What Law School Grads Wish They Knew Before They Started

 Recommended For:
Law School

Description:
Beginning with "A Look At Yourself," the author walks prospective law students through a series of chapters designed to help them think through the decision to attend law school and eventually become a lawyer. "The Lawyer Personality" and "It's a Lawyer's Life" discuss necessary character traits (good work ethic, perseverance, humility, the ability to listen, good judgment) and the realities of daily life as a lawyer. "Where the Lawyers Are" and a chapter on specialties explore career options, with information on salaries, expected hours, and the culture prevalent in large law firms, public interest organizations, and such fields as health or entertainment law. "Resourceful You" raises the issue of the time and monetary commitment that law school represents, and offers advice on how to pay for it. In "Choosing A Law School," the author shifts gears, discussing the myriad factors that influencing school selection. Little information on individual schools is provided.

Evaluation:
This niche book designed for those thinking about, but not yet committed to, law school begins with a quote: "So you want to go to law school. Maybe." Advice and information about choosing and applying to schools is also included, but the heart of this book, and half of its pages, are devoted to helping prospective students decide if they really want to be a lawyer. The author paints a "realistic picture of the landscape of the legal profession." Once students are sure law school is their goal, he offers a wealth of advice on planning the undergraduate and prelaw experiences. This book is not designed for prospective students completing applications in those harried fall months senior year. It emphasizes life goals, taking stock of one's strengths and weaknesses, planning a financial strategy, and putting into place an application strategy that maximizes the odds of admission at students' target school(s).

Where To Find/Buy:
Bookstores and libraries.

THINKING ABOUT LAW SCHOOL
A Minority Guide

 Recommended For:
Law School

Description:

This short booklet guides prospective law students through the decision of whether law school is a good choice for them and the process of researching and applying to law schools. The first chapter addresses topics such as: "Is law school right for you?" and "Evaluating Your Chances." Subsequent chapters discuss the LSAT and the role of undergraduate GPA in admissions. "Building Your Case: Assess Yourself" helps applicants consider their strengths and resources. "Financial Considerations: Calling All Resources" presents an overview of how much law school is likely to cost and how students typically pay for it, with an emphasis on problem-solving for applicants with financial limitations. The second section walks applicants through the school selection and application process itself. Chapter 8 covers the personal statement and letters of recommendation. "Behind the Scenes: The Admission Office" offers insights on what law schools look for and how admissions decisions are made.

Evaluation:

The Law School Admissions Council (LSAC), publishers of the LSAT/LSDAS Registration and Information Book, publish this free booklet for persons of color considering law school. Both resources are available at the LSAC website (http://www.lsac.org/ reviewed on page 156) and at law school admission offices and prelaw advisor offices. The LSAC has done an excellent job with this guide; it's informative, interesting and current—and free! We liked the way that personal stories of current and former law students of color are woven throughout the informational presentation. Each chapter presents the nuts-and-bolts information students need, along with valuable insider advice for students of color. The emphasis is on self-assessment: How do I choose a school that will be a good fit for me? How much can I afford to take on in student loans? What are my chances of admission? This guide is a must-read for all persons of color considering law school!

Where To Find/Buy:

To order this free publication, contact the LSAC at http://www.lsac.org, or phone (215) 968-1001.

Overall Rating
★★★★
Captivating personal stories and great guidance on law school

Design, Ease Of Use
★★★★
Readable and informal

1–4 Stars

Publisher:
Law School Admission Council

The Law School Admissions Council is a nonprofit corporation that provides services to the legal education community. Its members are 194 law schools in the U.S. and Canada.

Edition:
1998

Price:
Free

Pages:
85

ISBN:
0942639529

Media:
Book

Principal Focus:
Law School

Of Interest To:
Persons of Color

II. Law School

Overall Rating
★★★★
Detailed law school descriptions plus online applications, and more!

Design, Ease Of Use
★★★
The Law School Matchmaker slower than it should be

1–4 Stars

Publisher:
Embark.com

Embark.com (formerly CollegeEdge) is a California-based company "dedicated to helping people fulfill their life's learning and career aspirations."

Media:
Internet

Principal Focus:
Law School

EMBARK.COM: GOING TO LAW SCHOOL

 Recommended For:
Law School

Description:

Embark.com's law school portion has its own main page, detailing its contents. There are three topical sections: Choose the Right Law School, Apply to Law School, and Finance Your Education. Each section contains an Introduction, Advice & Information articles, and an interactive forum for joining discussions or posting messages. The sections have unique features as well. In Choose the Right Law School, a Law School Matchmaker matches users to schools based on field of study, degree type, location, cost, and institutional resources. Results produce a list of school names accompanied by user options: "view details," "apply online," "send inquiry" (via e-mail), and a link to the school's website. Click "view details" to see a three-page profile of the school. The profile includes an overview of the law school, contact info and admissions requirements, plus information on faculty, enrollment, student services, tuition, and housing. In Apply to Law School, users can apply online to Embark's partner schools. (A list of partners is provided.) Also featured: admissions, application, and LSAT tips. Finance Your Education covers finance sources, such as loans, work-study, and grants; "expert" advice, and a Free Application for Federal Student Aid (FAFSA) calculator are also provided.

Evaluation:

Not all of Embark's partner schools support online applications (at the time of this review, many are marked "coming soon"), but this is a formidable resource. The law school profiles are among the most detailed on the Web. They cover the same information as other sites, and more, including overviews of both the entire law school and specific programs, stats and facts on admissions, applications, enrollment, faculty, and tuition, plus information housing, environment/transportation, and financing. They even provide a "First-Year Enrollment/Student Profile." For students applying to the schools that do have online applications, this site means one-stop shopping. The online applications let users pay the application fee with secure check submission, help references complete recommendations electronically, and promise confidentiality. Embark.com will even check the application for errors before submission. Users will also find some good articles and tips in Finance Your Education, but some of the site's other advisory sections are lackluster. For instance, this site isn't the best place to go for LSAT prep. Still, the outstanding school descriptions, online applications, and interactive forums (which people actually use) make this a great site.

Where To Find/Buy:
On the Internet at http://www.embark.com/law

INTERNET LEGAL RESOURCE GUIDE

 Recommended For:
Law School

Description:

The Internet Legal Resource Guide is the trailhead for most law-related sites on the Web. It contains a categorized index of 4,000 websites from 238 nations, as well as more than 850 locally stored web pages and other files. It was established in 1995 by Prescott Caballero to "bring together only the finest and most substantive legal resources online in a comprehensive and meaningful capacity." Some of the site's most popular features site are: a law school course outline archive; a section on legal study abroad programs; a series of law school rankings; a survey of the "top" 100 law firms in the U.S.; a legal forms archive; and a U.S. federal case law search. The latter allows users to search (for free) the online databases of the U.S. Supreme Court and all circuit courts. In addition to the on-site features, the Guide contains an extensive set of links to legal sites on the Internet. A listing of legal usenet (law-related newsgroups) is also available.

Evaluation:

This guide is the place to start for law-related research on the Internet. The guide contains enough on-site information to warrant a four star rating and is also the best place to learn about other legal sites on the Web. One of its most interesting features is a series of law school rankings. The site is now the new home of the well-known Wehrli Law School Rankings. This section includes all the major published American law school rankings, along with an explanation of the various methodologies used to rate schools. The Guide presents its own unique cost/benefit analysis of American law schools by comparing median post-graduation salaries after adjusting for cost of living. Law students will appreciate the "Law School Course Outlines Archive," which features 31 free downloadable outlines for Civil Procedure, Constitutional Law, Contracts, Criminal Law, Property, Torts, and other common law school courses. Be sure to stop by the Pre-Law page at http://www.ilrg.com/pre-law.html/

Where To Find/Buy:

On the Internet at http://www.ilrg.com/

Overall Rating
★★★★
The place for information on law school rankings

Design, Ease Of Use
★★★
Some areas still under construction

1–4 Stars

Publisher:
Internet Legal Resource Guide

Created in 1995 by Prescott Caballero, a graduate of University of Texas Law School, the Internet Legal Resource Guide is one of the first sites dedicated to becoming a comprehensive online legal resource guide. It became a commercial entity in 1996.

Media:
Internet

Principal Focus:
Law School

II. Law School

Overall Rating
★★★
Excellent resource for those considering Harvard or any of the top-tier schools

Design, Ease Of Use
★★★
Clear, commonsense advice; needs an index for improved navigation

1–4 Stars

Author:
Willie J. Epps

Willie J. Epps, Jr., Esq., is a graduate of Harvard Law School, where he was elected student-body president. He is currently a military officer serving as a judge advocate in the United States Air Force.

Publisher:
Contemporary Books
(Tribune New Media/Education)

Edition:
1996

Price:
$16.95

Pages:
372

ISBN:
0809232529

Media:
Book

Principal Focus:
Law School

Of Interest To:
Persons of Color

HOW TO GET INTO HARVARD LAW SCHOOL
Invaluable Advice On Applying & A Look At Successful Application Essays From Current Students And Recent Grads

 Recommended For:
Law School

Description:
The author, a successful Harvard Law grad, has written this book to "relay to you what works and what doesn't work" when applying to the school. The first chapter describes daily life at Harvard Law, and the second discusses some of the strengths and weaknesses of the program to help students decide if Harvard is the right school for them. Chapter 3 is filled with commonsense advice on the application process, including strategies and time-management steps. Chapter 4 offers an insider look at how the admission committee makes its decisions. Chapter 5, by far the longest, profiles 50 current and former law students, providing their answers to a questionnaire about LSAT scores, undergraduate GPAs, extracurricular activities, undergraduate honors, and miscellaneous personal factors. The profiles cover career aspirations and financial background (How are they paying for their law school education?) Chapter 6 includes 50 essays culled from the personal statements of successful applicants.

Evaluation:
While numerous books cover the general topic of law school admissions, this is the only one we've found that focuses on one particular school. It is designed specifically for those who have set their hearts on attending Harvard Law, but the insights, tips, and strategies found here are transferable to any of the highly competitive, top-tier law schools. Reading this book is like having a helpful "friend of a friend" offer advice on navigating the application maze. We found it filled with first-rate advice, particularly on choosing people to write recommendation letters and writing a personal statement. The profiles of current and former Harvard Law students can also be a source of encouragement for prospective students whose grades, LSAT scores, and career paths may not make them a "shoo-in" for admissions. Included are former actresses, middle-aged career changers, and others who don't fit the preppie right-out-of-college stereotype. One caveat: while the author's advice and meaty profiles are excellent, we would like an index to help find topics of interest. In its present form, readers must scan every page to find profiles of specific interest (e.g., female, middle-class, African-American). An index would make this illuminating resource even better.

Where To Find/Buy:
Bookstores and libraries.

SO YOU WANT TO BE A LAWYER
A Practical Guide To Law As A Career

 Recommended For:
Law School

Description:

This guidebook provides information and advice about applying to law schools and working as a lawyer in order to help readers decide whether a legal career is right for them. The book opens by describing the range of reasons people go to law school and distinguishing between facts and myths. The book lists the skills and characteristics that make for a good lawyer and explains what lawyers actually do in different settings and specialties. The law school experience is overviewed, with brief descriptions of the Socratic method and courses. Four chapters are devoted to explaining where to get information about law schools, how to evaluate them, and how to apply, based on a self-assessment, which determines a student's personal needs and strength of application. The authors describe the relationship of the LSAT to admissions and counsel what sort of preparations to make. They also describe the admissions process from the inside, explaining how, when, and by whom decisions are made. Financing an education is also briefly addressed. Fifty pages of appendices include a geographic guide to law schools and a list of prelaw readings.

Evaluation:

Written by the people who produce the LSAT, this authoritative little book does what it sets out to do—it gives readers the facts they need when considering whether to go to law school, from what a lawyer really does to the skills needed to make it in school and in the field. More valuable, however, are the chapters devoted to the school search and admissions process, which this group of authors knows well. In the chapter on preparation and self-assessment, they address the concerns of college graduates and working people, as well as high school students already on the law track. They list all possible sources of information on law schools and, in their most useful chapter, provide an extensive, descriptive list of the factors that can influence the choice of which schools to apply to, such as faculty heterogeneity. They also list questions for evaluating a school's clinical courses. Also useful are the guidelines they give for writing personal statements and the specific stages for readying an application. This inside view of the admissions process will help readers make decisions and weather the wait for admission. Too bad the book is so dryly written and offers little insight into the real challenges of life in law school.

Where To Find/Buy:

Bookstores and libraries.

Overall Rating
★★★
Detailed information and advice on admissions process and selecting a law school

Design, Ease Of Use
★★★
Concise but fairly dry

1–4 Stars

Author:
Law School Admission Council

The Law School Admission Council (LSAC or Law Services) is a nonprofit association of Canadian and American law schools.

Publisher:
Broadway
(Bantam Doubleday Dell)

Edition:
1998

Price:
$13.00

Pages:
154

ISBN:
0767901606

Media:
Book

Principal Focus:
Law School

II. Law School

★★★★

Overall Rating
★★★★
Explores law school politics and why some schools are better for women than others

Design, Ease Of Use
★★★
Straightforward writing; index and table of contents ease navigation

1–4 Stars

Author:
Linda Hirshman

Linda Hirshman is a law professor at Brandeis University. After graduating from the University of Chicago Law School, she practiced for thirteen years before teaching. She is co-author of *Hard Bargains: The Politics of Sex.*

Publisher:
Penguin

Edition:
1999

Price:
$14.95

Pages:
290

ISBN:
014026437X

Media:
Book

Principal Focus:
Law School

Of Interest To:
Women

A WOMAN'S GUIDE TO LAW SCHOOL

Description:

Why a woman's guide to law school? Hirshman begins her book by answering that question. First, law school is a competitive, often expensive technical education; women should be sure, before they apply, that such an education is right for them. To help readers with their decision, she explores law school outcomes (types of jobs available, etc.) and the types of interests and motivations that lead women to consider law. Second, not all law schools are created equal. After gathering statistical data on, and conducting interviews with, the class of 1997, Hirshman concluded that some schools are better at fostering women and their interests and talents. She explains how "schools where women succeed" differ from "schools where women don't succeed as well," shows readers how to "pick a compatible law school," and presents her rankings of 158 accredited law schools (in which schools are ranked by the "success" of female students). She also explains how women who choose to go to less woman-friendly schools can succeed despite the obstacles. Also provided are advice and insights on the application process, the "dreaded first year," class and exam study habits, and the job interview.

Evaluation:

This is not a book for readers who eschew controversy. It's not that the book's central theme—that law schools vary in their ability to foster female students—is so controversial; gender and racial bias in schools of all types is a frequent topic of debate. But Hirshman's work will shock some readers with its indictments. (She's particularly scathing in her criticism of University of Chicago's Law School, her alma mater.) She uses interviews with students to demonstrate how some schools "pressure" women to adopt the school's political beliefs and agendas. She uses school course catalogs to prove that: for example, while on school advertised courses like "Gender-based Discrimination," the courses weren't offered in two consecutive semesters. She teaches women how to determine whether a school has compatible political beliefs by investigating its private contributors and their agendas. And, of course, she ranks 158 schools by their "Femscore"—a ranking of schools by woman-friendly factors. Hirshman's judgments are blunt and unapologetic; she isn't afraid to name names. Whether one agrees with her personal politics, this book is a thought-provoking read. For future female law students, especially for those interested in public interest law, this book tackles subjects that are worth knowing about, yet seldom discussed.

Where To Find/Buy:

Bookstores and libraries.

PRINCETON REVIEW BEST LAW SCHOOLS 2000

★★★★

Description:

The first eight chapters comprise a series of articles, covering such topics as women in law school, diversity and affirmative action, admission trends, and alternative careers in law. The bulk of the book is made up of two-page profiles of each ABA-accredited law schools. Each profile contains two sidebars with factual information on admissions (number of applications received, acceptance rate, percentage of acceptees attending), financial facts (tuition, percentage of students receiving aid, average graduation debt), academics (student/faculty ratio, percentage female faculty, percentage minority faculty), employment (grads employed by field, average starting salary) and students (enrollment, percentage male/female, average age). Information from student surveys is included in the text. This book differs from similar guides in its coverage of some non-ABA accredited schools, which are approved by the California Committee of Bar Examiners.

Evaluation:

This law school directory stands out for its decidedly non-stuffy tone and its incorporation of student input in its school profiles. The introductory materials in the early chapters are current and informative. Women and prospective law students of color will enjoy the thorough treatment of issues of interest to themselves. The authors buck conformity by including profiles of certain schools not accredited by the ABA. They tip their hand by including a chapter-long interview with Dean Lawrence Velvel of the Massachusetts School of Law (who has a long-standing dispute with the ABA over its accreditation process), which begins with the question, "Does the ABA hold a 'monopoly' on legal education?" Overall, readers receive a conversational discussion of each school with minimal factoids and plenty of input from students.

Where To Find/Buy:

Bookstores and libraries.

Overall Rating
★★★★
Conversational and informative with plenty of student input

Design, Ease Of Use
★★
Text is small and difficult to read at times

1–4 Stars

Author:
David Hallander & Rob Tallia

David Adam Hollander and Rob Tallia, co-authors of this book, run the Princeton Review Law Division, Worldwide.

Publisher:
Princeton Review
(Random House)

Edition:
1999

Price:
$20.00

Pages:
560

ISBN:
0375754644

Media:
Book

Principal Focus:
Law School

Of Interest To:
Women
Persons of Color

II. Law School

Overall Rating
★★★
Fun, stats-and-facts introduction to law school research; lots of rankings

Design, Ease Of Use
★★★★
Offers a personalized school search

1–4 Stars

Publisher:
U.S. News and World Report

Online U.S. News is the Internet home of the print publication, *U.S. News & World Reports*.

Media:
Internet

Principal Focus:
Law School

U.S. NEWS ONLINE: LAW

Description:

The "Law" section of U.S. News Online's "Graduate School" segment functions as its own site. Its main page acts as a home page, detailing the section's contents. There are six content areas: Find Your Law School, Compare Law Schools, Rankings, Specialties, Web-exclusive Rankings, and Articles. Find Your Law School allows users to search for schools by name or via a personalized search based on such criteria as location, LSAT score, and full/part-time programs. Search results provide a match or matches. Users then click on a school's name for contact information and a statistical overview. Overviews cover data on admissions, deadlines, tuition, and student demographics. The Compare Law Schools feature lets users select up to four schools for side-by-side comparisons on over 30 criteria (e.g., acceptance rates, costs). Rankings, Specialties, and Web-exclusive Rankings offer school rankings for Top Schools, for such specialties as Environmental or International Law, and for specifics such as Highest or Lowest LSAT scores. Articles include "Career Outlook," "Finding a Niche," and tips for "Getting In." Access to U.S. News Online graduate school advice forums on admissions and financial aid is also provided.

Evaluation:

Like the "Business" and "Medicine" subsections of U.S. News Online's "Graduate School," "Law" is best used by first-time researchers as an introductory tool, or by those who base their decisions largely on numbers. The articles are good, if not plentiful, and the advice forums (part of "Graduate School" and accessible from the Toolbox) are well worth a click. We must emphasize, however, that the heart of this site is its numbers: the statistics offered by the Find Your Law School search, the side-by-side numbers of Compare Law Schools, and the Rankings. Comparison shopping via Compare Law Schools is somewhat informative; at least, students will learn which of their choices costs the most, which has the highest percentage of women, and which is closest to their home. And students can identify which school is ranked "number 1" and which has the Most Part-Timers, the Highest Acceptance Rate, or the Graduates With Least Debt. All of this information can be useful, especially for those who have just begun their school search. However, we advise applicants not to take it too seriously; numbers aren't everything. A fun site and a good starting point for more serious research.

Where To Find/Buy:

On the Internet at http://www.usnews.com/usnews/edu/beyond/bclaw.htm

AMERICAN BAR ASSOCIATION GUIDE TO APPROVED LAW SCHOOLS

Description:

This American Bar Association guide presents profiles of all ABA-accredited schools, but does not provide any ranking or evaluation of the relative merits of the law schools included. School statistics are presented in two-page tables. "The Basics" include application deadlines, student faculty ratios, and housing data. "Faculty" contains detailed information on the number, gender, and race of the instructors. "Library" offers a glimpse of the capacity and depth of the law library. "Enrollment & Attrition" breaks these figures down by gender and minority status; it also provides the total number of JD degrees conferred. "Curriculum" covers typical first-year section size, and the availability of simulation courses, seminars, field placements, moot court and other courses. Other sections present GPA/LSAT, Financial Aid, Career Placement and Bar Passage statistics.

Evaluation:

This guide is not the only directory of law schools available. We rank it slightly below its LSAC competitor (*The Official Guide To U.S. Law Schools 2000*, reviewed on page 135) because it relies on tables and charts to inform readers. This is especially apparent in the two-thirds of the book comprised of law school profiles. Data is presented in charts with no interpretation or insight offered. Its best feature is the comparison chart chapter, which allows readers to compare law schools by such factors as type and location of employment and bar passage rate. A second chart compares expenses, faculty, and student body, and a third provides admissions data, such as percent admitted and total matriculations. Other chapters provide a visual geographic representation of law schools and bar admissions requirements. For updated information on law schools from the ABA, we suggest a visit to the Internet version of this book at http://www.abanet.org/legaled/approved.html.

Where To Find/Buy:

Bookstores and libraries.

Overall Rating
★★★
Loads of details help with law school comparisons

Design, Ease Of Use
★★★
Will appeal to the visually-oriented who prefer tables to prose

1–4 Stars

Publisher:
IDG Books Worldwide

Edition:
1999

Price:
$21.95

Pages:
480

ISBN:
0028628241

Media:
Book

Principal Focus:
Law School

II. Law School

Overall Rating
★★★
All the basic information needed to start the law school selection process

Design, Ease Of Use
★★★
Table and text format make for easy reading and comparison

1–4 Stars

Author:
Gary A. Munneke

Gary A. Munneke teaches Torts, Professional Responsibility, and Law Practice Management at Pace University School of Law. He is also the author of *Barron's How to Succeed in Law School.*

Publisher:
Barron's Educational Series

Edition:
13th (1998)

Price:
$14.95

Pages:
554

ISBN:
0764104314

Media:
Book

Principal Focus:
Law School

BARRON'S GUIDE TO LAW SCHOOLS

Description:

Now in its 13th edition, this Barron's guidebook profiles 179 ABA-approved law schools and 21 non-ABA-approved schools. The first 85 pages provide general information about choosing a law school. Questions, such as "Should I go to law school?," "How do I apply?," and "What should I expect?" are answered, with the help of tables listing basic admissions statistics, placement services, and records for the 179 profiled law schools, and a sample law school application. The section on taking the LSAT includes a full-length model LSAT test with answers. Individual law school profiles are presented on two-page spreads with one-paragraph descriptions of admissions requirements, procedures, and information for minority and disadvantaged students; costs and financial aid; required and elective courses; a list of on-campus organizations; contents of the library; makeup of the faculty; and composition of the student body. Application requirements, enrollment statistics, and tuition are encapsulated in table form, as are placement statistics. The non-ABA approved schools are presented in table format only.

Evaluation:

This guidebook presents information about law schools in both table and text form, an approach that makes it particularly usable. Numerous tables compare basic school information for quick reference. While these tables sometimes repeat information, they make for easy access to answers for the basic questions—tuition, test score and GPA requirements, etc.—before reading more about the school. One disappointment: While student body is broken down by gender, race, and age, the faculty breakdown only includes gender, degrees earned, and ratio of teachers to students. The sample LSAT test is an added, though limited, bonus, which will give applicants a first chance to gauge their abilities. The introductory material is just that: a general overview answering basic questions. It is written especially for this volume in a straightforward, factual style. The chapter, "What Should I Expect in Law School?," also written by Munneke, is an except from his book *How to Succeed in Law School* (reviewed on page 147). It offers an amusing, and enlightening description of the ups and downs of the first year of school and of law school culture.

Where To Find/Buy:

Bookstores and libraries.

BARRON'S HOW TO SUCCEED IN LAW SCHOOL

Description:

Written by the author of numerous books for law students and lawyers, this guidebook focuses on the keys to success in law school. Following an outline format typically used by law students, the author describes the law school structure and gives advice for succeeding in the classroom and on exams. The book opens with a short chapter discussing some of the factors to consider when choosing a law school and emphasizes that success depends on the fit of school and student. The author then describes the law school experience, from the milestones that mark the first year of "boot camp" to the types of professors and students encountered there. The next two chapters provide study skills to maximize what you learn in the classroom and to succeed on exams. The author provides a model for briefing cases and practice exam questions with answers. He also offers advice on time, money, and stress management, as well as avoiding "life in the fast lane." A full chapter is devoted to the issues of "diverse students" and another to the second and third years of law school. Appendices include suggested readings, and cases and materials on various law topics.

Evaluation:

This book, written primarily for those about to enter law school, is as much about attitude as study skills. The author first asks readers to think about how they define success and then describes the inherent dangers and rewards of different definitions. Throughout the book, he wisely encourages readers to remember what their goals are, and to remember attitude and commitment are, in fact, the keys to success. His time and stress management models, in particular, are founded on this belief. His advice is logical and realistic, and his commonsense approach allays many of the anxieties that other books inadvertently create by stressing the trauma of first-year law school and offering only study tips. Reading this book is much like listening to a serious talk on what to expect and how to cope with law school, but the author's sense of humor and vivid analogies spur self-confidence and understanding. This book is a good choice for preparing for law school. It is not for those looking for advice on which law school to attend nor is it particularly helpful to "diverse students." The chapters on law school choice and diversity are cursory at best.

Where To Find/Buy:

Bookstores and libraries.

Overall Rating
★★★
Valuable advice on preparing for and succeeding in law school

Design, Ease Of Use
★★★
Outline structure; useful model briefs and practice exams

1–4 Stars

Author:
Gary A. Munneke, JD
Mr. Munneke teaches Torts, Professional Responsibility, and Law Practice Management at Pace University School of Law. He is also the author of *Barron's Guide to Law Schools* and *The Legal Career Guide*.

Publisher:
Barron's Educational Series

Edition:
2nd (1994)

Price:
$9.95

Pages:
262

ISBN:
0812014499

Media:
Book

Principal Focus:
Law School

II. Law School

Overall Rating
★★★
Lively stories from a diverse array of law graduates

Design, Ease Of Use
★★★
Writing uneven, but always engaging; good use of sidebars to highlight career paths

1–4 Stars

Author:
National Association for Law Placement

Established in 1971, the NALP is a nonprofit organization serving as a source of information for legal career-planning and recruitment. Its mission is to meet the needs of all participants in the legal employment process for information, coordination, and standards. Members include every ABA-accredited law school and legal employers.

Publisher:
Harcourt Brace Legal & Professional Publications, Inc.

Edition:
1998

Price:
$17.95

Pages:
180

ISBN:
015900182X

Media:
Book

Principal Focus:
Law School

Of Interest To:
Women
Persons of Color

BEYOND L.A. LAW
Break The Traditional "Lawyer" Mold

Description:

A compilation of short profiles of 47 law school graduates who have taken a diverse array of career paths, this book is designed to give readers an idea of what can be achieved with a law degree. These "subjective success stories" are written by career counselors, lawyers, recruiters, and admissions officers. The editors note "common threads" running through these stories. All the interviewees cite the key role played by mentors in their success. They all share a passion for their work, and they all view their education and careers as a "process of self-discovery." Each profile comprises a sidebar with a current job description and career highlights, and a 2–3 page biography. Most chronicle the interviewee's education and career, and feature numerous quotes. Among those profiled are an attorney and legal advisor to the U.S. Department of the Interior, an attorney for a large media corporation, a woman who works as director of a private foundation and travel writer, a lawyer specializing in trademark and copyright law who moonlights as a professional musician, a single mother who is an attorney in international project finance, and a magistrate in juvenile court.

Evaluation:

This book debunks stereotypes about lawyers and their careers. For prospective law students and those already practicing law, it offers inspiration and insight that they won't get from course catalogs and law reviews. The book comprises profiles written by ten career counselors, lawyers, recruiters, and admissions officers, not professional writers, and it is edited by a nonprofit association. As a result, perhaps, the writing is uneven. At times, the punctuation confuses, and the prose ramble, but we liked the overall tone. The profiles portray people who love their work, and their passion is apparent. What better way to inspire young students and law professionals who have gotten into a rut? We also like the diverse background of the lawyers profiled. Their stories show students that law can open many doors—to fame, fortune, and often to rewarding careers in service of society. A good read for those considering law as a career and for law students who want to break the mold.

Where To Find/Buy:

Bookstores and libraries.

THE COMPLETE LAW SCHOOL COMPANION
How To Excel At America's Most Demanding Post-Graduate Curriculum

Description:

In its second edition, this book reflects the changes that have occurred in law and legal education since the publication of the first edition in 1984. These changes include an increase in the number of women, minority, and older applicants, more practical curricula, enhanced technology, and new legal issues. Finally, of crucial importance to law students, is the shrinking job market for new lawyers in the mid-1990s. Because of the intense competition, the author encourages students to get good grades in school in order to stand out from the pack and gain the necessary know-how. This book focuses on helping the law student be as successful as possible, using the Legal Concept Management (LCM) System, composed of strategies for surviving in the classroom, briefing cases, creating course outlines, preparing for and taking exams, and writing papers. After four chapters in which the author discusses the profession, the admissions process, and law school itself, the bulk of the book focuses on the LCM System, with a specific, detailed explanation of study techniques, complete with sample test questions, outlines, and briefs, and "emergency" help for exams.

Evaluation:

This book provides a useful approach to law school success: the LCM system, which he used in school and claims will "catapult you to the head of your profession." Given the massive amount of information that law students must absorb, such a systematized approach may be the best way to master the work and remain sane. The LCM System is a step-by-step approach to using class notes, creating "master outlines" of courses, using the outline and other lists to prepare for exams, taking the exams themselves, and writing papers. Will this technique work for all students? Its approach is flexible enough that students can combine it with their personal study techniques. The author's sharp focus on study technique means this book is less helpful on other aspects of law school, but students will find the "hands-on" approach useful.

Where To Find/Buy:
Bookstores and libraries.

Overall Rating
★★★
Detailed, specific study techniques combined with solid advice for law school success

Design, Ease Of Use
★★★
Personable tone and clear presentation

1–4 Stars

Author:
Jeff Deaver
Jeff Deaver is an author and an attorney. He is a cum laude graduate of the Fordham University School of Law.

Publisher:
John Wiley & Sons

Edition:
2nd (1992)

Price:
$15.95

Pages:
229

ISBN:
047155491X

Media:
Book

Principal Focus:
Law School

II. Law School

Overall Rating
★★★

A solid introduction to the LSAT, plus vital stats for 178 law schools

Design, Ease Of Use
★★★

Users will need Adobe Acrobat to download the Law School Directory

1–4 Stars

Publisher:
Kaplan Educational Centers

Kaplan, a subsidiary of The Washington Post Company, is a leading producer of test preparation materials. Their products include prep courses, books, and software.

Media:
Internet

Principal Focus:
Law School

KAPLAN ONLINE: LAW

Description:

Kaplan's "Law" segment has its own "home" page and sidebar table of contents. Users have six content areas to choose from: LSAT, School Selection, Admissions, Financial Aid, First-Year Success, and Careers in Law. LSAT provides an overview of the exam, its components, and its scoring. An introduction describes the test, while Flash Feedback details the contents of the most recent LSAT. Registration information and test dates are given, together with practice questions for Logical Reasoning, Reading Comprehension, and Writing. Also included is free test-prep software: "Kaplan's Digital Test Booklet," a simulated test users can take to receive feedback on their performance. To help students choose a school, School Selection offers a downloadable Law School Directory (in PDF). The Directory presents vital stats on 178 schools, including contact addresses, application deadlines, and tuition costs. The Admissions section deals with trends, application "dos and don'ts," and tips on personal statements, essays, and recommendations. Loan options, such as KapLoan, are discussed in Financial Aid, while insights from current students are presented in First-Year Success. Finally, Careers in Law contains links to pertinent resources.

Evaluation:

As is the case with any site, there are elements of Kaplan's "Law" that work and those that don't. We like the section on the LSAT. For students who have just begun to research the law school option and are unfamiliar with LSAT basics, this section is a terrific place to start. All components of the exam are covered, including how its scored and structured. There are even instructions for canceling previous LSAT scores. "Flash Feedback" is a good way to get a secondhand feel for the test, while the practice questions provide firsthand experience. The test-prep software is free (download it at the site) and worth checking out. (Do keep in mind, however, that Kaplan is a commercial enterprise; its software doubles as an advertising vehicle.) The Law School Directory works, too, but students need Adobe Acrobat to open the PDF file and must supply their name and e-mail address to download. For those concerned about privacy or the downloading hassles, we recommend U.S. News Online's searchable law school database. (http://www.usnews.com/usnews/edu/beyond/bclaw.htm; reviewed on page 144) So what doesn't work at Kaplan Online: Law? The rest of the site. Admissions and First-Year Success address valid topics, but they do so in a superficial, inadequate manner; they're decidedly unhelpful. The LSAT section is the real "score" here.

Where To Find/Buy:
On the Internet at http://www1.kaplan.com/view/zine/1,1899,5,00.html

LAW SCHOOL BASICS
A Preview Of Law School & Legal Reasoning

Description:

Written by a successful lawyer, this guide presents an overview of law school, legal reasoning, and legal writing. The first section of the book provides a glimpse of daily life in law school and explains important topics including how to write a case brief, the dynamics of competition for law review slots, and the process leading up to postgraduate employment. A second chapter explains the federal and state judiciary systems in the United States. "The Common Law Reasoning Process" briefly covers common law and how legal "rules" develop. "The Legal Research Process" presents an overview of case law; "Legal Writing: How Lawyers Write about Cases" explains how lawyers write about the law, with examples of legal analysis, including a legal memoranda and an appellate court brief. "Writing Hints" offers 15 pages of tips for success in a legal writing class. A series of appendices provide sample law school outlines.

Evaluation:

Born out of the author's own frustrating law school experience, this book was written to teach students what he wishes he had known before starting law school. Hricik's book is not designed to help students to choose a law school, nor does it help them decide whether law school is a better vehicle for them to reach their career goals than, say, business school. The value of this book is as a Law School Basics 101 of sorts, helping students approach course work and writing more effectively. According to the author, most law school curricula fail to explain the "big picture" of the judicial system and the basics of the trial process; instead they focus on teaching legal reasoning through reading cases. Hricik, a law school instructor, presents background information and sage advice to help law students excel in school, and to give prospective students a taste of what awaits them.

Where To Find/Buy:

Bookstores and libraries.

Overall Rating
★★★
Gives students a taste of legal reasoning and writing

Design, Ease Of Use
★★★
Written in the voice of a helpful uncle

1–4 Stars

Author:
David Hricik

David Hricik graduated with honors from Northwestern University School of Law and practices law at the law firm of Baker & Botts, L.L. P. He has also taught legal writing at the University of Houston Law Center, helped create the Law School Basics computer course on America Online, and published articles and lectured on legal ethics, patent litigation, and judicial reform.

Publisher:
Nova

Edition:
1997

Price:
$14.95

Pages:
249

ISBN:
1889057061

Media:
Book

Principal Focus:
Law School

Overall Rating
★★★
Good insights on the current job market and employment trends

Design, Ease Of Use
★★★
Best navigated via detailed site index

1–4 Stars

Publisher:
National Association for Law Placement

Since 1971, the National Association for Law Placement (NALP) has served as a source of information for legal career planning and recruitment. The nonprofit organization's members include virtually every American Bar Assocation-accredited law school and legal employers throughout the U.S.

Media:
Internet

Principal Focus:
Law School

Of Interest To:
Women
Persons of Color

NATIONAL ASSOCIATION FOR LAW PLACEMENT

Description:

Visitors to the National Association for Law Placement's (NALP) home page have two menus to choose from. A sidebar menu details the sections of the site that explain the background and mission of the NALP, while the top-border menu provides access to the student-oriented segments: Pre-Law, Schools, Trends. The Pre-Law section features tips for choosing a law school, directories and professional references, a starting salary chart, and essays on "Exploring Your Career Options." The salary chart displays median starting salaries by associate year and firm size, while the essays in "Exploring" include several pages on how and why lawyers make career decisions. In Schools, users will find law school rankings and a national directory of law schools. The Trends section offers studies on hiring trends, associate retention, and women and minorities' gains in the profession. The site has other features of interest to students too, such as the Forums segment, which contains an "Open Letter to Law Students" from law school deans across the country. The letter warns applicants to minimize the role that law school rankings play in their decision-making process.

Evaluation:

The best reason for potential law students to visit this site is that it is *not* for students only. Some sections are designed especially to help students choose and assess law schools, but this pre-law fodder found in many resources. This site is a winner because it provides plenty of industry and career-oriented information. True, some of the essays state the obvious, but many provide fascinating reading. "Significant Changes in Lawyer Demographics" delves into who is entering the legal profession and where they are finding employment. Applicants looking ahead to the post-graduation job scene will find several sections offering interesting analysis and commentary on the legal job market. The Trends and Salaries sections are also worth reading. They provide solid data on specific topics, such as entry-level and lateral hiring, and trends in the hiring of women and minorities. Before entering law school, it's a good idea to understand where that JD will take you; this site gives students a much better idea. Another high point of the site is the "Open Letter" from law school deans. It may change student views on school rankings.

Where To Find/Buy:

On the Internet at http://www.nalp.org/

ONE L
The Turbulent True Story Of A First Year At Harvard Law School

Description:

First published in 1977, this personal account chronicles the trials and traumas of Scott Turow's first year at Harvard Law School, the oldest and most prestigious law school in the country. Written in journal style, with dated entries, (though Turow admits rewriting most of them when the year was done), it follows his day-to-day progress from student orientation to final exams as a "1-L," the year that promises law students "wholesale drama" and makes many harried, fearful, and weary. He describes his first interaction reading a case ("harder than hell"), portrays different teaching styles (the dreaded, and adversarial, Professor Perini vs. the younger, gentler Morris, the only one to critique the educational system), and takes the reader straight into the stresses, neuroses, and personal politics of the classroom and exam preparation. Though initially curious about the Socratic style used in classes, Turow finds it creates antagonisms between teacher and student, and intense competitiveness between the students themselves. He concludes that while he was proud to be a law student, legal education should be more humane and just.

Evaluation:

The first book by a best-selling novelist, this narrative is probably his most controversial. Turow describes in intimate detail the bitter, and out-of-control, emotions he developed in response to the intense pressure and competitiveness of law school. For this, he has been called by some (usually law students of the 90s) a wimp. While Turow now admits that he may have overreacted, many of the criticisms that he leveled against the Socratic method and the structure of legal education have been acknowledged, and many schools have, in fact, adopted more humane techniques. This autobiography takes the reader into the heart of legal education, from the trial by fire of cold-calls to the confusion of learning "Legal," from the competitiveness over grades to the nuts-and-bolts of first-year classes. All of this is valuable inside material for the future law student. Ultimately, Turow reminds the reader who the enemy is: While his first chapter insinuates that it is the power of an institution like Harvard, in the end, he realizes it is his own power-hunger and fear. This is something for all law students to watch out for.

Where To Find/Buy:

Bookstores and libraries.

Overall Rating
★★★
Detailed account of one student's trial-by-fire as a first-year law student

Design, Ease Of Use
★★★
Engrossing personal story

1–4 Stars

Author:
Scott Turow

Scott Turow is best known for his legal suspense novels including *The Burden of Proof* and *Presumed Innocent.*

Publisher:
Warner

Edition:
1997

Price:
$12.99

Pages:
269

ISBN:
0446673781

Media:
Book

Principal Focus:
Law School

II. Law School

Overall Rating
★★★
One of the best law school databases; includes relatively detailed school profiles

Design, Ease Of Use
★★★
Users may have to backtrack while navigating

1–4 Stars

Publisher:
Peterson's

Peterson's is a publisher of education guides and a producer of test preparation materials and courses. It is part of the Lifelong Learning Group within Thomson Learning.

Media:
Internet

Principal Focus:
Law School

PETERSONS.COM: THE LAW CHANNEL

Description:

Although "The Law Channel" is a portion of Petersons.com, it functions as its own site. The main page details the featured articles on admissions and applications, as well as the five content areas: Law School Search, Resources on Financing Your Law Education, LSAT Test Preparation, Pre-Law Materials, and a discussion board. Law School Search is a database of information on more than 180 law schools. Users can search by school name, or conduct an Advanced Law Program Search by location, 1997 average LSAT, 1997 enrollment, and concentration. A search results in a two-page "Research Profile" of the school, including data on enrollment, demographics, applicant statistics, faculty, application requirements, tuition, and degree options, as well as contact information and a description of the law school's library resources. Resources on Financing features tips on loans (from the Access Group.) The LSAT section includes an overview of the exam, "hot tips," and free test-prep software users can download. The software (for Windows or Macs) allows users to complete a full-length test and a half-length diagnostic that result in a customized score report and study plan. A book list appears in Pre-Law Materials.

Evaluation:

When it comes to law school databases, Peterson's is one of the best. While the "Research Profiles" are just starting points for more in-depth research, they provide more information than the school profiles offered at comparable sites. These profiles include the typical statistical overview, with data on demographics, tuition, and so forth, but they also contain lots of "extras": school history, application requirements, percentage of first-year courses taught by full-time faculty, etc. The description of the law school's library is a rare yet wonderful inclusion. Not only does it detail the number of staff members, volumes, periodicals, and seats the library has, it notes the number of computer work stations and the availability of Internet access, WESTLAW, LEXIS-NEXIS, or CD-ROM players. For initial research on law schools, Petersons.com is an excellent tool. Of the site's other features, the free test-prep software is the most notable. Unlike other free offers, this one gives users a full-length test to take. Downloading is simple, though it may be time-consuming with a slow modem: the software is 1.4MB for Windows, 1.8MB for Macs. (Users should keep in mind that the "customized" score report and study plan includes references to Peterson's many for-sale test-prep materials.)

Where To Find/Buy:

On the Internet at http://www.petersons.com/law

INSIDE THE LAW SCHOOLS
A Guide By Students For Students

Description:

Goldfarb's guide covers 112 of the 176 American Bar Association (ABA) accredited law schools in the U.S. The book opens with introductory chapters briefly considering the decision to go to law school, school choice, admission, and finances. The bulk of the guide comprises 3–4 page descriptions of individual law schools. Basic data on the school, such as enrollment figures, admission rates, tuition, application and financial aid deadlines, and placement figures are presented in the introductory section for each school. Following these figures are several pages of text describing various aspects of the school, its social life, the relative quality of the faculty, the "flavor" of its student body, and the advantages and disadvantages of the school's geographic location. Student life at each school is given special emphasis. The author often comments on the level of competitiveness among students, manageability of course load, and teaching methods.

Evaluation:

Unlike the directories of law schools published by the Law School Admissions Council and the ABA, this book is not an "objective" guide focused on statistics. Rather, it is a subjective presentation of the strengths and unique characteristics of each school. The tone is informal, that of an "insider" offering insights into the schools. Students more interested in getting a "feel" for a school than knowing the number of full-time law librarians will appreciate this approach. One of its disadvantages is the lack of detail in statistics that matter. For example, you won't find detailed racial or gender breakdowns for faculty or students. And readers must gauge their chances for successful admission from a median LSAT and GPA figure, instead of the LSAT/GPA admission profiles found in other guides. The data on placement and bar passage are most detailed. Another disadvantage: the school profiles have not been updated significantly in the new edition.

Where To Find/Buy:

Bookstores and libraries.

Overall Rating
★★★
A good resource for gaining a "feel" for a specific school

Design, Ease Of Use
★★
Well-written, but only the stats are updated in latest edition

1–4 Stars

Author:
S.F. Goldfarb

S.F. Goldfarb, a graduate of Yale Law School, is a lawyer in New York City.

Publisher:
Plume (Penguin)

Edition:
7th (1998)

Price:
$16.95

Pages:
365

ISBN:
0452279461

Media:
Book

Principal Focus:
Law School

II. Law School

★★★

Overall Rating
★★★
A convenient way to register for the LSAT and LSDAS

Design, Ease Of Use
★★
The REGGIE system only accepts credit card orders at present; no fee waiver packets

1–4 Stars

Publisher:
Law School Admission Council

The Law School Admission Council (LSAC or Law Services) is a nonprofit association of Canadian and American law schools.

Media:
Internet

Principal Focus:
Law School

Of Interest To:
Persons of Color

LAW SCHOOL ADMISSIONS COUNCIL ONLINE

Description:

The LSAC is best known for administering the Law School Admission Test (LSAT) and the Law School Data Assembly Service (LSDAS). (This service allows applicants to submit biographic and academic information to the LSDAS who then forwards copies to schools, reducing the paperwork required in the admissions process). This website focuses on law school admissions. The "Law School Forums" page of the site offers information on one- and two-day law school forums held in seven major cities each year. At the forums, students meet face-to-face with admission professionals and law students and collect admission materials, catalogs, and financial aid information. Prospective law students who would like to register for the LSAT, the LSDAS, or the CRS (Candidate Referral Service) or the Minorities Interested in Legal Education (MILE) project can do so online. The site also includes financial aid information, special advice for gay, lesbian, and bisexual applicants, and links to law school home pages. Students can also access the Internet edition of *The Official Guide to U.S. Law Schools* (print version reviewed on page 135).

Evaluation:

The central feature of this site is the REGGIE program, which allows users to register for the LSAT and subscribe to the LSDAS and other LSAC-sponsored services (requires a credit card). Users should stop by and order a free copy of the latest LSAT/LSDAS Registration and Information Book, a good starting point for preparing for the LSAT. Persons of color looking into law school should check out the MILE project. It is an effort to address the under-representation of minorities in the legal profession by providing minority students with reliable information about preparation for law school. Readers can order a free copy of "Thinking About Law School: A Minority Guide" and peruse articles from the MILE Markers newsletter, such as "Is Affirmative Action Dead? Don't Believe the Hype." Interested persons can also order a free Disabilities Accommodations Request Packet and a Fee Waiver packet.

Where To Find/Buy:

On the Internet at http://www.lsac.org

PRINCETON REVIEW ONLINE: LAW SCHOOL

Description:

A sidebar menu on the "Law School" main page provides access to this site-within-a-site's main features: School Search, Get Into School, LSAT & MBE, The Transition, Scholarships & Aid. In School Search, students can search for a school based on personal criteria (location, cost, admissions ranking, etc.) or by name. The result is an overview of school demographics, admissions, and costs. Also included are lists of the top-ranked schools by categories, such as Academic, Facilities, Pressure, and Social Life. (Survey results are based in part on a survey of 11,000 current law students.) Get Into School contains a series of topical articles, such as "Beyond Numbers," "Affirmative Action & Higher Education," "A First Year Re-Evaluates His Choice," and "Advice for Women." In LSAT & MBE, students will find a practice LSAT, an article on "What Your Scores Mean," and an outline of LSAT structure and scoring. Stress management and exam strategies are among the subjects addressed in The Transition section. Scholarships & Aid offers a primer on Federal and institutional aid for law school and supplies links to a commercial loan program. Other features include a discussion forum for law students and database of tutors.

Evaluation:

As with many Internet sites geared to law students, this site is sponsored by a company with something to sell, in this case, an LSAT review course. However, the creators have kept the commercial pitch low-key and offer some very readable and practical articles. The content is current, relevant, and well-written. The section on financial aid is particularly well-done; students should stop and read the articles before signing up for any loan programs. This site is one of the few acknowledging the importance of Federal financial aid programs; it even supplies links for ordering and submitting the Free Application for Federal Student Aid (FAFSA) online. The School Search is a good tool for finding introductory information on particular schools, but there is one problem: it requires users to "log on" and provide their e-mail address before accessing results. The search is free, but those leery of giving out their e-mail address may want to find another directory. Aside from that, the tool is easy to use, and the search criteria can be as broad or as narrow as the user likes. Without logging on, users can still read the law school rankings, which are based on student surveys and thus come "straight from the trenches."

Where To Find/Buy:

On the Internet at http://www.review.com/Law/

Overall Rating
★★★
A solid introduction to law school admissions and financing; includes a school search

Design, Ease Of Use
★★
Clear and direct format; users must "log on" to get school search results

1–4 Stars

Publisher:
Princeton Review

The Princeton Review is a leading test preparation organization; it produces preparation classes, books, and educational software.

A portion of the larger Princeton Review Online, this site-within-a-site focuses on business schools. Sections include a business school search feature, tips on getting in and interviewing, and advice on making the transition. Also included is information on registering and preparing for the GMAT, and for finding scholarships and financial aid. An online discussion forum is also featured.

Media:
Internet

Principal Focus:
Law School

II. Law School

Overall Rating
★★
A brief how-to guide for the application process

Design, Ease Of Use
★★★★
Straightforward without being simplistic

1–4 Stars

Author:
Thomas H. Martinson, JD, &
David P. Waldherr, JD

"Two of America's top LSAT coaches."

Publisher:
Arco (Macmillan)

Edition:
3rd (1998)

Price:
$12.95

Pages:
148

ISBN:
002862498X

Media:
Book

Principal Focus:
Law School

ARCO'S GETTING INTO LAW SCHOOL TODAY

Description:
Written to prospective law students, this guide is essentially a "how-to" book for the application process. It begins with an overview of the structure of legal education in America. Chapter Two devotes 14 pages to the admission process as a whole. Subsequent chapters delve into specific aspects of the process, including "Targeting Schools" which lists various factors to consider when choosing where to apply. The two longest and most detailed chapters focus on writing a personal statement (with sample personal statements) and the LSAT. This last chapter devotes considerable space to the analytical reasoning, logical reasoning, and reading comprehension sections. Appendix A offers "Guidelines for Writing a Letter of Appraisal (recommendation) for a Law School Applicant." Subsequent appendices offer a "Historical Perspective" on law school and a listing of American Bar Association accredited law schools.

Evaluation:
Arco publishes one of the shortest (and cheapest) how-to-get-into-law-school guides. In 148 pages, it provides the information found in the introductory sections of the larger law school directories. The authors present a very clear discussion of "indexing" (the practice of initially scoring candidates based on a formula applied to their GPA and LSAT scores). They also provide an excellent explanation of what admission committees are looking for. The authors write in a commonsense, accessible style, honed no doubt in their many years teaching admissions seminars and workshops on law school admission. Their book's strongest sections are the chapters on writing personal statements and taking the LSAT. Because the authors have taught LSAT prep courses for a number of years, they offer solid test-taking advice and strategies for attacking all three test sections. Appendix A is a unique feature: advice for those asked to write letters of recommendation. A good focused resource for those applying to law school.

Where To Find/Buy:
Bookstores and libraries.

THE PENGUIN GUIDE TO AMERICAN LAW SCHOOLS

Description:

Written for prospective law students, career counselors, faculty, and administrative officers seeking information on law school, this resource tool describes nationally accredited public and private law schools. The author first explains the contents of the school listings and how readers can best use the information provided. He then presents descriptions and admissions statistics of law institutions and their parent school (if applicable). Each entry contains a brief history of the school, current tuition and fees, general characteristics, and contact information. Descriptions include enrollment, faculty, and graduation figures. Admissions requirement sections list all credentials necessary for application, whether students are transferring, international, or in a concurrent degree program. Application fee requirements and a special application assistance service are also covered. An abbreviation key, helpful organization and relevant website information, and a school selection checklist are included. Nine indexes round out the book.

Evaluation:

This up-to-date resource offers potential law students and those who counsel them the pertinent information they will need to narrow school choices according to individual needs. It will be especially helpful for students starting at ground zero. Written in plain English by a college administrator, the information is presented objectively and well indexed. Smooth writing and good organization ease navigation and make this book an effective quick reference tool. Readers will appreciate the abbreviation key, which lists examination abbreviations and degree information, details that many books commonly assume readers know. The inclusion of financial aid options for each school and financial aid organizational contacts eases the reader's research burden. For students starting the law school search and career counselors, this book is recommended.

Where To Find/Buy:

Bookstores and libraries.

Overall Rating
★★
A useful and up-to-date law school directory

Design, Ease Of Use
★★★★
Thorough, concise, and well-organized; several indexes

1–4 Stars

Author:
Harold R. Doughty

The author, a management and educational consultant, has held various administrative positions at numerous universities. He is also the author of *Guide To American Graduate Schools* and *The Penguin Guide To American Medical And Dental Schools.*

Publisher:
Penguin

Edition:
1999

Price:
$17.95

Pages:
307

ISBN:
014046994X

Media:
Book

Principal Focus:
Law School

Overall Rating

★★

Weak on school descriptions but a good source of info on financial aid

Design, Ease Of Use

★★★

Excellent graphics and easy to read

1–4 Stars

Author:

Ruth Lammert-Reeves

Ms. Reeves has been a college administrator for more than 20 years, 17 of those years with Georgetown University Law Center, where she has been the assistant dean of financial aid since 1990.

Publisher:

Kaplan (Simon & Schuster)

Edition:

1999

Price:

$20.00

Pages:

282

ISBN:

0684859580

Media:

Book

Principal Focus:

Law School

KAPLAN NEWSWEEK LAW SCHOOL ADMISSIONS ADVISOR

Expert Advice To Help You Get Into The School Of Your Choice—2000 Edition

Description:

The first section frames the issues involved in selecting a school, such as: "Is Law School Really For You?" "Evaluating Law Schools," and "How Will You Fit In?" Part Two provides 54 pages on the application process, including when to apply and how you'll be evaluated. Part Three, "Financing Your Law Degree," covers planning for the three-year investment of time and tuition, applying for financial aid, and taking on debt. A short chapter on "What Law School Students and Grads Say" is included before the directory of school profiles, which takes up the last 100 pages. The school profiles present very basic information, including application and admission numbers, median GPA/LSAT, tuition, numbers of students, percent female, percent minority, and average age. A section on academic specialties allows students to research school specialties, such as energy law or insurance law. A final section lists schools offering joint degree programs, such as a JD-MBA, and a LSAT sampler round out the book.

Evaluation:

Any book attempting to "do it all" is bound to fall short on one or two topics. This book is no exception. Its weakest section is the profiles of the ABA-accredited law schools. These descriptions offer only a superficial glimpse at the schools and do not provide anywhere near the level of detail supplied by other directories of law schools. However, for students who already have a good handle on their target schools and are more interested in guidance on the admissions and financial aid process, this book is a good choice. It offers the best discussion of the financial aspects of going to law school that we've found. The author rightly emphasizes accessing federal loans and money from the law schools themselves, the two most realistic sources of financial assistance for law students. She also writes in a down-to-earth manner with helpful sidebars on every page and graphics galore. Topical Internet URLs are sprinkled throughout the book, a sign that the author is up on current sources of information.

Where To Find/Buy:

Bookstores and libraries.

REA'S AUTHORITATIVE GUIDE TO LAW SCHOOLS

Description:

The bulk of this softbound guide comprises profiles of American Bar Association accredited, non-accredited, and Canadian Law Schools. Each profile covers two pages, with most entries including a quarter-page photo. A chart begins each profile, listing key statistics, such as degrees offered, application figures and acceptance rates, enrollment, mean GPA/LSAT scores, percentage men/women, percentage minority, tuition, and application deadlines. Following this box is a series of paragraphs on various aspects of the school, including The University, Admissions, Student Body, Placement Records, Costs, Financial Aid, Minority Programs, Student Organizations, Faculty, Curriculum, Library, Publications, Special Programs and Merits, Application Procedures, and Contact Information. A 15-page introduction to the law school admissions process begins the guide. All ABA-Accredited schools are compared in an "At-a-glance" chart.

Evaluation:

Our favorite aspect of this guide is the book's uncluttered presentation of information. The editors have included a large number of photos and plenty of white space. The result is an eye-pleasing and very readable design. The editors have also chosen not to evaluate or rank any of the schools. This directory is intended to provide basic information to potential applicants looking at law schools where they might apply. For example, students might use this guide to create a list of ABA-Accredited law schools in their home state. The guide is not much help in gaining a "feel" for a school—competition among students, the relative quality of its faculty, or the all-important reputation of a school within the law community. To gain these insights, students must look elsewhere. Because this guide is such a preliminary tool, we recommend students use it at their library or career center and save their money for more detailed resources.

Where To Find/Buy:

Bookstores and libraries.

Overall Rating
★★
Basic information and stats on schools

Design, Ease Of Use
★★★
Easy-to-read; photos a nice touch

1–4 Stars

Publisher:
Research & Education Association

Edition:
1997

Price:
$21.95

Pages:
482

ISBN:
0878914781

Media:
Book

Principal Focus:
Law School

II. Law School

Overall Rating
★★
General survival guide for
first-year law students

Design, Ease Of Use
★★
From-the-hip style peppered
with jokes; no index and
rudimentary table of contents

1–4 Stars

Author:
Greg & Shannon Gottesman

Greg Gottesman graduated from
Stanford University and currently
attends Harvard Law School.
Shannon Gottesman did her
undergraduate work at the
University of Southern California
and the University of Washington.
She is now at the Boston College
Law School.

Publisher:
Arco
(Simon & Schuster Macmillan)

Edition:
1998

Price:
$12.95

Pages:
240

ISBN:
0028622960

Media:
Book

Principal Focus:
Law School

Of Interest To:
Persons Of Color

ARCO'S LAW SCHOOL SURVIVAL
A Crash Course For Students By Students

Description:

This resource was written by two current law school students and includes significant contributions from 15 others, most of whom are attending prestigious schools in the Boston or New York area. Individual chapters address most aspects of the law school experience. The book is addressed primarily to soon-to-be first-year law students. It opens with the authors' philosophy for success and sanity in law school: "Remember who you are," and "Do what works for you." They describe first-year classes, then advise readers on how to read casebooks and brief cases as a study tool. They offer tips for handling cold calls, asking questions, preparing for exams (including a list of study aids), and taking exams. A chapter on financial aid explains how financial aid works and gives advice on dealing with the financial aid office. The authors stress the importance of a life outside of the classroom and devote separate chapters to summer jobs, extracurricular activities, social life, and involvement in law reviews and journals. The final chapter briefly describes issues related to the minority experience.

Evaluation:

This book is, as the title says, a survival guide, complete with horror stories from law students who have "been there" and tips culled from real-life experiences in the competitive world of first-year law school. The emphasis is on showing potential students the ropes, not on explaining law; the authors offer no advice on getting into law school. Reading this book is like sitting down with a bunch of law school students eager to regale you with their war stories, tricks of the trade, and jokes. In fact, the book is really a transcript of such bull sessions. There is at least one joke in every paragraph—the first word of the first chapter is "Sucker"—and a cartoon "1-L" named Justin Case pops up between chapters. While the content is "lite," the general overview and the advice are good. Most important is the authors' warning against taking law school—or yourself—too seriously. One caveat: While each chapter has ample subheadings, navigation is tough. The table of contents is rudimentary at best, and there is no index. The lake of navigational tools makes it hard to follow the authors' own recommendation—"Please do not read every page." You'll have to if you want to find what you're looking for.

Where To Find/Buy:

Bookstores and libraries.

THE EIGHT SECRETS OF TOP EXAM PERFORMANCE IN LAW SCHOOL

★ ★

Description:

Success on law school exams is the most important factor in determining class standing, job opportunities, and access to prestigious activities, such as positions on the law review. This book, written by a law professor, describes his formula for overcoming the "Intimidation Factor" and maximizing exam scores. Each chapter explains one of the author's eight secrets of top exam performance. The first seven chapters focus on the hypothetical fact pattern essay, which is the most common exam question, while the last chapter offers tips for other types of exam questions. Included is advice on setting time allocations, learning how to read questions and organize answers before writing, and using IRAC (Issue-Rule-Application-Conclusion) without falling into traps. Secret #7 describes how to tailor the technique to the particular course and professor. The author also offers advice on how to figure out what a professor is likely to test on. Each chapter ends with a brief summary, as does the entire book. The appendix includes sample exam questions and answers.

Evaluation:

This little book has a very specific purpose—to teach law students the organizational skills necessary to beat the time constraints of exams and write a cogent answer. The author repeatedly stresses that these organizational skills are crucial to success and that carefully reading questions and organizing answers is time well-spent. The author uses a direct, "I've-got-the-answers" style. He describes his technique thoroughly in short, concise chapters. He points out which student habits are a waste of time and provides some valuable rules of thumb. Be forewarned, however: this book focuses on taking tests, not on teaching law or explaining class content. In fact, it has little advice on actually studying for exams, though students will benefit from the author's tips on identifying what a professor is likely to ask on a test. Nevertheless, this resource provides valuable tools and perspective when exam time draws near.

Where To Find/Buy:

Bookstores and libraries.

Overall Rating
★★
Important advice on managing time and writing cogent answers for law exams

Design, Ease Of Use
★★
Easy-to-read; short chapters; no index

1–4 Stars

Author:
Charles H. Whitebread

Charles Whitebread is the George T. Pfleger Professor of Law at the University of Southern California Law Center, a member of the American Law Institute, and a frequent lecturer at judicial conferences. He is also the author of Criminal Procedure and Children in the Legal System.

Publisher:
Harcourt Brace Legal & Professional Publications

Edition:
2nd (1995)

Price:
$9.95

Pages:
99

ISBN:
0159003237

Media:
Book

Principal Focus:
Law School

II. Law School

Overall Rating

★★

Covers a range of topics, from preparing for and applying to law school, to career options

Design, Ease Of Use

★★

Conversational tone; lots of white space

1–4 Stars

Author:

Harry Castleman & Christopher Niewoehner

Mr. Castleman is an attorney with Gaffin & Krattenmaker, P.C., in Boston. He is a graduate of Boston University Law School and the coauthor of eight books. Mr. Niewoehner is a graduate of Harvard College and Harvard Law School.

Publisher:

John Wiley & Sons

Edition:

1997

Price:

$14.95

Pages:

204

ISBN:

0471149071

Media:

Book

Principal Focus:

Law School

GOING TO LAW SCHOOL?

Everything You Need To Know To Choose And Pursue A Degree In Law

Description:

Written by a practicing lawyer and a recent Harvard law school graduate, this book addresses preparing for and applying to law school, as well as issues facing newly minted graduates heading into the legal profession. "Do You Want To Be A Lawyer?" discusses lawyers' personal qualities and professional traits, as well as the financial and time commitment represented by law school. The next three chapters cover what to expect during law school. Three subsequent chapters consider post-graduation issues, such as the bar and options for legal careers. Part Two contains a chapter on how to make the most out of college, and one on when to go to law school. The second half of the book presents information on the application process, with a full chapter devoted to the LSAT. The final chapters address such questions as: How many applications should I complete? When should I start the application process? and, How can I put together an exceptional application?

Evaluation:

The authors attempt to cover a broader range of topics than other how-to-win-the-law-school-admissions game guides. About half of the book is devoted to topics of concern before and after the application process. Because the post-graduation discussion includes an analysis of possible legal career paths, it can be helpful for those who are still deciding if law school is right for them. However, we found that in their attempt to cover a broad range of issues, the authors do not adequately address the application process itself. They give short shrift to essential topics, such as the personal statement and letters of recommendation. Certain aspects of the law school selection and application process are well-done, such as the discussion of financial aid in "Which Law Schools Can You Afford?" However, prospective law students looking for a guide to give them an edge in the application process will want to choose a more detailed, focused guide.

Where To Find/Buy:

Bookstores and libraries.

LAW SCHOOL WITHOUT FEAR
Strategies For Success

Description:

This book, written by husband and wife law professors, grows out of conversations the couple had with their son, who decided to become a lawyer. Their goal is to guide students past the "patterns of intellectual confusion and emotional tensions" from which many students suffer by offering simplified explanations of law terminology, concepts, and analytical techniques, and by addressing the psychological environment of law school. In separate chapters, the authors explain the workings of the Constitution, legislation, and courts; how to brief a case; the concepts of precedent and procedures; the roles of judge and jury; and a host of other subjects taught in the first year of law school. The authors explain how to interpret legal terminology and devote a chapter to legal writing. A chapter on studying and reviewing gives basic suggestions for studying effectively, with a focus on time management, while another explains how to approach and answer exam questions. The final chapter offers tips for dealing with the "mind game" of legal education, in particular explaining the professor's role and the Socratic method.

Evaluation:

This book does not offer any advice for getting into law school, but it may be an important tool to keep on your desk once you get in. Its beauty lies in the fact that it is written by law professors with an emotional investment in helping their audience (principally their son) succeed. Stepping away from the Socratic method associated with law school classes, the authors provide their readers a framework for understanding the foundational ideas of law, as taught in first-year curricula. They define and describe confusing elements in a readable and progressive manner, so that students will come to the classroom better prepared. The chapters on legal writing, exams, and briefing are particularly useful guides to law school study skills. In the chapter on briefing cases, the authors dissect a case and explain what factors to focus on (they do not, however, include a sample case or brief, which would have been helpful). Much of what makes these chapters, and the advice on dealing with the psychological strains of law school, so valuable, is the authors' perspective as teachers. They explain the professor's point-of-view, especially when using the Socratic method, thus taking some of the mystery, fear, and pressure out of the law school experience. "What does the professor want?" Find out here.

Where To Find/Buy:

Bookstores and libraries.

Overall Rating
★★
Good introduction to course preparation; little on law school life

Design, Ease Of Use
★★
Detailed table-of-contents, but no index

1–4 Stars

Author:
Helene Shapo & Marshall Shapo

Helene and Marshall Shapo have taught in law schools for a combined half-century. They are currently professors of law at Northwestern University School of Law.

Publisher:
Foundation

Edition:
1996

Price:
$15.95

Pages:
200

ISBN:
1566624284

Media:
Book

Principal Focus:
Law School

II. Law School

Overall Rating
★★
A satisfactory guide for law school study

Design, Ease Of Use
★★
Heavy at times; lacks focus

1–4 Stars

Author:
Steven J. Frank

The author is an honors graduate of Harvard Law School and a partner in a Boston law firm. He lectures and has written magazine articles on law and technology.

Publisher:
Citadel (Carol)

Edition:
2nd (1997)

Price:
$16.95

Pages:
205

ISBN:
0806518715

Media:
Book

Principal Focus:
Law School

LEARNING THE LAW
Success In Law School And Beyond

Description:

Written for aspiring attorneys, this book introduces legal reasoning and logic, and explains how to succeed in law school and beyond. In three main sections, the author offers general overviews of the law, law school, and the professional world. In Part One, he explains the lawmaking process, including how each branch of government functions. He uses case examples to show how to compare and relate facts and general issues to get a feel for legal reasoning. In Part Two, he addresses what to do once accepted to law school and what approach works best for each individual. He offers advice on study groups, extracurricular activities, study aides, and coping strategies. Sample exam questions and formats provide readers with an idea of what to expect and how to get a "head start" on exam preparation. In Part Three, the author explains what students can expect when taking the bar exam, including how testing results and styles vary by state. He explores employment options, approaching law firms for jobs, and setting up a private practice, and offers interviewing, résumé, and goal-setting tips. An index follows the text.

Evaluation:

This guide is most useful for students already accepted to law school who are preparing for their first year. If readers can muddle through the first five chapters, which are chockfull of legal jargon, they will find some practical advice for the first year. Particularly helpful is Part Two in which the author explains how to get the most out of classes and study tools. He clearly explains study strategies and offers helpful advice on dealing with professors. An honors graduate of Harvard Law School, the author presents a more caring and understanding approach in Part Two. However, his terminology is still a bit heavy for novices. Overall, his book lacks focus and requires a basic understanding of our legal system and logic. Thus, his early chapters are difficult for newcomers and redundant for those familiar with the law. Some good information is hidden here and there, but readers will soon tire of the searching. Furthermore, the book offers little help for readers who want to evaluate law schools and assess their own chances for admissions.

Where To Find/Buy:
Bookstores and libraries.

SLAYING THE LAW SCHOOL DRAGON
How To Survive—And Thrive—In First-Year Law School

Description:

The author's "law school dragon" refers to the fear of failure, anxiety, competition, lack of time, and memory lapses that plague most first-year law students. He provides an overview of how law school works and advice on handling classes, studying for exams, and generally building student self-confidence. The book lays down steps to take in the month before law school starts in order to get a jump on the coming year. These include familiarizing yourself with law books (with an explanation on how to skim and what the text means) and people who can be of help. He describes an "overview system" for preparing for classes, and a study method for reading, understanding, remembering, and discussing cases. He explains the common law basis of the American law system and describes the four primary first-year courses: contracts, torts, crimes, and property. He also gives advice on studying and taking exams, and writing an "energizing" brief. The book concludes with brief discussions on different types of law practices and tips on where to practice and how to get clients. Includes selected law review readings and a glossary.

Evaluation:

Time and a relaxed attitude are the most valuable assets of a law student, according to the author of this first-year guide, but swamped with reading assignments in "legalspeak" and a new way of thinking, time and relaxation are usually what first-year law students lack most. To help these students get ahead of the game, the author introduces the study methods that made him a successful law student, most of which rely on being prepared. This book should be read at least one month prior to the start of school as his program hinges on getting a headstart on the reading. The author's study method is unique: He stresses reading, and rereading, the case (rather than writing a brief) until it is clearly understood, then considering it from numerous perspectives, with notes written right on the case itself. This system, he insists, saves time and energy, and helps students understand and remember cases better. Readers can decide for themselves if this approach works. We found the author's basic principle—prepare in advance—a valid one, but we were unimpressed by his meandering presentation. His book also suffers from a dated layout and lack of navigation tools.

Where To Find/Buy:
Bookstores and libraries.

Overall Rating
★★
Detailed discussion of the first year of law school and study methods

Design, Ease Of Use
★★
Dated layout hampers navigation; no subheadings, bulleted text, or index

1–4 Stars

Author:
George Roth
A graduate of New York University Law School, George Roth was in private practice in California and served as a California Deputy Attorney General. In the latter capacity he argued three cases before the U.S. Supreme Court.

Publisher:
John Wiley & Sons

Edition:
2nd (1991)

Price:
$16.95

Pages:
182

ISBN:
0471542989

Media:
Book

Principal Focus:
Law School

II. Law School

Overall Rating
★
Law schools receive little in-depth coverage

Design, Ease Of Use
★★
Cramped; little white space

1–4 Stars

Publisher:
Peterson's

Edition:
33rd (1999)

Price:
$34.95

Pages:
1,989

ISBN:
1560799862

Media:
Book

Principal Focus:
Law School

PETERSON'S GRADUATE PROGRAMS IN BUSINESS, EDUCATION, HEALTH, INFORMATION STUDIES, LAW & SOCIAL WORK

Description:

This thick resource includes information on graduate and professional programs in the fields of business, education, health, information studies, law, and social work. After a section entitled "The Graduate Adviser," which includes advice and information about applying to grad school, the book is divided according to field of study. A chapter is devoted to legal education in the U.S. Each section is broken down into a "directory" of basic information about each program (degrees awarded, student demographics; tuition, admissions requirements, contact information, and more), cross-discipline announcements, and a few full-page profiles submitted by schools.

Evaluation:

Considering the vast amount of information gathered in this book, it is relatively easy to use. Students may need a magnifying glass to read the program profiles, but they will be rewarded with practical information for whatever branch of law they may be interested in. Peterson's is a well-regarded reference book publisher, and one can rely on the accuracy of their information. This particular resource strives to cover a lot of ground—nearly 2,000 pages of coverage adds up to a bulky book. As a reference source, applicants to law school programs will find very basic information, helpfully classified by program type. It may be particularly useful for applicants who have no idea what kind of legal program they would like to apply to. Those looking for a bird's eye view of the different academic and professional programs in law will be pleased with the book. Eventually, however, they will need to find a resource that offers a closer, more detailed look at the individual programs; this resource is simply inadequate for that purpose.

Where To Find/Buy:

Bookstores and libraries.

PLANET LAW SCHOOL
What You Need To Know (Before You Go) . . . But Didn't Know To Ask

Description:

In this comprehensive book designed to "forewarn" prospective law students, the author presents his opinions about law school and what he believes students should consider before applying. Drawing on personal experience, others' opinions, and media portrayals, he attempts to paint a complete picture of law school reality. Part I looks at the curriculum, materials, and methodologies used law school. The author explores the roles of professors and how they can affect students' experiences. In Part II, he presents first-year "secrets of success" and lists resources for additional support and information: books, audiotapes, CDs, organizations, etc. He suggests moneysaving ideas and provides tips for a head start in the first year, for example, how and when to use study groups and how to prepare for exams. Part III and IV focus on fine-tuning skills during the second and third years while working on résumé preparation and employment options. Here he stresses the importance of internships, assistantships, and clerkships. In Part V, the author returns to the original question—Do you really want to attend law school?—and offers advice on how to prepare, as early as in high school.

Evaluation:

The author's tone clearly indicates some "issues" with his law school experience and law school itself. For example, he complains about law professors' high salaries relative to the few hours they teach and the piles of homework they assign students. He seems to hold a grudge and provides plenty of reasons to question the law school choice. He also raises some important issues about testing styles and grading systems. Readers will have to wade through this "attitude" to find sincere advice and valuable insights into the realities of law school. However, the author's humor and metaphors make the journey bearable. The best advice focuses on being prepared for the first year and relying on one's own thoughts, instincts, and notes, rather than professors or study groups. The author's all or nothing approach—that students only attend if they are determined to excel, not simply pass—is also valuable. For those who choose law school, and get in, this author's honest advice and up-to-date information will give them a step up on the competition.

Where To Find/Buy:

Bookstores and libraries.

Overall Rating
★
Interesting blend of satire, humor, and advice about law school; "nameless" author lacks credibility

Design, Ease Of Use
★★
A dense read

1–4 Stars

Author:
Atticus Falcon
The author, who writes under a pseudonym, is a recent law school graduate.

Publisher:
Fine Print

Edition:
1998

Price:
$19.95

Pages:
404

ISBN:
1888960027

Media:
Book

Principal Focus:
Law School

II. Law School

II. Law School

Overall Rating

★

General advice for the law school years

Design, Ease Of Use

★★

Clear and to the point

1–4 Stars

Author:

Paul M. Lisnek, JD, PhD, Steven J. Friedland, JD, LLM, & Chris M. Salamone, JD

Paul M. Lisnek is the Director of Academics and Faculty of the National Institute for Legal Education. Steven Friedland is a visiting professor at Georgia State University School of Law. Chris Salamone is the founder and Executive Director of the National Institute for Legal Education.

Publisher:

Princeton Review (Random House)

Edition:

1995

Price:

$15.00

Pages:

228

ISBN:

0679761500

Media:

Book

Principal Focus:

Law School

THE PRINCETON REVIEW LAW SCHOOL COMPANION

The Ultimate Guide To Excelling In Law School And Launching Your Career

Description:

This book is a "companion" to all three years of law school, written by three professionals in the field. It is intended as a guide to provide students with "insights into the law school experience, as well as with strategies and techniques to help (them) navigate the often confusing and intimidating maze" of the first year. The first two chapters give an overview of law school and the profession, including ways that students can prepare before law school begins. Chapter 3 focuses on the first-year experience, giving a taste of what to expect in classes, coursework, teaching methods, study guides, and more. Chapter 4 explains how to win "the exam game," with sample exam questions and answers. The second and third years of law school are covered in the next two chapters, with a look at classes and curriculum, extracurricular activities, and the bar exam. The final chapter discusses what to expect in law practice. Appendices include sample course outlines and job-hunting tips.

Evaluation:

This book is most useful as a bird's eye view of the law school experience. A lot is covered, but in a broad manner, making this guide most helpful to students just entering law school. This broad treatment has its advantages and disadvantages: the book is a quick read and will let students grasp the essentials of the law school experience in a relatively short time. However, it may leave them wanting a deeper investigation of such crucial topics as briefing cases, using study guides and study groups, writing course outlines, and preparing for exams. Coverage of some issues is minimal at best. While this book contains some specific advice, law students will want to look elsewhere for in-depth treatment of law school success strategies.

Where To Find/Buy:

Bookstores and libraries.

THE INSIDER'S BOOK OF LAW SCHOOL LISTS

Description:

Wondering which law schools offer joint degrees in law and political science? Check out "For Those Who Really Just Want to Run for President." This book presents a series of lists, some serious, most tongue-in-cheek. The first section, "Getting In and Staying In," has the highest percentage of serious lists. Prospective law students can learn which schools offer specialized programs, such as environmental, international or family law. They can also learn which schools have the largest and smallest core class enrollments. The "Lifestyle" section presents such lists as "Most Exotic Student Body" (schools with the highest percentage of international students) and "For the Old Fogies" (schools where the average age of students is 29 or older). In the "Entertainment Value" section, there are lists on vital factors, such as "Near the Beach" or "Near Great Microbreweries." A final section includes "Highest Average Starting Salaries" and "Graduates on the Supreme Court."

Evaluation:

Whether you find the author's style cheeky and entertaining or polemical and offensive may depend on your political leanings. For example, his list of Schools for Arch Conservatives includes the University of Idaho because ". . . Idaho has more than its fair share of survivalist groups and right wing militias." Even Baker's purportedly serious lists miss the mark. The "Schools with Women as Faculty" list, which, if done well, could help students find schools with women in major teaching and administration roles, is useless as it rates schools by the percentage of full- and part-time female faculty members. It would be more informative to know which schools have a solid percentage of tenured, full-time female faculty members. The book also suffers from a serious lack of quality control. Throughout the book, we found numerous slip-ups, such as "In each medical school on the following list . . ." Someone remind Mr. Baker that this is the Law School version! At best, this book is good for a chuckle during coffee breaks. It offers little to those choosing and applying to a law school.

Where To Find/Buy:

Bookstores and libraries.

Overall Rating
★
Designed to be lighthearted, it sometimes crosses the line to mean-spiritedness

Design, Ease Of Use
★
Too many slips of "medical" for "law" school—Someone wake up the copy editor

1–4 Stars

Author:
Mark Baker

Mark Baker is the author of eight other nonfiction books, including two bestsellers.

Publisher:
Simon & Schuster

Edition:
1997

Price:
$12.00

Pages:
177

ISBN:
0684841770

Media:
Book

Principal Focus:
Law School

II. Law School

AMERICAN BAR ASSOCIATION APPROVED LAW SCHOOLS (INTERNET)

Non-Rated Resource

Description:
At the American Bar Association's site, law school applicants can look up ABA-approved law schools under several indexes: an alphabetical list with links where applicable; a state list; a public/private list; and a visual display of U.S. law schools in each region of the country.

Publisher:
American Bar Association

The American Bar Association (ABA), founded in 1878, is the national organization of the legal profession. With about 35,000 members and 35,000 law student members, the ABA is the world's largest voluntary professional association.

Media:
Internet

Principal Focus:
Law School

Where To Find/Buy:
On the Internet at http://www.abanet.org/legaled/approved.html

FINAID: LAW SCHOOL RESOURCES

Non-Rated Resource

Description:
This site is part of the larger "FinAid Smart Student Guide To Financial Aid" website. "Admissions Guides" links to a site sponsored by the Law School Admission Council Online. "Loans" provides lengthy and detailed descriptions of five private lenders (some offer Bar Exam Loan Programs in addition to loans for law school). "Award Programs" describe the Food and Drug Law Institute Scholarships and links to the program homepage.

Author:
Mark Kantrowitz

Mr. Kantrowitz is a Research Scientist at Just Research, the US software laboratory for Justsystem Corporation of Japan. He is the author of three books, including one on financial aid, and has created several popular websites.

Publisher:
FinAid Page, L.L.C.

Media:
Internet

Principal Focus:
Law School

Where To Find/Buy:
On the Internet at http://www.finaid.org/otheraid/law.phtml

II. Choosing, Getting Into, & Excelling In Medical School & Other Health Science Programs

In 1999–2000, the American Association of Medical College Application Service (AMCAS) will process applications from approximately 40,000 applicants to 116 medical colleges and programs. The number of applicants admitted each year has hovered around 17,000 since the early 1990s. Approximately 15,000 medical students are awarded MD degrees each year.

Clearly, the competition for medical school is tough. It is no easier for students applying to dental school, and only one-third of all applications to veterinary medical schools were accepted in 1999.

Nursing students comprise more than one-half of all health-professional students, and their role as frontline healthcare professionals is expected to grow as the healthcare industry changes. Experts predict a growing demand for nurses with advanced training, including nurse practitioners and nurses with Master's or PhDs, in the years ahead.

In this chapter, we look at resources designed to help students make the decision about attending medical school and other health sciences programs. Most resources also discuss how to select target schools, how to prepare applications and what to do when accepted, or rejected. Several resources examine life as a doctor, to help applicants decide if they are really cut out for the profession.

We begin with medical school, the focus of most of the resources reviewed here. Then we move on to briefly discuss the admissions processes for dental schools, nursing programs, and veterinary medical schools.

Making The Decision: Do I Really Want To Become A Physician?

As you read our descriptions of resources, you'll note that some contain sections designed to help prospective medical students examine the appealing, and not so appealing, aspects of life as a medical school and physician in the late 1990s. These resources give applicants a feel for the coursework, clinical experiences, and lab work. These resources may also discuss character traits commonly found in successful physicians and reasons why some would-be physicians have decided that the doctor's life is not for them.

In addition to reading one or more of these resources, we urge students and graduates to take advantage of the services provided at their alma mater's career planning center or academic advising office. These facilities are especially important to medical school applicants because most medical schools require a composite letter of recommendation from the applicant's alma mater.

This letter is written by a prehealth committee or prehealth advisor on behalf of the applicant. The committee or advisor go over the applicant's letters of recommendation, transcript, résumé, essay, outside activities, and notes from a formal applicant interview, and then write a composite letter highlighting the applicant's strengths and accomplishments. The letter may also address any academic weaknesses that the applicant may have and reinforce the applicant's promise for future success.

Students should also take advantage of the many books and publications available at the centers free of charge. Prehealth advisors can also help students and alums narrow their list of target schools and prepare their applications.

Researching Schools And Narrowing Choices

If students are convinced they really want to be a doctor, it is time to start researching schools. Many applicants have their heart set on a particular school, but most will need help researching additional schools to choose the dozen or so where they'll apply. As with other graduate and professional programs, these will include a few "reach" schools, where their MCAT, GPA, and all-around profile place them in the possible but not likely category of admission. Most will be schools where the applicant has a reasonably good chance of admission, and the final three or so will be "safety" schools where the applicant is fairly confident of gaining admission. Remember that medical schools, even private ones, often show preference for in-state residents.

For the first round of research, when applicants are developing a list of potential medical schools, a number of medical school directories are available. Some are Internet-based searchable databases.

For a list of accredited medical schools in the U.S. and Canada, see the website of the American Association of Medical Colleges (AAMC) (http://www.aamc.org/meded/medschls/start.htm).

Those interested in osteopathic medicine should check out the website of American Association of Colleges of Osteopathic Medicine (http://www.aacom.org, reviewed on page 196) for information about and links to the 17 Colleges of Osteopathic Medicine.

Medical schools are also profiled in a variety of hefty paperback guides. Some present only objective data on schools, such as the cost of tuition, number of students enrolled, average MCAT scores, affiliated teaching hospitals, and any special programs. Others feature subjective information on the schools' reputation, or strengths in a particular area, such as research or clinical exposure.

As students narrow their search, they may turn to resources, which rank schools based upon a pre-determined set of criteria. Such ranking is controversial, but most students and advisors take a look. We recommend some resources, which rank medical schools, but we strongly suggest students and advisors also consider such factors as the school's student and faculty characteristics, program strengths, cost, and, of course, location.

Applying To Medical School

According to the AAMC, in 1998, 41,000 applicants competed for 16,170 first-year medical school positions. That's down slightly from recent years, but applicants are still facing stiff competition for medical school.

Medical school admissions committees report that the MCAT score and GPA are the two most important elements of the medical school application. The mean GPA of 1996–1997 successful applicants to medical school was 3.54. Average MCAT scores for these successful applicants are above 30, out a total of 45.

Most medical schools assess applications on a rolling basis. That means applicants have a better chance of getting in if they apply early. Medical school is unique in that most applicants apply in the summer, a year prior to their anticipated attendance.

We've reviewed numerous books and websites, which focus on how to apply to medical school, but we reserve our recommendations for those that go a step beyond the nuts and bolts how-to manuals to provide practical tips and insider advice. We like these resources because they help applicants establish an application to-do list and a realistic series of deadlines for accomplishing the various tasks along the way.

The AMCAS

The task of submitting applications to a dozen or more schools is greatly simplified by the American Medical College Application Service (AMCAS) and its osteopathic equivalent, the American Association of Colleges of Osteopathic Medicine Application Service (AACOMAS).

The AMCAS is a nonprofit, centralized application processing service for applicants to 110 participating U.S. medical schools. Students have the option of submitting their application electronically through AMCAS-E, a software program that allows applicants to complete their application on a personal computer and submit the data to AMCAS on computer diskette.

Applicants can obtain an application from their premed advisor or the AMCAS directly at:

> AMCAS
> Section for Student Services
> Association of American Medical Colleges
> 2450 N St. NW, Suite 201
> Washington DC 20037-1131
> phone: (202) 828-0600

For more information on the AMCAS-E website (http://www.aamc.org/stuapps/admiss/amcase/start.htm/), see our non-rated review on page 224.

Applicants to the 17 accredited osteopathic medical schools submit their applications to the AACOMAS, operated by the AACOM. To obtain an application, contact a premed advisor or AACOM directly at:

> AACOM
> 6110 Executive Boulevard, Suite 405
> Rockville, MD 20852
> phone: (301) 468-2037

For more information on the AACOMAS website (http://www.aacom.org/applic.htm/), see our non-rated review on page 224.

Through both these services, students can file one application, and a single set of official transcripts, MCAT scores, and an essay. The service then verifies and distributes these to each of the institutions designated by the applicant. About a dozen U.S. medical schools (and 16 Canadian schools) do not accept the AMCAS. Also, some schools that do accept the AMCAS may send a secondary application to candidates screened through the service.

The MCAT

The Medical College Admission Test (MCAT) is a standardized, multiple-choice exam required by almost every medical school in the U.S. The grueling 7–8 hour test is offered twice a year in April and August. We urge applicants to take the April test to be sure their scores reach the schools early in the rolling admissions process. Applications for the MCAT are available from a premed counselor or at:

MCAT Program Office
P.O. Box 4056
Iowa City, IA 52243
phone: (319) 337-1357

For online information, visit http://www.aamc.org/stuapps/admiss/mcat/start.htm.

Letters Of Recommendation

For medical school, letters of recommendation are not included in the application sent to the AMCAS. Letter-writers send their completed recommendations to the applicant's prehealth advisor or committee or the Student Affairs Office, which then forwards the letter to the institutions to which the applicant is applying. These letters also play a role in the composite letter prepared at the applicant's undergraduate school.

As with business, law, and graduate programs, well-known professors or professional figures may catch the eye of admissions committees, but it is more important to provide a letter that adds something to the applicant's presentation. Applicants should look for letter-writers who can make personalized and favorable recommendations.

The Essay

Admissions committees read thousands of essays, so it is a good idea to take the time to distinguish oneself with a thoughtful and highly personalized essay. Applicants should spend some time brainstorming, talking to teachers or acquaintances in the medical field, then sit down and write about what really matters to them. They should also be sure to proofread, spell check, and run the essay past a trusted friend or professor.

The Interview

Practically all medical schools review their applications and invite approximately 10–20 percent of the better applicants to come for an interview. Being invited for an interview is good news! It means the applicant has made it through a series of screens and has a good chance of acceptance.

The bad news is the applicant has to go to the interview! The prospect can be stressful, but with a little preparation, applicants can shine, and learn more about the program they are applying to. We recommend consulting the prehealth advisor for help preparing, with a mock interview or even a video.

Interviews vary in format. Some are one-on-one; others are with a group of candidates; and still others involve a single applicant in front of an admissions panel.

Our recommended resources include some strong chapters on interviewing. It helps to know what kind of questions are asked, how best to respond, even what to wear. A little research up-front can be a great confidence-builder.

Excelling In Medical School And Staying Human

If getting in wasn't hard enough, four years in medical school can grind down the most indomitable spirit. Maintaining a balanced life is not easy during these hectic years, but we've found several good resources on surviving and thriving in medical school. Some offer background information on coursework, including clinical rotations. Others offer study strategies, time management coaching, and encouragement for the weary. Medical school represents an enormous commitment, but with careful preparation and research, students can not only survive—they can excel and go on to a satisfying career.

Applying To Dental School

In this guidebook, we have reviewed relatively few resources on applying to and excelling in dental school, because far fewer resources are available on this topic.

Prospective dental students will, however, benefit from asking themselves the same questions their colleagues considering medical school do. We also urge them to talk to their alma maters' prehealth advisors, current dental students, and dentists in the field. As with the medical school application, dental school applications require the composite letter written by the prehealth advisor or committee.

The AADSAS

The dental school application process is similar to that for medical schools. Applications are processed by the American Association of Dental Schools Application Service (AADSAS), a centralized processing service for applications to 51 participating dental schools. Prospective dentists often apply to 10–15 schools, so this service saves a lot of time and energy.

For application materials, students can pick up the AADSAS brochure at the career counseling center or contact the AADSAS.

American Association of Dental Schools
1625 Massachusetts Avenue, NW, Suite 600
Washington, DC 20036-2212
phone: (800) 353-AADS (2237)
e-mail: aadsas.appl@aads.jhu.edu

The DAT

The Dental Admission Test (DAT) is a standardized multiple-choice examination, which assesses the applicant's mastery of basic science concepts, problem-solving ability, writing skills, and critical thinking. It is held twice a year, in April and October. Most advisors recommend taking the test in April in order to get applications in early and, if necessary, allow enough time for retaking the test.

Applicants can request information on the DAT from the American Dental Association at http://www.ada.org/cgi-bin/test-app.html, or at:

American Dental Association
Department of Testing Services
211 E. Chicago Avenue, Suite 1840
Chicago, IL 60611-2678
phone: (312) 440-2689

The Essay

With so much competition, dental school applicants need to use the personal essay to show the admissions committee why they are special. As with essays for medical school, applicants should not rush through the essay-writing process. We urge them to take some time to talk to teachers, acquaintances in the field, and prehealth advisors, and to carefully assess themselves, then sit down and write. As always, proofreading and spell checking are musts, and it is always a good idea to get a second, or third, opinion on an essay before submitting it.

Letters Of Recommendation

Dental schools usually require three letters of recommendation. The golden rules of recommendations hold true with dental school as they do with all professional schools:

- Recommendations from well-known individuals are good, but personalized letters are better.

- Timely submission of recommendation letters to the admissions office is essential.

Overly general or late letters of recommendations do nothing to support an application. Applicants should think carefully before asking an individual to write a recommendation.

Applying To Nursing Programs

Nursing is the largest, and one of the most rapidly changing, fields in the healthcare industry. As healthcare becomes more complex, the demand for nurses with advanced training is growing.

In this chapter, we review several resources that discuss nursing as a profession and the admissions process. Baccalaureate, Master's, and doctoral degrees are available in nursing. Here we focus on the admissions process for graduate programs.

Admissions requirements for graduate nursing programs vary, but most require a bachelor's degree from an accredited school of nursing; a state RN license; a minimum GPA; scores from the GRE, or in some cases, scores from the Miller Analogies Test (MAT); college transcripts; letters of recommendation; an essay; and an interview.

The GRE

The GRE General Test measures verbal, quantitative, and analytical reasoning skills. It is currently offered as a computer-based test. The traditional paper-based format is only used at international test sites and for specific subject tests.

Nursing school applicants planning to take the GRE must obtain a copy of the GRE Bulletin. This free publication describes the test, provides registration instructions, and features sample test questions.

For more information about the GRE, or to download a copy of the GRE Bulletin, see our full-page review of GRE Online on page 39. Most career planning centers will have copies of the Bulletin on hand.

To contact the Educational Testing Service, which administers the GRE, contact:

Graduate Record Examinations
Educational Testing Service
P.O. Box 6000
Princeton, NJ 08541-6000
phone: (609) 771-7670
email: gre-info@ets.org

The Miller Analogies Test

The Miller Analogies Test (MAT) is a standardized test of verbal analogies used to assist graduate departments and schools in their admissions process. The test comprises 100 analogies, given in a timed, 50-minute test period. It is given at "Controlled Test Centers," usually on college and university campuses around the United States. For registration information, contact:

The Psychological Corporation
Miller Analogies Test
P.O. Box 96152
Chicago, IL 60693
phone: 1-800-622-3231

Other Elements Of The Application

Letters of recommendation—Our advice for selecting medical and dental school letter-writers holds true here. Choose wisely and make sure they get the letters in on time!

The Essay is an important tool for distinguishing oneself.

Interviews are a great way to personalize an application and to get to know more about the program and campus environment. Resources reviewed here suggest applicants prepare carefully—thinking about what they have accomplished so far and what they hope to achieve with a nursing degree.

Applying To Veterinary School

Admission to veterinary medical schools can be as competitive as that of medical or dental schools. According to the Association of American Veterinary Medical Colleges (AAVMC), only 35 percent of all applications resulted in acceptance in 1998. In 1999, 6,695 applicants submitted over 24,000 applications for 2,301 first year openings. That means only 32.8 percent were accepted.

For those set on a career as a vet, thorough and timely preparation is essential. In this chapter, we review *The Veterinary Medical School Admission Requirements in the United States and Canada*, which together with the AAVMC website (http://www.aavmc.org/), is the main source of information about veterinary school admissions.

These resources recommend that applicants apply as early as possible. The deadline for applications for the vast majority of veterinary schools is October 1. Deadlines for the remaining dozen or so stretch into the spring, but students are advised to apply early.

Veterinary school prerequisites are strict, so prospective vets need to research requirements early in their undergraduate careers. Course requirements, which vary from school to school, and a list of pre-application tasks are available at the AAVMC's prevet page (http://aavmc.org/prevet.htm) and in brochures from the individual schools.

Admissions requirements vary from school to school. While most require the GRE, a handful ask for the GMAT or the Veterinary College Admission Test (VCAT).

The VCAT

The VCAT is designed to measure achievement in areas critical for success in veterinary medical school. The three-hour multiple-choice test comprises five content areas: verbal ability, biology, chemistry, quantitative ability, and reading comprehension. The test is administered three times a year in October, November, and January.

For registration information, contact:

> The Psychological Corporation
> Veterinary College Admission Test
> P.O. Box 96152
> Chicago, IL 60693
> phone: 1-800-622-3231

For admissions requirements at individual schools, including information on which test is required, applicants should check the AAVMC website and the program profiles included in *The Veterinary Medical School Admission Requirements in the United States and Canada.*

The VMCAS

Applications to 23 of the 27 U.S. veterinary medical schools and two of the four Canadian veterinary medical schools participate in the Veterinary Medical College Application Service (VMCAS). The VMCAS is a centralized application process designed to collect, process, verify, and distribute applicant data to participating institutions. For information about the service, contact:

> Veterinary Medical College Application Service
> 1101 Vermont Avenue, NW, Suite 411
> Washington, DC 20005
> Phone: (202) 682-0750/Toll free: 1- 877-VMCAS-40 (1-877-862-2740)
> e-mail: vmcas@aavmc.org
> http://www.aavmc.org/

Other Elements Of The Application

Application requirements vary from school to school. Most require a written statement and letters of recommendation; many ask students to come in for an interview. Applicants should contact the individual institutions for details.

Overall Rating
★★★★

An excellent and sympathetic guide for medical school applicants early in the process

Design, Ease Of Use
★★★★

Articulate and lively; well-organized and presented

1–4 Stars

Author:
Sanford J. Brown, MD

Sanford J. Brown, MD, wrote this book as a senior medical student in the early 1970s. It is now in its eighth edition, and he presently runs his own practice "providing fee-for-service medicine in a rural area."

Publisher:
Barron's Educational Series

Edition:
8th (1997)

Price:
$11.95

Pages:
279

ISBN:
0812096479

Media:
Book

Principal Focus:
Health Sciences

BARRON'S GETTING INTO MEDICAL SCHOOL
The Premedical Student's Guidebook

 Recommended For:
Health Sciences

Description:

In its eighth edition, this book was first penned by a medical student who wished to share his experiences as "an atypical premed who had somehow made it into medical school." Today he runs a private practice in a rural area and works as an advisor to premedical students who have contacted him after reading his book. The book's introduction and preface discuss current changes in the field of medicine; they are followed by two chapters on choosing a college and a major, the role of the college advisor, and the "premed syndrome." The MCAT is covered in Chapter 3. "Applying to a Medical School—When, Where, and How" follows, including a section on minority applicants. Chapter 6 talks about alternatives for rejected students. Chapter 7 consists of "amazing success stories" of atypical applicants, including the author's own experience. The future of medicine is explored in a final section. Appendices provide a list of summer premed programs, a directory of U.S. medical schools, and a list of useful websites.

Evaluation:

A caring, intelligent voice rings throughout this book, rendering an often cold and objective process a little more human and offering excellent advice on almost every aspect of the application process. This book offers a vision of medicine's future, which few potential doctors can afford to ignore. With the perspective of a seasoned "solo practitioner" in practice for 20 years, it provides an exceptional introduction not only to the basic steps of applying to medical school, but also to today's medical profession. Particularly valuable are the sections describing how to choose a course of study at college beyond the typical science grind, and those that deal with minority students, women, and other "nontraditional" candidates. The "amazing success stories" are an inspiration to all unusual applicants. Finally, the last chapters provide a fascinating and sobering look at how medicine may be practiced in the future. These chapters should serve as a wake-up call to many applicants. This book is a good basic resource for college students considering medical school.

Where To Find/Buy:

Bookstores and libraries.

GUIDE TO MEDICAL SCHOOL & THE MCAT

 Recommended For:
Health Sciences

Description:

Written by two authors with extensive backgrounds in medicine, education, and test preparation, this guidebook provides information and advice about applying to medical school and taking the MCAT. The first part of the book consists of nine chapters on the application process, including such topics as: making the decision to pursue a medical career; preparing for medical school in high school and college, and through internships and premed programs; medical school itself; the future of medicine; requirements for admission; financial considerations and options; and alternatives for rejected applicants. Part 2 focuses on preparing for and taking the MCAT. This section includes a practice MCAT with scoring and analysis, which allows the reader to prepare a personalized review plan. Review methods, study skills, and test-taking techniques are all discussed in this section. Appendices include information and statistics for medical schools in the U.S. and Puerto Rico.

Evaluation:

Glib entertainment tactics are left far behind in this serious and informed approach to the medical school admissions process. Readers will find excellent advice on all the essentials, compiled by two seasoned experts in medicine and education. The book is nicely balanced with thoughtful organization (great table of contents and index) and honest discussion of the future of medicine and the advantages and disadvantages of a medical career. Extensive tables list valuable information on summer internships; premed and post-baccalaureate programs; medical school acceptance rates by mean MCAT scores; and minority student admission rates. The hefty Part 2 focusing on the MCAT provides some superb tips and information on meeting this challenge physically, emotionally, and intellectually. (Both authors have significant experience in the field of test preparation.) Medical school hopefuls will find this resource a very valuable guide.

Where To Find/Buy:

Bookstores and libraries.

Overall Rating
★★★★
An informed guide to medical school admissions and the MCAT

Design, Ease Of Use
★★★★
Lucid, straightforward writing

1–4 Stars

Author:
David A. Hacker, MA, & Kenneth Ibsen, PhD

David Hacker is Director of Medical Education at *National Medical School Review*. Kenneth Ibsen served as a faculty member at University of California, Irvine, College of Medicine until 1993, and currently works for *National Medical School Review* as Director of Faculty Development.

Publisher:
Williams & Wilkins

Edition:
1997

Price:
$19.95

Pages:
298

ISBN:
0683006797

Media:
Book

Principal Focus:
Health Sciences

II. Medical School &
Health Science Programs

Overall Rating
★★★★
Comprehensive admissions tool

Design, Ease Of Use
★★★★
In-depth; organized and navigable layout

1–4 Stars

Publisher:
Association Of American Medical Colleges

Founded in 1890, AAMC is a nonprofit association comprising the 125 accredited U.S. medical schools, the 16 accredited Canadian medical schools, teaching hospitals, professional societies, medical students and residents.

Edition:
50th (1999)

Price:
$25.00

Pages:
291

ISBN:
1577540115

Media:
Book

Principal Focus:
Health Sciences

MEDICAL SCHOOL ADMISSION REQUIREMENTS
United States & Canada 2000–2001

 Recommended For:
Health Sciences

Description:
Designed for potential medical school applicants and premed advisers, this guide, published by the Association of American Medical Colleges (AAMC), profiles 125 U.S. and 16 Canadian accredited medical schools and provides information on premedical preparation and admission requirements. The first three chapters explain general medical school curriculum, premedical planning, and what qualities to look for in a school. Chapters 4–6 address the individual's chances of getting in and financing school, and what admission advisors want from applicants. Medical College Admission Test and American Medical College Application Service requirements are explained and samples provided. In Chapters 7–9, the AAMC lists resources for financial planning and explains the process of accelerated study and which schools offer those programs. Part 2 contains school profiles—two-page comprehensive descriptions outlining seven major characteristics of each program, such as enrollment figures, and application and acceptance policies. Numerous charts and table are included.

Evaluation:
This clearly written, well-organized reference tool provides students and advisers with practical advice regarding each medical school application process. The AAMC looks candidly at students' chances of acceptance, without being discouraging, and warns of the financial struggles, too. For example, credit card debt and poor credit will nearly destroy a student's chance to get loans and greatly affect debt management after graduation. This resource provides practical solutions, including informative leads for financial aid, including sources for women and minorities. A discussion of career trends and numerous charts and figures help complete the admission picture, with details on who is actually accepted to what specialties and where. The two-page profiles are the best we've seen—comprehensive in content and laid out with clear headings and effective use of text boxes and tables. This book is one of the most complete medical admission and information resources we've found, packed with useful and practical advice. Highly recommended.

Where To Find/Buy:
Bookstores and libraries, or from the Association of American Medical Colleges, Dept. 66, Washington, DC 20055 (Phone: (202) 828-0416; fax (202) 828-1123) On the Internet at http://www.aamc.org

MEDICAL SCHOOL ADMISSIONS
The Insider's Guide

 Recommended For:
Health Sciences

Description:

First penned in 1989 and recently revised and updated, this book covers the gamut of issues pertaining to the medical school application process. The authors are recent grads, now serving residencies or on the staff of major hospitals. The book's credo is summed up neatly in the introduction: "We believe that the whole admissions process is a formula, a game with set rules. If you play the game by the rules, you'll get in." The authors' goal is to help the reader understand the rules, providing information gleaned from their experiences as well as from admissions committee members. The first three chapters discuss "premedical preparation" (choosing a college, courses to take, post-baccalaureate programs), tips for getting good grades, and MCAT preparation. Chapter 4 is a sequential overview of the steps in the actual application process. Chapters 5–6 give an in-depth look at interviews and writing essays. Nearly 100 pages at the end of the book are reserved for "Fifty Successful Application Essays."

Evaluation:

This book offers lots of savvy advice, such as to "go ahead and learn to scuba dive or take a course on Emily Dickinson," as it may help students stand out from the pack. Life experience, honesty, and passion for the profession are brought to the fore here, along with advice on getting good grades and scoring well on the MCAT. But the heart of this book (and the heart of the medical school application) is the section on the personal essay and the 50 sample essays that follow. This discussion is simply invaluable for any applicant, offering practical advice about writing the essay, from editing and style issues to introspection about one's motivation for becoming a doctor. The essays themselves range from the truly astonishing and moving to the merely egotistical and boring, each offering a lesson in itself. Although this book pulls no punches about the difficulty of the application process, it acknowledges a more humane side and helps applicants understand that the best doctors are, ultimately, "thoughtful, caring, well-rounded people with wide-ranging interests." No index, but detailed table of contents aids navigation.

Where To Find/Buy:
Bookstores and libraries.

Overall Rating
★★★★
A savvy "insider's view" of the application process

Design, Ease Of Use
★★★★
Readable, user-friendly style

1–4 Stars

Author:
John A. Zebala, Daniel B. Jones, & Stephanie B. Jones

John A. Zebala and Daniel B. Jones are serving their residencies at University of Washington Medical Center and Barnes-Jewish Hospital in St. Louis, respectively. Stephanie B. Jones is currently on the staff at Barnes-Jewish Hospital.

Publisher:
Mustang

Edition:
4th (1997)

Price:
$12.95

Pages:
189

ISBN:
0914457772

Media:
Book

Principal Focus:
Health Sciences

II. Medical School & Health Science Programs

Overall Rating
★★★★

A fun introduction to medical schools; includes school comparisons, rankings, articles, tips

Design, Ease Of Use
★★★★

Well-formatted; searching for schools is simple and effective

1–4 Stars

Publisher:
U.S. News and World Report

Online U.S. News is the Internet home of the print publication, *U.S. News & World Reports*.

Media:
Internet

Principal Focus:
Health Sciences

U.S. NEWS ONLINE: MEDICINE

Recommended For:
Health Sciences

Description:

U.S. News Online's "Graduate School" segment includes this subsection dedicated to medical schools. "Medicine" functions as its own site. Its first page acts as a home page, describing the section's six main areas: Find Your Medical School, Compare Medical Schools, Rankings, Specialties, Web-exclusive Rankings, and Articles. In Find Your Medical School, users can find information on a specific school or perform a personalized search to find school matches based on their own criteria (e.g., location, MCAT scores, special courses). The search produces a statistical overview of relevant schools, providing data on admissions, deadlines, tuition, and student demographics, as well as contact addresses. The Compare Medical Schools produces side-by-side summaries of four schools, comparing over 30 different criteria (e.g., acceptance rates, costs). Rankings, Specialties, and Web-exclusive Rankings offer lists of school rankings in a variety of categories. Also included are lists of Top Schools in such specialties as Women's Health or Geriatric, as well as rankings for Lowest MCAT Scores or Most Research Money. In Articles, "Getting In" and "Career Outlook" are among the pieces presented.

Evaluation:

Since "Medicine" is a subsection of U.S. News Online's "Graduate School" site (http://www.usnews.com/usnews/edu/beyond/bchome.html; reviewed on page 188), it links to lots of other resources in addition to those specific to medical schools. From the sidebar menu, visitors access advice forums on admissions and financial aid, and an internal link to "Health" (another subsection of "Graduate School"), which contains information on nursing schools and midwifery. Other features—all accessible from "Medicine's" main page—include rankings for "Best Hospitals" to work at, links to "hot jobs," and links to relevant websites, such as the American Medical Association. (Note: There's nothing here for future osteopathic doctors, except a link to the American Association Of Colleges Of Osteopathic Medicine site; this is strictly a MD resource.) Users should also note that, despite the amenities, most of the information found here is number-oriented. That is, the school overviews are number-based; the side-by-side comparisons are number-based; and the rankings are number-based. It's important to keep in mind that numbers aren't everything. School rankings can be useful in the early stages of research; plus, they're fun. But applicants shouldn't spend all of their time at this terrific site searching for "Number 1." The rest of the site is of equal, if not greater, value.

Where To Find/Buy:

On the Internet at http://www.usnews.com/usnews/edu/beyond/bcmed.html

ASSOCIATION OF AMERICAN MEDICAL COLLEGES

 Recommended For:
Health Sciences

Description:

The AAMC's site is enormous, with segments on Government Affairs & Advocacy, Meetings & Conferences, Research, Medical Education, and "About the AAMC." For students, the segment titled Student, Applicant & Advisor Information is of greatest interest. It is divided into subsections, including Admission to Medical School, Applicant Information, Minority Programs, and Financial Aid. (An outline of the subsections and their contents is provided.) In Admission to Medical School, users can learn about AMCAS-E, the online application service, and about the MCAT, including registration deadlines, score distribution, and the MCAT Fee Reduction Request Form. Applicant Information, which has its own table of contents, covers information for women, minorities, non-U.S. citizens, and U.S. citizens transferring from foreign schools. There are also articles on medical careers, as well as contact info for all U.S. and Canadian medical schools. Minority Programs presents AAMC programs and services dedicated to increasing the number of minority medical students. Financial Aid offers details on scholarships and loans, plus a debt-management guide.

Evaluation:

This site is absolutely overflowing with helpful information and advice for future medical students. It includes in-depth information on the MCAT, contact information for all medical schools (no school profiles), even admissions tips. The Financial Aid subsection offers explanations of federal loans and MEDLOANS, as well as details on loan repayment/forgiveness programs. And there's AMCAS-E, the online application service for medical schools. (The same list of medical schools that provides contact info identifies which schools use AMCAS.) What distinguishes this site from all others is the specific, and very pertinent, advice for women, minorities, non-U.S. citizens, and students who have attended foreign medical schools. Minority applicants can learn about the Med-MAR, a registry circulated to all medical schools wishing to directly contact minority students to encourage applications, and the Minority Medical Education Program, which assists minority students by providing clinical and laboratory exposure and academic opportunities. Women will find links to women's medical associations and advice on contacting the Women's Liaison Office at their school of choice. For users interested in medicine, this site is an absolute must.

Where To Find/Buy:

On the Internet at http://www.aamc.org

Overall Rating
★★★★
An absolute must for future medical students; extremely helpful info and advice

Design, Ease Of Use
★★★
Some information duplicated under different headings; lots of overlap

1–4 Stars

Publisher:
Association Of American Medical Colleges

Founded in 1890, AAMC is a nonprofit association comprising the 125 accredited U.S. medical schools, the 16 accredited Canadian medical schools, teaching hospitals, professional societies, medical students and residents.

Media:
Internet

Principal Focus:
Health Sciences

Of Interest To:
Women
Persons of Color

II. Medical School &
Health Science Programs

★★★★

Overall Rating
★★★★
A valuable medical school application guide for minorities

Design, Ease Of Use
★★★
Helpful information presented clearly; some chapters outstanding

1–4 Stars

Author:
Edited by Edward J. James, MD, MBA & Karen E. Hamilton, PhD

The editors of this book are successful medical school graduates, who are now pursuing MD/PhD degrees, serving residencies, holding fellowships, working in public health or group practice, or teaching at medical schools.

Publisher:
Williams & Wilkins

Edition:
1996

Price:
$12.50

Pages:
198

ISBN:
0941406512

Media:
Book

Principal Focus:
Health Sciences

Of Interest To:
Persons of Color

GETTING INTO MEDICAL SCHOOL
A Planning Guide For Minority Students

 Recommended For:
Health Sciences

Description:
Edited by several successful medical school graduates currently practicing, teaching, or working in the field of medicine, this book is intended to provide underrepresented minorities essential information about applying to medical school. In the preface, one editor notes that "lack of information about how to approach the rigorous premedical academic course requirements, medical school applications, and admissions procedures is a major reason why many minority undergraduates are unsuccessful medical school applicants." Chapters cover strategies for academic success; extracurricular and summer opportunities; "beating the MCAT"; choosing a school; interviewing; and receiving financial aid. Extensive appendices include lists of summer enrichment and post-baccalaureate programs, tuition at U.S. medical schools, and information about the Student National Medical Association, an organization devoted to the concerns of medical students of color.

Evaluation:
Often faced with unique challenges on their path to medical school, minority applicants need support and information, and this book provides just that. It offers clear, accurate advice about the application process. Some chapters are of particular value to the minority applicant; these include the sections on the interview ("You should approach the interview with pride in your cultural heritage"), financial aid, and particularly on choosing a medical school. By far the best part in the book, this chapter exposes some myths and issuing a few warnings about potential difficulties. One editor also shares his experiences as a person of color at Princeton. One wishes that the whole book was made up of such chapters, including more stories and personal experiences by the editors, and more in-depth exploration of the issues as they pertain to minorities. Such a book would be a milestone—but this book is a great first step. We recommend it!

Where To Find/Buy:
Bookstores and libraries.

THE INTERACTIVE MEDICAL STUDENT LOUNGE

 Recommended For:
Health Sciences

Description:

The "Lounge" is primarily a web guide, comprising links to online resources, such as websites, email lists, discussion areas, and personal home pages. The site's target audience is allopathic medical and premed students, but it features sections for dental students and students of osteopathic medicine, and such medical specialties as sports medicine and podiatry. The home page details the site's contents on a sidebar menu. In "Applying," users will find links to organizations and sites offering application advice, such as the Association of American Medical Colleges (AAMC) and the Princeton Review, plus links to current and recently graduated medical students' homepages, like "Bobby's Arizona Pre-Med Information Home Page." Also featured are email lists and links to "premed advisors" who help students with personal essays and offer premed advice. Other features include "discussion areas" for medical, premed, and dental students in the form of email lists, lists of contacts, and lists of volunteers. The volunteer lists let users talk to a current student at a specific school. One example: a volunteer posted a message saying "If you have any questions on Mount Sinai, feel free to ask. It is an awesome school," along with an email address.

Evaluation:

This site is one of the most elaborate web guides available to medical students; it is a fantastic resource. In this short space, it's hard to do justice to the site when it offers so many pages of links—on such a wide array of topics. Included are links to medical references, journals, e-mail lists, news, libraries, and schools, plus links to subject-specific sites and sites providing advice on applying and succeeding in school. Other areas address financial aid and testing, present calendars of events, or sell textbooks and software. The best thing about this site is its inclusion of "mainstream" *and* "independent" resources. Most web guides focus on the "mainstream": medical school homepages, large commercial sites (such as Princeton Review), medical organizations, national associations, and the like. Overlooked are some of the most valuable and underrated sources of information on the Net: "independent" sites, the home pages of individuals or discussion groups offering pithy advice, commentary, and evaluations. The inclusion of so many of these "independent" sites in the "Lounge" makes it a "must-see" for students. They will find hands-on experience, insider advice, and insight from the real experts: current and recently graduated medical students.

Where To Find/Buy:

On the Internet at http://www.medstudents.net

Overall Rating
★★★★
Future medical students should bookmark this page!

Design, Ease Of Use
★★★
A site map would be helpful

1–4 Stars

Author:
Nancy Sween & Katlinel Shlasko

Publisher:
Nancy Sween

Media:
Internet

Principal Focus:
Health Sciences

Overall Rating
★★★★

The best site for learning about osteopathic medicine, plus lots more!

Design, Ease Of Use
★★★

Could use an all-inclusive, explicit site map; some features are "hidden"

I–4 Stars

Publisher:
OMEGA

OMEGA is a nonprofit organization.

Media:
Internet

Principal Focus:
Health Sciences

OSTEOPATHIC.COM
The Osteopathic Medicine Resource

 Recommended For:
Health Sciences

Description:

Osteopathic.com features four main sections, each of which are detailed on the home page's side-bar menu. The first is About Osteopathic Medicine, an introductory section describing what a Doctor of Osteopathic Medicine (DO) is, as well as the history of the profession. Next are two sections for students: Premeds and Med Students. The student sections share some features, such as access to the OCom Lounge (a chat room) and to OCom FAQ, a question-and-answer forum where users ask questions of the resident osteopathic physicians or a current medical student. "Premeds" also features a PreMed FAQ page, which, like About Osteopathic Medicine, functions as an introduction to the field, and a Resources page. The Resource page offers internal and external links to student resources; it is organized into four "steps" to walk students through the research process. Step 1: Introduction to Osteopathic Medicine includes links to medical schools, to DOs' home pages, and to medical associations. Step 2 has links for exploring the field. Step 3 covers applying to school with a link to the American Association of Colleges of Osteopathic Medicine (AACOM) site. Step 4: Have Additional Questions? sends users to Q & A forums. The site's fourth section is aimed at physicians and contains a Professional's Center.

Evaluation:

Since there are fewer osteopathic medical schools than allopathic schools, it is not surprising that there are also fewer osteopathic-related websites. This site reflects the inherent advantage to this field's smaller numbers: choice websites can be easily organized into an effective web guide. One of the best features of Osteopathic.com is the step-by-step link guide found in "Premeds: Resources." It covers all of the basics and will be especially useful to students who are just beginning their research. The site also links to another web guide: "Gregory's Osteopathic Links" (http://www.osteopathic.com/gregory/). Gregory is a student at Nova Southeastern University's College of Osteopathic Medicine (class of 2003). His guide includes links to Important Starting Points for Pre-Medical Students, Medical Schools, and Homepages of Medical Students. Also of note are the site's many FAQ pages, the interactive Lounge and the "expert" Q & A forum. (Replies to questions are posted within 48 hours.) Navigation can be a little tricky; valuable features like Gregory's guide don't appear on the home page or site index. We noticed it in a banner "ad" on the top of one page. Still, for those interested in osteopathic medicine, this site is worth strolling through.

Where To Find/Buy:

On the Internet at http://www.osteopathic.com

BARRON'S ESSAYS THAT WILL GET YOU INTO MEDICAL SCHOOL

 Recommended For:
Health Sciences

Description:

This guide, part of a series of books on how to get into Ivy League schools, is designed to help individuals create an effective essay when applying to medical school. The authors show readers how to gather information and create strategies for essay writing. First, they help readers determine who their audience is and how to choose an essay theme. They provide writing exercises, which help applicants illustrate their best assets. The first section of the book explains how to make a list of goals, accomplishments, and experiences, and how medical essays differ from other school application essays. Part Two explains how to write an outline and work it into a strong statement through extensive rewrites and editing. The authors provide advice on editing, style, grammatical preferences, and overall structure. Interview preparation and sample questions are the focus of Part Three. Part Four, nearly one-half the book, consists of 40 original essays from diverse applicants, all accepted to at least one medical school. An Essay Index follows the essays, so readers can access those that best mirror their own needs. A general index rounds out the book.

Evaluation:

Based on the concept, "a beautifully written essay isn't going to get you into medical school, but a poorly written one could keep you out," the authors show readers what not to write in a personal statement. They emphasize the importance of the essay as an evolving work and provide practical advice and exercises to help readers focus. Exercises also help individuals discover personal qualities they may have overlooked. Readers will learn what admission officers are looking for, and what they have already seen too much of. The authors help readers build on one idea or theme using a unique angle and creating a persuasive essay. Their step-by-step outline directions and editing tips will help even the most confident applicants. The authors' best advice? Take a personal approach and don't try to look smart by using a bunch of "big" words. This book is a winner because it will continue helping students with writing projects throughout medical school and into their professional careers. The information on interviewing skills is another plus.

Where To Find/Buy:

Bookstores and libraries.

Overall Rating
★★★
Practical advice; an effective essay-writing tool

Design, Ease Of Use
★★★
Well-organized tool

1–4 Stars

Author:
Daniel Kaufman, Chris Dowhan, & Amy Burnham

The authors work for Ivy Essays, an Internet-based company offering editing and consulting services to prospective college and graduate school students.

Publisher:
Barron's

Edition:
1998

Price:
$10.95

Pages:
145

ISBN:
0764106112

Media:
Book

Principal Focus:
Health Sciences

II. Medical School & Health Science Programs

Overall Rating
★★★
A thoughtful discussion of "staying human" during the medical school admissions process

Design, Ease Of Use
★★★
Well-written, with a real authorial "presence"

1–4 Stars

Author:
Keith Russell Ablow, MD
The author is a graduate of the Johns Hopkins University School of Medicine and served his residency at Tufts in Boston. With J. Raymond DePaulo, Jr., MD, he co-wrote *How to Cope with Depression: A Complete Guide for You and Your Family.*

Publisher:
St. Martin's

Edition:
1990

Price:
$14.95

Pages:
144

ISBN:
031204349X

Media:
Book

Principal Focus:
Health Sciences

MEDICAL SCHOOL
Getting In, Staying In, Staying Human

 Recommended For:
Health Sciences

Description:
Dr. Ablow, the author of this guide to getting into, and staying in, medical school, is a graduate of the Johns Hopkins University School of Medicine. He discusses the more general issues of medical school admissions, with advice about how to "stay sane" from the premed years through the application process, and into medical school itself. The first chapter discusses the decision to become a physician, including what to expect from the premed and medical school years, new trends in medicine that are changing the way doctors practice, and personal motivations for becoming a doctor. The next two chapters include the dos and don'ts of premed preparation in high school and college. The MCAT, the application process, admissions essay, and interview are all discussed next, with examples of successful essays. The last three chapters focus on what to do "once you make it," what to do "if you don't make it," and what to expect during the medical school years.

Evaluation:
Forgoing tables, grids, and graphs, this book offers a thoughtful and practical discussion of how to "stay human" while successfully completing the medical school admissions process. The author rejects the "cookbook" mentality of other guides, which offer lots of lists and addresses; instead he presents a considered exploration of medical school admissions, while keeping in mind that "dealing with stress and completing the educational process with your sensitivity and outside interests intact—as a whole person—is more important than your test scores in biology and anatomy." This book offers a welcome change from the "win at all costs" mentality of similar books on the subject, and should offer comfort and needed perspective for medical school applicants and students alike. Applicants may find, however, that they need to supplement this general perspective with a more detailed resource on medical school programs and admissions.

Where To Find/Buy:
Bookstores and libraries.

PETERSON'S GUIDE TO NURSING PROGRAMS
Baccalaureate & Graduate Nursing Education In The U.S. & Canada

 Recommended For:

Health Sciences

Description:

This specialized guide lists more than 2,000 nursing programs at 600-plus schools in the United States and Canada. All of the programs profiled in this guide are four-year and graduate level programs; no comparative or evaluative information is provided. The programs are all accredited or have candidate-for-accreditation status in the U.S., and Canadian programs are all chartered or accredited. The first section includes articles on nursing careers today, how to finance a nursing education, and tips for returning students. A second section contains program profiles, organized alphabetically by state and province. The profiles range in length from one-quarter page to a page and a half and contain information on enrollment, academic facilities, student life, contact information, expenses, and programs offered. In-depth descriptions of the nursing programs, written by the schools, are provided in a third section. These essays are approximately two pages long; Peterson's does not take responsibility for their content (Not all schools chose to be included in this section). A final section comprises a series of indexes by program concentration, program name, and institution name.

Evaluation:

Peterson's has produced several good guidebooks, and this one is no exception. It brings a lot of valuable information together in one easy-to-use volume. Peterson's does not evaluate the programs they profile; information is provided by the colleges and universities and consists largely of statistics on enrollment and basic information on the programs, expenses, and student life. This information is helpful in deciding which schools to contact for further information and provides students with a general idea of what expect in course load and expenses. One of this guide's strengths is its three indexes, which make it possible to find specific information easily. Because the in-depth program profiles are provided by the schools, students should be sure to look elsewhere for evaluations and comparisons of these programs.

Where To Find/Buy:

Bookstores and libraries.

Overall Rating
★★★

Lots of information; take the "in-depth descriptions" with a grain of salt

Design, Ease Of Use
★★★

Listed alphabetically by state, province; indexes by study areas, programs, name

1–4 Stars

Publisher:
Peterson's

Edition:
4th (1998)

Price:
$24.95

Pages:
632

ISBN:
1560799986

Media:
Book

Principal Focus:
Health Sciences

II. Medical School & Health Science Programs

Overall Rating
★★★
Offers overviews of all 19 osteopathic colleges, plus an application service

Design, Ease Of Use
★★★
Small, effective site; no frills, but none are necessary

1–4 Stars

Publisher:
American Association Of Colleges Of Osteopathic Medicine

The American Association Of Colleges Of Osteopathic Medicine (AACOM) serves the administration, faculty, and students of its 19 member osteopathic medical schools through its centralized application service (AACOMAS), government relations, finance, and research and information departments.

Media:
Internet

Principal Focus:
Health Sciences

AMERICAN ASSOCIATION OF COLLEGES OF OSTEOPATHIC MEDICINE

Description:
Sponsored by the American Association of Colleges of Osteopathic Medicine (AACOM), this site provides information on osteopathic medicine and the 19 accredited osteopathic colleges. From the home page, users access all of the main sections: About AACOM, Osteopathic Medicine, Osteopathic Medical Education, Osteopathic Colleges, and AACOMAS, a centralized application service. In Osteopathic Medicine and Osteopathic Medical Education, users will find introductory essays on the field and practitioner statistics. The essays include descriptions of "Osteopathic Physicians" and a biography of the "father" of osteopathic medicine, Dr. Andrew Taylor Still. The Osteopathic Colleges section features information on all 19 osteopathic schools in the U.S.; listings are arranged alphabetically. By clicking on a college, users can access a school overview, detailing the curriculum, entrance requirements, admission process, deadlines, and costs. AACOM also offers students a centralized application service, AACOMAS, through which students can file a single application and a single set of official transcripts/MCAT scores. AACOMAS then distributes these to the colleges designated by the student. Students can download paper or electronic AACOMAS applications from the site.

Evaluation:
The number of osteopathic physicians has increased 50 percent in the last decade, making osteopathic medicine one of the fastest-growing health professions in the U.S. Students considering medical school may be confused about the difference between Doctors of Osteopathic Medicine (DO) and the traditional MD; this site may be helpful in clarifying some of the distinctions. (According to AACOM, DOs are physicians fully trained to diagnose illness, prescribe drugs and perform surgery. The federal government and the American Medical Association recognize DOs and MDs as equals. DOs, like MDs, are licensed to provide comprehensive medical care in all 50 states). The introductory essays offered here are not as informative as they could be; they give only brief glimpses into the history and philosophy of osteopathic medicine and cannot take the place of in-depth research. They do provide a valuable starting place, however, as do the college overviews. If you have only begun to consider osteopathic medicine as an educational choice, this site is a fine place to go to learn the basics. For the "I'm sure this is what I want" future DO, the AACOMAS centralized application service is the reason to visit. With AACOMAS, you can easily send transcripts and MCAT scores, etc., to as many schools as you like.

Where To Find/Buy:
On the Internet at http://www.aacom.org/

BARRON'S GUIDE TO MEDICAL & DENTAL SCHOOLS

Description:

In its eighth edition, this thick book combines up-to-date information and advice about applying to medical and dental school. Among the many changes incorporated in this volume are updated profiles on all medical and dental schools; discussions of memory techniques and how to succeed as a premedical student; admission of disabled students; chapters on opportunities for women and summer programs for minorities; as well as a chapter on osteopathic medicine and "Physicians and Medicine in the Twenty-First Century." The book is intended as a guide from the premed years through postgraduate training and should be of use to readers applying to medical or dental school or considering further training and employment opportunities. Readers will also find such tools as a self-assessment admissions profile, sample medical school application forms and personal essays, and tracking tables for all stages of the application process.

Evaluation:

This book presents an informed view of the application process, complete with accurate statistics, tables, and information about medical and dental schools. And it is more than a dry compilation of facts; it distinguishes itself with its excellent discussion of the crucial issues involved in becoming a doctor or dentist, such as the changing face of medicine and the special issues affecting women, minorities, and disabled people, and fascinating historical background. Lacking is thorough coverage of the all-important personal statement. The MCAT and DAT are the focus here. The book also includes information on osteopathic medicine, as well as foreign medical schools (opportunities and words of warning), but it is not as extensive as the information on medical schools. The book contains extensive sections on dentistry as a career, dental school applications, the DAT, and more. This information tended to be thin, however, and not as current as we would like. Overall, this is a well-organized, thoughtfully designed, and carefully researched book, but it is time for an update and more thorough coverage of dentistry and osteopathic medicine.

Where To Find/Buy:

Bookstores and libraries.

Overall Rating
★★★
Thorough treatment of some aspects of the medical and dental school application process

Design, Ease Of Use
★★★
Well-written; clear and usable information tables, profiles, and lists; weaker on dentistry and osteopathic medicine

1–4 Stars

Author:
Dr. Saul Wischnitzer, with Edith Wischnitzer

The author has extensive experience in career guidance for the health professions and as a college advisor. Currently he works as a private medical career consultant.

Publisher:
Barron's Educational Series

Edition:
8th (1997)

Price:
$16.95

Pages:
612

ISBN:
0812097882

Media:
Book

Principal Focus:
Health Sciences

Of Interest To:
Women
Persons of Color

II. Medical School & Health Science Programs

Overall Rating

★★★

Vivid, and critical, account of the third year of medical training

Design, Ease Of Use

★★★

Eloquently written; small, dense print

1–4 Stars

Author:

Melvin Konner, MD

An anthropologist, teacher, and writer, Dr. Konner is a professor of anthropology at Emory University, a contributing editor of *The Sciences*, and a columnist on health and behavior for *The New York Times Magazine*. His most recent book is *Medicine at the Crossroads: The Crisis in Healthcare*.

Publisher:

Penguin

Edition:

1988

Price:

$13.95

Pages:

390

ISBN:

0140111166

Media:

Book

Principal Focus:

Health Sciences

BECOMING A DOCTOR
A Journey Of Initiation Into Medical School

Description:

An anthropologist who had spent two years studying the !Kung bushmen in Africa and then became a professor, the author decided to attend medical school at age 33. He draws on this unusual perspective to chronicle his four years of medical school with the anthropologist's "participant observation." The book focuses on the third year of medical school, when students begin treating real patients, consolidating skills, assuming responsibility, and learning to act reflexively. It is also the year in which students adopt the values of physicians, as modeled by their physician-teachers. Konner takes the reader on his rotations through the many wards of Galen Hospital, from emergency ward surgery to gynecology, describing in detail his interactions with patients, doctors, and other hospital staff. He emphasizes not only the pressures and stresses of medical school, but the competitiveness and arrogance of many clinicians. In his view, these attitudes instill a sense of power in students, but ultimately undermine their compassion for patients.

Evaluation:

Dr. Konner attended medical school in the early 1980s, but this controversial book is still a valuable eye-opener for those considering medical school. It is also a reminder of the need for compassion, as well as skill, in the medical profession. This book is not your average recounting of a year in graduate school—the author's age and experiences, particularly those living in Africa, give him an unusual perspective that makes him more reflective and perceptive than most students. He is also a gifted writer. Konnor's detailed accounts of life as a medical student are valuable in themselves for portraying the overwhelming, and empowering, reality of hospital life. However, by taking on the medical school establishment, Konner presents insightful criticism that those considering the doctor's life should be aware of. The honesty with which he portrays the pressures of medical training and the power of teachers as models, not only of technical skills but also of interpersonal skills, is insightful and troubling. His thesis that the stress of clinical training itself alienates doctor from patients is also convincing. Fascinating reading, though with its small, dense print, not a quick read.

Where To Find/Buy:

Bookstores and libraries.

II. Medical School & Health Science Programs

GET INTO MEDICAL SCHOOL!
A Guide For The Perplexed

Description:

This book covers a broad range of topics related to medical school admissions. The author's background includes experience as a professor, practitioner, and researcher in the field of medicine. Chapters cover such topics as the different medical specialties; osteopathic medicine; medical school admissions requirements (with a detailed table listing the requirements of all U.S. medical schools); financial aid; and "Waiting For, Choosing Among, and Accepting Offers." Especially detailed chapters discuss women, minority, and "unconventional" applicants; foreign medical schools; and the all-important interview. Included along the way are extremely detailed charts and tables with such information as "Estimated Percentage Increase in Physician Specialties—1991–2000 and 1991–2010," "Percentage of Women Residents and Fellows in Selected Specialties," and "Average MCAT Scores for Applicants and Matriculants." Appendices include lots of contact information for medical schools, programs, and organizations.

Evaluation:

For those who don't mind wading through page after page of dense print with little white space, and spending time squinting at charts and tables, this book offers a wealth of valuable information. The author provides a thorough treatment of the topic in a personable writing style. Chapters of particular interest are those on "nontraditional" applicants and on the interview process, which takes students all the way from choosing the proper attire ("Appropriate dress can help you a little. The wrong outfit will destroy you"), packing for the interview trip, preparing questions as well as preparing for theirs, and entering and exiting the interview with assurance and grace. The chapter on foreign medical schools offers specific, reliable information along with excellent words of advice and caution. All the charts and tables, while a little hard on the eyes, provide crucial data that might be difficult to obtain elsewhere. A thorough resource, great for counselors and libraries.

Where To Find/Buy:

Bookstores and libraries.

Overall Rating
★★★
Thorough and informed resource on medical school admissions

Design, Ease Of Use
★★★
Straightforward, clear writing; good navigational tools

1–4 Stars

Author:
Kenneth V. Iserson, MD

The author is a medical teacher, clinician, and researcher, with a background as Professor of Surgery and director of the Residency Program in Emergency Medicine at the University of Arizona College of Medicine.

Publisher:
Galen

Edition:
1997

Price:
$34.95

Pages:
495

ISBN:
1883620236

Media:
Book

Principal Focus:
Health Sciences

Of Interest To:
Women
Persons of Color
Disabled
International Students

II. Medical School & Health Science Programs

Overall Rating

★★★

Real insider's perspective on medical schools

Design, Ease Of Use

★★★

Engaging profiles, but inconsistent content and a lot of typos

1–4 Stars

Author:

Ivan Oransky, MD; Eric Pousen, MD; Darshak M. Sanghavi, MD; & Jay K. Varma, MD

All four of the editors are physicians, recent medical school graduates, and former editors of *Pulse* (the medical student section of the Journal of the American Medical Association).

Publisher:

Peterson's

Edition:

1999

Price:

$21.95

Pages:

336

ISBN:

0768902037

Media:

Book

Principal Focus:

Health Sciences

PETERSON'S INSIDER'S GUIDE TO MEDICAL SCHOOLS, 1999

Description:

Part of the U-Wire Student-to-Student Guides (in conjunction with Peterson's), this guidebook was written by students for students. Four physician/writers wrote the introductory chapters, then solicited profiles from current upper-class students or recent graduates at 122 allopathic medical colleges and 16 osteopathic schools. Introductory chapters describe what to look for in a medical school (with an emphasis on prestige, location, clinical training and cost); how to get in (or "ways to load the dice in your favor"); how to survive medical school; and types of residencies, practice scenarios, and nonclinical professional opportunities awaiting graduates. The program profiles are written in text form and vary in length, style, and detail, based on the individual writer's preferences. Each profile describes the school's overall image, the admissions process and financial aid, preclinical and clinical curriculum, social life, the student body, housing, and the locale. Data is also included on the number of applicants, size of the entering class, and percentage of men and women.

Evaluation:

By relying exclusively on students or former students to describe the 138 institutions profiled in this book, Peterson's has taken a risky but generally successful leap toward creating a true "insider's guide." The writing is generally lively, even funny (especially in the introductory chapters), and goes in to the kind of depth applicants need to begin their search and make a sound decision. The program profiles vary in depth and content, however, and most contributors conclude with a positive, and relatively generic, "Bottom Line." Nevertheless, the profiles describe in some detail how these programs function at each school, what clinical training centers are like and the populations they treat, and which specialties are recommended. They also provide insight into important areas such as social life, the student body (not merely men vs. women, but mothers, musicians, etc.) and the atmosphere of the school and the larger community. The criticisms, gripes, and accolades, along with straight descriptions, create a good picture of each school. In their introductions, the editors aptly remind readers which factors are most important in the selection process. While the basic principles of all medical schools are the same, they say, the clinical training and ensuing residency program determine one's future career. Definitely worth a look.

Where To Find/Buy:

Bookstores and libraries.

ARCO'S GETTING INTO MEDICAL SCHOOL TODAY

Description:

This book opens with a graphic description of an intern's first day in the emergency room, interspersed with information about medicine as a career. Subsequent chapters discuss such "premed" activities as preparing in high school and college; selecting a major; fulfilling core requirements; maintaining science grades; studying successfully; choosing college extracurricular; and working at a part-time job. The basic steps of the application process are then outlined, from the MCAT, recommendation letters, and the C.V. to deciding where to apply, dealing with the interview, and applying for financial aid. Special issues pertaining to minority, female, and older applicants are discussed next. A chapter on what to do if you don't get in follows. The last three chapters discuss what to expect in medical school and residency. A list of accredited U.S. medical schools is featured at the back of the book. Many chapters end with lists of helpful publications and resources.

Evaluation:

This book offers a conservative, "safe" look at the medical school application process. After a hair-raising description of an intern performing an emergency procedure on a young patient, the book gives accurate, if uninspiring, information about the entire admissions process. Applicants who want to cover all their bets will find this book thorough, from its explanation of emergency drop procedures during college to its advice on careful selection of science courses. The sections on the interview and on letters of recommendation reveal an insider's know-how—and the authors' mentality—a sort of general craftiness, which seems to say "Admission at any price, and to heck with honesty or passion." For those who prefer a narrow approach to medical school, this may be a good resource, but others will find the authors' approach rigid and limiting.

Where To Find/Buy:

Bookstores and libraries.

Overall Rating
★★★
Sound, conservative overview of the important issues

Design, Ease Of Use
★★
Straightforward writing style; no index

1–4 Stars

Author:
Scott H. Plantz, MD, Nicholas Y. Lorenzo, MD, & Jesse A. Cole, MD

Dr. Plantz is the Assistant Chairman of the Department of Emergency Medicine at Mt. Sinai Medical Center, and Assistant Professor of Emergency Medicine at the Chicago Medical School. Dr. Lorenzo is a peripheral nerve fellow in the Department of Neurology at the Mayo Clinic. Dr. Cole is currently in private practice in Minneapolis.

Publisher:
Arco (Macmillan)

Edition:
4th (1998)

Price:
$14.95

Pages:
168

ISBN:
0028625005

Media:
Book

Principal Focus:
Health Sciences

Of Interest To:
Women
Persons of Color

II. Medical School & Health Science Programs

★★★

Overall Rating
★★★
Extensive overview of admission criteria

Design, Ease Of Use
★★
Alphabetical program listing; no chapter headings; navigation somewhat difficult

1–4 Stars

Author:
Association of American Veterinary Medical Colleges

AAVMS represents more than 4,000 faculty, 5,000 staff, 10,000 veterinary students, and 3,000 graduate students in the U.S. and Canada. It coordinates the affairs of the 27 U.S. Veterinary Medical Colleges, four Canadian Colleges of Veterinary Medicine, Departments of Veterinary Science and Comparative Medicine, and animal medical centers, and foster each membership's teaching, research and service missions, nationally and internationally.

Publisher:
Purdue University

Edition:
15th (1999)

Price:
$16.50

Pages:
170

ISBN:
155731684

Media:
Book

Principal Focus:
Health Sciences

VETERINARY MEDICAL SCHOOL ADMISSION REQUIREMENTS IN THE UNITED STATES AND CANADA
1999 Edition For 2000 Matriculation

Description:

This handbook, updated annually by the Association of American Veterinary Medical Colleges (AAVMC), provides students with current admission and application information for 31 accredited veterinary schools in the U.S. and Canada. In this 15th edition, AAVMC describes the various career paths veterinarians can follow. They explain the structure of the Veterinary Medical College Application Service, which some institutions require students to use. Two sections cover contracting agreements, which allow state institutions without veterinary schools to send students to states where programs are offered. These sections list states and provinces that contract with other schools and the schools that accept applications from nonresident or non-contracting states. Also briefly addressed are standard required testing and financial aid options. The bulk of the book consists of school profiles, which include institution background, application deadlines and fees, admission prerequisites, requirements, and procedures, and tuition. Numerous application and enrollment tables round out the book.

Evaluation:

This guide offers students essential direction in the veterinary school admission process. Because there are so few veterinary schools, students need to know where the schools are and how they can apply to a school outside their state and still receive in-state tuition benefits. Contracting arrangements are important in veterinary school admissions. For example, students from Alaska, which does not have a vet school, can apply to Colorado State University, which contracts with Alaska, and pay Colorado resident tuition. This book does a good job explaining these arrangements. We also like the school descriptions, which provide a clear picture of the school setting and offer plenty of important details, like average GPA and required credits. The program profiles are the meat of this book. We would have liked more specific details on contract agreements between schools, as well as phone numbers and email addresses for the contracting agencies. Nevertheless, this book is a great tool for those heading into veterinary medicine.

Where To Find/Buy:

Bookstores and libraries.

FROM RESIDENCY TO REALITY

Description:

Designed as a career and business management tool, this book show medical students and residents how to use networking and self-marketing tools to approach practice opportunities with confidence. Drawing on information gathered from interviews and other resources, the authors, a physician search consultant and a freelance writer, explain how individuals can create a medical career that suits their personal and professional needs. They hope this "how-to" book will help physicians at various career stages deal with "the realities of the medical marketplace." They provide an overview of the future of medicine and how changes will affect specialty decisions. They also offer advice on how to use specific communication strategies to build a professional network. Chapters IV through VII help readers determine what type of practice is right for them—partnership, private, group—on the basis of personal needs and lifestyle choices. Chapters VIII through X take readers through the interview process, including wardrobe suggestions and tips for negotiating contracts, and into the nuts and bolts of what is needed to begin a practice. The last chapter offers advice for those leaving an established practice to go onto new business ventures.

Evaluation:

While dated (this book was published in 1988), some of the authors' advice is helpful. Newly minted MDs will benefit from the authors' tips on professional attitude, peer relationships, and interview techniques. They offer plenty of "food for thought" for those new to the field, though their discussion of insurance costs, HMO policies, and potential workload is outdated. Few will appreciate the grooming and wardrobe suggestions, however. Times are a-changing, and the shelf life on such advice is short. New doctors will find the chapter on setting up and managing a practice helpful; included is a good basic checklist, one of the highlights of this book. However, overall this resource lacks punch and timeliness. We do not recommend it.

Where To Find/Buy:

Bookstores and libraries.

Overall Rating
★★
Food for thought for would-be doctors; needs updating

Design, Ease Of Use
★★★
Practical layout mirrors authors' practical approach

1–4 Stars

Author:
Patricia Hoffmeir & Jean Bohner

Hoffmeir is senior vice-president for a physician search consulting firm. Bohner is owner of Writer at Work and Assistant Professor of English at the University of Delaware.

Publisher:
McGraw-Hill

Edition:
1988

Price:
$24.00

Pages:
208

ISBN:
0070292124

Media:
Book

Principal Focus:
Health Sciences

Overall Rating

★★

Offers a quick overview of the MCAT, plus useful test dates, registration info, links

Design, Ease Of Use

★★★

Lots of advertising—some clearly labeled, some hidden

1–4 Stars

Publisher:

Kaplan Educational Centers

Kaplan, a subsidiary of The Washington Post Company, is a leading producer of test preparation materials. Their products include prep courses, books, and software.

Media:

Internet

Principal Focus:

Health Sciences

KAPLAN ONLINE: MEDICINE

Description:

Structured as its own site (it is actually part of Kaplan Online), Kaplan Online: Medicine's main page features a sidebar menu that details its content areas: MCAT, School Selection, Admissions, Financial Aid, First-Year Success, and Healthcare Careers. The MCAT section serves as an introduction to the exam. Test dates, registration how-to, and "Top 10 MCAT Tips" are provided, along with practice questions for the test's Science, Verbal, and Writing segments. Also included: an explanation of MCAT scoring and an overview of the entire exam. Visitors can download "Kaplan's Digital Test Booklet," free test-prep software that allows users to take a simulated test and receive feedback on their performance. The School Selection and Admissions sections offer advice and essays, including "MD Pros & Cons," "Accredited vs. Non," and "Application Dos & Don'ts." Admissions gives tips on personal statements, recommendations, and interviews, too. Users will find details on loan options (i.e., KapLoan), plus a timeline for applying in Financial Aid; "What Medical School is Really Like" is addressed in First-Year Success. Healthcare Careers discusses allied medical fields and schools, as well as the tests required to pursue them.

Evaluation:

Since Kaplan produces MCAT test preparation courses and materials, it is no surprise that this site features a fair amount of advertising. Approximately one-third of the MCAT section is devoted to promoting Kaplan's for-sale items. The "Student Survey" page, for example, displays a pie chart indicating which MCAT-prep courses students prefer. Guess who has the biggest chunk of the pie! Discounting this "survey," most of the advertising is clearly labeled and avoidable. And, despite the advertising, there is plenty worth visiting, especially the sizable introduction to the MCAT. For students unfamiliar with the exam, this is a good place for a quick, easy overview. Scoring is explained, as is test structure, and the practice questions are particularly helpful. There are only a few practice questions in each category, but that's enough to give students a "sneak peak." This isn't the place to learn everything about the MCAT, but it is a helpful starting point. The site's other sections, with the exception of Healthcare Careers, are disappointing. The advice is too superficial to be useful. Healthcare Careers, however, works nicely as a very basic introduction to allied medical fields/schools, including dental, optometry, pharmacy, and veterinary schools.

Where To Find/Buy:

On the Internet at http://www1.kaplan.com/view/zine/1,1899,4,00.html

PETERSON'S U.S. & CANADIAN MEDICAL SCHOOLS
400 Accredited MD & Combined Medical Degree Programs

Description:

This guidebook opens with a "career and education advisory" section with articles, written by various career services professionals, a school dean, and others, on such subjects as practicing medicine in the future, choosing and applying to medical schools, accreditation, and financial aid. The heart of the book follows with profiles of 400 accredited MD and combined degree programs in the U.S. and Canada. Profiles are organized alphabetically and contain general information on the institutions as well as specific information on medical school programs, such as number/gender/degrees of faculty; research emphasis; library holdings; hospital and research affiliations; degree programs; curriculum teaching methods; available clerkships; a student profile (total enrollment, women/men, minority, acceptance rate, percentage of students receiving top three residency choices, etc.); and tuition and financial aid information. Indexes list combined degree programs and medical schools by state. A sample MCAT is also included.

Evaluation:

Peterson's has put together a number of guidebooks to undergraduate and graduate schools, colleges, and universities. This guide to U.S. and Canadian medical schools follows the basic format: information is gathered from surveys sent out to school officials and other secondary sources, such as medical school catalogs and the Internet, and subsequently checked for accuracy (though we found a few errors). The result: a resource with relatively reliable information about the schools, but not much else. No effort is made to rate or otherwise categorize the schools by strengths (or drawbacks). This will disappoint readers looking for rankings. And besides, applicants can gather most of this information for themselves. Why shell out almost $25 for a guidebook of this type? Readers looking to save themselves some time and a few phone calls may find this book worth their while, but others will want information straight from the schools and a more analytical resource for comparisons.

Where To Find/Buy:

Bookstores and libraries.

Overall Rating
★★
School profiles offer little more than basic data

Design, Ease Of Use
★★★
Readable layout and clear design

1–4 Stars

Publisher:
Peterson's

Edition:
1998

Price:
$24.95

Pages:
248

ISBN:
1560798866

Media:
Book

Principal Focus:
Health Sciences

Overall Rating

★★

Basic overview of the stages of medical school, most useful as an introduction

Design, Ease Of Use

★★★

Well-written and organized

1–4 Stars

Author:

Mary Ross-Dalen, MD; Keith Berkowitz, MD; & Eyad Ali, MD

Dr. Ross-Dalen is a clinical fellow in child and adolescent psychiatry at Columbia-Presbyterian Medical Center/Columbia College of Physicians and Surgeons. Dr. Berkowitz and Dr. Ali are both residents at North Shore University Hospital.

Publisher:

Princeton Review (Random House)

Edition:

1996

Price:

$15.00

Pages:

179

ISBN:

0679764623

Media:

Book

Principal Focus:

Health Sciences

THE PRINCETON REVIEW MEDICAL SCHOOL COMPANION

The Ultimate Guide To Excelling In Medical School & Launching Your Career

Description:

Written by three medical school grads currently serving residencies (and a fellowship), this book hopes to provide "companionship" and information about what to expect in medical school, as well as tips on how to succeed. After a brief chapter covering the basics of the application process, chapters move in a chronological fashion through the various stages of medical school: the first year (coursework, teaching methods, exams); the second year (growing exposure to clinical hospital work, physical diagnosis, and the National Boards, Part I); the third year's "transition from the classroom to the hospital" and its attendant rotations in the various medical specialties; and the fourth year's challenges, choices and opportunities (sub-internships, electives, applying for residency, and studying for the Boards). The appendices offer descriptions a nd contact information for residencies and fellowships, as well as a list of recommended textbooks and review books.

Evaluation:

This book should prove informative for medical school applicants and matriculants alike. For applicants, its specific and often vivid presentation of medical school adventures will make for eye-opening reading, and perhaps provide a better sense of what medical school is all about. For medical students, this book should provide helpful survival tips and a good look at what lies ahead. The authors' advice is sound, from the perspective of people who have survived the trials and tribulations of medical school. One does sense, however, that the average medical school student will probably learn from experience much of what is offered here: the information is pretty basic, and few would turn to this source to find out how to take a patient's history when the time comes. Overall, this book is most helpful as a broad overview of medical school for those who have yet to experience it.

Where To Find/Buy:

Bookstores and libraries.

REA'S AUTHORITATIVE GUIDE TO MEDICAL & DENTAL SCHOOLS

Description:

This directory is intended to help "you, the prospective medical or dental school student, gain insight into the admissions process while learning about all types of medical and dental school programs." To this end, readers will find brief discussions of the professions and application information and checklists for allopathic, osteopathic, podiatric, chiropractic, and dental schools. But the bulk of the book comprises profiles, which contain up-to-date data on all the accredited schools in the U.S. and Canada, with tables listing accreditation, number of students applied and admitted, mean GPA and MCAT/DAT, percentage men, women, and minorities, tuition, and application deadlines. Information follows about the university itself, admissions requirements, undergraduate preparation required, and financial aid. Each school description is accompanied by a photograph or drawing.

Evaluation:

For sheer scope of information about all accredited medical, osteopathic, podiatric, chiropractic, and dental schools in the U.S. and Canada, this book can't be beat. It is big and bulky, but school profiles are nicely laid out and not too injurious to the eyes. One drawback—the dark, grainy photos accompanying the profiles—but many books of this type don't have any pictures. Each section begins with a helpful "at-a-glance" chart of basic facts on each school, together with very basic descriptions of the field, the application process, financial aid, and careers. The key word here is "basic"; a book of this sort is designed to provide a bird's eye view of all the schools, without rankings or ratings, and without much in-depth information on the schools themselves. Don't expect anything on student quality of life or program specialties and strengths. Potential users of this resource should consider their need for such a broad, but limited, look at all the schools before investing in this purchase.

Where To Find/Buy:

Bookstores and libraries.

Overall Rating
★★
An immense, but basic, compilation of information on the schools

Design, Ease Of Use
★★★
Clear layout of school profiles, marred by grainy photos

1–4 Stars

Publisher:
Research & Education Association

Edition:
1997

Price:
$21.95

Pages:
564

ISBN:
087891479X

Media:
Book

Principal Focus:
Health Sciences

Overall Rating
★★
Inspiring interviews with non-traditionally aged students; unscientific sampling of interviewees

Design, Ease Of Use
★★
No table of contents or index; not for browsing

1–4 Stars

Author:
Bryan Goss

A second-year student at Northwestern Medical School when this book was published, Mr. Goss was formerly a Pharmaceutical Sales Representative.

Publisher:
Lakeshore-Pearson

Edition:
1997

Price:
$15.00

Pages:
201

ISBN:
0966394402

Media:
Book

Principal Focus:
Health Sciences

Of Interest To:
Women

APPLYING TO MEDICAL SCHOOL FOR THE NON-TRADITIONAL STUDENT
From Decision To Admission–Interviews With Successful Applicants

Description:

In his book, Goss interviews 15 older medical school applicants from various backgrounds in an attempt to share and explore their experiences. In the Introduction, he outlines the types of questions asked in each interview. All interviewees are asked to describe their background, their premed program, and their strategies for choosing premed courses. Goss also delves into the students' study habits, their involvement in the medical community, and their experiences balancing school work and outside jobs. Each student then discusses the medical school application process: selecting a school, finding advisors, choosing sources of recommendations, and deciding what to include on the standardized medical school application. The interviewees also discuss the MCAT: when to take it, and how and how long to study for the test. All of the interviews end with closing thoughts and advice. A list of the individuals interviewed follows the Introduction. Among the interviewees are Therese, a 29-year-old mother who previously worked in the engineering industry, Howard, a 41-year-old husband who worked in health care, and Lisa, a 30-year-old former nurse.

Evaluation:

Despite its title, this book is not a how-to-apply guide. The interviewees share their experiences as applicants, including what the MCAT was like for them and how they filled out applications, but the author doesn't add general how-to information. No MCAT test dates here, no tips on registering or fee waivers, and no how tos for essays or entrance interviews. This book is strictly a collection of interviews, offering firsthand accounts from older medical school applicants and students. The interviewees candidly recall sacrifices made, obstacles overcome, and doubts quelled in pursuit of their medical school dreams. One woman explains how a friend helped her overcome her misgivings: "[I]f I ended up having another baby while I was in school, have it. Be happy, take a little time off. It's not the end of the world." The individuals interviewed come from very different backgrounds, though race and genders are not dealt with in any detail. Despite their diverse backgrounds, all interviewees share a certain optimism and self-acceptance. This inspirational attitude makes this book shine. Clearly, older students face an arduous journey; this resource offers inspiration and the realization that they are not alone.

Where To Find/Buy:
Bookstores and libraries.

BECOMING A PHYSICIAN
A Practical And Creative Guide To Planning A Career In Medicine

Description:

The authors, a mother and daughter team, began this book when Jennifer Danek was applying to medical school. They wanted to write a book that would "describe the nuts and bolts of getting into medical school but also address the human issues: Is medicine right for me? Do I have what it takes to prepare for the field? How can I become a physician without sacrificing the other things in life that I love?" The book is divided into three parts: the first offers a general discussion of the "big picture," including how to decide if medicine is right for you, understanding what the practice of medicine entails and how it will change in the future, medical specialties, and practice settings. Part Two discusses the premed years: choosing a college and realizing both personal and academic goals. Part Three discusses the nuts and bolts of the application process, from taking the MCAT and choosing a school to preparing for the interview and "making the transition to medical school."

Evaluation:

This book offers a unique combination of practical suggestions and psychological support. The supportive side, perhaps stemming from the fact that one of the authors is a professor of counseling, comprises genuinely creative advice on how to set goals, examine motivations in terms of becoming a physician (including a helpful exercise on how to "envision your future as a physician"), and dealing with stress while developing one's potential. This aspect of the book is truly helpful and may not be found in other resources on the subject. The second aspect of the book is more "nuts and bolts." The book's second half discusses the medical school application process itself. This half of the book is not as helpful as the first, offering only general information about taking the MCAT, writing the essay, etc. Medical school applicants will find the empathetic first half more beneficial.

Where To Find/Buy:

Bookstores and libraries.

Overall Rating
★★
A uniquely supportive perspective on the medical school admissions process

Design, Ease Of Use
★★
Warm, personable style

1–4 Stars

Author:
Jennifer Danek & Marita Danek

Jennifer Danek is a student at the University of California School of Medicine, San Francisco. Marita Danek, PhD, is a professor in the Department of Counseling at Gallaudet University in Washington, DC.

Publisher:
John Wiley & Sons

Edition:
1997

Price:
$14.95

Pages:
217

ISBN:
0471121665

Media:
Book

Principal Focus:
Health Sciences

II. Medical School & Health Science Programs

Overall Rating

★★

Good tips on admissions and self-test for would-be dentists, but lacks authority

Design, Ease Of Use

★★

Detailed table of contents helpful; no index or resource lists

1–4 Stars

Author:

Carla S. Rogers, PhD

Formerly assistant dean of admissions for the Medical College of Ohio (Toledo), the author has much experience in medical education, working as a professor, researcher, and counselor. She is also author of many scientific articles, as well as *How to Get into the Right Medical School* and *How to Get into the Right Nursing Program.*

Publisher:

VGM Career Horizons

Edition:

1997

Price:

$14.95

Pages:

155

ISBN:

0844264547

Media:

Book

Principal Focus:

Health Sciences

HOW TO GET INTO THE RIGHT DENTAL SCHOOL

Description:

This book was written by a former assistant dean of medical school admissions with extensive experience on admissions committees. It opens with a discussion of what it means to be a doctor and the skills it takes to survive in medical school. The first four chapters focus on how to prepare for medical school (the "written" and "unwritten" requirements), what schools look for in an applicant, the application itself, and the basics about the MCAT. Chapters 5–7 describe alternative degree programs, the medical school admissions committee, and provide information for nontraditional or minority candidates. Interviewing techniques are discussed next, with a list of "favorite questions" of interviewers. Chapter 9 tells how to juggle acceptances, rejections, and waiting lists. The final chapters introduce topics related to becoming a successful (and healthy) medical student, the residency, and managing finances. An appendix follows a day in the life of an ER physician.

Evaluation:

This book offers an inside look at what dental school admissions committees look for in students and their applications. The author also provides a good self-test for students: Do you really want to be a dentist? Would you be good at it? Her quick list of career characteristics—Detail; Eye-hand coordination and Esthetics; Need; Teeth; Interpersonal skills; Service: and Teamwork—it may be gimmicky, but it gets her point across. Dentistry is a tough field of study and work. Prospective dentists have to love this field to make it work for them. The same is true of most advanced degree programs, and for dentistry, this author offers a nice introduction. Her book lacks, however, the perspective of recent applicants or any references to outside sources of support and information. Another minus: much of the text on admission committee criteria and selected portions of other chapters are taken verbatim from Rogers' *How to Get into the Right Medical School.* The information may be applicable, but the cookie-cutter approach shows that this book isn't finely tuned to the needs of the would-be dental student.

Where To Find/Buy:

Bookstores and libraries.

HOW TO GET INTO THE RIGHT MEDICAL SCHOOL

Description:

This book was written by a former assistant dean of medical school admissions with extensive experience on admissions committees. It opens with a discussion of what it means to be a doctor and the skills it takes to survive in medical school. The first four chapters focus on how to prepare for medical school (the "written" and "unwritten" requirements), what schools look for in an applicant, the application itself, and the basics about the MCAT. Chapters 5–7 describe alternative degree programs, the medical school admissions committee, and provide information for nontraditional or minority candidates. Interviewing techniques are discussed next, with a list of "favorite questions" of interviewers. Chapter 9 tells how to juggle acceptances, rejections, and waiting lists. The final chapters introduce topics related to becoming a successful (and healthy) medical student, the residency, and managing finances. An appendix follows a day in the life of an ER physician.

Evaluation:

This book's chief value is that it allows a glimpse into the admissions process from the other side of the admissions desk. As such, it provides a unique look at how admissions officers evaluate students and their applications. The chapters on the nuts-and-bolts of the application process are quite helpful, as are the sections on the important elements that admissions committees look for in an application. Unfortunately, these strengths are undermined by what the book lacks: the kind of in-depth, "been through the wringer," perspective of recent applicants. The sections on how to prepare for the MCAT, acquire successful study habits, and create a well-rounded undergraduate course selection are relatively weak compared to other books on the subject. This book offers a helpful "official" perspective, but medical school applicants may find they need a more balanced applicant-insider's view.

Where To Find/Buy:

Bookstores and libraries.

Overall Rating
★★
Helpful look at the admissions process from an "official" perspective

Design, Ease Of Use
★★
Readable and personable

1–4 Stars

Author:
Carla S. Rogers, PhD

Formerly assistant dean of admissions for the Medical College of Ohio (Toledo), the author has much experience in medical education, working as a professor, researcher, and counselor. She is also author of many scientific articles, as well as *How to Get into the Right Dental School* and *How to Get into the Right Nursing Program*.

Publisher:
VGM Career Horizons
(NTC Publishing Group)

Edition:
1996

Price:
$19.95

Pages:
137

ISBN:
084424161X

Media:
Book

Principal Focus:
Health Sciences

Of Interest To:
Women
Persons of Color

II. Medical School &
Health Science Programs

Overall Rating

★★

An informative but brief overview of the basics of applying to medical school

Design, Ease Of Use

★★

Personable and clear

1–4 Stars

Author:

R. Stephen Toyos, MD

The author is a graduate of the University of Illinois College of Medicine and is currently a resident in ophthalmology at Northwestern University in Chicago.

Publisher:

Career

Edition:

1997

Price:

$16.99

Pages:

187

ISBN:

1564142728

Media:

Book

Principal Focus:

Health Sciences

THE INSIDER'S GUIDE TO MEDICAL SCHOOL ADMISSIONS

Description:

This book divides its pages between information about applying to medical school and medical school itself. It was written by a medical school grad now serving a residency in ophthalmology at Northwestern University. This edition has been expanded with sections on preparing for the MCAT, data on U.S. medical schools, and a National Boards study guide. The first chapter focuses on the steps of the application process. Chapter 2 discusses MCAT preparation and test-taking strategies, with samples from each section of the test. A discussion of the interview, and options for those who are not accepted follow. The last three chapters of the book focus on what to expect during the medical school years, including strategies for success. Comprehensive appendices include a directory of medical schools with basic vital information; a list of sources for further information on medical specialties; a review section for clerkship tests and the Boards; and a "Medical Potpourri" of interesting anecdotes from the history of medicine.

Evaluation:

This book attempts to be both guide to medical school admissions and a guide to medical school itself. It covers the basics of the application process while giving the applicant a glimpse at what awaits: lectures and coursework; rotating clerkships; choosing a specialty; and the residency-matching program. This Janus-faced approach has its benefits and its drawbacks: readers gain a more holistic view of the whole process, but sacrifice depth on such vital topics as premed coursework and majors, letters of recommendation, and extracurricular opportunities. The coverage of four years of medical school—while potentially engrossing for premed students—isn't of much use to prospective students. There is a useful chapter on the MCAT, with sample questions, but other sections, such as the lengthy appendix A with its study notes for clerkship tests and Boards, seem out of place. This is a book longing to be two books, with more in-depth, useful discussions of the disparate topics of applying to, and succeeding in, medical school.

Where To Find/Buy:

Bookstores and libraries.

KAPLAN'S GETTING INTO MEDICAL SCHOOL
Expert Advice For Navigating The Admissions Process

Description:

This large guide to medical school admissions is written by two medical school grads and put out by Kaplan (of testing preparation fame). It is divided into three major sections: Part One, "Selecting a School," focuses on the decision to become a doctor and researching medical schools, including 142 pages devoted to in-depth profiles of all licensed allopathic and osteopathic schools in the U.S. and Puerto Rico. Part Two, "Getting In," addresses the application process itself: fulfilling requirements; dealing with the MCAT; writing the personal essay; AMCAS and Non-AMCAS applications; the interview; and an "inside view" of how admissions committees judge applications. Part Three, "Financing Your Degree," discusses tuition, scholarships, and loans. The last part of the book includes anecdotes from real medical school students and grads. An appendix includes admissions worksheets and forms.

Evaluation:

This book has the virtue of being both comprehensive and accurate. The thick, 142-page directory of medical schools is particularly useful, listing such vital information as admission requirements, average MCAT scores and GPAs, types of curricula, facilities, tuition, and financial aid. The section on the MCAT (as one might expect from Kaplan) is informative, though too brief, with no sample questions (perhaps enticing the reader to take a Kaplan prep course?). Included are good discussions of financial aid and the important factors in choosing a medical school (curriculum, location, diversity, affiliated teaching hospitals, etc.). Despite all this, the book has a decidedly "generic" quality, lacking the experienced voice and personal insight that other books offer. It also doesn't contain a discussion of medicine's future, which, due to the changing climate, is indispensable to potential applicants. However, as a basic information source, this book will serve well.

Where To Find/Buy:

Bookstores and libraries.

Overall Rating
★★
Comprehensive guide to the application process with profiles on medical schools

Design, Ease Of Use
★★
Friendly, non-intimidating style

1–4 Stars

Author:
Amy Baxter, MD, & Rochelle Rothstein, MD

Dr. Baxter is currently a resident in Pediatrics at University of Cincinnati Children's Hospital. Dr. Rothstein graduated from University of California at San Diego Medical School, and is now the Vice President of Medical Programs at Kaplan.

Publisher:
Kaplan (Simon & Schuster)

Edition:
1997

Price:
$20.00

Pages:
304

ISBN:
0684836904

Media:
Book

Principal Focus:
Health Sciences

Of Interest To:
International Students

II. Medical School & Health Science Programs

Overall Rating
★★

With few sites dedicated to nursing, this one is worth checking out

Design, Ease Of Use
★★

Needs a design overhaul: cumbersome navigation; no internal search features

1–4 Stars

Publisher:
NursingNet

NursingNet was created by Mark and Mary Carraway. Mary is an RN with PEDS, ICU, and Emergency Nursing experience. Mark is an RN and BSN; he is currently employed in the operating room at a teaching facility.

Media:
Internet

Principal Focus:
Health Sciences

NURSINGNET

Description:

NursingNet is an interactive community site and a web guide; it targets an audience of students and nursing professionals. Among its interactive features are a Q & A forum for discussing issues, a Nursing Lounge chat room, and a web board for students. On the student web board, students post messages on such topics as "most valuable prerequisite," "new nursing student," and "looking for a nursing school in northwest Indiana." As a web guide, the site offers links to other online resources in four categories: Nursing Information; Nursing Student Information; Other Medical Information; and Other Information. Under Nursing Information are links to sites related to specific fields of practice, (e.g., critical care, geriatric care, and nurse midwifery), plus links for nurse practitioners, nursing associations, and nursing journals. The student section features links for student help, NCLEX review programs, and nursing school homepages. (Nursing school links are arranged alphabetically by school name.) Other Medical Information and Other Information include links to hospitals on the Internet, disease references, and search engines.

Evaluation:

One of the most attractive features of NursingNet is the exuberance of its design and attitude. Visitors are not just welcomed; they are embraced by a hostess who cannot contain her excitement at all of the features she has to offer. Punctuated by plenty of exclamation marks and descriptions proclaiming every feature "great," the home page rolls on and on, and on. The design tries to be friendly, but it is not functional. Navigation and format are the main problem areas for this site. The home page scrolls on for five pages and is the only navigation tool; no other menus or links are featured. To move from one section to another, users must backtrack, returning to the top of the home page—which means scrolling again (and again) through five pages of similar-looking headings. (All section headings are in the same color, font, and style.) The content warrants at least one visit. The interactive chat rooms and web boards are well-used; the student web board is a particularly fine place for feedback from current students. Aside from the links to nursing schools and a handful of other sites, the student-oriented "web guide" portions are far less developed than those directed at professionals. Students may want to explore the professional-oriented material, but in general, this site is thin on content and difficult to navigate.

Where To Find/Buy:

On the Internet at http://www.nursingnet.org

THE PENGUIN GUIDE TO AMERICAN MEDICAL & DENTAL SCHOOLS

Description:

All nationally accredited/approved medical, dental, and osteopathic schools in the United States are profiled in this reference book. A brief introduction explains admissions materials typically required by these programs and includes addresses for testing agencies and application-processing services. Program profiles, written in short, incomplete sentences, briefly outline general characteristics of the parent institution, the medical/ health science center or hospital complex, and the medical and dental schools. Information on the library system, affiliated hospitals used for clinical experiences, special facilities, and special programs, such as institutes, summer-abroad programs, internships, and minority programs, are included, together with tuition and housing costs for 1998–99. Admissions information includes required undergraduate preparation and materials; admissions stats, including state/resident ratios; median MCAT and DAT scores and grades; and program ranking information based on a number of sources. Eight indexes (Medical/dental/osteopathic; medical/dental by state; private/public; and combined or joint degree programs) are included, along with a checklist for comparing schools and an application calendar.

Evaluation:

This book is intended as a first source of information for potential medical and dental school applicants. To that end, it is a good basic choice—it covers every program in the United States and lists an impressive amount of data for each one. The parent institution and each program (medical, osteopathic, or dental) are covered separately. Information on the first is quite limited, however; for example, school environment and location are not covered. Plenty of objective information on specific programs is provided, however, from costs and enrollment statistics to National Institutes of Health awards and grants. Application processes and requirements are covered in some detail, including deadlines, fees, types of recommendations required, and specific information for international or combined degree students. This objective information (which is supplied by the schools) will help readers make informed preliminary decisions, based on schools' offering and applicants' needs and credentials. Skip the opening chapter, however. It just glides over the surface, making sweeping generalizations with convoluted language.

Where To Find/Buy:

Bookstores and libraries.

Overall Rating
★★
Comprehensive data on all accredited medical, dental, and osteopathic schools

Design, Ease Of Use
★★
Indexed by discipline, state, private/public, combined and joint degree programs

1–4 Stars

Author:
Harold R. Doughty

Mr. Doughty is a management and educational consultant. He is the former Executive Vice President and COO at American Commonwealth University, VP for Admissions, Financial Aid and Enrollment at U.S. International University, as well other administrative posts. He is also author of *The Penguin Guide To American Law Schools* and *Guide To American Graduate Schools*.

Publisher:
Penguin

Edition:
1999

Price:
$17.95

Pages:
312

ISBN:
0140275150

Media:
Book

Principal Focus:
Health Sciences

II. Medical School & Health Science Programs

Overall Rating
★★
Accurate, but uneven—most helpful for those outside allopathic medicine

Design, Ease Of Use
★★
Programs arranged by category; profiles cramped

1–4 Stars

Publisher:
Peterson's

Edition:
33rd (1999)

Price:
$34.95

Pages:
1,989

ISBN:
1560799862

Media:
Book

Principal Focus:
Health Sciences

PETERSON'S GRADUATE PROGRAMS IN BUSINESS, EDUCATION, HEALTH, INFORMATION STUDIES, LAW & SOCIAL WORK

Description:

This heavy-duty resource includes information on graduate and professional programs in the fields of business, education, health, information studies, law, and social work. After a section entitled "The Graduate Adviser," which provides advice and information about applying to grad school, the book is divided according to field of study. A chapter is devoted to programs in health-related professions, including sections on allied health, nursing, and public health programs. The chapter on medical programs includes sections devoted to chiropractic, dentistry, medicine (allopathic, osteopathic, etc.), optometry and visions sciences, oriental medicine and acupuncture, pharmacy and pharmaceutical sciences, and veterinary medicine and sciences. Each section is broken down into a "directory" of basic information about each program (degrees awarded, student demographics; tuition, admissions requirements, contact info., etc.), cross-discipline announcements, and a few full page profiles submitted by schools.

Evaluation:

Although this is an enormous guide, it offers slim pickings for the applicant researching "traditional" medical school programs in the U.S. Small, "capsule" profiles of the programs in allopathic medicine offer little beyond basic information, reduced to about an inch or less. However, applicants to other types of medical programs, such as osteopathic, podiatric, and chiropractic medicine, as well as programs in optometry, acupuncture, and pharmacy, will find this resource more thorough, as these types of programs also chose to include helpful in-depth profiles of their offerings. One might be hard-pressed, for instance, to find better coverage of programs in naturopathic medicine, which tends to be overshadowed or simply overlooked in other reference books on medical programs in the U.S. In a nutshell, applicants to programs in allopathic medicine won't find much help here, but applicants to different or atypical medical programs will find this resource well worth a look.

Where To Find/Buy:

Bookstores and libraries.

PRINCETON REVIEW ONLINE: MEDICINE

Description:

Formatted as a site-within-a-site, this medical school portion of Princeton Review Online has its own "home" page. From a sidebar menu, users can access all of the main sections: School Search, Get Into School, Tests, The Transition, Scholarships & Aid. In School Search, students search a database of medical schools by name or by a criteria of their choosing, such as location, tuition, and average MCAT. Search results provide a statistical overview of the school, with details on academics, demographics, and costs. Get Into School covers the admissions process, offering articles on interviewing, essays, and completing applications. The Tests sections includes a "Guide to the MCAT," which outlines the structure of the exam and scoring procedures, plus study tips. Stress management and advice on surviving the first year are among the topics discussed in The Transition. Scholarships & Aid looks at financial aid programs, loans commonly applied to in medical school expenses, grants and scholarships. The site also features an online practice MCAT and an online discussion forum for medical students. Additional articles are highlighted on the main page, including "When Should I Apply To Medical School?" and "What's Allopathic Medicine?"

Evaluation:

The Princeton Review sponsors well-known MCAT preparation courses, and plugs for these courses and Princeton Review-sponsored loan programs are woven into this site, though not in an obtrusive manner. The MCAT study tips, test dates, and registration information are routine but pertinent, as is the rest of the content. The admission tips and transitioning advice are standard fare, helpful to the novice but not particularly insightful. The School Search is a good tool for first-time seekers, but it has one drawback: it requires users to "log on" and provide their e-mail address before accessing results. The search is free, but those leery of giving out their e-mail address may not want to browse school stats here. The best portion of the site is Scholarships & Aid, a solid introduction to the varied types of aid available. The subsection on Grants & Scholarships (within Scholarships & Aid) includes a discussion of service-based scholarships, such as those provided by the Federal government in exchange for a commitment to work in an agency, such as the Veterans Administration. In general, students in the early stages of exploring medical school will benefit most from a visit here. Those further along in their research won't be satisfied by these beginner basics.

Where To Find/Buy:

On the Internet at http://www.review.com/medical/

Overall Rating
★★
Useful for students in the preliminary stages of exploring medical school

Design, Ease Of Use
★★
Easy to navigate, but users must "log on" to get school search results

1–4 Stars

Publisher:
Princeton Review

The Princeton Review is a leading test preparation organization; it produces preparation classes, books, and educational software.

A portion of the larger Princeton Review Online, this site-within-a-site focuses on business schools. Sections include a business school search feature, tips on getting in and interviewing, and advice on making the transition. Also included is information on registering and preparing for the GMAT, and for finding scholarships and financial aid. An online discussion forum is also featured.

Media:
Internet

Principal Focus:
Health Sciences

Overall Rating
★
Upbeat look at foreign study options, but lacks credibility

Design, Ease Of Use
★★★
User-friendly layout; clearly written with lots of helpful contact info

1–4 Stars

Author:
Nilanjan Sen

Publisher:
Indus

Edition:
1997

Price:
$12.95

Pages:
158

ISBN:
1890838004

Media:
Book

Principal Focus:
Health Sciences

THE COMPLETE GUIDE TO FOREIGN MEDICAL SCHOOLS IN PLAIN ENGLISH

Description:

The author of this guide explains where, why, and how prospective medical students can apply to schools outside the U.S. He also provides a general overview of what to look for in foreign medical schools, noting their reputation and financial aid possibilities. He cautions students to check the legitimacy of a school's financial division for possible scams and provides tips for finding pertinent information. Chapter 3 describes the process of returning to the U.S. to complete a residency training program and outlines examination requirements, who to contact for help, and how to use the National Residency Matching Program. Next is "The Best of the Bunch," in-depth descriptions of three "top" programs. These profiles include the location, curriculum, clinical affiliation list, admission requirements, tuition, financial aid, student life, recent residency appointments, and general contact information. Also included are comments from students, recent graduates, and school officials. Brief profiles of 14 additional schools, grouped by region, follow. A list of international medical schools, statistics from U.S. medical schools, Internet resources, and appendices follow the school profiles.

Evaluation:

Using charts, graphics, checklists, and a simple design, the author provides students with a positive and realistic look at medical schools overseas. Especially useful are the tips on checking financial aid services and lists of U.S. contact addresses for most schools profiled. However, without an index, navigation is a bit rough, and we wondered how the author determined which schools were "the best of the bunch." Overseas medical schools don't have a great reputation, so the author needs to be extra careful ranking these institutions. We also wondered who the author was. An author bio speaks to the credibility of any resource, and without one, the reader has to wonder. The author's comments on financial aid scams and school facilities are good eye-openers for students and their families, but overall we find this resource lacking, in content and presentation. It may be better than nothing—and there is very little available on this topic—but it lacks the professionalism we expect.

Where To Find/Buy:

Bookstores and libraries.

PETERSONS.COM: MEDICAL SCHOOLS

Description:

Structured as its own site, Petersons.com Medical Schools features a main home page from which users access the three content areas: Medical Schools, Resources on Financing Your Education, and MCAT Test Preparation. Medical Schools includes two searchable databases: one for allopathic medicine and one for osteopathic medicine. Users can search both databases by school name; the names appear alphabetically in a scroll box; simply scroll down to select a school. By selecting a name, a Quick Overview of the school will appear, together with a direct-link list of the institution's Areas of Graduate Study. Users then click on the area of interest, such as Medicine, for a 1998–99 "Program Profile," which features faculty and student demographics, application deadlines, entrance requirements, and contact info. In some cases (designated by an envelope icon), users can send an e-mail inquiry to the school. Resources on Financing features an introduction to federal and private loans provided by the Access Group (a loan provider). An explanation and overview of the MCAT, "hot tips," and sample questions comprise MCAT Test Preparation.

Evaluation:

Petersons.com features fine home pages for graduate, law, and business schools; Medical Schools is the black sheep in this family. The other sections have abundant resources—excellent databases, free test-prep software, discussion forums, featured articles; Medical Schools has but a few crumbs. Limiting medical school database searches to school names is ridiculous. Forcing users to scroll through an alphabetical list, instead of typing in the name, is outrageous. True, the crude search mechanism is less of a hardship for visitors interested in osteopathic medicine, since there are only 19 accredited osteopathic schools. But users looking for schools that offer MDs—of which there are well over 100—need extraordinary patience, especially if they don't know exactly which school to select. The search tool would be less annoying if the results were worth the wait. They aren't. All students get are a few basic stats, and even those can only be accessed through an intermediary page, the list of "Areas of Graduate Study." As for the MCAT and financial segments, don't bother. There are too many good medical school sites to waste time with this one.

Where To Find/Buy:

On the Internet at http://www.petersons.com/medical

Overall Rating
★
Very basic program information on medical schools

Design, Ease Of Use
★★★
Some backtracking required

1–4 Stars

Publisher:
Peterson's

Peterson's is a publisher of education guides and a producer of test preparation materials and courses. It is part of the Lifelong Learning Group within Thomson Learning.

Media:
Internet

Principal Focus:
Health Sciences

II. Medical School &
Health Science Programs

Overall Rating
★
Humorous and potentially useful guide to medical school "extras"

Design, Ease Of Use
★★
Funny, easy to read

1–4 Stars

Author:
Mark Baker

Mark Baker is a published nonfiction author whose works include *The Insider's Book of Business School Lists* and *The Insider's Book of Law School Lists*.

Publisher:
Kaplan (Simon & Schuster)

Edition:
1997

Price:
$12.00

Pages:
196

ISBN:
0684841789

Media:
Book

Principal Focus:
Health Sciences

KAPLAN'S INSIDER'S BOOK OF MEDICAL SCHOOL LISTS

Description:

This book was written as an "extracurricular" information source for students considering medical school. Part One, "Getting In and Staying In," includes lists of schools with the least expensive to most expensive tuitions; schools with "snob appeal" (i.e. with low acceptance rates); schools with special programs in OB-GYN, osteopathy, and plastic surgery; schools with the most financial aid; and more. Part Two, "Lifestyle," includes lists of schools with "Most Eligible Men" and "Most Eligible Women"; "Big-City Schools" and "Schools in the Sticks"; "Crime Rates by Region"; and "Most Annual Precipitation." Part Three contains lists with "entertainment value," such as "Near the Beach"; "Near Natural Wonders"; "Near Legalized Gambling"; and "On the Lollapalooza Tour." The last section guides students to a future with schools with "Nobel Prize Winners as Alumni," "Schools with Graduates at the Mayo Clinic," and schools "Where the Living is Easy," and "Near the Jobs."

Evaluation:

As the introduction points out, if you are a medical school applicant, you have "committed yourself to one of the most demanding, stressful, pressurized lifestyles in America today, perhaps rivaled only by deep-sea diving underwater welders and air traffic controllers." Being human, you probably also want to have a little fun on the side. This book shows you how to figure in such essentials when choosing a medical school. As the author says, "Passion in life is a good thing." This includes not only passion for the medical profession, but passion for other aspects of life, which may, ultimately, make you a better doctor. This book is strictly humorous and does not want to persuade anyone to attend a medical school just because it is located "within 30 minutes of great skiing." But some of the information here may make a difference to medical students' quality of life, making them more well-rounded individuals with a life outside coursework, blood work, and exam cramming.

Where To Find/Buy:

Bookstores and libraries.

MEDICALSTUDENT.NET

Description:

As the name implies, this site is dedicated to helping and informing medical students—current and prospective. A sidebar menu on the home page details the contents, including the two main sections: Premeds and Med Students. Med Students discusses in-school issues, such as courses, while Premeds addresses such topics as Applications, MCAT, and Financial Aid. "Applications" features tips on when and where to apply, plus a sample essay. MCAT covers exam preparation, while Financial Aid provides links to pertinent resources. Also found in Premeds is the site's Medical School Database, which offers profiles and contact information for dozens of schools. Both the Premeds and Med Student sections employ a split-screen format and have their own table of contents. The table of contents appears in the center screen. By clicking on a topic, a new menu appears on the left screen, for navigating within that content area. For example, by clicking on the Medical School Database, a list of schools appears on the left screen. Schools are arranged alphabetically by state; users scroll to make their choice. Chat rooms, message boards, and a bookstore are among the site's other features.

Evaluation:

MedicalStudent.net is one of those sites that looks great—once it has loaded—but lacks substantial content. It is easy to navigate; the site uses its split-screen format well, though it lacks a search engine for the Medical School Database; users have to scroll through listings. Too bad the content is paltry, and loading is slowed by a multiple banner ads. The Database's school profiles are good for finding contact information but little else; the most beneficial MCAT segments are links to other sites; and the advice in Applications is rudimentary at best. Some good links are featured: Financial Aid provides a handful, and links to specific areas of study (e.g., anatomy, biology, genetics, etc.) are included. As for original content, there is only one example of note: the sample essay found in Applications. Supplied by one of MedicalStudent.net's past contributors, a student at Baylor's medical school, the essay isn't particularly well written, but it did get its author accepted. For that reason alone, it is worth a quick look. Unfortunately, the same cannot be said for the rest of the site.

Where To Find/Buy:

On the Internet at http://www.medicalstudent.net

Overall Rating

★

Mediocre content; only a few of the application tips are worthwhile

Design, Ease Of Use

★★

"Free" site clogged with ads; no search engine for database

1–4 Stars

Publisher:

MedicalStudent.net

MedicalStudent.net had its origins in 1994 as the *Pre-Med Companion*, an electronic book. In 1998, two Baylor medical students resurrected it as a website. Dr. Jim Henderson bought the partnership in 1999.

Media:

Internet

Principal Focus:

Health Sciences

Overall Rating
★
Many school profiles offer only the most basic information

Design, Ease Of Use
★★
Readable; profiles nicely laid out

1–4 Stars

Author:
Malaika Stoll & Paula Bilstein

Publisher:
Princeton Review
(Random House)

Edition:
1999

Price:
$20.00

Pages:
400

ISBN:
0375754652

Media:
Book

Principal Focus:
Health Sciences

PRINCETON REVIEW BEST MEDICAL SCHOOLS 2000

Description:

Three introductory chapters describe how to use the information in this book and discuss the medical school application process. The bulk of this resource comprises profiles of the "top" medical schools. Each profile provides basic address, telephone, fax, e-mail, and Internet address information, along with descriptions of "Academics," "Student Life," "Admissions," and "Financial Aid," many of which include student comments, criticism, and accolades gleaned from surveys sent out by the authors. Each profile also contains a sidebar with the school's Gourman Report rating (also found in the Gourman Report reviewed on page 313), demographics, admissions statistics, GPA and MCAT score averages, tuition and fees, financial aid, and overall "strengths," as reported by students on the surveys, and school officials.

Evaluation:

Medical schools are such complex systems that attempts to qualify them as "best" (or even "worst") can be meaningless: The best schools for research? For opportunities in affiliated teaching hospitals? For women? For minorities? In this book, "best" simply means accredited schools in the U.S. This book's unique angle is its student critiques and commentaries on schools. However, as the preface notes, the Association Of American Medical Colleges (AAMC) issued a memo expressing concern about the authors' research; as a result, only about two-thirds of AAMC-approved schools allowed them to contact students. This leaves a large hole in the data; many profiles contain only basic "official" information and no student commentary. The criteria used in the Gourman Report ratings are also never explained. This resource offers some useful information, and the student comments are often helpful, but applicants would do better to contact students on their own.

Where To Find/Buy:

Bookstores and libraries.

MEDICAL SCHOOL ADMISSIONS SUCCESS!
You Can Get In!

Description:

Written by a graduate of the Hahnemann University School of Medicine, this book combines information and advice on the medical school admissions process. It begins with a discussion of medicine and moves on to a section answering "commonly asked questions by applicants to medical school," which includes information about osteopathic medicine and allied health fields. The next section examines the application process itself, from obtaining strong letters of recommendation to writing the personal statement. Studying for and taking the MCAT, preparing for the interview, and dealing with financial aid are discussed in the next three sections, which include a list of common interview questions and the best ways to respond to them. An overview of the four years of medical school and information about residency specialties follow. The "Schools" section presents data on allopathic and osteopathic schools and degrees. A list of pertinent journal articles concludes the book.

Evaluation:

This book suffers from poor editing and strange punctuation, including a distracting overabundance of capitals. Its simple design—word-processor layout and spiral binding—would not be a problem if the content were of higher quality. However, the author's discussion of the medical school admissions process, while accurate, is overly general, offering little more than the standard advice found in dozens of other guidebooks. Most helpful are the applicant questions: for example, "Does my ability to pay tuition at a particular school have any effect on my chances of being accepted there?" The information about schools of allied health and publications on the medical specialties is also helpful, but overall, this is an inferior and dated resource.

Where To Find/Buy:

Bookstores and libraries.

Overall Rating
★
Overly general advice, with only a few genuinely helpful sections

Design, Ease Of Use
★
Poor editing and "homemade" layout

1–4 Stars

Author:
Stanley Zaslau, MD
The author is a 1994 graduate of the Hahnemann University School of Medicine in Philadelphia.

Publisher:
FMSG Publishing

Edition:
1995

Price:
$28.00

Pages:
182

ISBN:
1886468044

Media:
Book

Principal Focus:
Health Sciences

II. Medical School & Health Science Programs

AACOMAS APPLICATION KIT

Non-Rated Resource

Description:
The American Association of Colleges of Osteopathic Medicine (AACOM) offers prospective students a centralized application service for the 17 accredited osteopathic medical schools. Through AACOM's Application Service (AACOMAS), students can file one application, and a single set of official transcripts and MCAT scores. AACOMAS then verifies and distributes these to each of the colleges designated by the applicant.

Publisher:
AACOM

American Association of Colleges of Osteopathic Medicine (AACOM) offers prospective students a centralized application service for the 17 accredited osteopathic medical schools. Through AACOM's Application Service (AACOMAS), students can file one application, and a single set of official transcripts and MCAT scores. AACOMAS then verifies and distributes these to each of the colleges designated by the applicant.

Media:
Internet

Principal Focus:
Health Sciences

Where To Find/Buy:
On the Internet at http://www.aacom.org/applic.htm

AMCAS-E STUDENT & APPLICANT INFORMATION

Non-Rated Resource

Description:
AMCAS-E® is a software program for use by applicants to U.S. medical schools participating in AMCAS (American Medical College Application Service); it can be downloaded at this site (Windows only). Its major benefit to applicants is allowing applicants to complete and submit information required for the AMCAS application on diskette, instead of on paper. AMCAS-E software automates the process of converting official transcript grades to standard AMCAS grades.

Publisher:
Association Of American Medical Colleges

Founded in 1890, the Association of American Medical Colleges is a nonprofit association comprising 125 accredited U.S. medical schools, 16 accredited Canadian medical schools, more than 400 teaching hospitals, 90 academic and professional societies, and the nation's medical students and residents.

Media:
Internet

Principal Focus:
Health Sciences

Where To Find/Buy:
On the Internet at http://www.aamc.org/stuapps/admiss/amcase/start.htm

FINAID: MEDICAL SCHOOL RESOURCES

Non-Rated Resource

Description:
This site is part of the larger "FinAid Smart Student Guide To Financial Aid" website. It comprises three topical link directories. "Admissions Guides" offers links to three websites that provide articles on medical school admission. "Loans" gives a brief description of, and provides a link to, nine lenders who offer customized student loans. "Associations" includes only one listing, "The National Association of Residents and Interns."

Author:
Mark Kantrowitz

Mr. Kantrowitz is a Research Scientist at Just Research, the US software laboratory for Justsystem Corporation of Japan. He is the author of three books, including one on financial aid, and has created several popular websites.

Publisher:
FinAid Page, L.L.C.

Media:
Internet

Principal Focus:
Health Sciences

Where To Find/Buy:
On the Internet at http://www.finaid.org/otheraid/medical.phtml

THE MATURE MEDICAL STUDENT

Non-Rated Resource

Description:
Dr. Powell chronicles the ups and downs of being a "mature" medical student when the average age of an entering medical student is 22. The autobiographical essays cover: Universities and education; Jobs and work-related travel; Initial plans and prerequisites; and Marriage and family. A second section covers First Year; Second Year; Clinical Rotations; and A look at residencies. The writing is personal and inspirational, not analytical.

Author:
Charles W. Powell, MD

Dr. Powell is a "forty something" recent graduate of the University of Kansas School of Medicine. He has a wife and four children.

Media:
Internet

Principal Focus:
Health Sciences

Where To Find/Buy:
On the Internet at http://falcon.cc.ukans.edu/~cwpowell/index.html

THE MEDICAL EDUCATION PAGE

Non-Rated Resource

Description:
This site features a directory of Internet links of interest to medical and premed students. Some of the main headings include: News, Frequently Asked Questions & Ftp Sites; Educational Reference; Medical Indices; Medical Courses; Medical Specialties; Medical Schools; Interview Feedback Page; and Miscellaneous Links. The interview feedback page allows prospective students to browse questionnaires about medical schools completed by current students.

Author:
Gregory Allen

Mr. Allen is a medical student who is interested in "exploring the medium of the world wide web, bringing medical education resources to the masses."

Media:
Internet

Principal Focus:
Health Sciences

Where To Find/Buy:
On the Internet at http://www.scomm.net/~greg/med-ed/index.html

PREMEDICAL STUDENT FORUM

Non-Rated Resource

Description:
A popular discussion area for premed students, this site features questions and responses posted by visitors. Issues include: being a premed (what to do, majors); the application process (reapplying, interviews); the MCAT (Should I retake it? How to prepare?); getting in (What do I need to do?); interviewing experiences; and medical schools (Where should I go?).

Author:
Larry Chu & Bryan Chan

Editors Larry Chu and Bryan Chan are medical students at Stanford; they began the Medical World project to facility communication and exchange of medical information around the world.

Publisher:
Medical World

Media:
Internet

Principal Focus:
Health Sciences

Where To Find/Buy:
On the Internet at http://mednet.stanford.edu/cgi-bin/medworld/HyperNews/get.cgi/premed.html

II. Medical School & Health Science Programs

II. Financing A Graduate Or Professional Degree

The most common reason for abandoning a dream of attending graduate or professional school is the seemingly overwhelming financial burden associated with advance studies. The cost of tuition, living expenses, books, supplies, fees, and travel is daunting, especially to applicants who are still paying off student loans from college.

This is no time to panic, however. Graduate and professional school hopefuls should consider these reassuring facts:

- They aren't the first students to face the daunting challenge of paying for graduate or professional education. Every year thousands of applicants embark on the quest for financial aid, and a multitude of books, software programs, and websites beckon with information and advice on paying for advance studies. We have reviewed plenty and recommend several in this chapter to help students understand all aspects of graduate and professional school funding.

- The federal government recognizes both the value of higher education and the difficulty paying for it. There are many government programs with billions of dollars in grants and loans available to support higher education.

- An advanced degree is often an important step toward a more lucrative career, so most students may be able to take on more debt that they previously considered.

What Is Financial Aid And Where Does It Come From?

The term "financial aid" refers to an assortment of funding programs sponsored by federal and state governments, colleges and universities, private organizations, and commercial groups. It is designed to supplement the financial contribution that students (and their families) make toward the cost of attending college or graduate and professional school.

On the graduate level, student aid generally comes in three forms.

- Scholarships, fellowships, grants, and awards do not need to be paid back. Scholarships are outright awards from public, school, or private sources, which do not have to be repaid. Traditionally they have been merit-based, but some are targeted at specific groups and awarded on financial need. Fellowships are like scholarships, but they generally involve some kind of service by the recipient. Grants are outright awards—no strings attached. Awards are the same, though as the name suggests, they honor the recipient in some sense. Not surprisingly, scholarships, fellowships, grants, and awards are the preferred forms of student aid.

- Loans are an advance of funds, which requires repayment with interest under prescribed conditions. Subsidized loans may offer a below-market interest rate or other preferential financial treatment. For its Subsidized Stafford Loan, the government pays the interest accrued while the student is in school.

- Assistantships are school-based programs, which provide funds in return for some kind of service. They are usually merit-based and are paid in the form of paychecks, a tuition waiver, or tuition cut. Often universities cover a graduate student's tuition and offer a stipend in exchange for teaching or research. Federal work-study funds also may be available, but often they are earmarked for undergraduates.

How Is Financial Aid Distributed?

- **Need-Based Aid:** Most federal and state aid, and a portion of institutional aid are awarded on the basis of need. Simply put, financial need is the difference between the cost of attendance (a figure, which includes tuition, fees, room and board, books, supplies, and travel) and the student's ability to pay.

  To apply for need-based aid, students must submit the Free Application for Federal Student Aid (FAFSA). Financial data from this form is processed to calculate student need. The federal formula considers student savings, earnings during the school year, a spouse's earnings, and a percentage of the student's assets.

  For federal aid, undergraduates must meet strict criteria to prove they are financially independent of their parents, but graduate and professional students are automatically considered independent. That means parental financial data is not considered for federal aid. However, many graduate schools, especially professional schools, require parental income and asset data, and may figure a parental contribution from these figures. At the graduate level, most federal financial aid comes in the form of loans.

- **Merit-Based Aid:** Graduate and professional programs often award merit aid to attract highly qualified candidates. Merit-based aid is common in research Master's and PhD programs, but it is relatively rare in professional schools. Scholarships, fellowships, and grants sponsored by privately-funded groups may be merit- or need-based, although at the graduate level, these aid vehicles are usually based on a student's abilities.

- **Targeted Aid:** Some financial aid is earmarked for certain groups of students, such as those pursuing a certain field of study, veterans, or disabled or international students. Students who belong to a group traditionally underrepresented in a particular field, such as a women in engineering or racial minorities in the health sciences should look into targeted aid available from the schools themselves, the government, or privately-funded groups.

Financing A Master's Or PhD

According to the National Association of Graduate and Professional Students, about one-half of all doctoral and one-third of all Master's candidates receive financial aid.

Certain fields enjoy much higher levels of student funding than others do. The sciences have traditionally received more grant money for graduate students than departments in the humanities and social sciences.

Students considering advance degrees may have received adequate aid from their undergraduate institutions, albeit mostly in the forms of government loans, but many find that their graduate destinations offer less financial assistance.

Merit-based aid is limited and competitive. At most schools, the departmental committee, which makes admission decisions, also decides which students will receive departmental fellowships, grants, assistantships, and internships. Top-tier students may receive merit-based aid covering most or all of their expenses. More commonly, students receive a partial package, and they are required to fill the gaps themselves.

More than one-half of all graduate students finance their education by attending school part-time while working full- or part-time. This arrangement is much less common among PhD-track students, however, because they carry a much heavier course and research load.

Inevitably, many students take out loans to finance their advanced degrees. Loans are helpful tools, but we warn students to be prepared to carefully manage their debt. Many of the resources reviewed here offer valuable advice about debt management.

Financing A Professional Degree

Merit aid for professional students is rare; loans are abundant. Medical, law, and business students traditionally pay what they can from savings or the contributions of a working spouse, and borrow the rest. Even the most attractive professional school applicants are rarely offered institutional aid. These funds are almost exclusively disbursed on the basis of need, although the schools' aid formula may differ from that of the federal government. Only during slow years when the applicant pool is low do schools, particularly second- and third-tier schools, offer scholarships to attract the strongest candidates.

Navigating the financial aid process is easier with the help of the resources reviewed in this chapter. We have recommended several that present a useful overview of the financial aid system and help prospective students create a realistic, workable budget. Some offer advice on developing a financial plan and prioritizing funding sources. They also cover applying for federal financial aid and privately-funded fellowships; researching school-based funding opportunities; apply for privately-funded fellowships; evaluating financial aid offers; and calculating a responsible level of debt.

We also recommend taking full advantage of the services of the career planning centers and financial aid services at one's undergraduate institution. Career planning advisors can help steer students to aid that works for them.

Accessing Uncle Sam Online

The federal government provides a wealth of information and tools online to help students understand and apply for federal financial aid.

The Department of Education publishes several electronic guides.

- *The 1999–2000 Student Guide to Financial Aid; Funding Your Education* (http://www.ed.gov/prog_info/SFA/StudentGuide/1999-0/index.html)

- *Looking for Student Aid* (http://www.ed.gov/prog_info/SFA/LSA/)

Students can also request print versions of these materials by calling the Federal Student Aid Information Center at 1-800-FED-AID (1-800-433-3243).

The Department of Education also has several FAFSA materials available online.

- *FAFSA Online* (http://www.ed.gov/offices/OPE/express.html, reviewed on page 235)

- *The Guide to Completing the 1999–2000 FAFSA* (http://www.ed.gov/prog_info/SFA/FAFSA, reviewed on page 251)

Students can also access this information at their career counseling office.

Other government sites of interest include:

- The *Direct Loan* page (http://www.ed.gov/offices/OPE/DirectLoan/, reviewed on page 242)

- *The Guide to Defaulted Student Loans* (http://www.ed.gov/offices/OPE/DCS, reviewed on page 239).

All this information is consolidated on the U.S. Department of Education's Office of Postsecondary Education's *Financial Aid for Students* page (http://www.ed.gov/offices/OPE/Students/index.html).

The Office of Postsecondary Education also sponsors a website featuring a current directory of State Guaranty Agencies and State Higher Education Agencies and Governing Boards with direct links to agencies that maintain Web sites). The site is found at http://www.ed.gov/offices/OPE/Students/other.html

We urge students and advisors to visit these sites and familiarize themselves with the financial aid opportunities. There is money out there, but it takes smarts and perseverance to find it!

DON'T MISS OUT

 Recommended For:
Financing a Graduate or Professional Degree

Description:

This guidebook, now in its 23rd edition, is well-known and oft-recommended. It is divided into six parts. "Useful Things To Know" outlines trends in costs and debunks common myths and misconceptions. "The Fundamentals Of Financial Aid" defines the "players" in the financial aid process and the need-based aid concept; it walks the reader through the standard federal aid process, with an emphasis on "taking charge" to improve results. "Advanced Moves In Financial Aid" provides suggestions beyond the usual. "The Major Money Sources" explains the roles of colleges, Uncle Sam, and the states in providing money for higher education. "The Big Alternatives" briefly outlines company-sponsored education and the education benefits of military service. The book finishes with 40 pages (12 chapters) describing other aid sources, from scholarships for athletes to community money.

Evaluation:

The authors' writing style is crisp, blunt, and tongue-in-cheek. Their tone helps as you wade through page after page of information on where the money really is (The Federal government, according to these authors). The Leiders help students focus their efforts by debunking various financial aid myths and offering valuable perspective on trends in education costs. The chapters addressed to "fundamentals" are especially helpful, defining terms and participants, and leading the first-timer through the steps necessary to estimate costs, family contribution, and ultimately, to complete the FAFSA. The authors then offer dozens of suggestions to improve results, some obvious, all helpful. Chapters explaining the variety of ways educational institutions, Uncle Sam, and the states provide financial aid are necessarily complex but rich with concrete suggestions. Don't miss Chapter 24, "A Few Words About Graduate School." It is a great source of suggestions and contacts.

Where To Find/Buy:

Bookstores and libraries, or direct from the publisher at (703) 836-5480 or http://www.octameron.com/.

Overall Rating
★★★★
One of the best, most readable all-inclusive guidebooks on financing higher education

Design, Ease Of Use
★★★★
Crisp writing style and good organization make this an easy read

1–4 Stars

Author:
Anna Leider & Robert Leider

The authors are experienced independent college and financial aid counselors.

Publisher:
Octameron Associates

Edition:
(23rd) 1998

Price:
$8.00

Pages:
213

ISBN:
1575090325

Media:
Book

Principal Focus:
Financing a Graduate or Professional Degree

Of Interest To:
Women
Persons of Color

Overall Rating
★★★★

A great way to comparison shop for loans or just see "what's out there"

Design, Ease Of Use
★★★★

Easy to use; loan programs are displayed side by side

1–4 Stars

Publisher:
eStudentLoan.com, L.L.C.

eStudentLoan is a web-based organization offering information on student loans.

Media:
Internet

Principal Focus:
Financing a Graduate or Professional Degree

Of Interest To:
International Students

ESTUDENTLOAN.COM

 Recommended For:
Financing a Graduate or Professional Degree

Description:
The goal at eStudentLoan.com is to help students at all levels, parents, international students, lenders, and counseling professionals locate the best loan for their specific needs. To do this, the site's creators have compiled a database of student loans: government loans, alternative loans, loans in a student's name, and loans in a parent's name. They have "hand picked" 40-plus rate plans from ten lenders. (Lenders include Access Group, Bank America, American Express Educational Financing, Sallie Mae, and Citibank.) To search this database, users employ the LoanFinder. With it, users indicate whether they are looking for a private or government loan, then complete a questionnaire on financial need, time frame, need for a co-signer, and preferred repayment plan. The LoanFinder then produces a list of up to ten "matches": loans that meet the established criteria. Descriptions of the loans appear side by side for comparison, and include details on loan amount, total cost, average monthly payments, average interest payments, fees, terms, and rate. Online applications are available for all loans listed.

Evaluation:
What a wonderful tool! Not only does the LoanFinder ask specific questions about a user's repayment preferences, thus producing genuine "matches," it also presents the loan descriptions side by side for easy comparison. At a glance, users can see which loan has the highest total cost, which has fees attached, and which has the lowest APR. If a loan is particularly appealing, users just click for an online application or go to the lender's site for more information. The LoanFinder has separate search tools for graduate students, parents, and international students, so the results are "tailor-made." (For most loans listed, international students will need a U.S. citizen as co-signer to be eligible.) Plus the lenders, which include Access Group, Sallie Mae, and Bank America, are reputable and competitive. Ah, if only all loans could be found this way! (Due to the lengthy personal questionnaire the LoanFinder uses for search criteria, the entire LoanFinder process takes a little time.) The site also provides a quick introduction to alternative loans and Stafford loans. Comparison shop with the LoanFinder; it's worth the time and effort.

Where To Find/Buy:
On the Internet at http://www.estudentloan.com

FINAID: GRADUATE SCHOOL FINANCIAL AID RESOURCES

 Recommended For:

Financing a Graduate or Professional Degree

Description:

Mark Kantrowitz is the creator of the widely used and highly regarded "Financial Aid Information Page" Website at http://www.finaid.org. This graduate student page is a "chapter" of the larger site and a good starting point for graduate students seeking general information. It also includes pages specifically directed at medical, law , and business students. Three documents are available. The first, "Funding for Graduate School," written by Mr. Kantrowitz, provides an overview of the financial aid process. A similar, though dated document, "What Every Graduate Student Should Know About Financial Aid," is also offered. The third document, "CRAW Graduate School Information Kit," is intended to encourage more women to pursue advanced degrees in computer science and engineering. It includes a list of sources of graduate financial aid available to women in these fields. Links to other valuable "chapters" within Mark's site are sprinkled throughout.

Evaluation:

There is simply no better Internet resource for information on financial aid. Graduate and professional students combing the Internet for background information and insider tips should begin here and spend a couple of hours reading the bulletins and following links. Great up-to-date insights are provided "on-site," and students will benefit immensely from the detailed and comprehensive bibliography of financial aid resources on the Internet. Be sure to check out "Graduate Student Educational Resources" (http://www.finaid.org/finaid/educ/res-grad.html) for links to a dozen sites focusing on applying to and surviving graduate school. Also see "Scholarship and Fellowship Databases" (http://www.finaid.org/finaid/awards.html), which explains, with links, the various directories of fellowships open to graduate students. The FinAid site includes pages for medical, business, and law school resources, which we have reviewed separately.

Where To Find/Buy:

On the Internet at http://www.finaid.org/otheraid/grad.phtml

Overall Rating

★★★★

An excellent, up-to-date source of financial aid information for grad students

Design, Ease Of Use

★★★★

Begin your web search at this trailhead; includes links to most useful sites

1–4 Stars

Author:

Mark Kantrowitz

Mr. Kantrowitz is a Research Scientist at Just Research, the US software laboratory for Justsystem Corporation of Japan. He is the author of three books, including one on financial aid, and has created several popular websites.

Publisher:

FinAid Page, L.L.C.

Media:

Internet

Principal Focus:

Financing a Graduate or Professional Degree

Of Interest To:

Women

II. Financing A Graduate Or Professional Degree

Overall Rating
★★★★
You won't find a more thorough or well-written book on graduate financial aid

Design, Ease Of Use
★★★★
Stories from grad students and insider tips abound

1–4 Stars

Author:
Patricia McWade

Ms. McWade is the Dean of Student Financial Services at Georgetown University and has 25 years of experience in student financial aid administration.

Publisher:
Peterson's

Edition:
1996

Price:
$16.95

Pages:
180

ISBN:
1560796383

Media:
Book

Principal Focus:
Financing a Graduate or Professional Degree

Of Interest To:
Persons of Color
International Students
Women

FINANCING GRADUATE SCHOOL
How To Get The Money For Your Master's Or PhD

 Recommended For:

Financing a Graduate or Professional Degree

Description:
A chapter titled "Can You Afford to Go to Graduate School?" opens this guide to financing a master's or PhD program. Topics include financial planning, managing debt, and loan repayment. "Who Qualifies for Aid and How is Eligibility Determined?" provides an overview of the financial aid process, emphasizing need-based aid. Financial aid dispensed by the federal and state government is covered in the following chapter; included are Stafford, Perkins, and other loan programs as well as federal work-study. "Service-Related Awards and Loans" describes teaching and research assistantships, internships, residence assistantships and cooperative education. Private and institutional loan programs are described, with contact numbers for several commercial loan programs geared to professional school students. "Finding and Applying for Grants" walks students through preparing a proposal. The guide concludes with "Financial Aid for Specific Student Groups."

Evaluation:
This book has become the standard in its field, and for good reason. Here students will find help navigating the often confusing options for graduate school financial assistance. The author, a 25-year veteran of higher education administration, weaves profiles of students, their stories and insights, into her text. The result is a lively presentation of what can be a dry topic. McWade goes a step beyond explaining the process to counsel students about the opportunities and dangers at each step along the way. For example, her first chapter is filled with advice on creating a realistic budget and guidelines for credit card usage and creditworthiness. Current topics such as distance learning, tax treatment of student aid, and commercial loan programs are also covered. We appreciate the author's inclusion of insider tips, such as this gem: Students in the sciences must "have a key to the lab" (i.e., be a research assistant) in order to be in the loop. A wonderful resource.

Where To Find/Buy:
Bookstores and libraries.

FREE APPLICATION FOR FEDERAL STUDENT AID (FAFSA) ONLINE

 Recommended For:

Financing a Graduate or Professional Degree

Description:

Students have several options for submitting the Free Application for Federal Student Aid (FAFSA) electronically. Using FAFSA on the Web (www.fafsa.ed.gov), students can complete and submit the form via the Internet. (Requires domestic versions of Netscape 3.0–3.04 and 4.0–4.03 or Internet Explorer 4.0, and Windows 95 or Windows NT). The advantages to completing the FAFSA online are: you don't have to pick up the form from your school; mistakes are easily deleted and changed; and once you have completed the form, it is instantly submitted, reducing mail delays. For students whose modem or software do not meet the FAFSA on the Web requirements, FAFSA Express is a second option for electronic submission. FAFSA Express allows students to download the complete form, including directions. When completed, the form may be transmitted via modem. You must then print out, sign, and mail in the signature page.

Evaluation:

Kudos to the federal government for taking advantage of the Internet's timesaving virtues by allowing students to apply for federal financial aid online. Introduced in 1997, FAFSA on the Web greatly simplifies FAFSA submission. The browser requirements ensure the confidentiality of all the income and asset information you'll be sending over the Internet. FAFSA Express is a second-best option, slower and more cumbersome. You must download FAFSA Express software to your computer. FAFSA Express requires an IBM-compatible PC to download the electronic form and a modem to send your completed FAFSA form to the Department. FAFSA Express instructions walk you through the application process. A PDF (Portable Document Format) version of the FAFSA is also available on the site for those whose computers don't support an electronic FAFSA. You can print and mail the completed form.

Where To Find/Buy:

On the Internet at http://www.ed.gov/offices/OPE/express.html

---

Overall Rating
★★★★
Techies who enjoy doing things online will love sending the FAFSA via the Web

Design, Ease Of Use
★★★★
Several options available for electronic submission of the FAFSA

1–4 Stars

Publisher:
U.S. Department Of Education, Office Of Postsecondary Education

The U.S. Department of Education was established in 1980 by Congress. The Department is committed to assuring equal educational opportunities to all Americans and administers more than 200 programs.

Media:
Internet

Principal Focus:
Financing a Graduate or Professional Degree

II. Financing A Graduate Or Professional Degree

Overall Rating
★★★★
An excellent guide to managing student loan debt, with an overview of the loan system

Design, Ease Of Use
★★★★
Very readable treatment of a complex issue

1–4 Stars

Author:
Anne Stockwell

Ms. Stockwell is a journalist who financed her education with student loans. Currently the arts and media editor at *The Advocate*, she has worked for *Esquire*, *Rolling Stone*, and *New York* magazines.

Publisher:
HarperCollins

Edition:
1997

Price:
$14.00

Pages:
336

ISBN:
0062734350

Media:
Book

Principal Focus:
Financing a Graduate or Professional Degree

THE GUERRILLA GUIDE TO MASTERING STUDENT DEBT

Everything You Should Know About Negotiating The Right Loan For You, Paying It Off, Protecting Your Financial Future

 Recommended For:

Financing a Graduate or Professional Degree

Description:

The author is a journalist who financed her own graduate school education with student loans. Her book, divided into four parts, begins with a discussion of how to negotiate a student loan "before you sign on the dotted line"; it includes warnings on how loans can backfire and a table of monthly payments. Part 2 outlines the two major student loan systems (the Federal Family Education Loan Program, or FFELP, and the Direct Lending program) and details the history of federal loan programs. Part 3 discusses how all of this affects the student: how individual loans work; what repayment options exist (deferment, forbearance, and consolidation); what happens in delinquency and default; and what students can do to help themselves. Part 4 describes "how to live with your loans," including establishing or rebuilding credit, declaring bankruptcy, getting finances back on track, and the future of student loan programs. Three appendices include a Sallie Mae deferment guide, a directory of guaranty agencies, and a directory of secondary markets.

Evaluation:

Here is a personable and knowledgeable guide to the world of student loans. The author takes us from federal loans' historical beginnings with the GI Bill and the birth of the Guaranteed Student Loan Program, through the Carter and Reagan years, and into the 1990s with the Federal Family Education Loan Program and Direct Lending. In a readable and lively fashion, the author traces the outlines of the federal loan programs, how they work and who, exactly, is involved. Students who borrow money must have at least a basic grasp of the system in which they're taking part, as well as an understanding of the alternatives if they can't pay back on time. This book lays it all out in a down-to-earth, friendly manner, providing an excellent guide to the benefits—and dangers—of student loans. It is particularly helpful on defaults and delinquency, and on resurrecting one's personal credit rating. This book is well worth the purchase price; it teaches students how to manage loans and protect their financial future.

Where To Find/Buy:

Bookstores and libraries.

TAKE CONTROL OF YOUR STUDENT LOANS

 Recommended For:
Financing a Graduate or Professional Degree

Description:

Written by two attorneys, *Take Control Of Your Student Loans* walks readers through the world of student loans. The first three chapters introduce different types of loans, how they function, how to figure out exactly what type of loan you have, and who exactly is holding it. Chapter 4 helps readers make a workable budget, and find out how much they can afford to pay toward their loan. Chapter 5 discusses repayment options, such as standard, graduated, and extended repayment plans, and loan consolidation. The next chapter delineates strategies to follow when grads cannot pay off their loans: conditions for canceling or deferring a loan, and how to apply for a cancellation, deferment, or forbearance. Chapters 7–9 discuss collection methods, how to get oneself out of default, and what graduates of trade or vocational schools should do. The last two chapters discuss bankruptcy, conditions under which a loan can be discharged, and legal help beyond this book. The appendix include forms for recording student loan information, payments, monthly income, and budgets.

Evaluation:

Nolo Press is known for its line of legal "do-it-yourself" books that help ordinary citizens help themselves through such events as bankruptcy, divorce, and business ownership. Readers overwhelmed by the burden of student loans will find much help in this particular Nolo guide. With its clear advice and helpful charts and forms, it take readers step by step through estimating monthly payments, making a budget, and requesting a review or hearing on a loan. It defines such murky legal terms as "deferment" and "forbearance" and explains what to do if you can't make a payment or have already defaulted. The book is excellent reading for anyone in this situation, but particularly for recent graduates for whom the legal tangle and ominous vocabulary of student loans may be overwhelming. Until the loan system is simplified, books like this one should be required reading for anyone with student loan debt. Not only will it help pull readers out of dangerous waters, it will also help graduates avoid future troubles.

Where To Find/Buy:

Bookstores and libraries.

Overall Rating
★★★★
Effective, straightforward information and advice about dealing with loan debt

Design, Ease Of Use
★★★★
Clear writing and sample forms and letters make this book highly usable

1–4 Stars

Author:
Robin Leonard & Shae Irving

Ms. Leonard graduated from Cornell Law School and has worked at Nolo Press since 1987. Ms. Irving received her law and undergraduate degrees from University of California at Berkeley. She is editor and co-author of numerous Nolo Press books.

Publisher:
Nolo

Edition:
1997

Price:
$19.95

Pages:
285

ISBN:
0873373588

Media:
Book

Principal Focus:
Financing a Graduate or Professional Degree

II. Financing A Graduate Or Professional Degree

Overall Rating
★★★
A quick overview for busy folks

Design, Ease Of Use
★★★★
Masterful use of graphics and charts to present information

1–4 Stars

Author:
Ellen Lichtenstein

During her publishing career, Ellen Lichtenstein has overseen the development and publication of many of guidance, educational and consumer reference books. She has co-authored *The 10 Minute Guide to Applying to Grad School*.

Publisher:
Arco (Macmillan)

Edition:
1997

Price:
$10.95

ISBN:
0028611659

Media:
Book

Principal Focus:
Financing a Graduate or Professional Degree

Of Interest To:
Women
Persons of Color
Disabled
International Students

ARCO'S TEN MINUTE GUIDE TO PAYING FOR GRADUATE SCHOOL

Description:

Arco publishes a series of these "10 Minute Guides" to various topics in higher education. As the title suggests, they're designed to give an overview of the topic in twenty, ten minute lessons, or chapters. Each chapter approximates a step along the road to financing a graduate education, beginning with "Going to Graduate School," "Understanding Your Options," and "Estimating the Costs," and ending with "Understanding the Financial Award Package," "Understanding Federal Loan Repayment," and "Paying Back Your Loans." All possible types of financial aid (loans, grants, work-study, employee tuition assistance, teaching and research assistantships) are explained. Prospective graduate students who did not learn the intricacies of the financial aid system as an undergraduate will find the presentation of materials basic enough for them to follow. The author uses charts, graphics and sidebars with word definitions and tips throughout the text.

Evaluation:

While readers of this quick-and-basic guide will not find a lengthy discussion of some of the difficult decisions to be made on the road to graduate school (the pros and cons of attending graduate school, how to create a realistic graduate school budget) the book delivers what it promises, the essential information you need to pay for grad school in a no-frills format. The author does an excellent job of presenting federal and state financial resources to be tapped, and walks the student through the forms necessary for applying for government aid. For those stuck in the procrastination mode, there is a practical chapter on "Managing Deadlines." Although the author covers private grants and fellowships, and preparing grant applications, this guide is not the best resource for information about specific programs, or the art of grant application. Specific commercial loan programs for professional school students are not covered in this guide, an omission making the book less useful for these students.

Where To Find/Buy:

Bookstores and libraries.

GUIDE TO DEFAULTED STUDENT LOANS

Description:

If you've received collection notices on unpaid student loans, first check the notices to see which agency holds your defaulted loan (or call the Federal Student Aid Information Center at (800) 433-3243). Many defaulted Federal Family Education Loan Program (FFELP) loans are held by a guaranty agency, not the U.S. Department of Education. If your loan is held by a guaranty agency, that agency is the best source of information about your loan. (This site contains a complete list of guaranty agencies). Similarly, if your defaulted Perkins Loan is still held by your college, you should contact the college for more information. However, if your defaulted loan is held by the Department of Educaid, this site provides information that can help you resolve your default status. Subjects addressed here include: Repaying Your Defaulted Loan; the Consequences of Default; Loan Consolidation; Loan Cancellation and Discharge; Resolving Disputes; Loan Cancellation Forms; Going Back to School; and Contacting Us (which helps put students in touch with the agency servicing their loan).

Evaluation:

This site is a "must visit" for students in the unenviable position of being in default on student loans. Most of the information is applicable no matter who is servicing your loan, but some of the links are directed only to students whose loan is being serviced by the Department of Education. The site provides some information designed to motivate defaulters (click on "negative consequences" to learn what happens if you default and do not attempt to repay). It also provides plenty of information and advice to help defaulters who want to get back on track. The site describes loan rehabilitation and loan consolidation programs for both FFELP and Direct Loans. Two new options are also explained. The Income Contingent Repayment Plan bases monthly payments on annual income and loan amount. And some students will be happy to know that the Debt Collection Service now accepts both VISA and MasterCard. This government-sponsored site is well-written and thoughtfully designed.

Where To Find/Buy:

On the Internet at http://www.ed.gov/offices/OPE/DCS

Overall Rating
★★★
Lots of practical information on how to get defaulted loans back on track

Design, Ease Of Use
★★★★
A well-designed and well-implemented site

1–4 Stars

Publisher:
U.S. Department Of Education, Debt Collection Service

The U.S. Department of Education was established in 1980 by Congress. The Department is committed to assuring equal educational opportunities to all Americans and administers more than 200 programs.

Media:
Internet

Principal Focus:
Financing a Graduate or Professional Degree

II. Financing A Graduate Or Professional Degree

Overall Rating
★★★
Downloadable software provides a crash course in planning and managing school debt

Design, Ease Of Use
★★★
Lots of niceties, including online loan application

1–4 Stars

Publisher:
Access Group, Inc.

The Access Group is a nonprofit organization dedicated to providing access to education through affordable financing and related services.

Media:
Internet

Principal Focus:
Financing a Graduate or Professional Degree

ACCESS GROUP

Description:

The Access Group is a nonprofit financial institution that provides loans for graduate and professional students. Students who qualify for a Subsidized or Unsubsidized Federal Stafford Loan can apply for one through the Access Group. The Group offers private loan programs tailored to general graduate, medical, dental, law, and business students. Two less common programs are also available, providing loans for students taking the bar exam or completing a medical residency. All Access Group private loans are guaranteed by The Education Resources Institute (TERI), a private, nonprofit organization. Users can request a paper loan application, or apply for loans online. To determine whether a school is currently approved for Access Group's loan program, students can search a school database. In addition to detailing the various loans, this site includes a guide to "Good Financial Habits," tips on what students should ask before they borrow, and a series of pages on Debt Management. Also featured: "Access Advisor," a free, downloadable software program that acts as an interactive student financial planner. ("Access Advisor" is available for IBM-compatible and Mac systems.)

Evaluation:

Many financial institutions offering educational loans have websites; usually, the site's main function is to explain and advertise those loans. The Access Group's site is distinguished by its detailed descriptions of the wide variety of loans offered and the *general* information it provides on financial aid and financial planning. The advice provided in the "Good Financial Habits" guide and the Debt Management series delivers the goods, with no strings attached; these segments are no advertising vehicles for loans. Of particular note is the free software, available for download. There are two types to choose from: "Need Access Financial Aid Service" and "Access Advisor." The "Need Access" analysis program gathers information from graduate and professional students to determine their eligibility for institutional financial aid. "Access Advisor" helps students plan and manage educational debt. With it, students construct a simplified budget, project a starting salary, and estimate monthly student loan payments. It also includes practical background information to help students better understand the graduate/professional school financial aid process. (Users can apply for loans online or they can request a paper application on-site.)

Where To Find/Buy:

On the Internet at http://www.accessgrp.org/ Loan information is available by telephone at (800) 282-1550.

COLLEGE FINANCIAL AID MADE EASY

Description:

The opening chapter provides an overview of the financial aid process, including common myths, financial aid terms, and a summary of the process. Chapters 2 introduces the various financial aid programs, including Pell Grants, Stafford loans, Federal Supplemental Educational Opportunity Grants (FSEOG), work-study, and Perkins and PLUS loans. Chapters 3 through 6 offer step-by-step instructions and advice for filling out the Free Application for Federal Student Aid (FAFSA) or College Scholarship Service/Financial Aid PROFILE forms. These chapters include strategies for maximizing aid eligibility and estimating one's Estimated Family Contribution. Chapter 7, "The Award Letter and Package," helps students evaluate their financial aid package(s) and negotiate a better one. Chapter 8 introduces the loan process and covers details such as deferment of loan payments, capitalization of loans, forbearance, loan forgiveness, defaults, and repayment. "How to Pay for College Costs Not Covered by Financial Aid" briefly covers alternative funding sources. The book ends with a glossary of financial aid terms and several appendices, including contact numbers for state financial aid offices, a checklist for the financial aid process, and a financial aid log.

Evaluation:

Although the FAFSA and PROFILE forms come with an informational guide, it is always convenient (and sometimes necessary) to have additional guidance in answering the questions. Bellantoni, a Certified Financial Planner, has written a comprehensive guide that walks the student step by step through the process, answering anticipated questions and offering worksheets to help with the calculations. His advice can help families complete forms truthfully, while at the same time maximizing financial eligibility. Bellantoni helps speed the process by breaking the tasks into sequential steps. First, gather financial records (checklists of paperwork for the FAFSA and PROFILE needed are included). Second, evaluate strategies to increase aid eligibility (he includes a chapter on this). Third, conduct calculations and research required for the federal forms (several worksheets are included to help with this step). Finally, fill out the forms. The step-by-step approach really helps.

Where To Find/Buy:

Bookstores and libraries.

Overall Rating
★★★
A great book for students who need help completing the FAFSA and/or PROFILE

Design, Ease Of Use
★★★
A logical and sequential layout guides readers through the forms

1–4 Stars

Author:
Patrick L. Bellantoni, CFP

Mr. Bellantoni is a practicing Certified Financial Planner and President of Bellantoni Financial Advisory, Inc. He has been in the financial services industry since 1983 and earned the CFP designation in 1986.

Publisher:
Ten Speed

Edition:
4th (1998–99)

Price:
$16.95

Pages:
240

ISBN:
0898159830

Media:
Book

Principal Focus:
Financing a Graduate or Professional Degree

Overall Rating
★★★
Thorough coverage of Direct Loans

Design, Ease Of Use
★★★
Some information only available in PDF, which requires the Adobe Acrobat reader

1–4 Stars

Publisher:
The U.S. Department of Education

The U.S. Department of Education was established in 1980 by Congress. The Department is committed to assuring equal educational opportunities to all Americans and administers more than 200 programs.

Media:
Internet

Principal Focus:
Financing a Graduate or Professional Degree

DIRECT LOAN

Description:

Direct Loans are a relatively new financing option. The idea behind this "one-stop shopping" site is that students need only complete the Free Application for Federal Student Aid (FAFSA) to apply for their Direct Loan. The process saves a few steps and some administrative hassle. When students take out a Direct Loan, the government raises the loan funds, and borrowers make a single loan payment to the Department of Education for the life of their loans. One advantage is that students do not have to endorse bank checks because schools receive loan funds electronically from the government and disburse to students directly. The government offers repayment options, which may not be available with other lenders, including Extended, Graduated, and Income Contingent Repayment. Online guides are available on such topics as loan consolidation, PLUS loans, and repayment options. The site features two interactive calculators, one for planning and budgeting and the other for analyzing repayment options.

Evaluation:

This website provides all the information students and parents need as they consider whether to participate in the Direct Loan program. To find out if a particular school participates in the program (many in the list are linked to school's home page), click on "Financial Aid for Students" on the home page, then click on "SchooLinks." Common questions are answered in a frequently asked question section. Also included is a glossary for those confused by new terminology like "capitalization." (Anyone who thinks they're referring to upper case letters should consult the glossary which defines the term as: "Adding accumulated interest to the loan principal rather than having the borrower make interest payments. Capitalizing interest increases the principal amount of the loan and the total cost of the loan.") The site is well organized with plenty of menu choices, which allow users to quickly find the information they need.

Where To Find/Buy:

On the Internet at http://www.ed.gov/offices/OPE/DirectLoan

EARN & LEARN

Description:

This small booklet introduces cooperative education, programs that combine real-life work experience with Postsecondary education. Because 14,000 of the 200,000 students currently involved in cooperative education work for the federal government, Uncle Sam is the focus of the author's attention. He begins with an overview of various government and private programs, such as corporate internships, summer job programs, and the federal Student Educational Employment Program (SEEP). Students participating in SEEP earn an average of $8,500 per year toward college costs. Chapter 2 outlines which government agencies employ the most students, and in which career fields. Chapter 3 focuses on Job Information Centers, where students can check for the closest federal co-op opportunity in their field of interest. Chapter 4 discusses summer employment opportunities for high school and undergraduate students, as well as intern and fellowship programs for graduates. Chapter 5 lists agency contact points, addresses to request agency policies and programs. Chapter 6 lists participating schools.

Evaluation:

Cooperative education provides a creative way of making college and graduate education affordable—by combining education with work experience. Author Joseph Re does an excellent job explaining what cooperative education is, why it can be a great investment of time and energy for the right student, and how to access the some 50,000 corporate-sponsored student employment programs. His emphasis is right where it should be, on the federal government and its myriad of cooperative education opportunities. He also includes plenty of direction on how to apply and even provides a guide to preparing a student résumé. Cooperative education is less common among graduate students, primarily because their course load is more intense. Chapter 7 discusses options which may be more appealing to graduate and professional students: internships (such as the Presidential Management Internship) and fellowships. This booklet is a great deal for $5.00!

Where To Find/Buy:

Bookstores and libraries, or direct from the publisher at (703) 836-5480 or http://www.octameron.com/.

Overall Rating
★★★
Excellent introduction to a small piece of the financial aid puzzle, cooperative education

Design, Ease Of Use
★★★
Written to students in a conversational tone; small print tiring

---

1–4 Stars

Author:
Joseph M. Re

Publisher:
Octameron Associates

Edition:
17th (1998–1999)

Price:
$5.00

Pages:
36

ISBN:
1575090236

Media:
Book

Principal Focus:
Financing a Graduate or Professional Degree

Overall Rating
★★★
Provides useful information particularly regarding loans and borrowing options

Design, Ease Of Use
★★★
Excellent design; access information either topically or by one's step along the process

1–4 Stars

Publisher:
Sallie Mae

Through affiliated companies, the Sallie Mae Foundation is one of the nation's largest financial services companies, providing funds for education loans, account servicing to borrowers, and operational support services to lenders and colleges.

Media:
Internet

Principal Focus:
Financing a Graduate or Professional Degree

SALLIE MAE: STUDENT LOAN MARKETING ASSOCIATION

Description:

The Student Loan Marketing Association, or Sallie Mae as it is widely known, is primarily in the business of purchasing education loans from lenders. In fact, the association currently funds about 40 percent of all insured student loans outstanding. Its website offers 200-plus pages of information for prospective and current students and their families. Included are several downloadable brochures on topics such as: applying for financial aid; understanding financial aid awards; getting education loans; and finding a lender. The site includes several "calculators" to estimate essential figures, such as the cost of school, savings needed, expected family contribution (EFC), borrowing needs, and student loan payments. Students can also check the status of their Sallie Mae-held loans through an online account access feature. The site includes frequently asked questions and links to locate lenders who offer Sallie Mae's borrower benefits, such as incentives for automatic payments.

Evaluation:

This website could be renamed "Loans 101" because of the quality and breadth of information it presents on loans for graduate and professional school. We recommend starting at the Table of Contents, then clicking on "expand" to help locate pages of interest. The best features are "If you've never had a student loan before," and the loan calculators. The interactive tutorial, "Financial Aid 101," conveys the essentials of how to pay for school. Woven throughout the site are informational advertisements for the "borrower benefits" available to students choosing a Sallie Mae affiliated lender. These benefits include interest rate reduction for electronic payment, loan consolidation, and graduated or income-sensitive payments. The site offers help on a topic many financial aid resources ignore: how to responsibly manage education loans once you have them. The site is well-organized and easy to follow. Two navigational aids, a keyword search function and an extensive table of contents, help visitors zero in on relevant information.

Where To Find/Buy:

On the Internet at http://www.salliemae.com/

THE GOVERNMENT FINANCIAL AID BOOK

Description:

This newly revised paperback focuses on sources of financial aid from Federal and state government programs. It is divided into three main sections, the first an overview of the financial aid process. This section contains worksheets and instructions for calculating Expected Family Contribution. Sample forms give readers a better idea how to fill out the forms. The first section also covers new legislation on financial aid and a worksheet to help estimate student's school budget. Section II covers Federal grants and loans and include information on such topics as repayment schedules, borrower rights and responsibilities, and the average yearly income for entry-level positions by job title. Addresses that students will need to send away for information on state-sponsored aid programs come next. Copies of the Free Application for Federal Student Aid (FAFSA) and College Scholarship Service/Financial Aid PROFILE forms are included with tips for filling them out. Section III contains this edition's new chapters, offering strategies for reducing loan debts and shopping for loans. The book concludes with a glossary.

Evaluation:

Though designed with college students in mind, this book is an excellent resource for graduate and professional students researching Federal and state financial aid. It has a few advantages that set it apart from its peers: it is current, covers the essentials, and is affordably priced. It contains sections not seen in similar books, such as information on new legislation covering funding for higher education, loan repayment through community service, Internet resources, and an extensive list of state-sponsored aid programs. Each chapter also includes numerous helpful graphics, such as a pie chart showing financial aid sources and the central role played by the Stafford loan program, and plenty of "fast facts" and "quick tips." Several useful planning tools are included as well; these include a table presenting "15 Simple Steps to Financial Aid." Important phone numbers and addresses are listed in an appendix, and additional resources and references are listed throughout the book. This revised edition is definitely worth $15.

Where To Find/Buy:

Bookstores and libraries, or directly from the publisher at: Perpetual Press, PO Box 45628, Seattle, WA 98145-0628 (add $3.00 S/H for the first book, $1.00 for every additional copy).

Overall Rating
★★
Up-to-date information on state and federal financial aid programs

Design, Ease Of Use
★★★
Many helpful tables, graphics, and timelines

1–4 Stars

Publisher:
Student Financial Services/ Perpetual

Edition:
3rd (1998)

Price:
$14.95

Pages:
204

ISBN:
1881199037

Media:
Book

Principal Focus:
Financing a Graduate or Professional Degree

II. Financing A Graduate Or Professional Degree

Overall Rating
★★
Focuses on selling loans, but offers general financial aid info and an Estimated Family Contribution calculator

Design, Ease Of Use
★★
Shockwave needed to download the Estimated Family Contribution calculator; KapLoan info not on site

1–4 Stars

Publisher:
Kaplan Educational Centers

Kaplan, a subsidary of The Washington Post Company, is a leading producer of test preparation materials. Their products include prep courses, books, and software.

Media:
Internet

Principal Focus:
Financing a Graduate or Professional Degree

KAPLAN ONLINE: FINANCIAL AID

Description:

This site has three sections of interest for graduate students: Paying for Grad School, Money Management, and KapLoan. Paying for Grad School details student options, explores eligibility, and explains how to apply. Included are "Focus" pages on Stafford and Perkins loans, plus Free Application for Federal Student Aid (FAFSA) tips. In Money Management, users find advice on budgeting, plus a glossary of financial aid terms. The KapLoan section briefly describes KapLoan, the Kaplan Student Loan Information Program, a package of incentives available when taking out an educational loan through KapLoan. It consists of Application Editing (basically they look over the application and screen out missing or incorrect information that might result in delays); Credit Pre-Approval (a quick indication of whether parents are likely to be approved for a loan) and a free credit reevaluation service called The Second Look, which may assist in reversing a credit-denied status. To receive information and an application for KapLoan, users click on "Request Application & Info" or call a toll-free number. An Estimated Family Contribution calculator is also available for download; users must have Shockwave to use it online.

Evaluation:

While essentially offering federal and private loans for college students, this site and the KapLoan Program differ from their competitors in two ways. First, Kaplan itself is not a lender. Rather, it is an intermediary directing students and families interested in educational loans to a lender. Second, most sites whose raison d'être is selling educational loans offer little information about financial aid in general; Kaplan's site offers more helpful information than most. The tips are not unusual, but neither are they self-evident. Seasoned financial aid recipients may find the "Focus" pages for Stafford and Perkins loans rudimentary, but those just beginning their financial aid research will be grateful for the quick synopses of eligibility requirements, subsidized vs. unsubsidized aid, interest rates, etc. The calculator for estimating Expected Family Contribution is a useful tool as well, but users need Shockwave to use it online, and downloading can be a hassle. Still, it's free; similar software costs $40 at bookstores or on the Net. Ironically, this site's greatest shortcoming is the lack of detailed information on KapLoan; to get the specifics, users must register online or call the toll-free number (1-888-KAPLOAN).

Where To Find/Buy:

On the Internet at http://www1.kaplan.com/view/zine/1,1899,10,00.html

LOANS & GRANTS FROM UNCLE SAM

Description:

The first chapter provides an overview of financial aid eligibility and the application procedure. Chapter 2 deals with special situations, such as divorce, death, and independent status, and Chapter 3 covers "Verification, Ouch!" Chapter 5 begins in-depth coverage of federal loans and grants, and offers detailed information on: How does the federal aid system work? How much is wise to borrow? What happens if I default? What changes in programs can I expect? What is verification and what can I do if my application is subject to verification? Stafford, Perkins and loans for medical training are covered ins separate chapters, which explain how they work and how to apply. The book ends with a discussion of loan consolidation and repayment options, and a directory of guarantee agencies.

Evaluation:

The scope of this short booklet is limited to Federal financial aid, or money coming from "Uncle Sam" in Leider's words. Her tongue-in-cheek style will turn off some readers (she refers to loan defaulters as "pond scum"), but it may appeal to students. This guide is one of very few texts covering the electronic Free Application for Federal Student Aid (FAFSA), the PROFILE form, income contingent repayment options, and other current developments. Throughout the text, Leider offers insightful tips, including this gem from the introduction: "Apply for federal financial aid even if you're pretty sure you aren't eligible because many states and colleges won't consider giving you aid unless you can prove you were turned down for, or have financial need beyond that covered by federal aid." The author packs a lot of valuable information in a small package. Don't let its informal tone put you off; the information is current, concise, and comprehensive. Note that it does not offer step-by-step instructions for filling out the FAFSA.

Where To Find/Buy:

Bookstores and libraries, or direct from the publisher at (703) 836-5480 or http://www.octameron.com/.

Overall Rating
★★
Good introduction to federal grants and loans

Design, Ease Of Use
★★
Tone humorous and informal

1–4 Stars

Author:
Anna Leider

The author is experienced independent college and financial aid counselor and co-author of *Don't Miss Out.*

Publisher:
Octameron Associates

Edition:
6th (1999)

Price:
$6.00

Pages:
72

ISBN:
575090228

Media:
Book

Principal Focus:
Financing a Graduate or Professional Degree

Overall Rating
★★
Solid, basic information on the financial aid process

Design, Ease Of Use
★★
Good for quick answers

1–4 Stars

Publisher:
National Association Of Student Financial Aid Administrators

National Association of Student Financial Aid Administrators (NASFAA) is a nonprofit organization that supports financial aid professionals at colleges, universities, and career schools. Members include 3,000 postsecondary institutions and 260 individuals and organizations interested in student aid.

Media:
Internet

Principal Focus:
Financing a Graduate or Professional Degree

NATIONAL ASSOCIATION OF STUDENT FINANCIAL AID ADMINISTRATORS: PLANNING FOR COLLEGE

Description:

The National Association of Student Financial Aid Administrators (NASFAA) is a professional association whose members include some 3,200 postsecondary institutions. On this site, a series of essays answers questions: What Is Financial Aid? What Financial Aid Is Available? How Is Your Financial Aid Calculated? How Do You Apply for Financial Aid? An online version of the NASFAA's brochure, "Cash for College," is also featured. The electronic brochure includes sections on new tax provisions, which can offset some of the costs of a graduate education (namely, the Hope Scholarship tax credit and the Lifetime Learning tax credit). Also available online is the first chapter of the 1998–99 edition of "The Advisor: A Counselor's Guide To Student Financial Assistance." Though created to advise high school guidance counselors on the intricacies of the financial aid process, this guide is an excellent source of information for students and families as well.

Evaluation:

Grad students who didn't learn how the financial aid process works as an undergrad will appreciate this source of basic information on the nuts and bolts of applying for, and receiving money from the federal government. As with many financial aid resources, this one was designed primarily with high school seniors and their parents in mind. Nevertheless, grad students will enjoy the plain English explanations found here. This site is also one of the few resources we've found, in any format (Internet, book, software), that explains the new educational tax credits. Skip the "Academics, You Can Do It" section, but take a moment to explore the "Application Help" area of the "Financial Aid, Pay For It" section. If you're considering paying a financial aid consultant or scholarship search firm a fee for their services, read the background information here first! We concur that most students will be able to do their own research without the aid of a consultant.

Where To Find/Buy:

On the Internet at http://www.nasfaa.org/DoItAffordIt/publicfront.html

GETTING YOURS: THE COMPLETE GUIDE TO GOVERNMENT MONEY

★★

Description:

This book is essentially a directory of federal government grant, scholarship, and fellowship opportunities, with a focus on sources of money to start or expand a business. The author's purpose is to help readers access federal funds for endeavors ranging from establishing an earthquake preparedness center to conducting biomedical research. Students researching financial assistance for higher education will not find much information on the large, well-known federally funded programs (such as the Stafford Loan Program). This book focuses on many lesser-known education-oriented government programs. The chapter on the U.S. Department of Education covers 173 programs providing grants for a range of activities. Readers will find programs funding international research, nursing loans, and several programs for disabled students. Very few are grants open to individuals; most are funds funneled through nonprofit organizations, institutions of higher education, and state and local governments. A comprehensive index allows readers to check what programs are available across all federal agencies.

Evaluation:

Lesko's guide suffers from two major drawbacks. First, because it was last updated in 1987, the guide describes programs most likely modified or eliminated since publication. Readers can call to check on the status of programs of interest, though not all contact addresses and phone numbers are current. The second drawback is that the majority of programs are grants geared toward nonprofit organizations and state and local governments. To find programs of interest to individuals seeking money for higher education, readers must wade through much extraneous information. This guide will not be a worthwhile investment of time or dollars for most students seeking funds, but it may appeal to individuals researching financial aid for a very specific purpose, such as nursing education, or a group of people, such as Native Americans.

Where To Find/Buy:

Bookstores and libraries.

Overall Rating
★★
Most grant programs covered apply to nonprofits, not individuals

Design, Ease Of Use
★
Lacks specifics

1–4 Stars

Author:
Matthew Lesko

Lesko is a *New York Times* syndicated columnist, author of numerous books, and a regular guest on several nationally syndicated television programs. He focuses on uncovering obscure government programs that ordinary citizens know nothing about.

Publisher:
Penguin

Edition:
3rd (1987)

Price:
$12.95

ISBN:
0140467602

Media:
Book

Principal Focus:
Financing a Graduate or Professional Degree

II. Financing A Graduate Or Professional Degree

Overall Rating
★★
Perhaps the best source of information available on establishing residency

Design, Ease Of Use
★
Amateurish layout elements distracting

1–4 Stars

Author:
Daryl F. Todd, Jr.

Mr. Todd is an attorney who practices law in New Jersey; his legal expertise is in civil rights litigation. He is a graduate of Rutgers University Law School.

Publisher:
Atlantic Educational Publishing

Edition:
1st (1997)

Price:
$23.95

Pages:
325

ISBN:
0965758702

Media:
Book

Principal Focus:
Financing a Graduate or Professional Degree

HOW TO CUT TUITION
The Complete College Guide to In-State Tuition

Description:

In-state students pay, on average, 60 percent less for tuition at state-sponsored institutions than out-of-state students, a compelling reason to learn the ins and outs of establishing residency. Todd's guide provides detailed instructions on how to qualify for in-state tuition. Because laws vary dramatically from state to state, Todd includes a chapter on every state, describing the specific legal guidelines for each. "The Problem" discusses the differences in tuition rates and how residency is determined. "The Four Basic Elements" covers the durational requirement, financial independence, proof of residency, and nonacademic purpose. "The Solution" outlines a "game plan for success" and discusses appropriate record-keeping and procedures. "The Hardest and Easiest" charts the 10 Easiest and 10 Most Difficult States to Qualify for Residency. An Appendix lists public colleges and universities and the difference between in-state and out-of-state tuition at each.

Evaluation:

Anyone who has attended an out-of-state public college or university knows firsthand the dramatic difference between tuition costs for in-state and out-of-state students. Obtaining a new state residency can be a complicated, time-consuming process, but students motivated to make the change will benefit immensely from this how-to manual. Todd writes with undergraduate students and their parents in mind, but graduate and professional students attending public universities can also profit from the information and advice presented in this guide. They will appreciate the practical, can-do approach taken by Mr. Todd. Fortunately, the author, an attorney, refrains from "lawyer-speak." He spells out in clear language what must be done on a state-by-state basis to establish residency and qualify for in-state tuition. Unfortunately, readers must endure numerous stylistic bloopers, amateurish graphics, confusing page layout, and the like. We hope the book's design will be improved in future editions.

Where To Find/Buy:

Bookstores and libraries, or directly from the publisher: Phone (888) 266-5717; fax (609) 927-3278; mail Atlantic Educational Publishing, P.O. Box 296, Linwood, NJ, 08221. (Add $3.00 S/H).

THE ALLIANCE TO SAVE STUDENT AID

Non-Rated Resource

Description:
In the words of the Alliance, the purpose of this page is to "educate the public regarding the importance of federal aid . . . and to publicize the extent to which proposed cuts would reduce college participation." This site offers background information on federal funding, updates on congressional action, and activities for students who want to become politically involved.

Publisher:
Student Aid Alliance

The Alliance is a coalition of 60 organizations representing students, colleges, and universities. It is a political advocacy group whose activities include lobbying Congress to maintain a strong federal commitment to student aid.

Media:
Internet

Principal Focus:
Financing a Graduate or Professional Degree

Where To Find/Buy:
On the Internet at http://www.StudentAidAlliance.org

EDUCAID LOAN PROGRAMS: LOANS FOR GRADUATE STUDENTS

Non-Rated Resource

Description:
At this page, graduate students can learn about the variety of education loans, both federal and private, offered through Educaid, a division of First Union National Bank. In addition to information about the loans, the site also provides Loan FAQs, a Stafford Repayment Calculator (to calculate monthly payments), and advice on applying for loans. Online application is available.

Publisher:
First Union

Educaid, a division of First Union National Bank, has been providing education loans since 1984.

Media:
Internet

Principal Focus:
Financing a Graduate or Professional Degree

Where To Find/Buy:
On the Internet at http://www.educaid.com/eduloan/loanchtg.htm

GUIDE TO COMPLETING THE 1999–2000 FREE APPLICATION FOR FEDERAL STUDENT AID (FAFSA)

Non-Rated Resource

Description:
A companion to the online versions of the Free Application for Federal Student Aid (FAFSA), this government-run site clarifies the purpose of certain FAFSA questions and explains how information should be reported in unusual cases. For specific instructions, students can click right to the section of the FAFSA they need help with.

Publisher:
U.S. Department Of Education

The U.S. Department of Education was established in 1980 by Congress. The Department is committed to assuring equal educational opportunities to all Americans and administers more than 200 programs.

Media:
Internet

Principal Focus:
Financing a Graduate or Professional Degree

Where To Find/Buy:
On the Internet at http://www.ed.gov/prog_info/SFA/FAFSA/

II. Financing A Graduate Or Professional Degree

NATIONAL SCIENCE FOUNDATION GRAD STUDENT PAGE

Non-Rated Resource

Description:
On this site, NSF programs of interest to graduate students include the Graduate Research Fellowship Awards and the Graduate Research Fellowship Minority Awards. The NSF awards approximately 1,000 new three-year Fellowships each March. Other programs described on the page include travel grants, post-doc grants, and the Integrative Graduate Education and Research Training (IGERT) Program.

Publisher:
National Science Foundation

The National Science Foundation is an independent U.S. government agency responsible for promoting science and engineering through programs that invest over $3.3 billion per year in almost 20,000 research and education projects.

Media:
Internet

Principal Focus:
Financing a Graduate or Professional Degree

Of Interest To:
Persons of Color

Where To Find/Buy:
On the Internet at http://www.nsf.gov/home/students/start.htm#grad

NELLIE MAE

Non-Rated Resource

Description:
Nellie Mae's site offers information on the federal loans it provides, such as Federal PLUS loans and Stafford loans, as well as information on three types of private loans for graduate and professional students. Other features include an explanation of Loan Basics, a Glossary of terms, Calculators, and FAQs. Online application is available.

Publisher:
Nellie Mae

Nellie Mae is a national leader in student loan financing and services.

Media:
Internet

Principal Focus:
Financing a Graduate or Professional Degree

Where To Find/Buy:
On the Internet at http://www.nelliemae.com

II. SCHOLARSHIP DIRECTORIES & SEARCH SERVICES

In the previous chapter, we looked at resources that introduce government and institution-based funding opportunities for students pursuing a Master's or PhD and for students heading into professional graduate programs.

In this chapter, we narrow the focus to merit-based aid from schools and private sources, which does not require repayment. Here we use the term "scholarship" to refer to all scholarships, fellowships, and gift aid, which are awarded on the basis of merit and do not require repayment.

For graduate and professional students, this aid comes from three main sources.

- The largest pool of scholarships is awarded by the university departments and professional schools themselves. These funds are "non-portable" awards, meaning they are school-specific and may only be used at the school itself.

- A second source of graduate scholarships is the many privately-funded awards sponsored by corporations, foundations, professional associations, and fraternal, civic, religious, and community organizations. These scholarships are portable, meaning a student may use them at any accredited graduate or professional school.

- A smaller pool of scholarship funds is available from the federal and state governments.

To learn about the first group of non-portable scholarships, applicants should contact the schools where they are applying. That is the most direct way to learn about their funding opportunities. And remember—at the graduate level, most funding comes from the department, not the larger university.

To research the second group of privately-funded, portable scholarships, many students consult scholarship directories and scholarship search services. Scholarship directories are often thick paperback tomes, with small print and a mind-numbing number of program descriptions.

In this chapter, we review many of these directories. The directories we recommend have several features in common: They are up-to-date, comprehensive, and easy-to-use. Many are general, covering the gamut of privately-funded and portable awards. Others focus on funding for specific fields, such as the Social Sciences or Math. Several fine directories specialize in scholarships targeting specific groups of students, such as women, minorities, or international students, and American students considering overseas study or research.

We have also identified some great Internet databases, which feature thousands of scholarship opportunities. The appearance of these free, searchable databases of scholarships on the Internet is a fairly recent development, which has revolutionized scholarship searches.

We recommend a site that contains a huge database, which students access by completing a personal profile including information on their field of study, residency, GPA, and personal characteristics, such as gender, ethnicity, and religion. The computer then searches the database for scholarship matches.

Because these up-to-date, comprehensive, and *free* Web-based scholarship search services are so readily available, we do *not* recommend students pay a scholarship search company to do the work for them. Some of these companies are not reputable, and with a little effort, students can find all the information they need for free.

We also recommend students take advantage of their alma mater's career counseling center. The advisors there are familiar with scholarship search tools and the experiences of other alums. They also are aware of scholarship opportunities available locally and through alumni connections. The larger print directories and electronic databases often do not include locally-based programs, such as those sponsored by your town's Rotary Club or the local chapter of a professional association in the student's chosen field. That's why local advice is so important.

Researching scholarships, writing to request applications, asking for letters of recommendation, and writing essays all take time and, in many cases, yield few results. Scholarships at the graduate level are often more generous than those granted to undergraduates, but they are fewer in numbers and usually have more stringent, highly specialized criteria.

Overall, privately-funded scholarships account for less than 6 percent of all graduate student funding. We encourage applicants to focus first on the government and institution-based funding opportunities described in the previous chapter before investigating privately-funded scholarships.

II. Scholarship Directories & Search Services

Overall Rating
★★★★
Comprehensive and up-to-date source for 1,700 financial aid opportunities for women

Design, Ease Of Use
★★★★
Excellent indexing and clear presentation of each financial aid program

1–4 Stars

Author:
Gail Ann Schlachter

Dr. Schlachter has worked for two decades as a library manager, a library educator, and an administrator of library-related publishing companies.

Publisher:
Reference Service Press

Edition:
1999

Price:
$45.00

Pages:
578

ISBN:
0918276802

Media:
Book

Principal Focus:
Scholarship Directories & Search Services

Of Interest To:
Women

DIRECTORY OF FINANCIAL AIDS FOR WOMEN 1999–2001

 Recommended For:
Scholarship Directories & Search Services

Description:

This large hard-bound book describes nearly 1,700 scholarships, fellowships, loans, grants, awards, and internships designed primarily or exclusively for women. These programs are funded by various sponsors, including government agencies, professional organizations, corporations, sororities, foundations, religious groups, educational associations, and military and veterans groups. The first section lists 474 scholarships for undergraduates; 361 fellowships for study at the graduate, postgraduate, or postdoctoral levels; 69 loan programs; 526 grants (these programs provide funds for "innovative efforts, travel, projects, creative activities, or research"); 137 awards ("competitions, prizes, or honoraria"); and 109 salaried internships. A second section identifies state agencies to contact for information on educational benefits for residents. A third section contains an annotated bibliography of general financial aid directories whose programs are open to both men and women. The final section contains six indexes to search for funding opportunities by title, sponsor, geographic area, subject, and deadline.

Evaluation:

Reference Service Press has been publishing financial aid directories since 1977, the first year it published this title on financial aid for women. The company has an excellent reputation among librarians (the founder and President is a former research librarian) and publishes several titles on the subject of financial aid. While a bit expensive for personal use (its $45 price tag is about twice that of its competitors), it is a topnotch reference tool for women serious about their pursuit of scholarship and internship funding. It is more comprehensive than similar guides, containing not only traditional private scholarships but also awards, fellowships, and internship opportunities. Unlike many similar guides, the number of listings is not padded with non-portable "scholarships" offered by the educational institutions themselves. The section on state contacts is helpful as well. The indexing is the best organized and most comprehensive we've seen. A great resource for women.

Where To Find/Buy:

Bookstores and libraries, or directly from the publisher at: Reference Service Press, 1100 Industrial Road, Suite 9, San Carlos, CA 94070-4131, or call (415) 594-0743. Add $4.50 for shipping and handling; CA residents add 7.25% sales tax.

FASTWEB

 Recommended For:
Scholarship Directories & Search Services

Description:

With a database of 400,000 scholarships, FastWeb's Scholarship Search is one of its central features. To ensure that a search results in the maximum number of awards for which a student is eligible, users are asked to complete a detailed personal profile. In the profile, students enter biographical data about their state of residency, school/program, handicaps, ethnic heritage, race, gender, marital status, and parents. Users give information about their work experience, activities, hobbies, and career objectives as well. Once the profile is complete, the Scholarship Search takes a minute to produce results. "Matching" awards are then listed; students click on an award name for a description. The award descriptions contain contact info (including direct links to the sponsor's home page and e-mail), deadlines, and requirements. There's also a link to FastWeb's application request letter, which the site automatically customizes for users. (Users give their name and address before the Search.) Aside from the Scholarship Search, the site features a cost calculator, tips on admissions and financial aid, and a searchable college directory.

Evaluation:

It's easy to understand why this scholarship search service is so widely recommended. It is quick, easy-to-use, current, comprehensive, and most important, free (the ads are not obtrusive). As you scroll through the exhaustive lists of choices for personal interests, parent activities, majors, etc., you'll appreciate how comprehensive FastWEB's database of scholarships and grants is. The matching process is quick, and the form letter they provide for each award can be mailed as is; this feature is really helpful because it gets students over the first hurdle—writing to request applications. FastWEB also keeps each profile on file and matches it with additions to their database. Remember, however, to pursue private scholarship or grant money *after* taking all the steps to maximize your chances for federal and school-based aid. Many private awards are relatively small ($1,000 or so), so assess the cost and benefit of your efforts before applying. For students pursuing private money sources, this is the place to start.

Where To Find/Buy:

On the Internet at http://www.fastweb.com/, or by calling fastWEB at (800) 327-8932.

Overall Rating
★★★★
Current and comprehensive source of private money matches

Design, Ease Of Use
★★★★
Well-designed, easy to use, quick response, updates available

1–4 Stars

Publisher:
FastWEB

FastWeb was created in 1995 to help students use the Internet to find scholarships for college. Chairman/CEO Leon Heller joined FastWeb in 1996 and led the transformation of the formerly paper-based scholarship service to an online resource.

Media:
Internet

Principal Focus:
Scholarship Directories & Search Services

II. Scholarship Directories & Search Services

Overall Rating
★★★★
An exceptional resource

Design, Ease Of Use
★★★★
Includes thousands of programs, organized into well-indexed chapters

1–4 Stars

Author:
Gail Ann Schlachter & R. David Weber

Dr. Schlachter has worked for two decades as a library manager, a library educator, and an administrator of library-related publishing companies. Dr. Weber is the chair of the Social Sciences Department at East Los Angeles College. Both have written several other guides.

Publisher:
Reference Service Press

Edition:
1999

Price:
$37.50

Pages:
512

ISBN:
0918276764

Media:
Book

Principal Focus:
Scholarship Directories & Search Services

Of Interest To:
Persons of Color

FINANCIAL AID FOR AFRICAN AMERICANS 1999–2001

 Recommended For:
Scholarship Directories & Search Services

Description:

This guide introduces funding programs primarily or exclusively targeted to African Americans (Reference Service Press publishes similar guides to funding programs open to Asian Americans, Hispanic Americans, and Native Americans). Each program is introduced in a quarter-page description. Also included are an annotated bibliography of general financial aid directories and a series of six indexes. The 1,500 program listings are divided by type of funding (such as scholarship or award). In all of the indexes, each program is coded by type. Funding opportunities range from programs targeting high school and college students to those serving postdoctoral students and researchers. Government-sponsored programs are also featured, although the emphasis is on privately-funded scholarships and fellowships.

Evaluation:

A top quality publication from the folks at Reference Service Press! This guide is revised biennially, ensuring current contact and deadline information. The descriptions of each program are brief, but they contain enough information for readers to determine whether they should contact the program for more information and an application. Because the book categorizes programs by type of funding (scholarship or award) instead of by academic level (undergraduate, postdoc), graduate students will have to sift through the entries to find programs suitable to their needs. Although scholarships and fellowships do not play a significant role for students in general, members of historically underrepresented groups, such as African Americans, should invest some time researching the many programs that provide funding for minority students. This book is an excellent place to begin.

Where To Find/Buy:

Bookstores and libraries, or directly from the publisher at: Reference Service Press, 1100 Industrial Road, Suite 9, San Carlos, CA 94070-4131, or call (415) 594-0743. Add $4.50 for shipping and handling; CA residents add 7.25% sales tax.

FINANCIAL AID FOR STUDY & TRAINING ABROAD 1999–2001

 Recommended For:

Scholarship Directories & Search Services

Description:

More than 600 public and private agencies, organizations, foundations, and educational institutions have set aside funds to underwrite study and training abroad for U.S. citizens. This hard-bound book describes 1,106 scholarships, fellowships, loans, grants, awards, and internships offered by these organizations. The listings cover every major field of study and practically every country in the world. Entries are grouped by recipients, with sections for High School and Undergraduate Students, Graduate Students, Post-doctorates, and Professionals and Other Individuals. Each entry describes the purpose of the grant and any unusual benefits associated with it, eligibility qualifications, financial details, duration for which support is provided, and the total number of awards given each year. An annotated bibliography lists general financial aid directories, while five indexes group entries according to program title, sponsoring organization, geographic location, subject, and application deadline.

Evaluation:

The number of funding sources for study and training abroad has increased substantially in the last decade as the importance of understanding world cultures and languages has become more apparent. This comprehensive guidebook profiles a huge number of grants. It is sure to help fund-seekers tap into billions of dollars available for opportunities abroad. The listings are current, as Reference Service Press updates it biennially. That's a good thing, because nearly 75 percent of the funders had changed their addresses, requirements, benefits, or deadlines since the last edition was published. Entries are succinct, but they provide enough basic information for readers to decide to whether to pursue a source further—in fair-sized type that is gentle on the eyes. The book's organization is superb. Bravo to the authors for foregoing alphabetical listings and arranging the entries according to recipient's educational status. This feature, along with five excellent indexes, makes the search for appropriate funds a lot easier. Also unique to this book is a currency conversion table, which allows readers to calculate the value of awards offered in foreign currencies. A great print guide.

Where To Find/Buy:

Bookstores and libraries, or directly from the publisher at: Reference Service Press, 1100 Industrial Road, Suite 9, San Carlos, CA 94070-4131, or call (415) 594-0743. Add $4.50 for shipping and handling; CA residents add 7.25% sales tax.

Overall Rating
★★★★
Comprehensive list of funding sources for study and training overseas

Design, Ease Of Use
★★★★
Well-organized with five indexes

1–4 Stars

Author:
Gail Ann Schlachter & R. David Weber

Dr. Schlachter has worked for two decades as a library manager, a library educator, and an administrator of library-related publishing companies. Dr. Weber is the chair of the Social Sciences Department at East Los Angeles College. Both have written several other guides.

Publisher:
Reference Service Press

Edition:
4th (1999)

Price:
$39.90

Pages:
372

ISBN:
0918276640

Media:
Book

Principal Focus:
Scholarship Directories & Search Services

II. Scholarship Directories & Search Services

Overall Rating
★★★★
A wealth of funding sources

Design, Ease Of Use
★★★★
Extensive indexes and thorough categorization make its easy to find appropriate programs

1–4 Stars

Author:
Gail Ann Schlachter & R. David Weber

Dr. Schlachter has worked for two decades as a library manager, a library educator, and an administrator of library-related publishing companies. Dr. Weber is the chair of the Social Sciences Department at East Los Angeles College. Both have written several other guides.

Publisher:
Reference Service Press

Edition:
1998

Price:
$40.00

Pages:
350

ISBN:
0918276659

Media:
Book

Principal Focus:
Scholarship Directories & Search Services

Of Interest To:
Disabled

FINANCIAL AID FOR THE DISABLED & THEIR FAMILIES 1998–2000

 Recommended For:
Scholarship Directories & Search Services

Description:

This hardback volume describes over 900 funding programs available to the 43 million Americans with disabilities and members of their families. The funding programs serve applicants who are high school seniors, and graduate and professional students. Awards may be used to cover study, research, travel, training, career development, emergencies, assistive technology, specially-adapted housing, and other purposes. The guide also contains a list of state sources of benefits (including vocational rehabilitation offices). Funding programs are categorized under the following headings: Disabilities in General; Orthopedic and Developmental Disabilities; Hearing Disabilities; Visual Disabilities; Communication/Other Disabilities; and Families of the Disabled. Included are several indexes (Program Title; Sponsoring Organization; Residency; Tenability; Subject; and Calendar) to help students find appropriate programs.

Evaluation:

Reference Service Press has been in the business of compiling directories of funding programs for students for two decades. This directory of funding programs for the disabled and their families is comprehensive, current, and well designed. Although not all of the programs are geared toward students (some provide general financial assistance such as the "Kansas Income Tax Exemption for the Disabled," which exempts a portion of the income of Kansas residents who are disabled from state tax liability), included are many opportunities targeted at graduate and professional students. Not all programs listed are restricted to disabled persons or members of their families. Programs that merely encourage applications from disabled persons are also included. Finding a loan, grant, or scholarship to fit the reader's profile is facilitated by an extensive system of indexes and a thorough categorization of program entries.

Where To Find/Buy:

Bookstores and libraries, or directly from the publisher at: Reference Service Press, 1100 Industrial Road, Suite 9, San Carlos, CA 94070-4131, or call (415) 594-0743. Add $4.50 for shipping and handling; CA residents add 7.25% sales tax.

FUNDING FOR UNITED STATES STUDY
A Guide For International Students & Professionals

 Recommended For:
Scholarship Directories & Search Services

Description:

The Institute of International Education has been providing information on educational exchanges for over 75 years. This guide contains listings for 600-plus fellowships, grants, scholarships, and paid internships for undergraduates, graduate students, and postdoctoral students. The awards are not limited to tuition scholarships; they include awards for foreign nationals to study, teach, carry out research, or pursue other educational objectives in the U.S. The award sponsors are colleges and universities, as well as governments, foundations, corporations, associations, research centers, libraries, and other agencies. Some awards are institution-based—that is, they are only for use at a specific school. Many others are portable for use at a wide range of colleges and higher education institutions. Award descriptions comprise contact information (including email when applicable); the purpose of the award; the amount and type of financial support; location for use; number of awards granted each year; eligibility requirements, restrictions and duration; deadlines; and application instructions.

Evaluation:

This book is a gold mine for foreign nationals hoping to study or conduct research in the U.S. Award entries are organized first by geographical regions of nationality or residency. Also featured is a "Worldwide" section for awards that are open to foreign nationals from more than one region or for recipients from anywhere in the world. Indexes provide access by sponsoring institution, field of study, academic level and type of award, amount of support, destination, and any special conditions. The second half of the book contain directories of undergraduate and graduate institutions, with a very brief description on the type of degrees offered, costs and financial aid, and application deadlines. The editor has done an excellent job organizing the information to provide as many practical "handles" as possible. For example, Index V groups awards under headings such as: "Granting Agency Encourages the Participation of . . ." with categories including ethnic minorities, people with disabilities, women, those with economic disadvantages, and underrepresented groups.

Where To Find/Buy:

Bookstores and libraries.

Overall Rating
★★★★
International students will find hundreds of awards

Design, Ease Of Use
★★★★
Well-indexed; up-to-date

1–4 Stars

Publisher:
Institute of International Education

The IIE is the largest U.S. higher educational exchange agency. It is a nonprofit organization with over 600 college and university members in the U.S. and abroad, assisting international students wishing to study in the U.S. or Canada.

Edition:
1998

Price:
$39.95

Pages:
462

ISBN:
0872062198

Media:
Book

Principal Focus:
Scholarship Directories & Search Services

Of Interest To:
International Students

Overall Rating
★★★★
Extensive compendium of grant sources

Design, Ease Of Use
★★★★
Two indexes make for easy navigation

1–4 Stars

Publisher:
Peterson's

Edition:
5th (1998)

Price:
$32.95

Pages:
566

ISBN:
0768900190

Media:
Book

Principal Focus:
Scholarship Directories & Search Services

PETERSON'S GRANTS FOR GRADUATE & POSTDOCTORAL STUDY

Recommended For:
Scholarship Directories & Search Services

Description:
The Office of Research Affairs at the University of Massachusetts in Amherst has been identifying funding sources for graduate students for 20 years. This volume is their most recent compilation of information on fellowships, scholarships, research and travel grants, exchange programs, internships, training programs, and awards and prizes. To be included in this compendium, programs must provide funds for use in some aspect of graduate or postdoctorate study or research and must not be limited to those affiliated with a particular school. A 15-page essay explains the grant-seeking process, offers advice on identifying appropriate funding sources, and discusses the elements of proposal writing. Grants are listed alphabetically. Two indexes help users narrow their search. The first divides programs by subject; the second identifies programs by "special characteristics" of the target audience, e.g., minorities, women, and international students. Grant profiles comprise brief paragraphs describing the program, eligibility requirements, and application procedures, and deadline information.

Evaluation:
Over 1,400 funding sources are presented in this Peterson's guidebook, a remarkable range of funds to support research and education in fields as varied as Uzbek studies, pathogenesis, and remedial education. Funds can be used for fieldwork, course work, summer study, even study abroad. While the book itself doesn't come cheap, the payback can be great—a diverse range of programs is covered, and the introductory text on grant-seeking is worthwhile. The authors explain how to approach the process with a "productive attitude," treating it as a learning experience and a partnership between student and fund sponsor. They provide a detailed approach to defining one's personal funding needs and interests, and matching those needs and interests to appropriate sources of funding. They also offer valuable tips on what organizations look for in applicants, which areas are easiest to fund, and how to market oneself by identifying the sponsor's goals or needs. The text are readable, and the dual indexes make for easy navigation. A very useful guide on an important subject.

Where To Find/Buy:
Bookstores and libraries.

SCHOLARSHIPS & FELLOWSHIPS FOR MATH & SCIENCE STUDENTS
A Resource For Students Pursuing Careers In Mathematics, Science & Engineering

 Recommended For:

Scholarship Directories & Search Services

Description:

This book was originally designed as a scholarship guide for the students and alumni of the prestigious Research Science Institute, a summer program for academically gifted high school students. It has been expanded and edited over the years and is now published for the public. It begins with some hints on searching for funding programs and completing applications. Chapter 3 covers topics like choosing and applying to graduate school, selecting an advisor, and finding a thesis topic. Chapter 4 describes methods for estimating one's "financial need." Financial aid programs are presented separate chapters based on level of education. These include undergraduate scholarships; graduate fellowships; high school competitions; internships and summer employment programs; study and travel abroad; and honor societies and other miscellaneous sources. A final chapter discusses the tax status of scholarships and fellowships.

Evaluation:

Students looking for science and math related fellowships, internships, and award competitions will find this guide an excellent research tool. In addition to providing a comprehensive list of scholarships, it covers topics not found in similar books, including sections such as "Surviving the Qualifying Exams" and "After the PhD." The listings include some general scholarships, but most are targeted to students in science, math, and engineering. Some chapters, specifically "Contests and Competitions," "Internships and Summer Employment," and "Study Abroad" offer information not covered in most scholarship directories. The chapter covering tax implications for scholarships and fellowships provides a good deal of pertinent information for any student who is successful in the scholarship search. The authors can be brief and without nuance with their advice; in their section on marriage and children during graduate school, they simply readers to "postpone these entanglements."

Where To Find/Buy:

Bookstores and libraries.

Overall Rating
★★★★
An excellent directory including insider tips for thriving in grad school

Design, Ease Of Use
★★★★
Well-organized and easy to follow

1–4 Stars

Author:
Mark Kantrowitz & Joann P. DiGennaro

Mr. Kantrowitz is a Research Scientist at Just Research, the US software laboratory for Justsystem Corporation of Japan. He is the author of three books, including one on financial aid, and has created several popular websites. Ms. DiGennaro is President of the Center for Excellence in Education, and has been an instructor at several universities.

Publisher:
Prentice Hall

Edition:
1993

Price:
$19.95

Pages:
325

ISBN:
0130453374

Media:
Book

Principal Focus:
Scholarship Directories & Search Services

Overall Rating
★★★★
Extensive list of graduate school grants over $1,000—worth the effort

Design, Ease Of Use
★★★★
Excellent organization, with five indexes to narrow the search

1–4 Stars

Author:
Justin Cohen, Ali Mohamadi, Gail Ann Schlachter, R. David Weber, and the staffs of Yale Daily News and Reference Service Press

Justin Cohen is a member of Yale University's class of 2002 and on the staff of *The Yale Daily News*. Ali Mohamadi is a Yale graduate and former sports editor of *The Yale Daily News*. Gail Ann Schlachter is President of Reference Service Press, a former library administrator, and author of numerous award-winning reference books, as is R. David Weber. Weber is also Reference Service Press's chief editor.

Publisher:
Kaplan Educational Centers and Simon & Schuster

Edition:
1999

Price:
$25.00

Pages:
482

ISBN:
0684862816

Media:
Book

Principal Focus:
Scholarship Directories & Search Services

YALE DAILY NEWS GUIDE TO FELLOWSHIPS & GRANTS

 Recommended For:
Scholarship Directories & Search Services

Description:
Kaplan has combined the resources of *The Yale Daily News* (the oldest college daily paper in the U.S.) and Reference Service Press (the leading authority on fellowships and grants) to produce this guide for graduate students. To be included in the list of nearly 2,000 funding opportunities, grants and fellowships must be "portable," worth more than $1,000, and not require repayment. The directory features short descriptions of fellowships, grants, forgivable loans, loan repayment programs, competitions, and awards for college seniors and graduates, currently enrolled grad students, returning students, and graduate students at all levels of training. Programs are divided into two categories: study and training, and research and creative activities. Five indexes help readers further narrow the search by subject, residency, tenability, deadline, and sponsoring organization. *The Yale Daily News* staff provides introductory chapters on the application process, explaining how to determine eligibility, identify research grants, and narrow the search. They also offer advice on the application and the interview.

Evaluation:
Kaplan always offers a satisfaction guarantee on their books, and in this case, few readers will want to take them up on it. By combining the writing skills of *The Yale Daily News* reporters and the award-winning financial aid database of Reference Service Press, they've created a winner. The writing is lively and hip, sprinkled with quotes from grant winners, and full of good advice for the application process (includes a list of the best sites for grant and fellowship listings on the Internet). The program entries—while short—cover the basics needed to determine whether a grant is worth pursuing, and there are plenty of them. By focusing only on grants for graduate students, and skipping over smaller grants, which are hardly worth the application time and effort, and school-specific grants, the editors have created an effective guide for fund-seekers of the biggest and best bucks. The book is also easy to use—with its two-part organization based on purpose of the awards, and the five indexes that follow. This setup makes for quick and easy navigation, although the type used in the program entries is tiny and hard on the eyes.

Where To Find/Buy:
Bookstores and libraries.

GRADUATE STUDENT'S COMPLETE SCHOLARSHIP BOOK

 Recommended For:
Scholarship Directories & Search Services

Description:

Brought to us by the folks who have created and maintained the free, Internet-based scholarship search FastWeb (http://www.fastweb.com, reviewed on page 257), this scholarship guide contains 1,100-plus sources of funding representing more than 27,000 awards. The listings include both privately funded, portable (meaning they can be used at any accredited school) funding programs, and non-portable, school-specific funding opportunities. Included are awards for professional degrees in law, medicine, nursing, business and others. Other funding programs support a Master's, PhD, or postdoctoral study in academic graduate programs. The programs are listed in alphabetical order by program name, with descriptive icons to the side of the title. These icons represent major fields of study (education, business, fine arts, etc.) and "special criteria," such as disability, gender, ethnicity, GPA range, and religion. Indexes list awards by field of study, special criteria, and school.

Evaluation:

The primary advantage of this book is its exclusive focus on funding opportunities for graduate/professional students. Consulting one of the large scholarship directories that mix programs for undergraduates with those for graduate students can be frustrating. The icon system used in Sourcebooks' scholarship directories makes skimming for programs of interest easier, although paper-based scholarship directories will never be as easy to search as a well-constructed electronic database. One clear advantage of this guide is its freshness; because program deadlines, eligibility requirements and award amounts change frequently, it is essential to have an up-to-date database. As always, students must realize that the scholarships, fellowships, and awards described in such guides make up just a small portion of the grad/professional student funding picture. Students should research department- and government-sponsored funding, too.

Where To Find/Buy:

Bookstores and libraries.

Overall Rating
★★★★
Current and comprehensive

Design, Ease Of Use
★★★
Icons make skimming a breeze

1–4 Stars

Publisher:
Sourcebooks

Edition:
1998

Price:
$18.95

Pages:
177

ISBN:
157071195X

Media:
Book

Principal Focus:
Scholarship Directories & Search Services

II. Scholarship Directories & Search Services

Overall Rating
★★★
Hundreds of awards for study and research abroad

Design, Ease Of Use
★★★★
Well-indexed, with plenty of detail

1–4 Stars

Publisher:
Institute of International Education

The IIE is the largest U.S. higher educational exchange agency. It is a nonprofit organization with over 600 college and university members in the U.S. and abroad, assisting international students wishing to study in the U.S. or Canada.

Edition:
1996

Price:
$39.95

Pages:
280

ISBN:
0872062201

Media:
Book

Principal Focus:
Scholarship Directories & Search Services

FINANCIAL RESOURCES FOR INTERNATIONAL STUDY
A Guide For US Nationals

 Recommended For:
Scholarship Directories & Search Services

Description:

This guide contains listings for nearly 700 fellowships, grants, scholarships, and paid internships for undergraduates, graduate students, postdoctoral students, and professionals who wish to study or conduct research abroad. Information is based on a survey of 10,000 award-granting agencies in the US and overseas, conducted in 1995–1996 by the Institute of International Education. The guide is designed as a preliminary search tool. The editors advise readers to contact the administering agency for complete, and final, information. Award entries are first organized by geographical region, and within these regional sections, alphabetically by the name of the administering agency. A "Worldwide" section features awards that are "active" in more than one region, or "portable." The introductory text provides specific information on how to use the guide and how to plan overseas study and research, as well as general information on financial aid for overseas purposes. Award descriptions comprise contact information; the purpose of the award; the amount and type of financial support; location for use; number of awards granted each year; eligibility requirements; and application instructions. Seven indexes follow the award entries.

Evaluation:

For those heading overseas to study or conduct research, this guide is a wonderful first stop. It is informative and easy to use—with multiple pathways to the short but pithy award descriptions. Unlike many directories packed with number-heavy entries and little else, this guide provides real content in its introductory material. The editors cover various levels of study—from undergraduates to professionals and artists—as well as internships, work abroad opportunities, and traineeships. The extensive bibliography of related publications and websites is another big plus, with links to plenty of additional funding opportunities. For those in the brainstorming stage, this guide is a valuable tool with plenty of practical and easy-to-use features.

Where To Find/Buy:

Bookstores and libraries, or directly from the Institute of International Education at IIE, PO Box 371, Annapolis Junction, MD 20701-0371. (Handling charges are $4 per book for U.S. addresses; $16 per book outside the U.S., $8 each additional book).

MONEY FOR GRADUATE STUDENTS IN THE SOCIAL SCIENCES 1998–2000

 Recommended For:

Scholarship Directories & Search Services

Description:

Reference Service Press is known for its series of directories of funding programs for graduate students. This hardback volume covers nearly 1,000 funding programs for students researching or studying fields, such as accounting, advertising, criminology, economics, education, geography, law, management, political science, psychology, sociology, and tourism. Programs are presented in two sections, "Study and Training" and "Research and Creative Activities." Each quarter-page program description provides the basic information needed to contact the sponsor for details and an application. Brief paragraphs describe the program's purpose and eligibility. Financial data, duration, and deadlines are also covered. An additional chapter on state sources of information on educational benefits is included. The book concludes with a series of indexes to help students locate programs of interest.

Evaluation:

Reference Service Press, the publisher of this directory, has cured one of the biggest headaches in the search for funding. By narrowing the list of programs to a fairly small and specific subset (those open to graduate students in the social sciences), the publisher reduces the time and energy spent searching for relevant programs. As with all their books, Reference Service Press has done an excellent job of organizing and presenting information. Graduate students should realize, however, that a large portion of the funding available for them is not covered in this book. This directory lists only portable programs, those funding opportunities that can be used for study at practically any grad school. Much of the money for study in the social sciences is awarded by the institutions themselves for study and research in their programs. While this directory is an excellent resource for researching funding available from outside sources, students should first consider funding programs sponsored by the school they will attend.

Where To Find/Buy:

Bookstores and libraries, or directly from the publisher at: Reference Service Press, 1100 Industrial Road, Suite 9, San Carlos, CA 94070-4131, or call (415) 594-0743. Add $4.50 for shipping and handling; CA residents add 7.25% sales tax.

Overall Rating
★★★
A comprehensive list of portable funding programs

Design, Ease Of Use
★★★★
Clear, current, and comprehensive

1–4 Stars

Author:
Gail Ann Schlachter & R. David Weber

Dr. Schlachter has worked for two decades as a library manager, a library educator, and an administrator of library-related publishing companies. Dr. Weber is the chair of the Social Sciences Department at East Los Angeles College. Both have written several other guides.

Publisher:
Reference Service Press

Edition:
1998

Price:
$45.00

Pages:
330

ISBN:
0918276705

Media:
Book

Principal Focus:
Scholarship Directories & Search Services

Overall Rating
★★★
A good place to begin the hunt for fellowships

Design, Ease Of Use
★★★
Arranging programs by field of study seems to make more sense

1–4 Stars

Author:
Gail Ann Schlachter &
R. David Weber

Dr. Schlachter has worked for two decades as a library manager, a library educator, and an administrator of library-related publishing companies. Dr. Weber is the chair of the Social Sciences Department at East Los Angeles College. Both have written several other guides.

Publisher:
Reference Service Press

Edition:
1998

Price:
$45.00

Pages:
418

ISBN:
0918276691

Media:
Book

Principal Focus:
Scholarship Directories & Search Services

MONEY FOR GRADUATE STUDENTS IN THE SCIENCES 1998–2000

 Recommended For:
Scholarship Directories & Search Services

Description:

This hardback directory describes some 1,300 funding opportunities for research and study in scientific fields, such as agriculture, astronomy, automation, biology, chemistry, dentistry, engineering, environment, geology, genetics, mathematics, medicine, nursing, nutrition, pharmacology, physics, technology, and zoology. The types of funding programs described include fellowships, grants, awards, loans, and traineeships. Each funding program is described in approximately a quarter of a page, with contact names, addresses, and phone numbers included. The program's purpose, eligibility, financial data, duration, limitations, number awarded, and deadline are also included when appropriate. Additional chapters on state sources of educational funding and information, and an annotated bibliography of financial aid directories are also included. The book concludes with a series of six indexes.

Evaluation:

This directory describes a wide range of funding programs, from large government-sponsored grants to small, very specific awards (such as the Ralph W. Stone Award sponsored by the National Speleological Society for funding of cave-related thesis research). All of the programs are "portable," which means they can be applied to study at practically any U.S. graduate school. Therefore, although this is a good resource to research portable funding programs, students are advised to research funding opportunities sponsored by the school and department where they are attending, as a significant portion of funding for graduate students in the sciences comes from the colleges themselves. Readers may be frustrated because funding programs are not categorized by field of study, but rather by type of funding. This means readers will have to scan all of the entries listed in the subject index, then flip back through the body of the book, to find programs tailored to students in their field.

Where To Find/Buy:

Bookstores and libraries, or directly from the publisher at: Reference Service Press, 1100 Industrial Road, Suite 9, San Carlos, CA 94070-4131, or call (415) 594-0743. Add $4.50 for shipping and handling; CA residents add 7.25% sales tax.

DIRECTORY OF PRIVATE SCHOLARSHIPS & GRANTS

Description:

This directory contains 3,000 listings of scholarships, grants, competitions, fellowships, internships, and loans. Readers search for awards using an indexing system categorized by: field of interest, state of residence, memberships and activities, student or family employment, and other personal characteristics. The "field of interest" index is further indexed designating what year in school a student must be in to meet eligibility requirements. Each entry includes a description of the award, eligibility and application requirements, and contact information. This directory also contains hints and facts about the financial aid application process in general and provides examples of inquiry letters and essays required for most scholarship competitions. Student Financial Services recommends students first contact organizations to request application materials before sending letter of intent.

Evaluation:

This well-indexed database of financial sources will save students time and money. Rather than blindly sending application after application, readers can narrow their search to a few good matches. Unlike many large directories, this resource is laid out in a readable font on fairly sturdy paper. Finally someone considers the reader's eyesight! And cross-referencing saves readers a lot of time digging through irrelevant resources. While the majority of listings are for high school and undergraduate students, many serve graduate students, and a few are earmarked for postdoctoral and vocational education. Financial aid advisors will appreciate this thorough guide, as will the students they advise. Remember, however, that students should thoroughly research government aid programs before beginning the search for private funding.

Where To Find/Buy:

Order direct from Student Financial Services, P.O. Box 30414, Lansing, MI 48909-7914 or at (517) 324-3100 during business hours.

Overall Rating
★★★
Well-indexed financial aid directory

Design, Ease Of Use
★★★★
Easy-to-read format; great cross-referencing

1–4 Stars

Author:
Student Financial Services

Publisher:
American Collegiate Media

Edition:
6th (1998)

Pages:
601

Media:
Book

Principal Focus:
Scholarship Directories & Search Services

Overall Rating
★★★
Great resource on funding for travel/study abroad

Design, Ease Of Use
★★★★
Careful attention to detail marks this and other RSP books

1–4 Stars

Author:
Gail Ann Schlachter &
R. David Weber

Dr. Schlachter has worked for two decades as a library manager, a library educator, and an administrator of library-related publishing companies. Dr. Weber is the chair of the Social Sciences Department at East Los Angeles College. Both have written several other guides.

Publisher:
Reference Service Press

Edition:
1999

Price:
$45.00

Pages:
450

ISBN:
0918276632

Media:
Book

Principal Focus:
Scholarship Directories & Search Services

FINANCIAL AID FOR RESEARCH & CREATIVE ACTIVITIES ABROAD 1999–2001

Description:

The heart of this book is a directory of scholarships, fellowships, loans, grants, awards, internships, work experience programs, and on-the-job training opportunities for research, study, and "creative" activities abroad. Included are well-known and competitive programs, such as the Fulbright Teaching Program, and lesser-known but substantial programs, such as the Louise Wallace Hackney Fellowship for the Study of Chinese Art, which awards $8,000 per year for travel or translation into English of works on the subject of Chinese art. Contact addresses and phone numbers, as well as brief descriptions of on program eligibility, purpose and special features are included. Programs are presented in relevant chapters targeting high school/undergraduates, graduate students, post-docs, and professionals/others. Extensive indexes help readers access programs by area of study, geography, and other factors.

Evaluation:

Each year thousands of graduate students study or conduct research abroad, often at great expense. There are many programs sponsored by government, academic, civic, international, and fraternal groups for study and research abroad, but locating information on these programs can be difficult. Each year many hefty scholarship directories boasting of thousands of scholarships are printed, but students must wade through literally thousands of entries to find the handful of scholarship programs earmarked for study or research abroad. This guide is the only one of its kind that we have found. It is a treasure trove of information and easy to navigate. Programs are presented in chapters for graduate students, post-docs, etc., making finding applicable programs even easier. Considering the price, we suggest checking your library before purchasing.

Where To Find/Buy:

Bookstores and libraries, or directly from the publisher at: Reference Service Press, 1100 Industrial Road, Suite 9, San Carlos, CA 94070-4131, or call (415) 594-0743. Add $4.50 for shipping and handling; CA residents add 7.25% sales tax.

FINANCIAL AID FOR VETERANS, MILITARY PERSONNEL & THEIR DEPENDENTS 1998–2000

Description:

This product addresses the needs of a broad population: 23 million wartime veterans, 5 million peacetime veterans, 3 million active duty military personnel, and millions of their dependents. Numerous government, civic, community, and fraternal groups have developed scholarship programs to reward members of these groups. This guide describes nearly 1,000 such programs. Each program listing includes contact information and a brief description of the purpose, eligibility, financial data, special features, numbers awarded, and deadlines. Entries are grouped by type of program (e.g., scholarship, fellowship, or award) and recipient (veterans, military personnel, and their dependents). Programs are further subdivided in a series of indexes. A calendar index is included so "fundseekers" working with specific time constraints can locate programs by their deadline. Other chapters cover state sources of information on benefits and an annotated bibliography of general financial aid directories.

Evaluation:

When searching for graduate scholarships, fellowships, and other privately-funded study grants, students are well advised to use resources that are as specific as possible. There are plenty of general guides, but for veterans, military personnel, and their dependents, this directory is an excellent source of information. Its major drawback is that the programs are open to a wide range of study levels, from high school to postdoctoral study. Thus graduate students have some sifting to do. However, given the overall high quality of all Reference Service Press scholarship directories, students will want to comb through this guide to find valuable programs of interest.

Where To Find/Buy:

Bookstores and libraries, or directly from the publisher at: Reference Service Press, 1100 Industrial Road, Suite 9, San Carlos, CA 94070-4131, or call (415) 594-0743. Add $4.50 for shipping and handling; CA residents add 7.25% sales tax.

Overall Rating
★★★
A worthy resource; one of the best for this readership

Design, Ease Of Use
★★★★
Organized, detailed, and up to date

1–4 Stars

Author:
Gail Ann Schlachter & R. David Weber

Dr. Schlachter has worked for two decades as a library manager, a library educator, and an administrator of library-related publishing companies. Dr. Weber is the chair of the Social Sciences Department at East Los Angeles College. Both have written several other guides.

Publisher:
Reference Service Press

Edition:
1998

Price:
$40.00

Pages:
400

ISBN:
0918276667

Media:
Book

Principal Focus:
Scholarship Directories & Search Services

Overall Rating
★★★
A wide range of programs and sponsors

Design, Ease Of Use
★★★★
Easy to locate programs of interest

1–4 Stars

Author:
Gail Ann Schlachter &
R. David Weber

Dr. Schlachter has worked for two decades as a library manager, a library educator, and an administrator of library-related publishing companies. Dr. Weber is the chair of the Social Sciences Department at East Los Angeles College. Both have written several other guides.

Publisher:
Reference Service Press

Edition:
1st (1996)

Price:
$37.50

Pages:
298

ISBN:
0918276314

Media:
Book

Principal Focus:
Scholarship Directories & Search Services

MONEY FOR GRADUATE STUDENTS IN THE HUMANITIES 1996–98

Description:

In its first edition, this hardback directory contains information on some 900 fellowships, grants, awards, loans, traineeships and other funding opportunities for students in the Humanities. (Similar books are available for graduate students in the sciences and social sciences. These are reviewed on page 268 and page 267 respectively.) The funding programs are targeted to students researching or studying the fields of: architecture, art, communications, dance, design, film making, history, journalism, languages, literature, music, mythology, performing arts, philosophy, photography, religion, sculpture and writing. Programs are divided into two sections: "Study and Training" and "Research and Creative Activities." Chapters on state sources of information on educational benefits and a "Financial Aid Bookshelf" are also included. The book concludes with a series of six indexes, including listings by program title, sponsoring organization, residency, tenability, subject, and deadline.

Evaluation:

Graduate students in the humanities who have had tried to sift through larger, general scholarship directories will appreciate the time saved by having a volume devoted to their specialties. No more flipping through page after page of funding programs aimed at biologists and engineers—art history scholars, this one is for you! Take note, however, that the programs included here are limited to portable funding opportunities. These are generally fellowships and awards sponsored by the government or foundations for study at practically any graduate school in the U.S. Readers may be fortunate enough to find a program of interest within the listings, but keep in mind that these types of funding programs represent a very small proportion of the overall funding sources for graduate study in the humanities. In addition to checking this resources, be sure to explore funding available from the school you are attending as funding provided by the colleges and universities themselves is not included.

Where To Find/Buy:

Bookstores and libraries, or directly from the publisher at: Reference Service Press, 1100 Industrial Road, Suite 9, San Carlos, CA 94070-4131, or call (415) 594-0743. Add $4.50 for shipping and handling; CA residents add 7.25% sales tax.

AMERICAN JOURNALISM REVIEW NEWSLINK
Special Section On Awards, Grants And Scholarships

Description:

This site, developed by the *American Journalism Review*, lists awards, grants, fellowships, and scholarships. It is "published" each year in the October issue. Many of the competitions are annual events; if the deadline has passed, readers are encouraged to prepare for the next year. Most of the programs listed are of interest to students either practicing as a journalist or pursing a career in the media. The page lists approximately 50 financial aid opportunities with links to a longer description of each program. Many awards are for a particular kind of journalistic effort: for example, the Pro Football Writers' Association sponsors scholarships for Sports Journalism. Awards for civic journalism are among the opportunities available.

Evaluation:

Graduate and professional students interested in careers in broadcast, radio, online, and print journalism will find much of interest at this website. Included are mid-career programs for students already established in their career, as well as programs designed to attract talented students to journalism-related fields. Readers can look over a list of approximately 50 listings, then hit the link to a longer description of each program. The site could be improved by supporting links directly to each of the sources. As it works now, users must write down the contact address and send for more information and/or an application via snail mail. The editors have done a good job of selecting awards that appeal to a large number of applicants and offer a significant financial opportunity. A printed version of this online guide is available (Send $4.95 check or money order to AJR Awards Issue, University of Maryland, 1117 Journalism Building, College Park, MD 20742-7111. For addresses outside North America, send $6.50 U.S. currency).

Where To Find/Buy:

On the Internet at http://ajr.newslink.org/ajraw.html

Overall Rating
★★★
Many interesting opportunities are described

Design, Ease Of Use
★★★
Awards listed on one page, with links to in-depth descriptions of each program

1–4 Stars

Publisher:
American Journalism Review

American Journal Review magazine was formerly known as *Washington Journal Review*. AJR Newslink is a joint venture of *American Journal Review* magazine and the Newslink Association, an online research and consulting firm.

Media:
Internet

Principal Focus:
Scholarship Directories & Search Services

Overall Rating
★★★
One of the better free searches on the Web

Design, Ease Of Use
★★★
Lots of bells and whistles make this search fun to use

1–4 Stars

Publisher:
Universal Algorithms, Inc.

Launched in 1995, CollegeNET is a portal for applying to colleges over the Internet. Over 250 colleges and universities have contracted with CollegeNET to handle their official web-based admissions applications.

Media:
Internet

Principal Focus:
Scholarship Directories & Search Services

COLLEGENET MACH25 SCHOLARSHIP SEARCH

Description:

MACH25 is a scaled-down, Internet-based version of the huge Wintergreen/Orchard House Scholarship Finder database, published on the Internet by CollegeNET. According to the publisher, the database contains listings of more than 600,000 awards totaling over $1.6 billion. (Awards include college-specific grants/scholarships.) There are several ways to search MACH25. First, users can set their own search perimeters by gender, age, academic level, and including/excluding "school specific" (i.e., non-portable) awards. Then they can maintain these "filters" and search by keyword or category (i.e., academic subject, religion, etc.) or view all scholarships that fit the basic "filters." Another alternative is eliminating filters and simply searching by keyword or category. When a list of results is found, click on an award title for an overview of the award/scholarship and information on the sponsor. Overviews cover such pertinent details as type of award, deadlines, award statistics, award features (i.e., renewable or not), contact information, and applicant qualifications. Another feature of the database allows users to send listings "to a friend" or to view previous search results, thus keeping track of their research.

Evaluation:

MACH25 stands out in the increasingly crowded field of free scholarship searches offered on the Web because it helps students track their searches via the "View My List" feature and send results "To A Friend" or to themselves. The variety of search options is helpful as well, allowing users to search by "filters" in conjunction with keywords or category searches. The category list is expansive, ranging from academics and interests to clubs, disabilities, and ethnicity. Unfortunately, the site no longer offers the automatic letter of interest function, which gave students the option of copying the proposed letter (with their information typed into the appropriate fields) and pasting it into an email document to send to a scholarship coordinator via the Internet. Still, for a relatively easy search of 600,000-plus awards, this site is definitely the place to go. Remember, however, that students shouldn't waste time searching for scholarship money until they have exhausted the financial aid options outlined in our guidebook. (Keep in mind, too, that most of these awards are school-specific.) Even with the most technically advanced scholarship searches, students should not depend on any significant financial aid through this route—but hats off to those who beat the odds!

Where To Find/Buy:
On the Internet at http://www.collegenet.com/mach25/

THE FINANCIAL AID BOOK
The Insider's Guide To Private Scholarships, Grants & Fellowships

Description:

Like many of its competitors, this scholarship directory is a hefty paperback, but it offers information and advice not covered in similar products. Most scholarship books are essentially directories of grants and scholarships, organized by a system of indexes. This newly revised edition includes sections on how to organize the application process, how to write letters of request and letters of recommendation, and how to write scholarship essays. The bulk of the book is a directory of three categories of aid: scholarships and grants; student loans; and fellowships, internships, and research funding. Each listing includes the program name, address, phone, contact person, major/interest, amount of award, number of awards, deadline, and a brief description of eligibility criteria.

Evaluation:

This updated edition really shines when it comes to indexing. Each listing is numbered, and students can look under several groupings to target programs of interest. Groupings include college major; state of residence or study; student affiliations, family affiliations, religious affiliations and ethnic background. Students can tell by looking at the number whether a program is a scholarship or grant, a student loan, or a fellowship/internship/research funding program. This makes it easy to target programs that suit individual needs and interests. This book is a great resource for discovering interest-free and other subsidized, non-governmental loan options. Because most of the scholarship directories on the market exclude fellowships or research funding programs, this guide's section devoted to fellowships, internships, and research funding make it especially valuable for graduate students.

Where To Find/Buy:

Bookstores and libraries.

Overall Rating
★★★
Information on fellowships, internships, and research funding especially valuable for graduate students

Design, Ease Of Use
★★★
Extensive indexes make targeting scholarships easy

1–4 Stars

Publisher:
Student Financial Services/ Perpetual

Edition:
3rd (1999)

Price:
$24.95

Pages:
672

ISBN:
188199010

Media:
Book

Principal Focus:
Scholarship Directories & Search Services

Overall Rating
★★★
A great resource for students interested in nursing careers and nursing professionals

Design, Ease Of Use
★★★
Indexes make it simple to find scholarships and loans of interest

1–4 Stars

Publisher:
National League for Nursing

Edition:
1997

Price:
$16.95

Pages:
124

ISBN:
0887377300

Media:
Book

Principal Focus:
Scholarship Directories & Search Services

SCHOLARSHIPS & LOANS FOR NURSING EDUCATION 1997–1998

Description:

As the name implies, this 124-page paperback guide covers scholarships, awards, grants, and loans for nursing education. The first 16 pages cover general information such as choosing a school and applying for financial aid. The directory of scholarship programs is divided into four chapters: Scholarships and Loans for Nursing Education; Aid for Minority Students; Special Awards, Postdoctoral Study, and Research Grants; and Aid from NLN's Constituent Leagues for Nursing. Within these chapters, each program entry contains the program title, a paragraph or two describing the program, and a contact address. Every program entry has a numerical code next to its heading to help determine whether that program is appropriate for the student. Codes are listed for the following categories: beginning RN study; LPN study; baccalaureate completion for RNs; advanced clinical study for RNs; graduate study (master's or doctoral); doctoral study only; special grants, research, traineeships, or postdoctoral work; and for minority students primarily.

Evaluation:

The benefit of searching out a specialized book like this guide on nursing education is that programs may be uncovered that are not included in general, all-inclusive scholarship books and computer searches. Most of the programs listed are portable, that is they can be used at any accredited college; however, some are institution-based. This guide is best used to supplement (but not replace) the process of applying for financial aid from the federal government, as most nurses fund their education the way other students do, from a combination of savings, and loans and grants from Uncle Sam. Many of the programs listed offer significant financial support for nurses or students interested in nursing who fit their specific criteria. Those criteria range from students interested in becoming a nurse with a certain specialization (such as a pediatric nurse practitioner) to nurses hoping to do graduate study in a certain field (such as the prevention of epilepsy).

Where To Find/Buy:

Bookstores and libraries, or directly from the publisher at: National League for Nursing Press, 350 Hudson Street, NY, NY 10014. Publication #41-6789.

SCHOLARSHIPS, FELLOWSHIPS & FINANCIAL SUPPORT FOR JEWISH COLLEGE STUDENTS

Description:

Section I contains a brief overview of financial aid for college, with special attention to Californian students. An "expanded table of contents" serves as an index. It presents listings in 12 sections: Campuses with Scholarships for Jewish Students (total of 14); Scholarships/Internships for Jewish Students (10); Study in Israel Scholarships and Internships (11); Regionally-Specific Scholarships (5); Jewish Communal Scholarships and Internships (15); Scholarships for Recent Immigrants (2); Regional Loan Funds (3); Research—Jewish Fields (12); Research—Other Fields (3); Jewish Communal Graduate Fellowships (7); Once-In-A-Lifetime-Experiences (8); and Award and Contest Competitions (5).

Evaluation:

As stated in its prologue, this book aims to create a "bridge between resources in the Jewish community and the tremendous need for financial assistance" among students. The editor has done an excellent job compiling information on scholarships and other financial aid programs open exclusively to, or targeted at, Jewish students. However, the overview of the financial aid process included in Section I is brief, so students will need to consult other resources for a full discussion of how to apply for and receive financial aid. The program listings include plenty of detail, including eligibility criteria, contact addresses, and deadlines. Programs range from Kansas State University's Theater in Israel Program, which takes students to Israel to study Israeli theater, to the Jewish Free Loan Association-Becker Graduate Student Loan Fund, which provides interest-free loans up to $1,500 to graduate students.

Where To Find/Buy:

Order direct from the Hillel/FACETS program at (213) 259-2959 or 1600 Campus Road, Box F-10, Los Angeles, CA 90041.

Overall Rating
★★★
Contains many small programs for Jewish students that larger directories may not carry

Design, Ease Of Use
★
Has the look of a desktop publishing piece; lack of an index makes research cumbersome

1–4 Stars

Author:
Caty Konigsberg
Ms. Konigsberg is the Director of the Hillel/FACETS program.

Publisher:
Los Angeles Hillel Council/ FACETS

Edition:
6th (1998)

Price:
$18.00

Pages:
115

Media:
Book

Principal Focus:
Scholarship Directories & Search Services

Overall Rating
★★
A thorough and accurate source of information on a variety of known and lesser-known awards

Design, Ease Of Use
★★★★
Clear and attractive layout makes searching for awards easy

1–4 Stars

Author:
Laurie Blum

Laurie Blum is the author of more than 20 books on the subject of undergraduate and graduate school funding, including *Free $ For Foreign Study* and *Free $ For College*. She lives in Los Angeles.

Publisher:
Facts on File

Edition:
3rd (1996)

Price:
$15.95

Pages:
298

ISBN:
0816035636

Media:
Book

Principal Focus:
Scholarship Directories & Search Services

FREE MONEY FOR GRADUATE SCHOOL
A Guide To More Than 1,000 Grants And Scholarships For Graduate Study

Description:
In its third edition, this book gives complete and updated information on over 1,000 grants, awards, and scholarships for all fields of graduate study. It is divided into 8 sections, the first 5 focusing on sources of funding for: Humanities and Social Sciences; Biological and Agricultural Sciences; Physical Sciences and Mathematics; Engineering and Applied Sciences; and Business, Education, Health, and Law. The next 2 sections include awards for special applicants: "Women Only, Women Preferred, Women's Studies," and "Ethnic Only, Ethnic Preferred, Foreign Nationals." Grants for study and research abroad, and grants for all areas of study, follow. Application and contact information is included: addresses, telephone numbers, and contact names; descriptions and restrictions for the awards; money given; and deadlines. A bibliography of additional resources on the subject of graduate funding, as well as an index providing cross-referencing according to subject, organization, discipline, etc., are included.

Evaluation:
For students looking for more ways to finance their graduate education—besides federal loans and school-specific funding—this book may be helpful. Its clear layout and helpful index may hook students up to more than 1,000 awards for graduate study. Sources of funding range from the obscure ("National Speleological Society") to the well-known and respected ("Jacob K. Javits Fellows Program"). As the introduction mentions, there are lots of books out there that will tell students *how* to locate sources of funding, as well as expensive and hard to find reference books, but this book gives complete contact information, is very thorough, and relatively inexpensive. Drawbacks? These funding opportunities are extremely competitive (many offering less than 5 awards) and range greatly in terms of money granted ($100 to upwards of $15,000). Also, because the book contains awards targeting a wide range of scholars, students must wade through numerous listings to find programs of interest.

Where To Find/Buy:
Bookstores and libraries.

PRINCETON REVIEW SCHOLARSHIP ADVISOR 1999

Description:

To search through the 4,500-plus financial aid sources described here, readers use one or more "Locator" indexes, which group listings by eligibility criteria: major/career objective, hobbies, work experience, ethnicity, religious affiliation, disabilities, gender, military service, state of residence, college, and GPA. The information provided on each scholarship includes the award amount, the level of study, contact information, eligibility, deadlines, and the number of awards offered. Though the listings form the bulk of this directory, it also contains a guide to the college application process. The author, Mr. Vuturo, qualified for $885,000 in funds while applying to various undergraduate colleges. He expounds on his success "wowing" scholarship committees in chapters such as "Getting Your Application Together," "Writing the Essay," and "Preparing for the Interview." Commonly asked interview questions are presented and critiqued, as are sample essays. There is also a formula for composing a "distinguished" letter of inquiry. Graduate students have their own "special instructions."

Evaluation:

Mr. Vurturo's advice on the application process is sound, insightful, and valuable. This is, however, primarily a scholarship directory. The quantity of sources is commendable, and the "Locator" indexes, common to many such directories, are relatively extensive. However, despite the editor's efforts to facilitate easy searches, difficulties do arise. For instance, students interested in Spanish as a major will find 12 entries under that index heading. Some entries clearly describe eligibility requirements, but others, such as the "Mary Louise White Scholarship," are ambiguous. Only after looking up and reading the entry will readers see that this is a college-specific award for undergraduate students attending the University of Houston. The many indexes don't help distinguish levels of study or portability of aid resources. Print directories such as this simply can't compete with the cross-referencing capabilities of the Internet.

Where To Find/Buy:

Bookstores and libraries.

Overall Rating
★★
Comprehensive and informative; focused on the college years

Design, Ease Of Use
★★★
Relatively extensive search indexes; easy to use

1–4 Stars

Author:
Chris Vuturo

Mr. Vuturo graduated cum laude from Harvard University in 1993 and is now attending the London School of Economics. He plans to pursue a combined MBA/MA in Environmental management at Duke University. When applying to college, Mr. Vuturo qualified for $885,000 for undergraduate funding, a feat documented in *Life Magazine*.

Publisher:
Princeton Review (Random House)

Edition:
1998

Price:
$23.00

Pages:
852

ISBN:
0375752072

Media:
Book

Principal Focus:
Scholarship Directories & Search Services

Overall Rating
★★
Comprehensive and up-to-date but focused on undergraduates' needs

Design, Ease Of Use
★★
Well-organized and indexed; includes number of applicant per program

1–4 Stars

Publisher:
College Board

The College Board is a national association of schools, colleges, and other educational organizations dedicated to putting college within the reach of all students. College Board's services and products include the SAT, PSAT/NMSQT, AP programs, and "The College Handbook."

Edition:
1999

Price:
$24.95

Pages:
812

ISBN:
0874476275

Media:
Book

Principal Focus:
Scholarship Directories & Search Services

THE COLLEGE BOARD SCHOLARSHIP HANDBOOK
Scholarships, Grants, Internships & Loans For Undergraduate & Graduate Students

Description:

This thick softback includes information on over 2,800 programs and more than 700,000 awards from private, federal and state sources of funding for undergraduate and graduate students. College students are the primary audience, although programs for Master's, doctoral, and postdoctoral students are also covered. Each entry is listed under its sponsoring organization and includes information on the type of award, intended use, eligibility, basis for selection, application requirements, number and amount of award(s), number of applicants, deadline, and total amount awarded. All scholarships are indexed for quick access to find programs of interest. A total of 70 eligibility indexes are presented under the following major headings: Disabilities, Field of Study/Intended Career, Gender, International Students, Military Participation, Minority Status, National/Ethnic Background, Religious Affiliation, Returning Adult, and Study Abroad.

Evaluation:

We'll repeat our mantra on privately-funded scholarships (which make-up the majority of the listings in this and other scholarship directories): they play a very small role in the overall picture of graduate student funding. Less than 2 percent of the total dollars funding graduate education come from privately-funded scholarships. Thus, we counsel students to research and apply to the major sources of funding (federal and state government programs and institution-based programs) before spending precious time and hard-earned dollars on the scholarship search. Having said this, the College Board is a reputable and reliable source of information. Their directory is comprehensive and up-to-date, although graduate students will have to wade through a large number of programs targeted to undergrads. Though it includes information on federal and state loans, grants, and scholarships, this directory is not a good source of information on government funding. One unique feature of this guide is its inclusion of the "number of applicants," which can help students gauge the competition.

Where To Find/Buy:

Bookstores and libraries.

THE COMPLETE SCHOLARSHIP BOOK

Description:

This book is essentially a listing of private scholarships compiled by Student Services, Inc., a leader in the scholarship database field. More than 5,000 scholarships and grants are listed. About half are college-specific; the other half are portable to any accredited college. Indexes help students find the scholarships best suited to their profile. Each listing contains the scholarship name, the amount of the available award or awards, the deadline for submission, major or career objective, and an address for more information. Readers can look up scholarships by numerous categories, including athletics, disability, ethnic background, gender, GPA, heritage, marital status, military service, and religion. Another index lists scholarships by major or career objective. Icons next to each entry help readers to scan the listings. The introductory section includes 52 Tips for optimizing college funds.

Evaluation:

This book suffers from the limitation of every print resource listing scholarships: it just can't compete with a well structured online version with the same entries. This guidebook's indexes are better than many in similar books. For example, the "Special Criteria" index makes locating the most suitable scholarship competitions easier by breaking down high academic performance scholarships by GPA. Similarly, the major or career objective index allows students to find listings under, say, operations research or electrical engineering. The primary shortcoming of print resources such as this is that it is difficult to locate scholarships based on two or more criteria, such as engineering scholarships for women, or grants targeted at black medical students. Searching by multiple criteria is still easiest online. Another major draw back of this volume is that awards for graduate and professional students are mixed with those for undergrads.

Where To Find/Buy:

Bookstores and libraries.

Overall Rating
★★
Funding programs for grad students separate from undergrads

Design, Ease Of Use
★★
Multiple indexes, but it could use more

1–4 Stars

Publisher:
Student Services, Inc.

Edition:
1998

Price:
$22.95

Pages:
857

ISBN:
1570713901

Media:
Book

Principal Focus:
Scholarship Directories & Search Services

Overall Rating
★★
Wonderful introductory chapters, but the directory is skimpy

Design, Ease Of Use
★★
Icons make scanning a breeze

1–4 Stars

Publisher:
Sourcebooks

Edition:
1998

Price:
$18.95

Pages:
176

ISBN:
1570711933

Media:
Book

Principal Focus:
Scholarship Directories & Search Services

Of Interest To:
Women
Persons of Color

THE MINORITY & WOMEN'S COMPLETE SCHOLARSHIP BOOK

Description:

Student Services publishes several scholarship directories. This guide focuses on scholarships primarily for women and members of ethnic/racial groups. It also contains several listings for students with religious affiliations and people with disabilities, such as blindness, hearing impairments, or learning disabilities. A total of 1,200 sources of aid, including scholarships, fellowships, grants, and low-interest loans are included. About half the financial aid opportunities are school-specific, meaning students must attend a particular school to receive the aid. The other half are portable, meaning the funds may be used at any accredited school. Extensive indexes follow the scholarship information. A unique feature of this guide is the icon system, which allows readers to scan the directory for specific characteristics. For examples, some icons indicate major fields of study (medicine, engineering, business); others signal scholarships targeted at women or specific ethnic groups.

Evaluation:

The publishers of this book deserve kudos for including introductory chapters explaining financial aid's "big-picture" and the role of privately-funded scholarships in the aid-seeking process. We like the section "where financial aid comes from," which outlines the central role that government funding plays. We also like the explanation about the Free Application for Federal Student Aid (FAFSA). The book admonishes, "Do not rely on the opportunities listed in this book as your only potential sources of financial aid. It is always wise to pursue several options, including government and college-sponsored programs." Good advice. The series of 23 essay-length tips are also helpful. The directory itself is not as comprehensive as similar guides, and it is not always clear from the scholarship description whether the program is open to graduate students. The inclusion of non-portable scholarships is a mistake in our judgment, as these opportunities are very limited. Overall, a good supplementary resource for women and minorities.

Where To Find/Buy:

Bookstores and libraries.

MOLIS: MINORITY ONLINE INFORMATION SERVICE

Description:

MOLIS, the Minority On-Line Information Service, is a joint project of RAMS and FIE, the Federal Information Exchange. (FIE is a for-profit group contracted by the government to design pathways to improve online communication between higher education and the government.) The site's primary purpose is to provide information on Historically Black Colleges and Universities, Hispanic Serving Institutions, and Tribal Colleges and Universities. School information is arranged in two ways: by geographic location and institution name. An alphabetical list of schools appears in both categories; users click the school's name for a profile. Profiles include contact addresses, as well as data on housing, enrollment, degrees awarded, finances, and faculty. A secondary feature of this site is the scholarship search. The scholarship search page asks the user to create a personal profile, then delivers matching scholarships. MOLIS primarily posts information that is funded by its supporting agencies, such as NASA, the Environmental protection Agency, and the Department of Education, although some private scholarships are listed. Results of each scholarship search include contact, eligibility, and application information.

Evaluation:

While MOLIS's database of school profiles does not target postgraduates, per se, it is a useful place for students interested in Historically Black Universities, Hispanic Serving Institutions, and Tribal Universities to begin their research. The school profiles provide statistical information on the number of Master's and PhDs granted in each field, plus details on housing, costs, and the institution's research centers. The MOLIS scholarship search, however, is limited in its usefulness. Though MOLIS lists scholarships funded by its supporting agencies—including listings which may not appear elsewhere—it is not a comprehensive list of minority scholarships. The database is so small that most personal profiles—male or female, engineering or education major—will produce the same or similar matches. We suggest students follow the link on the scholarship search page to the Scholarship Resource Network (http://www.rams.com/srn, reviewed on page 286). Entering virtually the same personal information there yields a larger number of scholarships. Despite its scholarship search's weaknesses, however, MOLIS is worth a quick look.

Where To Find/Buy:

On the Internet at http://www.fie.com/molis/ir

Overall Rating
★★
Offers a database of minority-related school profiles, plus a scholarship search

Design, Ease Of Use
★★
No search interface for selecting schools; users scroll through names

1–4 Stars

Publisher:
RAMS-FIE

RAMS and the Federal Information Exchange (FIE) developed MOLIS to provide a research and institutional capabilities database on Historically Black Colleges, Hispanic Serving Institutions, and Tribal Colleges.

Media:
Internet

Principal Focus:
Scholarship Directories & Search Services

Of Interest To:
Persons of Color

II. Scholarship Directories & Search Services

★★

Overall Rating
★★
Not as comprehensive as some of the larger guides, but priced affordably

Design, Ease Of Use
★
Indexes adequate, but program listings lack detail

1–4 Stars

Publisher:
Garrett Park

Edition:
1996–1998

Price:
$5.95

Pages:
80

Media:
Book

Principal Focus:
Scholarship Directories & Search Services

Of Interest To:
Persons of Color

FINANCIAL AID FOR MINORITIES (SERIES)

Description:

This paperback series includes a volume for students with "any major," in addition to separate volumes for those pursuing degrees in business, law, education, engineering and science, the health fields, and journalism and mass communications. In each book, Section I presents introductory material on trends in enrollment for minority students and discusses types of financial aid. Section II, the heart of the booklet, is a directory of 300–400 scholarship and financial aid programs either restricted to, or showing preference to, minority students. "Minority" includes: Native Americans (Alaska Natives and American Indians), African Americans, Hispanic, and Asian Americans. In some cases, Asian Americans are not eligible for minority programs because they are already over represented in the field concerned. Section III presents a very brief outline of federal financial aid programs. Section IV lists other sources of information on financial aid and scholarships. Section V is a glossary of financial aid terminology. Section VI is an index of the financial aid programs listed.

Evaluation:

This inexpensive paperback series offers a mixed bag. Some entries are better than others. For example, in the general volume, entry 21, the American Historical Association, merely refers to a guide the Association publishes on scholarship opportunities for history majors. On the other hand, the Alpha Kappa Alpha Sorority, also cited in this volume, offers more than 700 individual scholarships. Most of the listings are for undergraduates, but several address graduate student needs, including some internships. Students should use this series together with some of the larger scholarship and financial aid directories. The series would be greatly improved by more detail in the program listings, especially the more substantial scholarship programs that offer full tuition and/or stipends.

Where To Find/Buy:

Order directly from the publisher at P.O. Box 190, Garrett Park, MD 20896, (301) 946-2553. $5.95 each, or $30 for set of all six booklets. Add $1.50 for shipping no matter how many are ordered.

THE GRADUATE SCHOOL FUNDING HANDBOOK

Description:

Three-fourths of this 162-page book is devoted to a directory of specific graduate-level fellowship and grant programs offered by institutions and external sources. The information presented will be most useful for students pursuing a master's or PhD, not for professional school students. In the overview of graduate financial aid offered in the first 40 pages, the author discusses institution-based aid (tuition remission, fellowships, assistantships, and work study) and external funding (grants and fellowships). Beginning with Chapter 3, she presents general information and application writing advice for different types of funding: individual fellowships (such as the Javits and Department of Defense graduate fellowships); study/research abroad (such as the Fulbright and Marshall Scholarships); research grants (such as the Presidential Library and Geological Society of America research grants); dissertation fellowships (such as American Association of University Women Educational Foundation Fellowships and Grants and Ford Foundation fellowships), and postdoctoral fellowships.

Evaluation:

Our major gripe with this book is its complete lack of information on federal and state financial need-based aid for graduate study. If a student used this book as their only source of information on graduate school funding, they would probably not submit a Free Application for Federal Student Aid (FAFSA) and thus be ineligible for any of the $200 million dispensed by the government each year for graduate study (these funds are mostly in the form of subsidized and unsubsidized loans). On the other hand, its coverage of specific grants and fellowships is outstanding. Students looking for a directory of major grants and fellowship programs will be well served by the detailed program information and practical tips offered for applying to each specific program. The chapters on research and study abroad and postdoctoral study are two of the strongest, and most unique, offerings. For students interested in institutional and private grants and fellowships for a Master's or doctoral degree in the arts and sciences, this guide is worth browsing.

Where To Find/Buy:

Bookstores and libraries.

Overall Rating
★★
More a directory of fellowship and grant programs than an overview of aid sources

Design, Ease Of Use
★
Visual presentation muddled

1–4 Stars

Author:
April Vahle Hamel

Ms. Hamel is the former Associate Dean of the Graduate School of Arts and Sciences at Washington University in St. Louis and is currently an independent researcher.

Publisher:
University of Pennsylvania

Edition:
1995

Price:
$14.95

Pages:
162

ISBN:
0812214471

Media:
Book

Principal Focus:
Scholarship Directories & Search Services

★★

Overall Rating
★★
The free search may yield some scholarships of interest

Design, Ease Of Use
★
8,000 programs and 150,000 awards worth a total of more than $35 million

1–4 Stars

Publisher:
Scholarship Resource Network

The Scholarship Resource Network is a for-profit group who leases its database of scholarship opportunities to high schools and colleges. It offers a free search of its database to students at this site, and produces a list of matching scholarships for the profile entered.

Edition:
1997

Media:
Internet

Principal Focus:
Scholarship Directories & Search Services

THE SCHOLARSHIP RESOURCE NETWORK

Description:

SRN is one of the many groups which maintain a database on scholarship opportunities which they then lease to high schools, colleges and universities. Students can access the database using the SRN Express free scholarship search found at this site. The profile we entered yielded a list of about 20 scholarships. Each scholarship is linked to a page listing information on eligibility criteria, a contact address, the award amount and deadlines. The database is moderate in size containing 8,000 programs and 150,000 awards worth a total of more than $35 million. (Compare to fastWEB with some 400,000 entries).

Evaluation:

In the battle to create the most comprehensive, state-of-the-art scholarship search, SRN has taken a back seat to fastWEB and others. When we changed the student profile we entered, the names of the scholarship "matches" did not change very much. Clearly the database contains quite a few generally targeted scholarships. The student profile is less extensive than others on the Web, another factor leading to a disappointing search result. Remember that all computerized scholarship searches contain mostly national, widely publicized programs. Your best bet may be a local scholarship offered by the Rotary or other civic, religious or service clubs. And these smaller, locally based programs are not found in any of the searches.

Where To Find/Buy:

On the Internet at http://www.rams.com/srn

DOLLARS FOR COLLEGE (SERIES)
The Quick Guide To Financial Aid

Description:

The publisher, Garrett Park Press, has been publishing financial aid guides for 25 years. The "Dollars for College" series focuses on specific majors and career paths, and on two special interest groups. Included are separate volumes for Art, Music, and Drama; Business and Related Fields, The Disabled; Education; Engineering; Journalism and Mass Communications; Law; Liberal Arts and Social Science; Medicine, Dentistry, and Related Fields; Nursing and Other Health Fields; Science; and Women in All Fields. Each guide begins with an introductory section, which offers tips for using the booklet, describes federal financial aid programs, and defines some basic financial aid terms. The bulk of the book is a listing of specific financial aid programs, some of which are small and very selective. Entries are numbered and indexed. Lists of useful books and related helpful organizations are also provided.

Evaluation:

While some of the entries in these directories describe meaningful programs with substantial awards, too many are for small awards or narrowly defined eligibility. Similarly, many of the entries simply indicate that a given school may offer scholarships or other forms of financial aid to business majors. For example, in the Business guide, entry 121 for Elmira College merely gives the school's address and phone number and states that "Among the awards available at Elmira are scholarships for majors in business, science and mathematics." We also found the indices overly general. This series is best used as a supplement to a more comprehensive guide.

Where To Find/Buy:

Order directly from the publisher at P.O. Box 190, Garrett Park, MD 20896, (301) 946-2553. $7.95 each, or $60 for set of all 12 booklets. Add $1.50 for shipping no matter how many are ordered.

Overall Rating
★
Contains many small awards and scholarships with narrowly defined criteria

Design, Ease Of Use
★★
Could use more indexing to make locating scholarships easier

1–4 Stars

Publisher:
Garrett Park

Edition:
1997

Price:
$7.95

Pages:
70–90

Media:
Book

Principal Focus:
Scholarship Directories & Search Services

Of Interest To:
Women
Disabled

WORLDWIDE GRADUATE SCHOLARSHIP DIRECTORY
America's Top 1,000 Scholarships And More Than 500 Others From 75 Countries Around The World

Overall Rating
★
An adequate list of private scholarships, less current than similar guides

Design, Ease Of Use
★★
Scholarship listings include minimal description

1–4 Stars

Author:
Dan Cassidy

Mr. Cassidy is the President of the National Scholarship Research Service and the new International Scholarship Research Service, the world's largest computer database services offering private scholarship research assistance to students.

Publisher:
Career

Edition:
4th (1995)

Price:
$26.99

Pages:
295

ISBN:
1564142094

Media:
Book

Principal Focus:
Scholarship Directories & Search Services

Description:

This directory primarily lists scholarships and grants, although some listings for loans, fellowships, and internships are included. The sources of funding are many and varied, including colleges, foundations, trust funds, associations, religious and fraternal groups, and private philanthropists. The fourth edition adds 500-plus international scholarships from 75 different countries. Scholarship entries are given a reference number. Each entry includes basic information on the award (program name, amount, contact address, deadline, field(s), and a brief description). Several indexes are provided for locating scholarships of interest. A "Quick Find" index lists reference numbers for scholarships with common eligibility requirements, such as residency, field of interest, race, religion, or physical challenge. A "Field of Study" index lists programs of interest to students in various fields of study. An alphabetical index lists scholarship program names. Organizations and publications of interest are listed in separate chapters.

Evaluation:

In our view, researching privately-funded scholarships, grants, and fellowships is a final step to be taken after students have thoroughly researched and applied for all available government and institutionally-based funding opportunities. In the overall picture of graduate student funding, privately-funded scholarships, grants, and fellowships play a very small role in addressing the financial needs of students. With this caveat in mind, prospective graduate students may be among the fortunate few who stumble upon a scholarship targeted at their profile. Cassidy's directory is well-indexed, so students can quickly learn if there are scholarships available to, for example, someone interested in studying vertebrate paleontology (there is!), or for female veterinary students (yes!). Cassidy could improve the guide by adding more substance to the introductory materials. As written, they do little more than explain (three times) how to use the book.

Where To Find/Buy:
Bookstores and libraries.

AMERICAN ASSOCIATION OF UNIVERSITY WOMEN EDUCATIONAL FOUNDATION FELLOWSHIPS & GRANTS

Non-Rated Resource

Description:
The American Association of University Women (AAUW) has helped more than 6,800 women reach their personal and professional goals through a variety of fellowships and grants. This website describes their 2000–01 fellowships and grants. Preference goes to women whose civic, community, or professional work shows a commitment to advancing the welfare of women and girls.

Publisher:
American Association Of University Women

The American Association of University Women (AAUW) has helped more than 6,800 women reach their personal and professional goals through a variety of fellowships and grants. This website describes their 2000-01 fellowships and grants. Preference goes to women whose civic, community, or professional work shows a commitment to advancing the welfare of women and girls.

Media:
Internet

Principal Focus:
Scholarship Directories & Search Services

Of Interest To:
Women

Where To Find/Buy:
On the Internet at http://www.aauw.org/3000/fdnfelgra.html

AMERICAN CHEMICAL SOCIETY MINORITY AFFAIRS

Non-Rated Resource

Description:
The American Chemical Society has created this directory of minority scholarships, fellowships and grants sponsored by organizations who target minority groups and promote the sciences. Included are pages listing scholarships specifically targeted to African American, Hispanic, and Native Americans, as well as a page with 53 entries for underrepresented minorities in general.

Publisher:
American Chemical Society

The American Chemical Society is an individual membership organization consisting of over 151,000 members; its goal is to promote understanding of chemistry and the chemical sciences, and to provide career development assistance for students and professionals in academia and private industry.

Media:
Internet

Principal Focus:
Scholarship Directories & Search Services

Of Interest To:
Persons of Color

Where To Find/Buy:
On the Internet at http://www.acs.org/pafgen/minority/main_2.htm

FEDERAL TRADE COMMISSION SCHOLARSHIP SCAM ALERT

Non-Rated Resource

Description:
The Federal Trade Commission operates this site to warn students of potential scams in the fee-based scholarship search business. It lists six warning signs and offers a number or website to contact if you feel that you may have been scammed. Warning signs include "money back guarantees" and pitches that "we'll need your credit card number to hold the scholarship." Visit this site before you consider paying for a scholarship search!

Publisher:
Federal Trade Commission

The Federal Trade Commission enforces a variety of federal antitrust and consumer protection laws. In general, the Commission's efforts target actions that threaten consumers' opportunities to exercise informed choice.

Media:
Internet

Principal Focus:
Scholarship Directories & Search Services

Where To Find/Buy:
On the Internet at http://www.ftc.gov/bcp/conline/pubs/alerts/ouchalrt.htm

ONELIST

Non-Rated Resource

Description:
At the ONElist site, students can register for "Scholarshiplist," a free periodic newsletter listing "general" scholarships available to most students. To ensure that "most everyone" can qualify for the scholarships, only awards with "minimal" academic, athletic, or special background requirements are chosen.

Publisher:
ONElist, Inc.

The Federal Trade Commission enforces a variety of federal antitrust and consumer protection laws. In general, the Commission's efforts target actions that threaten consumers' opportunities to exercise informed choice.

Media:
Internet

Principal Focus:
Scholarship Directories & Search Services

Where To Find/Buy:
On the Internet at http://www.onelist.com/subscribe/scholarshiplist

SALUDOS WEB EDUCATION CENTER

Non-Rated Resource

Description:
The "Education Center" on the Saludos website contains a listing of internship opportunities and scholarships, including those targeted specifically at Hispanic Americans and those that do not consider race or ethnicity. Program descriptions are brief. A series of links to other Web-based Hispanic educational resources is posted. Information is also available on Hispanic careers, employment, and cultural topics.

Publisher:
Saludos Hispanos Magazine

Created in 1967, *Saludos Hispanos* is a bilingual career and education magazine dedicated to encouraging Hispanics to strive for excellence in career and academic pursuits. Saludos Web is the print magazine's online product.

Media:
Internet

Principal Focus:
Scholarship Directories & Search Services

Of Interest To:
Persons of Color

Where To Find/Buy:
On the Internet at http://www.saludos.com/ed.html

SCHOLARSHIPS FOR WOMEN & MINORITIES 1998

Non-Rated Resource

Description:
Dr. Fung has compiled a directory of Internet links to: Searchable Databases; Scholarships for Women; Scholarships for Minorities; Scholarships for Undergraduates and Graduate Students; and General Scholarships for High School Seniors. She keeps the site up-to-date and often adds new sites. Most of the scholarships listed are either limited to, or strongly encourage applications from, women and/or members of minority communities.

Author:
Ella Y. Fung, PhD

Media:
Internet

Principal Focus:
Scholarship Directories & Search Services

Of Interest To:
Women
Persons of Color

Where To Find/Buy:
On the Internet at http://members.aol.com/ox13qr/webpages/eyfswm1.html

UCI SCHOLARSHIP OPPORTUNITIES PROGRAM

Non-Rated Resource

Description:
University of California, Irvine developed this scholarship directory to serve its own students, but anyone can apply for the awards. Scholarship listings are divided into the following selection categories: Essay, General, Graduate, Heritage, Internships, Major, Prestigious, Research, and Symposia. Most of the advice offered is for UCI students only.

Publisher:
University of California, Irvine

UC Irvine's Scholarship Opportunities Program is designed to help students win scholarships by identifying and organizing information about external scholarships and fellowships.

Media:
Internet

Principal Focus:
Scholarship Directories & Search Services

Of Interest To:
Persons of Color

Where To Find/Buy:
On the Internet at http://www.honors.uci.edu/sop.html

II. Of General Interest To Prospective Graduate & Professional Students

Though their career goals can range from becoming a district attorney to teaching high school English, graduate and professional students share many interests and face many common challenges. The resources reviewed in this final chapter serve the interests of a broad range of students.

For example, almost every application for graduate or professional school requires a personal statement where applicants must wax poetic about their goals, experiences, and unique qualifications. The personal statement offers applicants the chance to add a human dimension to the GPA and test scores at the top of their application.

In the Master's/PhD, Business School, and Health Sciences chapters, we introduced resources that focus on personal statements in those disciplines. Here we review several guides written to help all professional and graduate applicants brainstorm a topic, write an interesting and impressive statement, and check it for common mistakes. One recommended resource includes examples of personal statements and essays that inspire.

Many of the resources reviewed in this chapter are websites of interest to graduate and professional students. Several have been created by current or former students and provide support and useful information to those considering an advance degree or currently pursuing one.

We also include in this chapter several of the omnibus print directories of Master's, PhD, and professional programs, and websites, which provide search tools for all American colleges and universities.

General resources addressing the needs of international students considering study in the United States are also reviewed here. Included are print resources and websites accessible around the world.

We also look at several government websites providing information and support to students and prospective students, as well as two resources introducing AmeriCorps, a national service program that allows people 17 years and older to earn "education awards" in exchange for a year of service.

ACCESS AMERICA'S GUIDE TO STUDYING IN THE USA

 Recommended For:
Of General Interest

Description:

Written for international students, this guide aims to make applying to and attending college in the U.S. less difficult. The editors use checklists, questionnaires, and sample forms to show readers what to expect when they pursue an associate, bachelor, or graduate degree. The first three chapters explain the structure of the U.S. higher education system, including the types of degrees offered and accreditation. Throughout the book, they provide "reality checks"— bits of information and advice about American education and culture. In chapters Four through Six, they provide a step-by-step guide to school selection and the admissions process. Timelines and checklists help readers with essay preparation and recommendation letters. Chapter Seven focuses on preparing to come to the U.S.—Travel tips, living arrangements, medical insurance, student visas, and customs preparations. Culture shock, college living, and personal safety and health concerns are addressed in Chapters Eight through Ten. The authors also describe preliminary steps for employment searches. A glossary and additional resources round out the book.

Evaluation:

This guide is an excellent tool for international students preparing for study in the U.S. Its easy-to-use design guides students through all the basics, including postgraduate employment. It focuses on undergraduate study, but most of the information is applicable to students pursuing graduate degrees as well. The overall layout is pleasing to the eye and easy to use. The "reality check" sidebars provide some essential tips, including how to avoid the wrong classes; they also help dispel many myths about America, and we liked the use of headings and sidebars and the glossary of essential terms. The resource list was relatively thin; the books listed were a particular disappointment. Nevertheless, this self-proclaimed "one-stop-shopping" guide lives up to its cover blurb: "the essential resource for international students."

Where To Find/Buy:

Bookstores, libraries, or by direct order (800) KAP-ITEM or (312) 836-4400, ext. 3650 for International orders.

Overall Rating
★★★★
Thorough with upbeat and practical advice

Design, Ease Of Use
★★★★
Graphically friendly; interactive

1–4 Stars

Author:
Marilyn J. Rymniak et al

The editor is executive director of International Products and Programs at Kaplan Educational Centers.

Publisher:
Simon & Schuster

Edition:
1997

Price:
$20.00

Pages:
198

ISBN:
0684841533

Media:
Book

Principal Focus:
Of General Interest

Of Interest To:
International Students

Overall Rating
★★★
Intelligent, helpful guide to writing the graduate admissions essay

Design, Ease Of Use
★★★
Funny, lively writing

1–4 Stars

Author:
Donald Asher

Donald Asher is the author *The Overnight Résumé*, also published by Ten Speed Press.

Publisher:
Ten Speed

Edition:
2nd (1999)

Price:
$12.95

Pages:
128

ISBN:
1580080421

Media:
Book

Principal Focus:
Of General Interest

GRADUATE ADMISSIONS ESSAYS
What Works, What Doesn't, And Why

 Recommended For:
Of General Interest

Description:

The preface states, "This book's goal is to take all the mystery and most of the stress out of the graduate applications process, and guide the reader through drafting a compelling graduate admissions essay." The book provides brainstorming and writing techniques that can be used for any type of admissions essay to all types of graduate schools. The first two chapters focus on the admissions process. Chapter 3 describes how to get ready to write, with exercises and tips to get students writing, and help them figure out how to best present, and distinguish, themselves. The next chapter discusses the first draft, and elements of style and language. Subsequent drafts are explored in the next chapter, including "The Essay Hall of Shame," together with tips on editing for spelling and grammar. Chapter 6 contains sample essays from applicants in the fields of journalism, architecture, nursing, business, law, and medicine, and those applying for scholarships and fellowships. The last chapter discusses letters of recommendation.

Evaluation:

This book is a straightforward and intelligent discussion of the ins and outs of composing an effective essay. The book is concise enough to be read in one or two sittings and insightful enough to give the reader to a good sense of what makes a winning essay. Its broad coverage of essays for all graduate and professional school programs (The author leans toward business, law, and medicine) and various types of application essays (for scholarships, fellowships, etc.) has its disadvantages: readers must adapt the information and advice to their particular programs (such as deciding how much personal information is appropriate). However, the author provides a nice balance of writing tips and essay samples, as well as good, original advice on the application process. It's nice to read a book that exemplifies the elements of good writing. This author clearly knows what he is talking about. Finally, the sample essays are excellent—a source of inspiration for application writers.

Where To Find/Buy:

Bookstores and libraries.

OFFICE OF POSTSECONDARY EDUCATION HOME PAGE

 Recommended For:

Of General Interest

Description:

At the home page of Office of Postsecondary Education (OPE, the division within the U.S. Department of Education responsible for college financial aid), the Information For Students section provides a directory tailored to student needs. This sections contains links to the newly created Office of Student Financial Assistance Programs (OSFAP) website, where users will find the department's online "Student Guide to Financial Aid," as well as government sponsored pages covering Direct Loans, State Agencies, and Recognized Accrediting Agencies. Students wanting to complete the Free Application for Federal Student Aid (FAFSA) electronically can link to FAFSA on the Web. OSFAP offers the Title IV School Code Search Page (these codes are needed to record on your FAFSA which colleges you want to send your information to) as well as a link to the Guide to Defaulted Student Loans Page. Also in Information For Students are links to sites for advice on taxes, and two mini-web directories: College & Admissions Information and Other Higher Education Resources. College & Admissions covers links to colleges, universities, and business schools, plus College Board test dates and FA sites. Other Resources includes directories of educational resources by state/area and NASFAA resources.

Evaluation:

We do not usually review sites that are primarily designed to provide links to other online resources, but we make an exception in this case because families will benefit from a page that organizes and presents all of many resources and tools published by the U.S. Department of Education. There is more at the OPE Home Page than the Information For Students (described above), but that's the best place for students to begin. Use that section as a bookmark or portal to the various Department of Education resources. It may not look like much, with only a few sections offered, but its simplicity is a blessing. The Spartan design allows users to "see it all" easily—no bombarding with an enormous list of links. In addition to the Students page, the OPE has sections on News & Initiatives, to help students and families keep abreast of policy changes affecting student aid, and Resources For Institutions. In the latter section, financial aid administrators and other professionals will find the most current information, including a calendar, training program details, bulletins on various programs, and publications providing official guidance on topics of interest. In addition to its practical content, the site is attractive to look at with soft graphics and well-integrated photos.

Where To Find/Buy:

On the Internet at http://www.ed.gov/offices/OPE/home.html

Overall Rating

★★★

Functions as a directory to all Department of Education/ Office Of Postsecondary Education online offerings

Design, Ease Of Use

★★★

Easy to follow; straightforward

1–4 Stars

Publisher:

U.S. Department Of Education, Office Of Postsecondary Education

The U.S. Department of Education was established in 1980 by Congress. The Department is committed to assuring access to equal educational opportunity for every individual and administers more than 200 programs.

Media:

Internet

Principal Focus:

Of General Interest

Overall Rating
★★★

A "how to" guide for applications and admission requirements; not specific to grad schools

Design, Ease Of Use
★★★

Uses "practice" exercises to teach practical skills; includes lots of examples, charts

1–4 Stars

Author:
Moya Brennan & Sarah Briggs

Publisher:
NTC LearningWorks

Edition:
1998

Price:
$12.95

Pages:
163

ISBN:
0844224790

Media:
Book

Principal Focus:
Of General Interest

Of Interest To:
International Students

APPLY TO AMERICAN COLLEGES & UNIVERSITIES

Description:

Chapter 1 introduces international students to the U.S. system of higher education. Community colleges are distinguished from 4-year colleges and universities, and undergraduate degree programs are differentiated from graduate study. Charts illustrate these differences, as do "faux" profiles of students in a variety of situations. Subsequent chapters answer such questions as: "How do I get application and program information?" "What tests do I need to take?" "How do I complete the application form?" and "How do I pay for my studies?" Also included are instructions for writing the "personal statement," information-request letters, and letters of acceptance or refusal; and directions for registering for required tests (each test is described), providing financial certification, and applying for aid, and obtaining a visa. Sample forms for most of the paperwork—applications, academic certificates, TOEFL/TSE registration forms—are provided. "Q & A" segments and definitions of relevant terms (indicated by bold-type) are incorporated into the text, as are interactive exercises, which enable readers to "practice" as they learn the "answers" to the exercises appear in the Appendix.

Evaluation:

Although the authors explain how to request application and program information, the purpose of this guide is not to aid students in selecting the "right" college or university. Rather, the authors attempt to "walk" readers through the admission process, step by step. The language is plain and simple; terminology specific to university admissions is clearly defined and appears in bold-type. What distinguishes this resource from others are the interactive "learning" exercises, which teach students practical skills, such as where to locate necessary information. Applying to U.S. institutions requires a lot of paperwork; there are forms for everything from test registration to financial certification. This guide provides samples of almost all of the required forms, including the application, and exercises for completing the forms correctly. Another virtue is the authors' attention to detail. They include detailed guidelines for filling in the "personal information" segments of the application, including employment history, and ethnicity; there is even an explanation of "the signature." While other guides offer rhetoric, this guide offers concrete examples.

Where To Find/Buy:

Bookstores and libraries.

EDUPASS
The Smart Student Guide To Studying In The USA

Description:

To help international students, Kantrowitz has created an inclusive guide that focuses on all aspects of studying in the U.S.A. A site map outlines the seven topical sections: College Admissions, Financing College, English as a 2nd Language, Passports and Visas, Traveling to the USA, Cultural Differences, and Living in the USA. There is also an interactive "Ask the Advisor" Q&A forum and links to Other Resources, such as professional associations. College Admissions discusses general admissions issues for graduate and professional schools: tests, requirements, application preparation, and choosing a school. Financing College offers explanations and links for such financing options as school aid, scholarships, and loans. Special pages detail financial aid for Canadian and European students. The TOEFL is examined in English as a 2nd Language. Passports and Visas and Traveling to the USA cover changing or maintaining visa status, proving nonimmigrant intent, and finding budget air travel. A wide spectrum of subjects is addressed in Cultural Differences, including toilets, tipping, and American holidays. Housing, banking, and safety are among the topics presented in Living in the USA.

Evaluation:

The great benefit of this site to international students is its all-inclusive nature; in conjunction with its external links, eduPASS is a complete cultural introduction to the U.S. However, as a guide to admissions, per se, eduPASS falls short. While it does offer general guidance for graduate students, such as brief explanations of application requirements, the GRE, and GMAT, there aren't enough specifics on how to find particular programs or schools. Students will have to learn about individual universities and programs elsewhere. (Some links to individual schools are provided.) What is exceptional about this site is the segment on financial aid. The Financing College segment features a financial planning worksheet, help calculating costs, a list of schools with financial aid for international students, plus links to and lists of useful publications and organizations. The pages on scholarships and loans function as both educational articles and mini-web guides; they include links to relevant resources plus lengthy descriptions of these resources. For example, the scholarship page provides a link to and information on Stod & Stipendier AB, a Swedish grant search service for Europeans wishing to study abroad. The Loans page includes details on CanHELP for Canadians plus the International Student Loan Program.

Where To Find/Buy:

On the Internet at http://www.edupass.org

Overall Rating
★★★
Offers only a few tips on admissions, but terrific for financial aid education

Design, Ease Of Use
★★★
Great site map, but difficult to move within topic sections

1–4 Stars

Author:

Mr. Kantrowitz, creator of eduPASS, is a Research Scientist at Just Research, the US software laboratory for Justsystem Corporation of Japan. He is the author of three books, including one on financial aid, and has created several popular websites. eduPASS began as the international student section of FINAID (http://www.finaid.org/).

Publisher:
Mark Kantrowitz

Media:
Internet

Principal Focus:
Of General Interest

Of Interest To:
International Students

Overall Rating
★★★

Lets you know who offers what; not specific to graduate schools

Design, Ease Of Use
★★

Breakdown by state makes listing more practical

1–4 Stars

Publisher:
College Board

The College Board is a national association of schools, colleges, and other educational organizations dedicated to putting college within the reach of all students. College Board's services and products include the SAT, PSAT/NMSQT, AP programs, and College Online.

Edition:
22nd (1999)

Price:
$21.95

Pages:
695

ISBN:
0874476291

Media:
Book

Principal Focus:
Of General Interest

THE COLLEGE BOARD INDEX OF MAJORS & GRADUATE DEGREES 2000

Description:

This directory describes over 600 undergraduate and graduate programs at nearly 3,000 institutions. Information for the book was culled from the College Board's Annual Survey of Colleges. It is primarily designed to help high school students select a college that offers their intended major, in the location of their choosing. Majors (or graduate degree programs) are listed alphabetically, and schools offering that major/graduate degree are listed by state. After each entry is a degree code, such as M for Master's degree, D for doctoral degree, F for first professional degree, and W for work beyond doctoral or first professional degree. For prospective students researching options within a broad field, there is a list of "Major fields of study by discipline." Specific majors/graduate degrees (such as Art Therapy) are grouped under disciplines (such as Health). Brief definitions of each field of study are included.

Evaluation:

This guide has been used by high school guidance counselors for years to help their students find colleges offering their intended major(s), in geographic areas of interest to the student. It can be used by prospective graduate students as well, to research which institutions offer degree programs of interest. It offers the helpful organizational step of listing institutions by state, which makes it easier to find, say, all the schools in the state of Alabama offering a Master's Degree in Early Childhood Education. However, its usefulness ends there. There are no descriptions of the institutions or degree programs themselves. For this information, students must use other resources. This guide is one of the few resources highlighting special academic programs, such as schools offering a combined bachelor's/graduate program in medicine or law. Students who know what they want to study, but not who offers it, will find this a helpful reference. Look elsewhere for evaluations of the graduate degree and professional programs.

Where To Find/Buy:

Bookstores and libraries.

PETERSON'S GRADUATE & PROFESSIONAL PROGRAMS
An Overview (Book 1)

Description:

This reference work contains information on graduate programs and degrees at more than 1,600 institutions of higher learning. An introductory section discusses the graduate application process, finances, standardized tests, and accreditation. Next comes a list of 386 graduate and professional programs by field, with schools offering degrees in each field listed alphabetically. A second directory alphabetically lists the institutions and their graduate study offerings. A third directory introduces combined-degree programs. The heart of the book is its "profiles of institutions offering graduate and professional work," which include general information on the graduate schools and profiles of each college, including enrollment statistics, admission rates, number and types of degrees awarded, and application and contact information. In-depth, full-page descriptions of some institutions, in part provided by the schools themselves, rounds out the book. This guide contains two indexes.

Evaluation:

This guide is the granddaddy of Peterson's reference book series on graduate schools. Peterson's annually publishes six guides to graduate study in the U.S. and abroad. This guide, Book 1 in the series, includes (in microscopic print) a rundown of all the fields covered in greater depth in the other five guides. Thus, it is aimed at those who need help identifying which graduate programs they intend to pursue. Many applicants can bypass this step by heading straight to Peterson's program-specific guides or other guidebooks of this sort. Peterson's Guides have a reputation for providing accurate and up-to-date information. By nature, they cannot help students evaluate or otherwise assess these programs' strengths or weaknesses, and data gleaned from these guides should be supplemented with more in-depth or evaluative information sources. However, for that first step researching schools and gathering contact information, this book will steer students in the right direction.

Where To Find/Buy:

Bookstores and libraries.

Overall Rating
★★★
A broad but informative sweep of U.S. graduate institutions and programs

Design, Ease Of Use
★★
Tiny type makes reading difficult

1–4 Stars

Publisher:
Peterson's

Edition:
33rd (1999)

Price:
$39.95

Pages:
1333

ISBN:
1560799811

Media:
Book

Principal Focus:
Of General Interest

II. General Interest

Overall Rating
★★★
Part how-to guide, part entertaining guide to American culture and idiosyncrasies

Design, Ease Of Use
★★
Written in a student-friendly, casual tone

1–4 Stars

Author:
Ian Jacobs & Ellen Shatswell

Mr. Jacobs is a writer. Ms. Shatswell is Director of International Development with the Princeton Review.

Publisher:
Princeton Review (Random House)

Edition:
1996

Price:
$15.00

Pages:
207

ISBN:
0679769137

Media:
Book

Principal Focus:
Of General Interest

Of Interest To:
International Students

PRINCETON REVIEW INTERNATIONAL STUDENTS' GUIDE TO THE USA

Description:

There are currently about 450,000 international students attending institutions of higher learning in the United States. The audience for this guide is the untold number of students from foreign countries who would like to join their ranks. The book is divided into two sections. The first half addresses such issues as: Where to find information about schools, scholarships, and other funding sources; how to organize time and activities; how to prepare an admissions application; which admissions and English proficiency tests are required; what student visas are available and how to apply for one; what student employment and practical training opportunities to explore, and how to adjust to life in the U.S. The information and guidance offered in this section comes primarily from author Ellen Shatswell, a former official of the U.S. Immigration and Naturalization Service with ten years of experience in advising international students. The second half of the book addresses American cultural issues. Believing that students will adjust better if they understand cultural references and history, co-author Ian Jacobs presents a primer on American life.

Evaluation:

Students researching study in the U.S. quickly learn that they must jump through a number of hoops. This guide will help demystify the process of getting a visa, applying for admission, seeking financial aid, and attending college. Its tone is warm and conversational; the authors have an obvious care and concern for international students. Note: this book does not offer students and their families a directory of U.S. colleges with information about what courses of study they offer, nor does it offer any college-by-college information on financial aid available for international students or course information. It does do an excellent job of explaining standardized testing, visa options, and employment issues. The second half of the book contains an eclectic assortment of American trivia and cultural must-knows. How did the authors decide what information foreign students should know? Who knows, but they ended up including a recipe for chocolate chip cookies and an explanation of how to play baseball. Also included are a discussion of country western music and a glossary of favorite American acronyms (BYOB, AC, and MTV made the cut). For students looking for the "big picture" on study in America, this guide is helpful.

Where To Find/Buy:

Bookstores and libraries.

NATIONAL ASSOCIATION OF GRADUATE-PROFESSIONAL STUDENTS

Description:

The National Association of Graduate-Professional Students (NAGPS) is a nonprofit organization "dedicated to improving the quality of graduate and professional student life in the U.S." Its home page features a dropdown site directory (on a side frame) outlining the topical sections. For nonmembers, sections of interest include What's New and Hot Topics. What's New contains news stories related to trends and practices in graduate studies. The stories are arranged chronologically, from the newest updates to past articles. Hot Topics houses the site's main attractions: "Tax Issues for Graduate/Professional Students" and "The Student Aid Awareness Page." The "Taxes" page provides (in PDF) a "Student's Guide to Federal Income Tax," as well as links and articles on education tax credits and deductions, FICA and withholding, general IRS info, and tax resources and assistance. To help students keep abreast of political and legislative developments, the "Student Aid" page offers a NAGPS legislative fact sheet plus legislative updates on (among others) US PIRG, USSA, NASFAA, and ACE. Also included is information on direct lending and the problem of student debt.

Evaluation:

There is no better Internet source for keeping abreast of political, tax, and legislative issues affecting graduate and professional students. Those lost in the maze of taxation rules and regulations will find a gold mine of information and advice from a wide range of sources, including IRS briefs, journal articles, and NAGPS advisors. This site is the place to read up on developing issues of interest, too, such as taxation of scholarships and fellowships, and changing practices in graduate studies. The June 1999 articles in What's New include a piece on "Academic Departments and the Ratings Game." May 1999 stories include "Master's Degrees, Once Scorned, Attract Students and Generate Revenue." (Most stories are reprinted from the "Chronicle of Higher Education.") For quality information on taxes and student aid, plus several worthwhile articles, this site is worth bookmarking. However, note the format: while the site deserves an "A" for content, its design gets a flunking grade. Topical sections are vaguely titled, and the dropdown menu (the only site directory) is clunky.

Where To Find/Buy:

On the Internet at http://www.nagps.org/

Overall Rating
★★★
The place to find updates on tax, legislative and political issues

Design, Ease Of Use
★
Clunky navigation; sections lack introduction

1–4 Stars

Publisher:
National Association Of Graduate-Professional Students

National Association Of Graduate-Professional Students (NAGPS) is a nonprofit organization dedicated to improving the quality of graduate and professional student life in the U.S.

Media:
Internet

Principal Focus:
Of General Interest

Overall Rating
★★
Helpful "official" advice about writing the personal statement plus good essays

Design, Ease Of Use
★★★
Down-to-earth and readable

1–4 Stars

Author:
Richard J. Stelzer

The author is a consultant based in West Los Angeles, CA, who advises "a wide array of clients on winning strategies for written presentations," including applicants to graduate and professional schools.

Publisher:
Peterson's

Edition:
3rd (1997)

Price:
$12.95

Pages:
142

ISBN:
1560798556

Media:
Book

Principal Focus:
Of General Interest

HOW TO WRITE A WINNING PERSONAL STATEMENT FOR GRADUATE & PROFESSIONAL SCHOOL

Description:

This guide was written by a L.A.-based consultant for applicants to top graduate and professional schools. A brief beginning section discusses how to write a "winning" personal statement, including how to "set yourself apart" and "tell a story," and questions to ask yourself to prompt self-revelation. The majority of this book (59 pages) is comprised of actual essays by applicants to various graduate and professional programs, with an emphasis on application essays for law, business, and medical school. These are essays that manage, in the author's words, to "catch the reader's interest and set themselves apart," and in which there is a uniqueness that "distinguishes the applicant and stands out in the reader's mind afterward." The last section of the book offers an "inside perspective" on successful application essays, with advice from admissions officers at a number of graduate and professional schools; in particular, business, law, and medicine.

Evaluation:

Although this book is directed toward applicants to all types of graduate programs, its real thrust is toward personal statements for business, law, and medical school. Applicants to other programs will find helpful advice here, but the majority of the essays themselves is focused on these three types of programs. The most useful parts of this book are definitely the essays themselves (which make for inspiring reading) and the advice offered at the end from admissions representatives, which by themselves offer the best insights into what makes a "winning" personal statement. The first section of the book, offering the author's guidance on writing a successful essay, is all too brief—with only one in-depth look at writing the business school essay, and no equally detailed discussions of law or business school essays. It would behoove the applicant to such programs to find a resource offering a similar depth of advice on writing the personal statement, tailored to their individual programs.

Where To Find/Buy:

Bookstores and libraries.

ACCEPTED.COM

Description:

To help students write winning application essays, Accepted.com offers information about its for-fee editorial service as well as free advice, live chats, and more. On the home page, the for-sale services are detailed on the left sidebar menu; the top menu, with headings for Medical, Law, Grad, and MBA, leads to the free advice. In the Medical section, medical school applicants will find "Ten dos and don'ts" for AMCAS essays, suggested approaches for tackling common secondary questions/essays, plus nine sample essays. Sample essays include one from an anthropology student, one from a "non-traditional" student, and one for dental school. The Law and Grad sections also provide "Ten dos and don'ts" for creating a personal statement and sample essays. Prospective MBA students get writing tips, such as how to approach common application questions, "dos and don'ts," and sample essays, as well as assistance with interviews. Users can read over 100 "interview feedback" questionnaires, which were completed by past MBA applicants, and thus "see for themselves" what an interview is like. All sections—Medical, Law, Grad, MBA—feature tips for letters of recommendation and for "better writing."

Evaluation:

Accepted.com is a commercial enterprise trying to attract paying customers, so it is no surprise that much of their free advice leaves one wanting more: more depth, more details, and more samples. There is some worthwhile free content, however—the sample essays, for example. Not only are these samples interesting to read, well-written and often creative, they are authored by a wide variety of applicants with diverse interests. In the Grad section are samples from an engineering student, a public health applicant, and an environmental studies student. In the Law section, one of the authors is an archeology enthusiast, while another is returning to school after many years. The writing "dos and don'ts" (which appear in every section) are helpful, too, especially for applicants with minimal essay-writing backgrounds. While the Medical, Grad, and Law sections are worth a look, MBA applicants get the best deal. The MBA section provides writing advice and a terrific interview segment; the "interview feedback" questionnaires are great tools for interview preparation. This site is worth a look for essay-writing and MBA interview preparation, but don't buy into the for-fee essay critique service.

Where To Find/Buy:

On the Internet at http://www.accepted.com

Overall Rating
★★
Some good tips and sample essays for grad, law, medical, and business school applicants

Design, Ease Of Use
★★
Free material accessible from the top menu; hefty fees charged for essay critiques

1–4 Stars

Publisher:
Accepted.com

Founded in 1993, Accepted.com is an editing service that assists applicants to undergraduate, graduate, and professional programs with application writing. Accepted.com is the website of a commercial editing service, but it offers some free content to help students with application writing. Included are sections for applying to graduate school, medical school, law school, and MBA programs, each containing essay writing "do's and don't's" and sample essays. A live chat feature is also included.

Media:
Internet

Principal Focus:
Of General Interest

Overall Rating

★★

One-stop shopping for those interested in researching or applying for AmeriCorps

Design, Ease Of Use

★★

The site would be even more convenient if the application could be completed online

1–4 Stars

Publisher:

Corporation For National Service

Since 1993, the Corporation for National Service has engaged more than one million Americans in service to their communities, helping to solve community problems.

Media:

Internet

Principal Focus:

Of General Interest

AMERICORPS HOME PAGE

Description:

AmeriCorps is a national service program that allows people 17 years and older to earn "education awards" in exchange for a year of service. After one year (10–12 months) of service, AmeriCorps members receive an education voucher worth $4,725. These vouchers can be used to pay future college costs or to repay student loans. AmeriCorps members also receive a modest stipend and health insurance. At present, more than 25,000 AmeriCorps members serve in over 430 programs across the country. These programs address community needs in four primary areas: education, public safety, human services, and the environment. Interested persons can consult an AmeriCorps Program Directory to select a program of interest. An application can be printed from the Web but cannot be completed online. It must be printed, completed, signed and returned with the required letters of reference completed and signed.

Evaluation:

One of the best features of the Internet is that it provides "one-stop shopping" for users, which is exactly what this site offers. Those interested in serving in the AmeriCorps program can research service options, learn more about education awards, and print the application and reference letter forms. One of the most convenient features is the frequently updated directory of current AmeriCorps programs, important because applicants must apply for a specific program, one sponsored by a local group (such as a nonprofit tutoring center) or a nationally-run program. The two national programs are the AmeriCorps VISTA program (where members work for nonprofit groups and live in the low-income communities they serve) or through the AmeriCorps NCCC (where members serve on teams and live together in housing complexes). Anyone interested in learning more about the AmeriCorps program will find answers on this informative site.

Where To Find/Buy:

On the Internet at http://www.cns.gov/americorps/

ARCO'S PERFECT PERSONAL STATEMENTS
Successful Application Essays From Students At America's Top Graduate And Professional Schools

Description:

This book is designed to help applicants create winning, and original, personal statements that will help them stand out from the crowd. The book begins by taking a look at typical essay questions from a variety of graduate and professional schools, divided into categories (e.g., topics that "inquire about your motives, goals, and ambitions," topics that "invite you to explain blemishes, deficiencies, or gaps in your past," etc.). A discussion follows on how to write an effective personal statement in response to such questions. Part 2 of the book gives advice about letters of recommendation and interviewing. Part 3, the longest section, contains "Thirty Great Personal Statements by Successful Applicants" to a variety of schools and programs, and from a variety of backgrounds and perspectives. Interspersed among the essays are brief remarks on how/why they are successful. The last section contains advice from admissions officers at law, business, and medical schools.

Evaluation:

Any book that contains examples of successful (or unsuccessful) personal statements is bound to be of use to the grad school applicant, for whom even flipping through such essays can help give an idea of the size, scope, possibilities, and limitations of the application essay. This book, although it includes essays for all types of schools, is really geared toward the law, business, and medical school applicant—some advice offered may be less relevant for applicants to other programs. A drawback is that this book offers no critical evaluations of essays that don't work—often as enlightening as examples of great essays. Additionally, it tries to cover application essays for all types of schools, although medical school essays are often critically different than MBA essays, which are in turn very different from essays for law school. Readers should find this a generally useful tool to get started, but there are more useful books on this subject that focus specifically on personal statements for individual graduate programs.

Where To Find/Buy:

Bookstores and libraries.

Overall Rating
★★
Pretty good essays, but with little critical evaluation, and very general focus

Design, Ease Of Use
★★
Little breathing space between essays gives pages a "cramped" feel

1–4 Stars

Author:
Mark Alan Stewart

Publisher:
Arco (Macmillan)

Edition:
1996

Price:
$9.95

Pages:
114

ISBN:
0028610490

Media:
Book

Principal Focus:
Of General Interest

Overall Rating

★★

Online scholarship and school searches can be fun, but they aren't very informative

Design, Ease Of Use

★★

Designed for undergrads; not tailored to graduate students

1–4 Stars

Publisher:

College Board

The College Board is a national association of schools, colleges, and other educational organizations dedicated to putting college within the reach of all students. College Board's services and products include the SAT, PSAT/NMSQT, AP programs, and College Online.

Media:

Internet

Principal Focus:

Of General Interest

COLLEGE BOARD ONLINE

Description:

The most popular feature at this large site is the free college search software, ExPAN. Although designed primarily for high schoolers choosing a college, those interested in graduate and professional schools can refine their search to include a master's, PhD, or professional degree. Searches can then be narrowed by several criteria, beginning with field of study. Users then select other criteria important to them, such as maximum tuition, location, school size, and options like research and teaching assistantships, or financial aid for international students. Schools matching the search inquiry appear on the screen. To learn more about individual schools, users click to a brief description with charted information on application and financial aid deadlines. Users can also use a scholarship search program: by entering a student profile with information, such as degree, field of study, ethnic background, state of residence, etc., a hyperlinked set of "matching" scholarships is listed.

Evaluation:

One of the largest and most visited sites aimed at students and their families, the College Board website offers several interesting features. Because the scholarship search includes only a fraction of the fellowships and grants available to graduate and professional students, we don't recommend it. The school search may be helpful for those who happen to place importance on the criteria included in the search (location, availability of married housing, maximum tuition), but most graduate and professional students use more sophisticated criteria in selecting a school (presence of appropriate advisor, laboratory facilities, percent of faculty who are women or minority). If your school requires the PROFILE form (to disburse nonfederal aid), you can register online for $5. We like the "calculators" found at this site, tools for helping you estimate your Expected Family Contribution, and appropriate loan limits given your anticipated starting salary.

Where To Find/Buy:

On the Internet at http://www.collegeboard.org/toc/html/ tocstudents000.html

II. General Interest

COLLEGE & UNIVERSITY HOME PAGES

Description:

This website offers a simple listing of links to virtually all the college and universities home pages, principally in the U.S., but also worldwide as sites are discovered and added. The site is maintained by Christina DeMello, who started the list when she was at MIT. The links can be accessed through an alphabetical listing or a geographical listing. Mirror sites, several outside the U.S., are listed to facilitate quick access from anywhere. The author also conducted a survey designed to solicit input on the best examples of home pages. A list of results from this survey is presented, although DeMello no longer updates survey results. A list of FAQs about the site is also available.

Evaluation:

This site is a useful tool for accessing the home pages of most colleges and universities. These home pages vary widely in quality and focus, but are always useful to some degree when sampling college and graduate school alternatives. DeMello says she's working on converting the listing to a searchable database; she is also trying to add information within the database that would allow selection by specific criteria, such as degrees offered, but don't get your hopes up. This site hasn't been updated for at least three years. For now, the site is impressive given it is essentially a labor of love, maintained in the author's spare time, and most of the links are up-to-date. The FAQs and other pages were last updated in July 1996, so it looks like DeMello has gone on to other things. Too bad.

Where To Find/Buy:

On the Internet at http://www.mit.edu:8001/people/cdemello/univ.html

---

Overall Rating
★★
Useful links to college home pages; pages vary in quality & relevance

Design, Ease Of Use
★★
Basic point & click; useful alphabetical and geographic listings, but needs updating!

1–4 Stars

Author:
Christina DeMello

Media:
Internet

Principal Focus:
Of General Interest

Overall Rating
★★
A limited overview of 767 graduate colleges and universities

Design, Ease Of Use
★★
Organized and readable

1–4 Stars

Publisher:
Peterson's

Edition:
1998

Price:
$24.95

Pages:
692

ISBN:
1560797657

Media:
Book + CD-ROM

Principal Focus:
Of General Interest

PETERSON'S GRADUATE SCHOOLS IN THE U.S.
1998

Description:

Peterson's thick reference guide provides an overview of graduate and professional programs at 767 colleges and universities in the U.S. The book is accompanied by a CD-ROM, which offers in-depth description of 291 of these programs. The CD-ROM/book package is intended to serve as a "starting point for individuals who are thinking of attending graduate school and who would like to begin researching their options." Accordingly, readers will find, in the first few chapters, general information pertaining to the graduate school application process, including financial aid, graduate admissions tests, and accreditation information. A directory of programs by field follows with 386 fields of study and schools offering degrees in each field. After a similar directory listing combined-degree programs, the bulk of the book comprises school profiles arranged by state, including general information on the school and the individual graduate programs and degrees offered. An appendix with contact information follows these profiles.

Evaluation:

This resource contains very basic profiles of 767 colleges and universities offering graduate programs "classified by the Carnegie Foundation for their commitment to graduate education and research." As such, it focuses on the "best" graduate schools and may serve as a helpful preliminary filter for graduate school applicants. However, because the program information is so brief, this resource is best used by applicants unsure of their field of study or those who need to limit their search geographically. Applicants who are certain about their chosen field or aware of the schools offering their program will find little of value here. Certainly, other resources offer more in-depth lists of graduate programs. Peterson's own line of "Compact Guides" are a better choice. Individuals will not want to buy this book, but career counselors and libraries will want to keep a copy on hand for those in the earliest stages of the graduate and professional school application process.

Where To Find/Buy:

Bookstores and libraries.

STUDY IN THE USA

Description:

To help international students study in the USA, this site provides two tools: a searchable directory of U.S. colleges and universities (most entries refer visitors to intensive English-language programs); and a Resource Guide (available in Spanish and Japanese.) The directory arranges schools alphabetically in several categories: schools with locations throughout the U.S.; schools with international locations; distance learning programs; and schools in specific U.S. states. By clicking on a school name, users link to a one-page description of the school, which includes contact information and a link to the school's home page. In most cases, the school descriptions also include "request information" forms for requesting admissions materials. The Resource Guide explains the structure of U.S. education, differentiating between state/private colleges and universities, undergraduate and postgraduate programs, and Master's and PhDs. Also featured are articles on such topics as getting a visa, applying for admissions, choosing a college or university, and paying for education. Test dates for the SAT, GRE, GMAT, and TOEFL are included, as are tips on evaluating intensive English programs.

Evaluation:

According to the Study in the USA home page, its directory is a tool for accessing information on U.S. colleges/universities in general or for choosing an intensive English program. Currently, its only practical use is as a tool for choosing English programs, since such programs comprise the vast majority of directory listings. Only a few colleges and universities listings include general information—rather than information on their intensive English programs—but you wouldn't know that from the search interface. Finding the program of your choice (beside intensive English) is a hit-or-miss proposition. For example, a search of Law Schools turned up Colorado School of Mines and Tacoma Community College, two of dozens of schools that don't have law schools! They do have English programs targeting international students, however, and that's who this site is after. As a guide to such programs, the site is useful. A helpful feature: the online information request form. This tool can save students a lot of stamps and hassles, and the fill-in-the-blank format is easier than composing a letter, especially for those who do not read or write English well. The online Resource Guide is also worth a quick visit. Its articles provide tips, insider information, and commonsense advice for students new to the U.S.

Where To Find/Buy:

On the Internet at http://www.studyusa.com/

Overall Rating
★★

A directory of U.S. institutions with intensive English programs—don't look for grad or professional programs here

Design, Ease Of Use
★★

A time saver for international students researching intensive English options

1–4 Stars

Publisher:

Study in the USA, Inc.

Study in the USA publishes international admissions magazines that provide information about American education to international students.

Media:

Internet

Principal Focus:
Of General Interest

Of Interest To:
International Students

Overall Rating

★

Lots of hype, little substance

Design, Ease Of Use

★★★

Table of contents on every page makes for easy navigation; busy, busy interface

1–4 Stars

Publisher:

PowerStudents.com

PowerStudents.com was founded by two Harvard graduates. It comprises six networks: high school, college, graduate school, career, parents, and insideguide.com.

Media:

Internet

Principal Focus:

Of General Interest

POWERSTUDENTS.COM GRAD SCHOOL

Description:

This website is one of six networks for students and parents created by PowerStudents.com. It includes membership opportunities and a newsletter, interactive forums, chat, and free e-mail to help visitors connect with a larger student community. Each week, the website offers a different spotlight. The week devoted to relocating, for example, features short essays on living in a dorm, finding a roommate, and deciding whether to break up with a hometown sweetheart.

In the "Smart Talk" section, visitors can read student "diaries," describing different graduate programs, ask experts questions about business and medical school, and join forums on graduate school-related topics. Articles in the "Get Smart Zones" discuss getting into graduate school and specific programs. "Get a Life" offers tips on dating, entertainment, sports and recreation, health and lifestyle, and travel. The site's publishers also provide a list of recommended books and resources. Every page is bordered by a table of contents and offers readers the opportunity to respond to what they've read.

Evaluation:

According to the publishers, PowerStudents.com is the "largest cyber-learning center for high school, college, graduate and career-seeking students on the planet." After perusing the pages of the grad school site, it is hard to figure out what is being learned. Articles—all original—are consistently short and lacking in substance. Many fall on their face because they rely on humor and little else. For example, the piece on "When It's Not Worth Staying Together" is a list of ten silly reasons to break up. Other articles are personal manifestos by individuals who chose a particular career path; most offer little to readers. Useful advice is hard to find. While the "Get Smart Zones" seem to promise tips on graduate school success and money issues, they too follow the same format of fluffy articles in 300 words or less. The experts featured here have good credentials, but they offer general answers to user questions, answers covered in more detail in any good guidebook. As for the interactive forums, there's next-to-no action here. Someone named "LILI" pops up on every page and is clearly generating most of the questions and the answers. This site is big on hype but falls well short of its stated goals.

Where To Find/Buy:

On the Internet at http://www.powerstudents.com/gradschool/index.shtml

AMERICORPS: SERVE YOUR COUNTRY & PAY FOR COLLEGE

Description:

In 1993, President Clinton signed into law the National Community Service Trust Act, establishing the AmeriCorps program. This guide begins with "Profiles," inspiring stories and photos, of students involved in AmeriCorps. The bulk of the book is a state-by-state directory of National Service programs, in which AmeriCorps volunteers can participate. Each listing contains a description of the program, its location, number of AmeriCorps members, and a contact. Students interested in applying for AmeriCorps will find all the information they need to apply and designate a program of interest. Because programs change from year to year, students should contact the state commission in their home state to receive the latest information and updates. Students are eligible to perform community service in any participating program, not just programs within their state of residency.

Evaluation:

The AmeriCorps program is one means of financing higher education that appeals to young people committed to community service. AmeriCorps participants receive compensation in the form of a living stipend, and the opportunity to accrue educational awards, which can be used for future education or to pay back student loans. To be eligible, applicants must be 17 years or older; a U.S. citizen, national or legal resident; and, in most cases, a high school graduate or equivalent. Participants work in community-based programs. In exchange for one or two years service, students receive a living allowance (averaging $7,500/year), healthcare, and childcare benefits, and an educational award of $4,725/year to finance higher education or pay back student loans. This book can help interested students prepare the best application possible as the program is fairly competitive. In its first year, 100,000 applicants applied for 20,000 positions.

Where To Find/Buy:

Bookstores and libraries.

Overall Rating
★
A great resource for students interested in community service

Design, Ease Of Use
★
Very basic design—for information only!

1–4 Stars

Publisher:
Conway Greene

Edition:
1996

Price:
$12.95

ISBN:
1884669123

Media:
Book

Principal Focus:
Of General Interest

Overall Rating

★

Minimal background information provided; no listing of degree programs

Design, Ease Of Use

★

Thin pages and small font make for difficult reading

1–4 Stars

Publisher:

College Board

The College Board is a national association of schools, colleges, and other educational organizations dedicated to putting college within the reach of all students. College Board's services and products include the SAT, PSAT/NMSQT, AP programs, and College Online.

Edition:

12th (1998)

Price:

$21.95

Pages:

358

ISBN:

0874475937

Media:

Book

Principal Focus:

Of General Interest

Of Interest To:

International Students

THE COLLEGE BOARD INTERNATIONAL STUDENT HANDBOOK OF U.S. COLLEGES

Description:

Part I, "Applying to College in the U.S.," provides background information on higher education in the U.S. Topics include comparing and choosing colleges, as well as college costs and requirements. Information on tests and how colleges make their decisions, a planning calendar for U.S. study, and a glossary of college terms are also included. The second part, "Information on U.S. Colleges and Universities," provides two detailed tables listing colleges offering undergraduate and graduate study. These tables list basic information on the school, plus tests required, TOEFL minimum and average, student services, tuition and fees, living costs, and financial aid data. Several additional lists are included. One lists colleges that offer conditional admission to applicants whose English skills will not permit them to pursue academic course work their first term. Another lists colleges that require or recommend the SAT II. It concludes with "Sources of information and advising for your country."

Evaluation:

College Board publishes this guide primarily for undergraduate students from foreign countries researching the possibility of attending college in the United States. Information and advice tailored to graduate students is tacked on in a couple of chapters, but the focus is clearly on undergraduate students and their concerns. The background information on selecting and applying to a college is brief; most foreign students will need more details than provided. Information on individual colleges is also minimal. The tables list whether the schools offer a Master's or doctorate program, but there is no listing of degrees offered. What's more, readers cannot use this guide to research which colleges offer a Master's in Biology, for example, or a PhD in German Literature. Nor can they learn about professional schools (for example, Yale Law School or the UCLA School of Dentistry). The quality of the presentation is also poor: the font is small and difficult to read; and the pages are so thin the ink shows through. More comprehensive college profiles for International Students are available—so buyer beware.

Where To Find/Buy:

Bookstores and libraries.

THE GOURMAN REPORT
A Rating Of Graduate & Professional Programs In American & International Universities

Description:

Dr. Gourman, a former political science professor and CEO, has published his ratings of graduate and professional programs since 1980. He assigns each entity (whether a graduate program within a school, or a school as a whole) a numerical score based on a set of unspecified criteria of Dr. Gourman's choosing. These criteria are not explained, and they vary with each graduate program and type of professional school. Part I provides a series of charts ranking graduate programs in subjects ranging from oceanography to history. Each program is assigned a rank and a score, and only those programs rating a 4.0 or higher are listed. Parts II–VII rank professional programs (such as schools of law, medicine, dentistry, engineering, and MBA/Management) in a similar manner. Other charts include ratings of Gourman's top 50 doctoral programs and leading international universities. The final sections list criminal justice and education graduate programs NOT on his approved list. Numerous appendices follow.

Evaluation:

The value of the rankings in this book depends solely on the reputation of the ranker himself. However, Dr. Gourman provides no explanation of the criteria used to evaluate programs nor does he discuss the objectivity or subjectivity of the ratings. His wholly inadequate Preface merely lists reasons why many institutions scored poorly, such as the nebulous "students suffer from poor counseling." Any significance readers attach to the rankings and ratings found in this book depends on their confidence in the all-seeing, all-knowing powers of the author. We do not recommend any prospective student, administrator, or corporation use these rankings as a meaningful source of guidance. We also question the author's approach to advanced degrees in education: not a single education degree or major at any school meets his approval. His explanation: "Meaningless courses of no substance down grades (sic) the major. The major should be abolished by all institutions." So much for objectivity.

Where To Find/Buy:

Bookstores and libraries.

Overall Rating
★
No explanation of criteria used for evaluation

Design, Ease Of Use
★
A bare-bones series of charts begs for background information on the author's methods

1–4 Stars

Author:
Dr. Jack Gourman

Dr. Gourman is a former professor of political science and CEO. He has been assessing education programs for over 30 years. This volume is his eighth revision of this assessment of graduate and professional programs.

Publisher:
National Education Standards

Edition:
8th (1997)

Price:
$21.95

Pages:
302

ISBN:
0679783741

Media:
Book

Principal Focus:
Of General Interest

Overall Rating
★
Hand-holding services for international students with money

Design, Ease Of Use
★
Navigation fairly smooth ("back" button exits you); unclear how to access online application

1–4 Stars

Publisher:
International Education Service

The IES assists international students wishing to study in the U.S. or Canada. Its services include assistance in finding "appropriate institutions," getting your applications processed, and attracting international students. Currently, there are 500 IES member institutions, most of which accept a generic application supplied by IES.

Media:
Internet

Principal Focus:
Of General Interest

Of Interest To:
International Students

INTERNATIONAL EDUCATION SERVICE

Description:
Since 1983, the International Education Service has been an "agency dedicated to assisting students from all parts of the world who wish to study in the United States or Canada." The IES Placement Service will find "appropriate institutions" for students (based on financial, geographic, and academic needs) or process requests for institutions selected by students; there is no charge for this service, but students must complete the application information form and have a minimum of $10K per year for expenses (IES won't assist those who need financial aid). It also promotes institutions interested in attracting students from abroad. Currently, there are 500 IES member institutions. Through this website, students may contact these institutions via a geographic index and obtain info (email or online). The IES online resource, *American Education Magazine*, contains basic information on the U.S. educational system (I-20 form, selecting, applying, financial aid, housing, etc.). *The Foreign Students' Guide to American Schools, Colleges, and Universities* collects detailed information on the IES member schools and can be found at academic advising centers. Also offered is the "University/College ESL Application Form" accepted by most IES institutions.

Evaluation:
Though their mission statement says that they are an "agency dedicated to assisting students from all parts of the world who wish to study in the United States or Canada," this for-profit group exists for the benefit of colleges and university students (with adequate funds) who are interested in studying in the U.S. and Canada. Using their service may provide the kind of "hand-holding" that international students unfamiliar with the American college admissions process need (or assume they need), but most students would be better served by reading one of the printed guides to college admissions designed for international students. These guides are detailed and thorough, and will answer questions more completely than this website.

Where To Find/Buy:
On the Internet at http://www.ies-ed.com/

AMERICAN UNIVERSITIES

Non-Rated Resource

Description
The website team at the College of Liberal Arts and Sciences at the University of Florida maintains a list of direct links to American universities granting bachelor or advanced degrees. Most links lead to institution home pages, though a few connect to departments or college-level pages within a larger university. More than 1,500 links are included.

Publisher:
College of Liberal Arts and Sciences, University of Florida

The website team at the College of Liberal Arts and Sciences at the University of Florida maintains a list of direct links to American universities granting bachelor or advanced degrees. Most links lead to institution home pages, though a few connect to departments or college-level pages within a larger university. More than 1,500 links are included.

Media:
Internet

Principal Focus:
Of General Interest

Where To Find/Buy:
On the Internet at http://www.clas.ufl.edu/CLAS/american-universities.html#U

COLLEGENET

Non-Rated Resource

Description
The college search area of this site offers directories of MBA programs, medical schools, and nursing schools. Still under construction, the site has no search feature at this time; users simply scroll through school names. Contact information for each entry is provided. In some cases, hypertext links to institutions are included. Information on admissions/financial aid, campus life, and academics for each school is promised for the future.

Publisher:
Universal Algorithms, Inc.

Launched in 1995, CollegeNET is a portal for applying to colleges over the web. Over 250 colleges and universities have contracted with CollegeNET to serve their official web-based admissions applications.

Media:
Internet

Principal Focus:
Of General Interest

Where To Find/Buy:
On the Internet at http://cnsearch.collegenet.com/cgi-bin/CN/index

GENERAL EDUCATION ONLINE

Non-Rated Resource

Description
This website maintained at the University of West Florida, under the auspices of Web Spinners, an independent operating division of University Commons and Student Activities there. It comprises over 6,400 links to universities and colleges from over 160 countries, from Afghanistan to Zimbabwe. It claims to be the largest and most diverse university and college listing in the world.

Author:
Mike Viron

Mike Viron is Project Leader and Administrator for General Education Online, a web-based project supported by the efforts of web developers who have volunteered their time.

Media:
Internet

Principal Focus:
Of General Interest

Where To Find/Buy:
On the Internet at http://wsdo.sao.uwf.edu/~geo/

INFORMATION USA: EDUCATION IN THE USA

Non-Rated Resource

Description
This hyperlink web guide is designed to provide an introduction to the American system of higher education with practical information about study opportunities. It includes links to "overview" sites from the U.S. government, plus links to the United States Information Agency's Graduate Study guide, which contains a step-by-step plan for applying to U.S. schools.

Publisher:
United States Information Agency

Information USA is maintained by the U.S. Information Agency, an independent foreign affairs agency within the executive branch of the federal government.

Media:
Internet

Principal Focus:
Of General Interest

Of Interest To:
International Students

Where To Find/Buy:
On the Internet at http://www.usia.gov/infousa/educ/educate.htm

TEST OF ENGLISH AS A FOREIGN LANGUAGE (TOEFL)

Non-Rated Resource

Description
International students planning to attend graduate or professional school in North America may be asked to demonstrate their English proficiency level by taking the Test of English as a Foreign Language, as well as the Test of Written English. This site describes these tests and provides information on how, when, and where to register, the cost, and how scores are reported. Included are free test prep questions as well as a store to order test prep materials.

Publisher:
Educational Testing Service

Educational Testing Service (ETS) is a private, nonprofit organization that develops and administers millions of achievement and admissions tests each year in the U.S. and 180 other countries, including the TOEFL. Their website, http://www.ETS.org, was launched in 1996.

Media:
Internet

Principal Focus:
Of General Interest

Of Interest To:
International Students

Where To Find/Buy:
On the Internet at http://www.toefl.org/ or call (609) 771-7100, or fax (609) 279-9146, or email toefl@ets.org/

U.S. EDUCATION JOURNAL

Non-Rated Resource

Description
The U.S. Education Journal offers international students the opportunity to request information online from the Journal's database of featured U.S. colleges and universities. (About two dozen graduate programs are featured.) Visitors to the site will also find advice on getting a visa and English testing, plus travel tips and "Q and A."

Publisher:
U.S. Education Journal

Media:
Internet

Principal Focus:
Of General Interest

Of Interest To:
International Students

Where To Find/Buy:
On the Internet at http://www.usjournal.com

III

A Quick Guide To Internet Resources

III. A Quick Guide To Internet Resources

In the development of this guidebook, we have encountered hundreds of Internet resources. We include reviews of nearly 100, those that address the specific concerns of graduate and professional school students and their advisors.

Because our resource recommendations are based on our judgment of value, not only relative to alternatives in the same media, but against all available resource regardless of media, we present the full-page reviews of these Internet resources in our Resource Review section.

Here we provide a Quick Guide to Internet Resources for those readers who prefer going straight to the Internet.

These resources are arranged by Subject and Overall Rating. For ease of use, we include their Star Rating; the resource title; URL, or Internet "address"; and a reference to the page in this guidebook where the full-page review is located.

This guide is organized in the following topical sections:

- **Obtaining A Master's Or PhD**   319
- **Choosing, Getting Into, & Excelling In Business School**   319
- **Choosing, Getting Into, & Excelling In Law School**   320
- **Choosing, Getting Into, & Excelling In Medical School & Other Health Science Programs**   321
- **Financing A Graduate Or Professional Degree**   322
- **Scholarship Directories & Search Services**   323
- **Of General Interest To Prospective Graduate & Professional Students**   324

Obtaining A Master's Or PhD

★★★ **APA: Student Information/Education Programs**
http://www.apa.org/students/ and http://www.apa.org/ed/   See page 60

★★★ **Embark.com: Going To Graduate School**
http://www.embark.com/grad   See page 27

★★★ **Graduate Student Resources On The Web**
http://www-personal.umich.edu/~danhorn/graduate.html   See page 30

★★★ **Petersons.com: The Graduate School Channel**
http://www.petersons.com/graduate   See page 31

★★★ **U.S. News Online: Graduate School**
http://www.usnews.com/usnews/edu/beyond/bchome.htm   See page 32

★★★ **Association For Support Of Graduate Students**
http://www.asgs.org   See page 41

★★★ **GradSchools.Com**
http://www.gradschools.com/   See page 43

★★★ **Graduate Student Advice & Research Survival Guide**
http://www-smi.stanford.edu/people/pratt/smi/advice.html   See page 38

★★★ **GRE Online**
http://www.gre.org/   See page 39

★★★ **Kaplan Online: Grad School**
http://www1.kaplan.com/view/article/1,1898,3740,00.html   See page 37

★ **Getting In: An Applicant's Guide To Graduate School Admissions**
http://www.h-net.msu.edu/~burrell/guide0.html   See page 48

★ **Princeton Review Online: Graduate**
http://www.review.com/Graduate   See page 47

N/R **Council Of Graduate Schools: Student Page**
http://www.cgsnet.org/student/student.htm   See page 83

Choosing, Getting Into, & Excelling In Business School

★★★★ **Business Week Online's Business Schools**
http://www.businessweek.com/tocs/bschools.htm   See page 90

★★★★ **Embark.com: Going To Business School**
http://www.embark.com/mba   See page 95

★★★★ **Petersons.com: The MBA Channel**
http://www.petersons.com/mba   See page 96

★★★ **MBA Info**
http://www.mbainfo.com   See page 105

★★★ **MBA Plaza**
http://www.mbaplaza.com   See page 106

★★★ **Princeton Review Online: Business**
http://www.review.com/business/   See page 110

★★★ **U.S. News Online: Business**
http://www.usnews.com/usnews/edu/beyond/bcbiz.htm   See page 97

★★★ **GMAT Online: MBA Explorer**
http://www.gmat.org/   See page 113

★★★ **Kaplan Online: Business**
http://www1.kaplan.com/view/zine/1,1899,3,00.html   See page 111

★★★ **The MBA Page**
http://www.cob.ohio-state.edu/dept/fin/oldmba.htm   See page 115

N/R **Bschool.com**
http://www.bschool.com   See page 121

N/R **FINAID: Business School Resources**
http://www.finaid.org/otheraid/business.phtml   See page 121

N/R **GradAdvantage**
http://www.gradadvantage.org   See page 121

N/R **Top Ten**
http://www.top10.org   See page 122

Choosing, Getting Into, & Excelling In Law School

★★★★ **Boston College Online Law School Locator**
http://www.bc.edu:80/bc_org/svp/carct/matrix.html   See page 130

★★★★ **Embark.com: Going To Law School**
http://www.embark.com/law   See page 138

★★★★ **FindLaw**
http://www.findlaw.com   See page 131

★★★★ **Internet Legal Resource Guide**
http://www.ilrg.com/   See page 139

★★★ **Kaplan Online: Law**
http://www1.kaplan.com/view/zine/1,1899,5,00.html   See page 150

★★★ **Law School Admissions Council Online**
http://www.lsac.org   See page 156

★★★ **National Association For Law Placement**
http://www.nalp.org/   See page 152

★★★ **Petersons.com: The Law Channel**
http://www.petersons.com/law   See page 154

★★★ **Princeton Review Online: Law School**
http://www.review.com/Law/   See page 157

★★★ **U.S. News Online: Law**
http://www.usnews.com/usnews/edu/beyond/bclaw.htm   See page 144

N/R **American Bar Association Approved Law Schools**
http://www.abanet.org/legaled/approved.html   See page 172

N/R **FINAID: Law School Resources**
http://www.finaid.org/otheraid/law.phtml   See page 172

Choosing, Getting Into, & Excelling In Medical School & Other Health Science Programs

★★★★ **Association Of American Medical Colleges**
http://www.aamc.org   See page 189

★★★★ **The Interactive Medical Student Lounge**
http://www.medstudents.net   See page 191

★★★★ **Osteopathic.Com**
http://www.osteopathic.com   See page 192

★★★★ **U.S. News Online: Medicine**
http://www.usnews.com/usnews/edu/beyond/bcmed.htm   See page 188

★★★ **American Association Of Colleges Of Osteopathic Medicine**
http://www.aacom.org/   See page 196

★★★ **Kaplan Online: Medicine**
http://www1.kaplan.com/view/zine/1,1899,4,00.html   See page 204

★★★ **NursingNet**
http://www.nursingnet.org   See page 214

★★★ **Princeton Review Online: Medicine**
http://www.review.com/medical/   See page 217

★ **MedicalStudent.net**
http://www.medicalstudent.net   See page 221

★ **Petersons.com: Medical Schools**
http://www.petersons.com/medical   See page 219

N/R AACOMAS Application Kit
http://www.aacom.org/applic.htm   See page 224

N/R AMCAS-E Student & Applicant Information
http://www.aamc.org/stuapps/admiss/amcase/start.htm   See page 224

N/R FINAID: Medical School Resources
http://www.finaid.org/otheraid/medical.phtml   See page 224

N/R The Mature Medical Student
http://falcon.cc.ukans.edu/~cwpowell/index.html   See page 225

N/R The Medical Education Page
http://www.scomm.net/~greg/med-ed/index.html   See page 225

N/R Premedical Student Forum
http://mednet.stanford.edu/cgi-bin/medworld/HyperNews/get.cgi/
premed.html   See page 225

Financing A Graduate Or Professional Degree

★★★★ eStudentLoan.com
http://www.estudentloan.com   See page 232

★★★★ FINAID: Graduate School Financial Aid Resources
http://www.finaid.org/otheraid/grad.phtml   See page 233

**★★★★ Free Application For Federal Student Aid
(FAFSA) Online**
http://www.ed.gov/offices/OPE/express.html   See page 235

★★★ Access Group
http://www.accessgrp.org/   See page 240

★★★ Direct Loan
http://www.ed.gov/offices/OPE/DirectLoan   See page 242

★★★ Guide To Defaulted Student Loans
http://www.ed.gov/offices/OPE/DCS   See page 239

★★★ Sallie Mae: Student Loan Marketing Association
http://www.salliemae.com/   See page 244

★★★ Kaplan Online: Financial Aid
http://www1.kaplan.com/view/zine/1,1899,10,00.html   See page 246

**★★★ National Association Of Student Financial
Aid Administrators: Planning For College**
http://www.nasfaa.org/DoItAffordIt/publicfront.html   See page 248

N/R The Alliance To Save Student Aid
http://www.StudentAidAlliance.org   See page 251

N/R Educaid Loan Programs: Loans For Graduate Students
http://www.educaid.com/eduloan/loanchtg.htm   See page 251

**N/R Guide To Completing The 1999–2000 Free
Application For Federal Student Aid (FAFSA)**
http://www.ed.gov/prog_info/SFA/FAFSA/   See page 251

N/R National Science Foundation Grad Student Page
http://www.nsf.gov/home/students/start.htm#grad   See page 252

N/R Nellie Mae
http://www.nelliemae.com   See page 252

Scholarship Directories & Search Services

★★★★ FastWEB
http://www.fastweb.com/, or by calling fastWEB at (800) 327-8932. See page 257

★★★ American Journalism Review Newslink
http://ajr.newslink.org/ajraw.html   See page 273

★★★ CollegeNET MACH25 Scholarship Search
http://www.collegenet.com/mach25/   See page 274

★★★ MOLIS: Minority Online Information Service
http://www.fie.com/molis/ir   See page 283

★★★ The Scholarship Resource Network
http://www.rams.com/srn   See page 286

**N/R American Association Of University Women
Educational Foundation Fellowships & Grants**
http://www.aauw.org/3000/fdnfelgra.html   See page 289

N/R American Chemical Society Minority Affairs
http://www.acs.org/pafgen/minority/main_2.htm   See page 289

N/R Federal Trade Commission Scholarship Scam Alert
http://www.ftc.gov/bcp/conline/pubs/alerts/ouchalrt.htm   See page 289

N/R ONElist
http://www.onelist.com/subscribe/scholarshiplist   See page 290

N/R Saludos Web Education Center
http://www.saludos.com/ed.html   See page 290

N/R Scholarships For Women & Minorities 1998
http://members.aol.com/ox13qr/webpages/eyfswm1.html   See page 290

N/R UCI Scholarship Opportunities Program
http://www.honors.uci.edu/sop.html   See page 291

Of General Interest To Prospective Graduate & Professional Students

★★★ **eduPASS**
http://www.edupass.org   See page 297

★★★ **National Association Of Graduate-Professional Students**
http://www.nagps.org/   See page 301

★★★ **Office Of Postsecondary Education Home Page**
http://www.ed.gov/offices/OPE/home.html   See page 295

★★★ **Accepted.com**
http://www.accepted.com   See page 303

★★ **AmeriCorps Home Page**
http://www.cns.gov/americorps/   See page 304

★★★ **College Board Online**
http://www.collegeboard.org/toc/html/tocstudents000.html See page 306

★★★ **College & University Home Pages**
http://www.mit.edu:8001/people/cdemello/univ.html   See page 307

★★★ **Study In The USA**
http://www.studyusa.com/   See page 309

★ **International Education Service**
http://www.ies-ed.com/   See page 314

★ **PowerStudents.com Grad School**
http://www.powerstudents.com/gradschool/index.shtml   See page 310

N/R **American Universities**
http://www.clas.ufl.edu/CLAS/american-universities.html#U See page 315

N/R **CollegeNET**
http://cnsearch.collegenet.com/cgi-bin/CN/index   See page 315

N/R **General Education Online**
Internet at http://wsdo.sao.uwf.edu/~geo/   See page 315

N/R **Information USA: Education In The USA**
http://www.usia.gov/infousa/educ/educate.htm   See page 316

N/R **Test Of English As A Foreign Language (TOEFL)**
http://www.toefl.org/   See page 316

N/R **U.S. Education Journal**
http://www.usjournal.com   See page 316

IV

HELPFUL
ORGANIZATIONS

HELPFUL ORGANIZATIONS

In this directory, we provide contact information and a brief description of professional associations and national organizations, private and public, that provide information, advising, and referrals on specific areas of study, higher education in general, and professional schools. If local or regional offices are not listed, contact the national headquarters.

This directory is organized in the following topical sections:

- **Of General Interest**   327
- **Law School**   328
- **Health Sciences**   329
- **Business School**   331
- **Financial Aid & Scholarships**   333
- **Testing Services**   335
- **Professional Associations**   335
  - *Arts & Humanities*   335
  - *Psychology, Counseling, & Social Work*   338
  - *Other Social Sciences*   339
  - *Sciences & Engineering*   341
- **University Organizations**   343
- **Counseling & Career Planning Organizations**   344
  - *General Advising*   344
  - *Career Counseling*   344
  - *Prelaw Counseling*   346
  - *Prehealth Counseling*   347
  - *International Students & Overseas Study*   348

This directory is accurate to the best of our knowledge and does not represent an endorsement by the editor or publisher.

Of General Interest

American Association Of University Women

1111 Sixteenth St. NW
Washington, DC 20036

Phone: (800) 326-AAUW
Fax: (202) 872-1425
Email: info@aauw.org
URL: http://www.aauw.org

AAUW, with 150,000 members and more than 1,500 branches nationwide, is a national organization promoting education and equity for women of all ages. Its educational foundation funds pioneering research on young women and education, community action projects, and fellowships and grants for outstanding women around the globe. The AAUW Legal Advocacy Fund provides money and a support system for women seeking judicial redress for sex discrimination in higher education. Numerous grants and fellowships are available.

AmeriCorps

Corporation for National Service
1201 New York Ave. NW
Washington, DC 20525

Phone: (800) 942-2677
Email: acorps@infosystec.com
URL: http://www.americorps.org

AmeriCorps, part of the Corporation for National Service, is a service program in which members handle problems ranging from disaster relief to tutoring. Service usually lasts 10 months to one year. For all programs, members receive a modest living allowance; some programs provide housing. Members who successfully serve one year, full-time, are eligible to receive an education award of $4,725. Part-time members are eligible for a partial award. The award can be used to help finance higher education, pay off existing student loans, or pay for expenses incurred while participating in an approved school-to-work program. Members must be a US citizen, national, or legal permanent resident alien.

Association For Support Of Graduate Students

P.O. Box 4698
Incline Village, NV 89450-4698

Phone: (775) 831-1399
Fax: (775) 831-1221
Email: asgs@asgs.org
URL: http://www.asgs.org

ASGS is a service organization of graduate students, graduate-student organizations, and graduate-degree-granting institutions. Its goal is to assist students in completing their theses and obtaining their degrees. ASGS provides a news and reference bulletin, a moderated e-mail discussion list about doing a thesis, a professional consultant directory, and other services.

Council For Opportunity In Education

1025 Vermont Ave. NW, Suite 900
Washington, DC 20005

Phone: (202) 347-7430
Fax: (202) 347-0786
Email: mailbox@hqcoe.org
URL: http://www.trioprograms.org/home.html

Established in 1981, COE is a nonprofit organization dedicated to furthering the expansion of educational opportunities throughout the U.S. Through its numerous membership services, the Council works in conjunction with colleges, universities, and agencies hosting programs to help low-income Americans enter college and graduate. Federal TRIO Programs (Talent Search, Upward Bound, Upward Bound Math Science, Veteran's Upward Bound, Student Support Services, Educational Opportunity Centers, and the Ronald E. McNair Post-Baccalaureate Achievement Program) help students overcome class, social, academic, and cultural barriers to higher education. A directory of TRIO Programs and other publications are available.

National Association Of Graduate-Professional Students

207 Pennsylvania Ave. SE
Washington, DC 20003

Phone: (888) 88-NAGPS
Email: nagps@netcom.com-
URL: http://www.nagps.org

NAGPS is a nonprofit organization dedicated to improving the quality of graduate and professional student life in the U.S. Since 1986, it has actively promoted the interests and welfare of graduate and professional students in public and private universities, as well as in the public and private agencies at the local, state, and national levels. Through its national office and five regional networks, NAGPS acts as a clearinghouse for information on graduate and professional student groups at all stages of development. Call toll-free for regional office locations.

U.S. Department Of Education's Office Of Postsecondary Education

Regional Office Building 3 (ROB-3)
7th and D Streets, SW
Washington, DC 20202

Phone: (202) 708-5547
URL: http://www.ed.gov/offices/OPE

OPE formulates federal postsecondary education policy and administers programs that provide assistance to postsecondary education institutions and to students pursuing programs of postsecondary education. It also provides information and resources for students, parents, educators, and policy-makers.

United States Distance Learning Association

PO Box 376
Watertown, MA 02471-0376

Phone: (800)-275-5162
URL: http://www.usdla.org

USDLA is a nonprofit association formed in 1987 to promote the development and application of distance learning for education and training. It has chapters in all 50 states. In addition, USDLA holds annual meetings with leaders of distance learning programs in Europe and Asia. Individual membership is $125. Organizational memberships start at $500.

University Continuing Education Association

One Dupont Circle NW, Suite 615
Washington, DC 20036-1168

Phone: (202) 659-3130
Fax: (202) 785-0374
Email: postmaster@nucea.edu
URL: http://www.nucea.edu

Founded in 1915, UCEA consists of universities and colleges working to expand higher education opportunities for part-time and nontraditional students. It assists institutions of higher learning and affiliated nonprofit organizations to increase access through various educational programs and services. It also provides national leadership in support of policies that advance workforce and professional development. Association members include public and private accredited colleges and universities, as well as nonprofit organizations with a commitment to professional education.

Law School

American Bar Association

750 N. Lake Shore Drive
Chicago, IL 60611

Phone: (312) 988-5000
Fax: (312) 988-6281
Email: info@abanet.org
URL: http://www.abanet.org/

The American Bar Association has 400,000 members and can provide telephone numbers for referral services by state. It serves the needs of law students with student memberships, a Law Student Division, scholarships, competitions, and career publications.

Association Of American Law Schools

1201 Connecticut Ave. NW, Suite 800
Washington, DC 20036-2605

Phone: (202) 296-8851
Fax: (202) 296-8869
Email: aals@aals.org
URL: http://www.aals.org

Founded in 1900, AALS is a nonprofit association of 162 law schools working for "the improvement of the legal profession through legal education." It serves as the learned society for law teachers and is legal education's principal representative to the federal government and other national higher education organizations and learned societies. It conducts several workshops and conferences through out the year and one meeting each January. It publishes a Directory of Law Teachers and a quarterly newsletter, as well as other publications.

Earl Warren Legal Training Program

99 Hudson St. 16th Floor
New York, NY 10013

Phone: (212) 219-1900
Fax: (212) 226-7592
URL: http://spin.infoed.org/html/spinwww/progs/06516.htm

With varying amounts, Earl Warren Legal Training scholarships are for entering African-American law students who will focus on civil rights or public interest law. Applicants must be U.S. citizen or legal resident. Write or call for complete information.

Florida Endowment Education Fund

201 E. Kennedy Blvd., Suite 1525
Tampa, FL 33602

Phone: (813) 272-2772
URL: http://www.fl-educ-fd.org

FEF works for the advancement of African Americans, Hispanics, and Native Americans practicing law in Florida. The FEF's McKnight doctoral fellowship Program has increased the number of African Americans who have been awarded PhDs in historically underrepresented, crucial disciplines and fields of study. Up to 25 fellowships (renewable for up to five years) are granted each year to students pursuing a doctoral degree at one of ten participating institutions in the state of Florida. Each fellowship consists of $16,000 per year in tuition, fees, and stipend. Applicants must have at least a bachelor's degree from an accredited institution and wish to pursue a doctoral degree.

Law School Admission Council

Box 2000
Newtown, PA 18940-0998

Phone: (215) 968-1001
Fax: (215) 968-1119
Email: LSACinfo@LSAC.org
URL: http://www.lsac.org

The LSAC is a nonprofit organization that provides services to the legal education community. Its members are 194 law schools in the U.S. and Canada. It assists law schools in serving and evaluating applicants with the Law School Admission Test (LSAT) and the Law School Data Assembly Service (LSDAS).

Health Sciences

American Association Of Colleges Of Osteopathic Medicine

5550 Friendship Blvd., Suite 310
Chevy Chase, MD 20815-7231

Phone: (301)968-4100
Fax: (301)-968-4101
URL: http://www.aacom.org

The American Association Of Colleges Of Osteopathic Medicine (AACOM) serves the administration, faculty, and students of its 19 member osteopathic medical schools through its centralized application service (AACOMAS), government relations, finance, and research and information departments.

American Association Of Colleges Of Podiatric Medicine

1350 Piccard Dr., Suite 322
Rockville, MD 20850

Phone: (301) 990-2807
Email: aacpmas@aacpm.org
URL: http://www.aacpm.org/

AACPM is a national nonprofit educational association whose members include six colleges of podiatric medicine and approximately 160 hospitals and other types of institutions, which offer graduate or postdoctoral training in podiatric medicine.

American Association Of Dental Schools

1625 Massachusetts Ave. NW, Suite 600
Washington, DC 20036-2212

Phone: (202) 667-9433
Fax: (202) 667-0642
Email: aads@aads.jhu.edu
URL: http://www.aads.jhu.edu/

AADS seeks to lead the dental education community in addressing contemporary issues influencing education, research, and the health of the public. It provides support for student applicants and advisors, sponsors conferences and meetings, and publishes materials to support students, researchers, and dental schools.

American Dental Association

211 E. Chicago Ave.
Chicago, Illinois 60611

Phone: (312) 440-2500
Fax: (312) 440-2800
URL: http://www.ada.org/

ADA is the professional association of dentists dedicated to serving the public and the profession of dentistry. The association promotes the profession of dentistry by enhancing the integrity and ethics of the profession, strengthening the patient/ dentist relationship, and making membership the foundation of successful practice. It fulfills its public and professional mission by providing services and through its initiatives in education, research, advocacy and the development of standards.

American Medical Association, Student Section

515 N. State St.
Chicago, IL 60610

Phone: (312) 464-4742
URL: http://www.ama-assn.org/ mem-datat/special/ama-mss/ama-mss.htm

Founded in 1847, AMA is a partnership of physicians and their professional associations dedicated to promoting the art and science of medicine and the betterment of public health. It serves physicians and patients by establishing and promoting ethical, educational, and clinical standards for the medical profession and by advocating for the integrity of the physician/patient relationship. The AMA includes a Student Section and provides information about medical education and medical schools.

American Medical Student Association

1902 Association Dr.
Reston, VA 20191

Phone: (800) 767-2266
Fax: (703) 620-5873
Email: amsa@www.amsa.org
URL: http://www.amsa.org

AMSA, founded in 1950, is an independent U.S. association of physicians-in-training providing medical students a chance to participate in organized medicine. With nearly 30,000 members, it is committed to representing the concerns of physicians-in-training and continues its commitment to improving medical training and the nation's health. Members benefits include educational loan opportunities, subscriptions, life, auto, and health insurance, and numerous professional discounts.

American Naturopathic Medical Association

PO Box 96273
Las Vegas, NV 89193

Phone: (702) 897-7053
Email: webmaster@anma.com
URL: http://www.anma.com/

Founded in 1981, ANMA is a nonprofit, scientific, and educational organization dedicated to exploring the mind, body, medicine, and health. It is recognized by the World Organization for Alternative Medicine as the primary organization representing naturopathic medicine in the United States. Its membership is open to individuals with Doctor of Naturopathy or Doctor of Naturopathic Medicine degrees, as well as other health care credentials. Membership fees vary.

American Osteopathic Association

142 E. Ontario St.
Chicago, IL 60611

Phone: (800) 621-1773
Fax: (312) 202-8000
Email: info@aoa-net.org
URL: http://www.aoa-net.org/

AOA is organized to advance the philosophy and practice of osteopathic medicine by promoting excellence in education, research, and the delivery of quality, cost-effective healthcare in a distinct, unified profession. It produces numerous publications and promotes education in the discipline with Divisions of Continuing Medical Education, Postdoctoral Training, and Certification.

Association For Academic Psychiatry

330 Mt. Auburn St.
Cambridge, MA 02238

Phone: (617) 499-5008
Email: info@aapsych.org
URL: http://www.aapsych.org/

AAP promotes education in psychiatry from the beginning of medical school through lifelong learning for psychiatrists and other physicians. It attempts to help psychiatrists who are interested in careers in academic psychiatry develop skills and knowledge in teaching, research, and career development. It provides a forum for members to exchange ideas on teaching techniques, curriculum, and other issues and to work together to solve problems. It also works with other professional organizations on mutual interests and objectives.

Association For The Advancement Of Blacks In Health Sciences

42 Charles St. E.
Toronto, Ontario M4Y 1T4
Canada

Phone: (416) 928-9201
Fax: (416) 928-3325
URL: http://www.aabhs.org

AAABHS is a nonprofit organization of African-American professionals who work or are in training in the health sciences. It promotes and encourages youth to pursue a higher education in the health sciences, works to optimize health services delivered to the African-American community, and educates the community about health issues.

Association Of American Veterinary Medical Colleges

1101 Vermont Ave. NW, Suite 710
Washington, DC 20005

Phone: (202) 371-9195
Fax: (202) 842-0773
Email: Ljohnston@aavmc.org
URL: http://www.aavmc.org/

AAVMS represents more than 4,000 faculty, 5,000 staff, 10,000 veterinary students, and 3,000 graduate students in the U.S. and Canada. It coordinates the affairs of the 27 U.S. Veterinary Medical Colleges, four Canadian Colleges of Veterinary Medicine, Departments of Veterinary Science and Comparative Medicine, and animal medical centers, and foster each membership's teaching, research and service missions, nationally and internationally. AAVMC is involved in the collection and publication of statistical data and the publication of the *Journal of Veterinary Medical Education* and *Veterinary Medical School Admission Requirements in the United States and Canada*. It also operates the

Veterinary Medical College Application Service (VMCAS Application Request Phone, (202) 682-0750), the central distribution, collection and processing service for applications to the veterinary medical colleges.

Association Of Schools & Colleges Of Optometry

6110 Executive Blvd., Suite 510
Rockville, MD 20852

Phone: (301) 231-5944
Fax: (301) 770-1828
URL: http://home.opted.org/asco/

Founded in 1941, ASCO is a nonprofit education association representing the interests of optometry education. ASCO's membership encompasses the 17 schools and colleges of optometry in the United States and Puerto Rico. A number of foreign optometry schools are affiliate members. ASCO is committed to achieving excellence in optometry education and to helping its member schools prepare well-qualified graduates for entrance into the profession of optometry.

Council On Naturopathic Medical Information

PO Box 11426
Eugene, OR 97440-3626

Phone: (541) 484-6028
Email: dir@cnme.org
URL: http://www.cnme.org/

CNME is recognized by the U.S. Secretary of Education as the national accrediting agency for programs leading to the Doctor of Naturopathic Medicine degree. Its purpose is to ensure that accrediting agencies provide reliable evaluations of the quality of education and training offered by the colleges and programs they accredit.

Institute Of Medicine

2101 Constitution Ave. NW
Washington, DC 20418

URL: http://www4.nas.edu/IOM/
IOMHome.nsf

As a component of the National
Academy of Sciences, the Institute
of Medicine strives to advance and
disseminate scientific knowledge to
improve human health. The Institute
provides timely and authoritative
information and advice concerning
health and science policy to
government, the corporate sector,
the professions, and the public.
Members are elected on the basis of
their professional achievement and
serve without compensation in the
conduct of studies, conferences, and
other Institute inquiries into matters
of national policy for health.

National Medical Fellowships, Inc.

110 W. 32nd, 8th floor
New York, NY 10001

Phone: (212) 714-0933
URL: www.nmf-online.org

Established in 1946, NMF is a
nonprofit organization seeking
to improve the quality of and access
to health care in America, especially
in minority and underserved
communities, by increasing the
number of minority physicians.
Efforts focus on encouraging
African-Americans, mainland Puerto
Ricans, Mexican-Americans, and
Native American medical students
to achieve academic excellence
and to pursue careers that promote
primary care and wellness, academic
medicine and research, and leadership
development in all phases of health
and medicine. Programs include
need-based scholarships for medical
education, workshops, seminars, and
publications.

Student Senate—American Medical Women's Association

801 N. Fairfax St., Suite 400
Alexandria, VA 22314

Phone: (703) 838-0500
Fax: (703) 549-3864
Email:
wumsamwa@medicine.wustl.edu
URL: http://medicine.wustl.edu/
~wumsamwa/senate

AMWA, founded in 1915, is a
national organization of 10,000
women physicians and medical
students dedicated to promoting
women's health, improving the
professional development and
personal well-being of members,
and increasing the influence of
women in all aspects of the medical
profession. At the local level,
student branches provide support for
women in medical school through
mentorships and special programs.

The American Association Of Colleges Of Nursing

One Dupont Circle NW, Suite 530
Washington, DC 20036

Phone: (202) 463-6930
Fax: (202) 785-8320
URL: http://www.aacn.nche.edu

AACN is a national voice for
America's baccalaureate- and higher-
degree nursing education programs.
It works to establish quality standards
in nursing education, assist deans and
directors to implement those standards,
influence the nursing profession to
improve health care, and promote
public support of baccalaureate and
graduate education, research, and
practice in nursing.

Business School

American Assembly Of Collegiate Schools Of Business

600 Emerson Rd., Suite 300
St. Louis, MO 63141-6762

Phone: (314) 872-8481
Fax: (314) 872-8495
URL: http://www.aacsb.edu

AACSB is a nonprofit society of
educational institutions, corporations,
and other organizations devoted to
promoting and improving higher
education in business administration
and management. Organized in 1916,
AACSB is a accrediting agency for
bachelor's, master's, and doctoral degree
programs in business administration and
accounting. Its membership consists of
over 670 U.S. educational institutions,
over 140 international educational
institutions, and approximately 60
business, government, and nonprofit
organizations. AACSB represents the
combined influence of its member
universities, including more than
30,000 faculty and 700,000 students
majoring in business.

American Management Association

1601 Broadway
New York, NY 10019-7420

Phone: (800) 262-9699
Fax: (212) 903-8168
Email: consumercare@amanet.org
URL: http://www.amanet.org/
start.htm

AMA is a nonprofit, membership-
based educational organization
assisting individuals and enterprises
in the development of organizational
effectiveness. Programs are geared to
various levels of professionalism. Some
are for beginners who are about to
take the first steps into management;
some are for middle management
professionals who are seeking to keep
their skills up-to-date. Other programs
are for upper and middle managers
interested in learning the latest trends
and techniques of management.
Student programs are also available.

American Marketing Association

311 South Wacker Dr., Suite 5800
Chicago, IL 60606

Phone: (800) 262-1150
Fax: (312) 542-9001
Email: info@ama.org
URL: http://www.ama.org

AMA is an international professional society of individual members with an interest in the practice, study, and teaching of marketing. With chapters across North America, it publishes a variety of periodicals and offers 20 topical seminars in addition to tutorials and training programs, which provide members with information on current industry policies.

Business Professionals Of America

5454 Cleveland Ave.
Columbus, OH 43231

Phone: (614) 895-7277
Fax: (614) 895-1165
Email: bpa@ix.netcom.com
URL: http://www.bpa.org

BPA is a national student organization for students enrolled in business, office, and technology education programs at the middle school, secondary school, and Postsecondary school levels. It contributes to the preparation of workforce professionals through the advancement of leadership, citizenship, academic, and technological skills for students.

Catalyst

120 Wall St.
New York, NY 10005

Phone: (212) 514-7600
Fax: (212) 514-8470
Email: info@catalystwomen.org
URL: http://www.catalystwomen.org/home.html

This nonprofit organization works toward the advancement of women in business and, since 1977, has tracked women's progress through boardrooms, sales territories, and management ranks of the American workplace. Since 1990, it has published the annual Catalyst Census and 22 other publications. Research studies cover two main areas: women's leadership development; and work and family issues. Catalyst advisory services works with corporations and professional firms to identify issues and develop action strategies related to the recruitment, retention, and advancement of women.

Consortium For Graduate Study In Management

200 S. Hanley Rd., Suite 1102
St. Louis, MO 63105-3415

Phone: (888) 658-6814
Fax: (314) 935-5014
Email: cgsmfrontdesk@mail.olin.wustl.edu
URL: http://www.cgsm.wustl.edu:8010

CGSM is a 12-university alliance working to facilitate the entry of minorities into managerial positions in business. The universities recruit college-trained African American, Hispanic American, and Native American U.S. citizens and invite them to compete for merit-based fellowships for graduate study leading to a Master's Degree in Business. Founded in 1966, the Consortium was organized to assist qualified minorities in the process of enrolling in accredited graduate business programs. Since its inception, the Consortium has increased the number of annual fellowships awarded from 20 to over 350. These fellowships are funded by various American businesses and the 12 universities affiliated with the Consortium. Awards cover full tuition and fees; second-year support is contingent upon satisfactory progress in the first year.

Future Business Leaders Of America

1912 Association Dr.
Reston, VA 20191-1591

Phone: (800) 325-2946
Fax: (703) 758-0749
Email: general@fbla.org
URL: http://www.fbla-pbl.org

The mission of FBLA is to bring business and education together in a positive working relationship through innovative leadership and career development programs. Members interact with community businesses, experience the rewards of volunteerism, and enjoy travel and special activities. FBLA is open to all secondary students interested in a business or business-related career. FBLA Phi Beta Lambda is open to all collegiate or Postsecondary students pursuing a business or business-related career. Membership is also open to businesspersons, educators, school administrators, former FBLA-PBL members, and parents.

Graduate Management Admission Council

1750 Tysons Boulevard, Suite 1100
McLean, VA 22102

Phone: (703) 749-0131
Fax: (703) 749-0169
Email: gmacmail@gmac.com
URL: http://www.gmat.org

GMAC is a nonprofit organization of graduate business schools worldwide whose purpose is to create access to graduate business education, and provide products and services that add value to graduate business schools and their applicants and students. These products and services include: The Graduate Management Admission Test (GMAT); Self-study preparation guides in print and on software; MBA Forums for one-stop information on MBA programs; MBA LOANSSM and Executive MBA LOANSSM programs for financing an MBA education;

Destination MBA and other diversity initiatives; and Pre-MBA CD-ROM interactive educational programs designed for nonbusiness majors.

National Society Of Hispanic MBAs

8204 Elmbrook St. 235
Dallas, TX 75247

Phone: (877) 467-4622
Fax: (214) 267-1626
Email: rdelrio@gsm.udallas.edu
URL: http://www.nshmba.org

NSHMBA fosters Hispanic leadership through graduate management education and professional development in order to improve society. It was founded in 1988 as a nonprofit organization and has 15 chapters with over 2,800 members throughout the U.S. The Scholarship Program provides financial assistance to Hispanic students pursuing a master's degree in management or business. Scholarships range from $1,000 to $3,000 and one for $10,000. In 1998, NSHMBA awarded $200,000 in scholarships to graduate students. Scholarship recipients are selected by a national review committee and are evaluated on academic achievement, community service, financial need, written essay, and letters of recommendations.

Net Impact: New Leaders For Better Business

609 Mission Street, Third Floor
San Francisco, CA 94105

Phone: (415) 778-8366
Fax: (415) 778-8367
Email: Mail@Net-Impact.Org
URL: http://www.srbnet.org/

Net Impact is a network of emerging business leaders committed to using the power of business to create a better world. It comprises an association of 1,500 students and alumni representing 100 graduate business schools across North America and beyond. Originally founded as Students for Responsible Business in 1993, Net Impact offers a portfolio of programs to help members broaden their business education, refine their leadership skills, and pursue their professional goals, while they build their network.

Financial Aid & Scholarships

Committee On Institutional Cooperation

302 E. John St., Suite 1705
Champaign, IL 61820-5698

Phone: (217) 333-8475
Fax: (217) 244-7127
Email: cic@uiuc.edu
URL: http://ntx2.cso.uiuc.edu/cic/index.html

CIC, established in 1958, is the academic consortium of 12 major teaching and research universities: the University of Chicago, University of Illinois, Indiana University, University of Iowa, University of Michigan, Michigan State University, University of Minnesota, Northwestern University, Ohio State University, Pennsylvania State University, Purdue University, and University of Wisconsin-Madison. CIC awards five pre-doctoral fellowships in the sciences and engineering to underrepresented minorities each year. The fellowships provide a stipend, full tuition, and all standard fees for the first academic year of graduate work toward the PhD. Each CIC university also offers pre-doctoral fellowships that are awarded on a competitive basis to minority students. Call or write for details.

Fulbright Scholar Program

Institute of International Education
809 United Nations Plaza
New York, NY 10017-3580

Phone: (212) 984-5400
URL: http://www.iie.org/fulbright

The Fulbright Program was established in 1946 to increase mutual understanding between the people of the U.S. and other countries through the exchange of persons, knowledge, and skills. Its primary source of funding is an annual appropriation made by the U.S. Information Agency and the Institute of International Education. Participating governments and host institutions also contribute financial support through direct cost-sharing, as well as through tuition waivers, university housing, and other benefits. Grants are made to citizens of participating countries, primarily for university teaching, advanced research, graduate study, and teaching in elementary and secondary schools. Postdoctorate fellowships are also available.

Harry S. Truman Scholarship Foundation

712 Jackson Pl. NW
Washington, DC 20006

URL: http://www.truman.gov

Established by Congress in 1975, the Foundation awards merit-based $30,000 scholarships to college students who have outstanding leadership potential, plan to pursue careers in government or elsewhere in public service, and wish to attend graduate school to help prepare for their careers. In 2000, the Foundation expects to award nearly 80 scholarships in many fields of study.

Indian American Scholarship Fund

2707 Rangewood Drive
Atlanta, GA 30345

Phone: (404) 299-5795
Email: ravi@iasf.org
URL: http://www.iasf.org/index.htm

IASF was started in 1993 under the direction of the India American Cultural Association, a nonprofit organization in Georgia. It tries to provide support, financial or otherwise, to students who seek its help. It offers several awards to high school, college, graduate, and doctorate students. Write for eligibility requirements and details.

National Association Of Student Financial Aid Administrators

1129 20th St. NW, Suite 400
Washington, DC 20036-3489

Phone: (202) 785-0453
Email: ask@nasfaa.org
URL: http://www.nasfaa.org

NASFAA supports financial aid professionals at colleges, universities, and career schools. Its primary focus is on student-aid legislation, regulatory analysis, and professional development for financial aid administrators. Members include nearly 3,000 postsecondary institutions and 260 individuals and organizations with an interest in student aid. The association works closely with higher education institutions, government agencies, and other associations to share knowledge that will improve financial aid administration. Membership includes numerous publications.

National Consortium For Graduate Degrees For Minorities In Engineering & Science, Inc.

P.O. Box 537
Notre Dame, IN 46556

Phone: (219) 631-7771
URL: http://www.nd.edu/~gem

GEM is a nonprofit corporation chartered in 1976 and is jointly sponsored by a consortium of university and employer members. It is governed by a board of directors comprised of one GEM representative from each university and employer member. Its primary mission is to enhance the value of the nation's human capital in engineering and science by increasing the participation of

underrepresented minorities (Native Americans, African Americans, Mexican Americans, Puerto Ricans, and other Hispanic Americans) at the masters and doctoral levels. It offers 250 fellowships a year for full tuition, fees, and stipend. Applicants must be a U.S. citizen at time of application.

Office Of The American Secretary—The Rhodes Scholarship Trust

P.O. Box 7490
McLean, VA 22106-7490

Email: amsec@rhodesscholar.org
URL: http://www.rhodesscholar.org

These scholarships bring outstanding students from around the world to the University of Oxford. Rhodes Scholars are selected by regional selection committees, which choose 32 scholars each year from those nominated by selection committees in each of the 50 states. Applications are sought from talented students without restriction as to their field of academic specialization or career plans, although the proposed course of study must be available at Oxford, and the applicant's undergraduate program must provide a sufficient basis for further study in the proposed field. Rhodes Scholars are appointed for two years of study in the University of Oxford, with the possibility of renewal for a third year.

Reference Service Press

5000 Windplay Dr., Suite 4
El Dorado Hills, CA 95762

Email: gails@rspfunding.com
URL: http://www.rspfunding.com

RSP is a service committed to collecting, organizing, and disseminating—in both print and electronic formats—the most current information available on scholarships, fellowships, loans, grants, awards, internships, and other types of funding opportunities. Founded in 1977, RSP specializes in the

development of print and electronic sources of information on financial aid for specific groups, including women, minorities, the disabled, individuals interested in going abroad, and veterans, military personnel, and their dependents. RSP awards a $2,000 fellowship (through the California Library Association) to a graduate student interested in preparing for a career in reference librarian.

The Foundation Center

79 Fifth Ave./16th St.
New York, NY 10003-3076

Phone: (212) 807-3677
Fax: (800) 424-9836
URL: http://www.fdncenter.org

The Center, an independent nonprofit information clearinghouse established in 1956, works to foster public understanding of the foundation field by collecting, organizing, analyzing, and disseminating information on foundations, corporate giving, and related subjects. Their audience includes grant seekers, grant makers, researchers, policy makers, the media, and the general public.

United Negro College Fund

8260 Willow Oaks Corporate Dr.
Fairfax, VA 22031

Phone: (800) 331-2244
URL: http://www.uncf.org

UNCF was incorporated in 1944 with 27 member colleges and a combined enrollment of 14,000 students. Today it is the nation's oldest African American higher education assistance organization, a consortium of 39 private, accredited four-year historically black colleges and universities. Though UNCF has broadened its focus by offering more programs designed to enhance the quality of education for America's brightest young minds, its commitment to providing financial assistance to deserving students, raising operating funds for member colleges and universities, and supplying technical assistance to member institutions remains unchanged. UNCF oversees more than 400 scholarship programs.

World Of Knowledge Foundation

Princeton Forrestal Village
125-250 Village Blvd.
Princeton, NJ 08540

Phone: (888) 953-7737
URL: http://www.worldofknowledge.org

This foundation helps people in America's culturally diverse communities, foreign national students, and immigrants succeed by providing funding for educational scholarships and programs. Scholarship money is awarded through student competitions. Students must be presently studying in the U.S.

Testing Services

Educational Testing Service

Corporate Headquarters
Rosedale Rd.
Princeton, NJ 08541

Phone: (609) 921-9000
Fax: (609) 734-5410
Email: etsinfo@ets.org
URL: http://www.ets.org

ETS helps students with admission to college or graduate school, test registration, test preparation, and financial aid planning. It also offers services for teachers, including professional development programs, occupational skill certification, educational research, and career exploration. ETS has seven regional offices with corporate headquarters in Princeton, NJ.

Test Of English As A Foreign Language

P.O. Box 6151
Princeton, NJ 08541

Phone: (609) 771-7100
Email: toefl@ets.org
URL: http://www.toefl.org

TOEFL program provides English proficiency testing services for international students planning to study in the U.S., Canada, or other countries where English is the primary language of instruction. The TOEFL test is made available worldwide to all persons, regardless of age, gender, race, nationality, religion, or political views. Educational Testing Service develops the test under the direction of the TOEFL Policy Council, a board comprised of professionals drawn from the higher education community.

Professional Associations

Arts & Humanities

American Classical League

Miami University
Oxford, OH 45056

Phone: (513) 529-7741
Fax: (513) 529-7742
Email: Info@aclclassics.or
URL: http://www.aclclassics.org

ACL was founded in 1919 to foster the study of classical languages in the U.S. and Canada. Membership is open to those committed to the preservation and advancement of classical inheritance from Greece and Rome. The League includes teachers of Latin, Greek, and Classics on elementary, secondary, and college levels. Students of classics will find information on membership in the membership brochure. Call or write for more information.

American Film Institute

2021 North Western Ave.
Los Angeles, CA 90027

Phone: (323) 856-7600
Fax: (323) 467-4578
Email: Info@afionline.org
URL: http://www.afionline.org/
home.html

AFI is an independent, nonprofit organization dedicated to preserving the heritage of film and television, and increasing recognition and understanding of the moving image as an art form. Institute programs emanate from the AFI campus in Los Angeles and the AFI Theater in the John F. Kennedy Center in Washington, DC. Its Center for Advanced Film and Television Studies (CAFTS) offers MFA degrees in cinematography, directing, editing, producing, production design, and screenwriting. AFI offers numerous educational opportunities, professional training, workshops, and seminars.

American Historical Association

400 A St. SE
Washington, DC 20003-3889

Phone: (202) 544-2422
Fax: (202) 544-8307
Email: aha@theaha.org.
URL: http://www.theaha.org

AHA is a nonprofit membership organization founded in 1884 and incorporated by Congress in 1889 for the promotion of historical studies, the collection and preservation of historical documents and artifacts, and the dissemination of historical research. It serves as the umbrella organization for historians. Among its 15,000 members are faculty, independent historians, and historians in museums, historical organizations, libraries and archives, government, and other areas. Numerous fellowships and awards are available. AHA publishes several journals, periodicals, and directories.

American Institute Of Architecture

1735 New York Ave. NW
Washington, DC 20006

Phone: (800)242-3837
URL: http://www.aiaonline.com

AIA, created in 1857, works toward a public environment that is responsive to the people it serves while representing the professional interests of America's architects through education, government advocacy, community redevelopment, and public outreach activities. AIA also works to fulfill its commitment to help coordinate the building industry. Local chapters frequently offer internships to help younger professionals. Membership includes over 59,000 licensed architects and associated professionals. Certain eligibility requirements apply. AIA operates a student website at http://www.aiasnatl.org.

American Mathematical Society

P.O. Box 6248
Providence, RI 02940-6248

Phone: (800) 321-4267
Fax: (401) 331-3842
Email: ams@ams.org
URL: http://www.ams.org

AMS works to further mathematical research and scholarship. Membership costs vary and include a subscription to the quarterly *Bulletin of the American Mathematical Society* and *Notices of the American Mathematical Society*, and discounts on numerous other publications. Other benefits include job listings, employment services, and funding opportunities. Fellowships and postdoctorate awards are available.

American Philological Association

University of Pennsylvania
291 Logan Hall
249 S. 36th St.
Philadelphia, PA 19104-6304

Phone: (215) 898-4975
Fax: (215) 573-7874
Email: apaclassics@sas.upenn.edu
URL: http://scholar.cc.emory.edu/scripts/APA/APA-MENU.html

Founded in 1869, APA is the principal learned society for classical studies in North America. Although its membership is composed primarily of North American universities and college teachers of classical studies, it also includes many secondary school teachers, scholars from outside the United States and Canada, and other individuals of classical studies. Membership rates are based on salary earnings. Student rates are $20.

American Philosophical Association

University of Delaware
Newark, Delaware 19716-479

Phone: (302) 831-1112
Fax: (302) 831-8690
Email: apaOnline@udel.edu
URL: http://www.udel.edu/apa

APA, a professional organization for philosophers, was founded in 1900 to promote the exchange of ideas among philosophers, to encourage creative and scholarly activity in philosophy, to facilitate the professional work and teaching of philosophers, and to represent philosophy as a discipline. Membership dues range from $35 to $140 per year, depending on income.

American Planning Association

1776 Massachusetts Ave. NW
Washington, DC 20036

Phone: (202) 872-0611
Fax: (202) 872-0643
Email: APA@planning.org
URL: http://www.planning.org

APA is a nonprofit public interest and research organization representing 30,000 practicing planners, officials, and citizens involved with urban and rural planning issues. The organization has 46 regional chapters and 17 divisions of specialized planning interests and publishes a monthly magazine and newsletter and offers numerous other materials. Student memberships and scholarships are available. The American Institute of Certified Planners is APA's professional and educational component, certifying planners who have met specific educational and experiential criteria and passed the certification.

Archaeological Institute Of America

Boston University
656 Beacon St.
Boston, MA 02215-2010

Phone: (617) 353-9361
Fax: (617) 353-6550
Email: aia@bu.edu
URL: http://www.archaeological.org

The mission of the AIA is to inform the public about archaeology and provide information derived from the sound professional practice of archaeology. A nonprofit agency, it promotes ideas about archaeology and scholarship through annual meetings and publications, regional lectures and symposia, the award of fellowships, and other appropriate activities. Over 11,000 professional archaeologists and interested amateurs belong to AIA. Fellowships and awards are available.

Association For Art History

Henry Radford Hope School of Fine Arts
Fine Arts 124, Indiana University
Bloomington, IN 47405

Phone: (812) 855-5193
Fax: (812) 855-9556
URL: http://www.indiana.edu/~aah

This association consists of professionals working in art history who are concerned with issues relevant and particular to the field. It welcomes all art historians, museum professionals, critics, and scholars, including graduate students. AAH focuses on the specific interests and concerns of its members. Call or write for scholarship information.

Association Of Collegiate Schools Of Architecture

1735 New York Ave. NW
Washington, DC 20006

Phone: (202) 785-2324
Fax: (202) 628-0448
URL: http://www.acsa-arch.org

ACSA is a nonprofit, membership association founded in 1912 to advance the quality of architectural education. It currently includes over 150 schools in several membership categories representing over 3,500 architecture faculty. The association maintains a variety of activities, such as scholarly meetings, workshops, publications, awards and competition programs, support for architectural research, policy development, and serves as a liaison with allied organizations. ACSA publishes *The Guide to Architecture Schools* for $19.95 per copy, plus $3 shipping and handling. In addition to general information about architectural education, internship, and practice, the directory includes a two-page entry for each school with an accredited professional degree program in architecture in the U.S. and Canada.

Center For American Archeology

P.O. Box 366
Kampsville, IL 62053

Phone: (618) 653-4232
Email: CAA@caa-archeology.org
URL: http://www.caa-archeology.org

CAA works for archeological discovery, educational outreach, and cultural stewardship. Members receive a newsletter subscription, annual reports, open house tour passes, museum store discounts, and more. Dues range from $30 to $1,000 and help support research, education, public outreach, and duration. Scholarships and internships are available.

College Art Association

275 Seventh Ave.
New York, New York 10001

Phone: (212) 691-1051
Fax: (212) 627-2381
Email: nyoffice@collegeart.org
URL: http://www.collegeart.org

Founded in 1911, CAA promotes excellence in scholarship and teaching in the history and criticism of the visual arts, and in creativity and technical skill in the teaching and practices of art. It facilitates the exchange of ideas and information among those interested in art and history of art, and advocates comprehensive and inclusive education in the visual arts. Over 13,000 artists, art historians, scholars, curators, collectors, educators, art publishers, and other visual arts professionals are individual members. Another 2,000 university art and art history departments, museums, libraries, and professional and commercial organizations hold institutional memberships.

Modern Language Association

10 Astor Place
New York, NY 10003-6981

Phone: (212) 475-9500
Fax: (212) 477-9863
URL: http://www.mla.org

MLA, with over 30,000 members, provides opportunities for its members to share their scholarly findings and teaching experiences with colleagues and to discuss trends in the academy. For over 100 years, members have worked to strengthen the study and teaching of language and literature. Membership costs $20 per year for students and $35 for non-students. MLA's graduate student caucus represents the interests of graduate students and provides them with an information and support network.

Society For Cinema Studies

c/o Journals Department
University of Texas Press
P.O. Box 7819
Austin, Texas 78713-7819

Phone: (512) 471-7233
Fax: (512) 320-0668
Email: Membership@CinemaStudies.org
URL: http://www.cinemastudies.org/index.htm

Founded in 1959, the SCS is a professional membership organization composed of college and university educators, filmmakers, historians, critics, scholars, and others concerned with the study of the moving image. The Society's goals are to promote all areas of media studies within universities and two-and four-year colleges. It rewards excellence in scholarship and writing, and facilitates the improvement of the teaching of media studies. It also works for the advancement of multicultural awareness and interaction.

Society Of Professional Journalists

16 South Jackson St.
Greencastle, IN 46135-1514

Phone: (765) 653-3333
Fax: (765) 653-4631
Email: spj@spjhq.org
URL: http://spj.org/spjhome.htm

Founded in 1909 as Sigma Delta Chi, SPJ is a professional organization working to ensure that the concept of self-government outlined by the U.S. Constitution remains a reality and stimulating high standards and ethical behavior in the practice of journalism. Professional, retired, student, post-graduate, and certain institutional memberships are available. Fellowships, awards, and internships are also available. Call for further details.

Psychology, Counseling, & Social Work

American Counseling Association

5999 Stevenson Ave.
Alexandria, VA 22304-3300

Phone: (800) 347-6647
Fax: (703) 823-0252
Email: lpeele@counseling.org
URL: http://www.counseling.org/

Founded in 1952, ACA is a nonprofit professional and educational organization dedicated to the enhancement of the counseling profession. It serves professional counselors in the U.S. and in 50 other countries. Members receive numerous benefits including professional publications, access to professional liability insurance programs, and discounts on workshops, conferences, and books. Professional and regular memberships are $106. Student and retired memberships are $80.

American Mental Health Counselors Association

801 N. Fairfax St., Suite 304
Fairfax, VA 22314

Phone: (800) 326-2642
Fax: (703) 548-4775
Email: vmoore@amhca.org
URL: http://www.amhca.org/

Founded in 1976, AMHCA represents mental health counselors on a range of professional issues: managed care, malpractice insurance, rights to practice, and patients' health care issues. It publishes a bimonthly newsletter. Membership options include four professional and student categories.

American Psychological Association Graduate Students

750 First St. NE
Washington, DC 20002-4242

Phone: (202) 336-6014
Email: apags@apa.org
URL: http://www.apa.org/apags

APAGS was established as a national graduate student association within the American Psychological Association in 1988. In 1994, APAGS was officially established as a continuing committee of the APA governance structure. The APAGS Committee meets twice yearly and also sponsors programs at the APA annual convention. APA Student Affiliates (and a member of APAGS) receive a quarterly newsletter, the monthly *APA Monitor* and *American Psychologist*, reduced rates for APA journals and books, health care eligibility, and opportunities for professional advancement.

American Psychological Society Student Caucus

American Psychological Society
1010 Vermont Ave. NW, Suite 1100
Washington, DC 20005-4907

Phone: (202) 783-2077
Fax: (202) 783-2083
Email: aps@aps.washington.dc.us
URL: http://www.psychologicalscience.org

APSSC acts as a voice for students in American Psychological Society (APS) policy decisions and as a national networking and informational source. APSSC membership numbers more than 4,000 in approximately 50 chapters. The APS, founded in 1988, is dedicated solely to scientific psychology. Its mission is to promote, protect, and advance the interests of scientifically oriented psychology in research, application, and the improvement of human welfare. Direct inquiries to APS.

Association For The Advancement Of Behavior Therapy

305 Seventh Ave., 16th Floor
New York, NY 10001-6008

Phone: (212) 647-1890
Fax: (212) 647-1865
Email: mailback@aabt.org
URL: http://server.psyc.vt.edu/aabt/

AABT is a nonprofit membership organization of over 4,500 mental health professionals and students interested in behavior therapy and cognitive behavior therapy. Founded in 1966, it serves as a centralized resource and network for behavior therapy and cognitive behavior therapy, promoting these therapies through its journals, newsletters, annual conventions, a website, and other educational publications and programs.

Council Of Social Work Education

1600 Duke St., Suite 300
Alexandria, VA 22314

Phone: (703) 683-8080
Fax: (703) 683-8099
Email: info@cswe.org
URL: http://www.cswe.org

CSWE is a national association working to preserve and enhance the quality of social work education for practice. It promotes the goals of individual and community well-being, and social justice. CSWE accredits bachelor's and master's degree programs in social work, promotes research and faculty development, and advocates for social work education. CSWE offers the Minority Fellowship Program for doctoral students of color and the Carl A. Scott Memorial Lecture Fund Book Scholarship. Call for more information.

National Association Of Social Workers

Clinical Registrar Office
750 First St. NE, Suite 700
Washington, DC 20002-4241

Phone: (800) 638-8799
Fax: (202) 336-8311
URL: http://www.naswdc.org

NASW is the largest organization of professional social workers in the world. It serves nearly 155,000 social workers in 55 chapters throughout the United States and abroad. NASW members constitute about 50 percent of the United States' social workers. The association was formed in 1955 in a merger of seven social work organizations to strengthen and unify the social work profession, promote the development of social work practice, and advance sound social policies.

Other Social Sciences

American Anthropological Association

4350 North Fairfax Dr., Suite 640
Arlington, VA 22203-1620

Phone: (703) 528-1902
Fax: (703) 528-3546
URL: http://www.aaanet.org

Founded in 1902, AAA is one of the largest organizations of individuals interested in anthropology. It promotes the science of anthropology, coordinates the efforts of American anthropologists, fosters societies devoted to anthropology, and encourages the publication of matter pertaining to anthropology. Membership now averages over 10,000 annually. Annual meetings draw more than 5,000 individuals, who attend over 300 sessions organized into a five-day program.

American Association Of Colleges For Teacher Education

1307 New York Ave. NW, Suite 300
Washington, DC 20005-4701

Phone: (202) 293-2450
Fax: (202) 457-8095
URL: http://www.aacte.org

AACTE is a national, voluntary association of colleges and universities with undergraduate or graduate programs. It prepares professional educators providing leadership for the continuing transformation of professional preparation programs. Its members include over 700 member institutions located in every state, the District of Columbia, the Virgin Islands, Puerto Rico, and Guam. Together, they graduate more than 85 percent of new school personnel entering the profession each year in the U.S. It also has a small but growing number of affiliate members, including state departments of education, educational laboratories and centers, and foreign institutions and organizations.

American Economic Association

2014 Broadway, Suite 305
Nashville, TN 37203

Phone: (615) 343-7590
URL: http://www.vanderbilt.edu/AEA

AEA is a professional association serving the economic field. Membership ($26 for students) includes a subscription to *American Economic Review, Journal of Economic Literature* and the *Journal of Economic Proceedings*. Those seeking a graduate education in economics can purchase the *Guide to Graduate Study in Economics and Agricultural Economics* available from the Publications Center, 1030 13th St. Boulder, CO, 80802. AEA also publishes a bimonthly listing of academic and nonacademic jobs in economics, *Job Openings for Economists* (JOE) available for $25 for nonmembers, and discounted price for members.

American Political Science Association

1527 New Hampshire Ave. NW
Washington, DC 20036-120

Phone: (202) 483-2512
Fax: (202) 483-2657
Email: apsa@apsanet.org
URL: http://apsanet.org

APSA is a professional society for people who study politics, government, and public policy in the U.S. and around the world with more than 13,000 members residing in over 70 countries. It brings together political scientists from all fields of inquiry, regions, and occupational endeavors to expand the awareness and understanding of political life. Membership fees are discounted for students and are based on income for nonstudents. APSA offers a free brochure, *Earning a PhD in Political Science,* for those interested in graduate education in political science.

American Sociological Association

1307 New York Ave. NW, Suite 700
Washington, DC 20005

Phone: (202) 383-9005
Fax: (202) 638-0882
URL: http://www.asanet.org

ASA, founded in 1905, is a nonprofit membership association dedicated to advancing sociology as a scientific discipline and profession serving the public good. With over 13,200 members, ASA encompasses sociologists who are faculty members at colleges and universities, researchers, practitioners, and students. About 20 percent of the members work in government, business, or nonprofit organizations. Working at the national and international levels, the Association aims to articulate policy and implement programs likely to have the broadest possible impact for sociology now and in the future.

Association For Public Policy

2100 M St. NW
Washington, DC 20037

Phone: (202) 261-5788
Fax: (202) 223-1149
Email: appam@ui.urban.org
URL: http://qsilver.queensu.ca/appam

APPAM encourages excellence in research, teaching, and practice in the field of public policy analysis and management. Operating through its annual fall and spring conferences, a newsletter, and the *Journal of Policy Analysis and Management*, its membership includes individual and institutional members, practitioners, scholars, and students. Officially formed in 1979, APPAM now has approximately 2,000 individual members and 75 institutional members. Numerous fellowships, internships, and educational activities are available. Membership in the Association is open to individuals, students, and institutions.

Association Of American Geographers

1710 16th St. NW
Washington, DC 20009-3198

Phone: (202) 234-1450
Fax: (202) 234-2744
Email: aia@aag.org
URL: http://www.aag.org/

AAG is a scientific and educational society founded in 1904. Today it has 7,000 members who share interests in the theory, methods, and practice of geography. The AAG holds an Annual Meeting and publishes two scholarly journals, the *Annals of the Association of American Geographers* and *The Professional Geographer*, as well as the monthly AAG Newsletter. Through its nine Regional Divisions and 49 Specialty Groups, it also conducts educational and research projects that further the group's interests and programs.

Association Of Professional Schools Of International Affairs

1400 K Street NW, Suite 650
Washington, DC 20005-2403

Phone: (202) 326-7828
Fax: (202) 326-7830
Email: apsia@erols.co
URL: http://www.apsia.org

APSIA is an association of 23 graduate schools of international affairs and 14 affiliated institutions based in the U.S. and abroad. Member schools are dedicated to advancing global understanding and cooperation by preparing individuals to assume positions of leadership in world affairs. It is a nonprofit, non-governmental organization that serves as a source of information on professional international affairs education, represents the interests of professional international affairs education in national and international forums, and coordinates activities among and for its member institutions.

International Society For Intercultural Education, Training, & Research

P.O. Box 467
Putney, Vermont 05346

Phone: (802) 387-4785
Fax: (802) 387-5783
Email: SIETAR@sover.net
URL: http://www.sietarinternational.org/

SIETAR International is an international professional association comprised of professionals from a wide range of disciplines who share a common concern for international and intercultural relations. It provides an opportunity for interaction with leaders in a wide range of professions who share an interest in intercultural practices and research. SIETAR's membership comprises consultants, trainers, educators, managers, scholars, researchers, artists, and other professionals who contribute to cross-cultural operations in both multicultural and international contexts.

National Women's Studies Association

7100 Baltimore Ave., Suite 500
College Park, MD 20740

Phone: (301) 403-0525
Email: nwsa@umail.umd.edu
URL: http://www.nwsa.org

NWSA was founded in 1977 to further the development of Women's Studies at every educational level. Membership includes teachers, students, independent scholars, program administrators, and community activists. NWSA has initiated and sponsored a number of major projects and publications to further scholarship and curriculum development in Women's Studies. Individual membership is open to persons interested in promoting Women's Studies education in schools, colleges and universities, or in the community. Group memberships are also available.

Social Science Research Council

810 Seventh Ave.
New York, NY 10019

Phone: (212) 377-2700
Fax: (212) 377-2727
URL: http://www.ssrc.org

Founded in 1923, SSRC is an independent, nongovernmental, nonprofit, international association devoted to the advancement of interdisciplinary research in the social sciences. It does this through a wide variety of interdisciplinary workshops and conferences, fellowships and grants, summer training institutes, scholarly exchanges, and publications.

Sciences & Engineering

American Association For The Advancement Of Science

1200 New York Ave. NW
Washington, DC 20005

Phone: (202) 326-6400
Email: membership@aaas.org
URL: http://www.aaas.org

Founded in 1848, the AAAS works toward the advancement of science and the development of technology across all disciplines. It comprises 24 major sections, each corresponding to fields of interest among AAAS members, ranging from the physical, biological, and health sciences to the social, economic, and applied sciences. Membership, open to scientists, full-time students, postdoctorates, and residents, includes the weekly magazine, *Science*, and a variety of other benefits, ranging from discounts on science books and journals to nomination for fellowships and grants and group rate life insurance.

American Astronomical Society

2000 Florida Ave., Suite 400
Washington, DC 20009

Phone: (202) 328-2010
URL: http://www.aas.org

AAS, established 1899, is a major professional organization in North America for astronomers, other scientists, and individuals interested in astronomy. Membership in the society requires a nomination by two full members of the AAS. Full, associate, and junior memberships are available. Junior memberships, usually suited for prospective graduate students, cost $35 per year for the first two years. Full and associate dues are $105.

American Chemical Society

1155 16th St. NW
Washington, DC 20036

Phone: (800) 227-5558
URL: http://www.acs.org

Founded in 1876, the ACS encourages the advancement of all branches of chemistry and promotes chemical research in both science and industry. Member benefits include numerous professional discounts, subscriptions to special publications, and educational opportunities. ACS Younger Chemists Committee (YCC) identifies the needs and concerns of younger chemists and develops programs responsive to their needs. YCC is for those not yet established in their careers. It is a joint board-council committee of the ACS whose members represent industry, government, and academia.

American Computer Scientists Association

6 Commerce Dr.
Cranford, NJ 07016

Phone: (908) 272-0016
Email: 77662.133@compuserve.com
URL: http://www.acsa2000.net

ACSA is a nonprofit, charitable research and education organization. The majority of its publications are distributed via Internet at little or not cost. Graduate student services are evolving. Membership in this organization is free.

American Geological Institute

4220 King St.
Alexandria, VA 22302-1502

Phone: (703) 379-2480
Fax: (703) 379-7563
URL: http://www.agiweb.org

AGI is a nonprofit federation of 34 geoscientific and professional associations representing over 100,000 geologists, geophysicists, and other earth scientists. Founded in 1948, AGI provides information services to geoscientists, serves as a voice of shared interests in our profession, plays a major role in strengthening geoscience education, and strives to increase public awareness of the vital role the geosciences play in the environment. AGI offers a minority geoscience scholarship available for graduate students or those applying for an advanced degree in geoscience (MA, MS, or PhD) during the academic year. It also offers a Russian/U.S. geoscience student exchange scholarship for those who have an interest in energy and mineral resources.

American Institute Of Biological Sciences

1444 I St. NW, Suite 200
Washington, DC 20005

Phone: (202) 628-1500 x 253
Fax: (202) 628-1509
Email: jkolber@aibs.org
URL: http://www.aibs.org/core/index.html

Established in 1947, AIBS is a nonprofit scientific organization working to advance research and education in the biological, medical, environmental, and agricultural sciences. As an umbrella society for other biological organizations, it is responsible for providing a unified voice for diverse disciplines. Membership rates start at $20 for undergraduate students, and increase to $90 for sustaining members. Publications and subscriptions are included in membership benefits.

American Society For Engineering Education

1818 N St. NW, Suite 600
Washington, DC 20036-2479

Phone: (202) 331-3500
Fax: (202) 265-8504
URL: http://www.asee.org

ASEE works to further education in engineering and engineering technology by promoting excellence in instruction, research, public service, and practice. The society encourages local, national, and international communication and collaboration. It hopes to influence corporate and government policies and involvement, and promotes professional interaction and lifelong learning. It recognizes outstanding contributions of individuals and organizations, and encourages youth to pursue studies and careers in engineering and engineering technology. It also works to influence the recruitment and retention of young faculty and underrepresented groups. Numerous fellowships are available.

Association For Women In Science

1200 New York Ave. NW, Suite 650
Washington, DC 20005

Phone: (202) 326-8940
Fax: (202) 326-8960
Email: awis@awis.org
URL: http://www.awis.org

AWIS is a nonprofit organization established in 1971, dedicated to achieving equity and full participation for women in science, mathematics, engineering, and technology. AWIS has over 5,000 members in fields of physical sciences, mathematics, social science, and engineering. Over half of its members have doctorates in their respective fields, and hold positions at all levels of industry, academia, and government. AWIS offers mentoring programs, numerous publication materials, and scholarships and internships for graduate students. Call for chapter locations and information.

Botanical Society Of America

1735 Neil Ave.
Columbus, OH 43210-1293

Phone: (614) 292-3519
URL: http://www.botany.org

BSA promotes research and teaching in all fields of plant biology, facilitates cooperation among plant biologists and other scientists worldwide, and disseminates knowledge of plants, algae, and fungi to help solve practical problems of humanity. BSA offers the Karling graduate student research award, which supports and promotes graduate research in the botanical sciences. Eligibility requires membership in BSA and full-time graduate student status. Applicants' faculty advisor must also a member of the BSA.

National Academy Of Engineering

2101 Constitution Ave. NW
Washington, DC 20418

Email: NAEMembershipOffice@nae.edu
URL: http://www.nae.edu/

Founded in 1964, NAE provides engineering leadership in service to the nation, and works to build and to articulate the implications of rapid technological change, affecting the way people work, learn, and play. Like other components of the National Academy of Sciences, NAE is a private, independent, nonprofit institution that advises the federal government and conducts independent studies examining topics in engineering and technology. Members are peer-elected and serve as leaders in government and private engineering organizations.

National Academy Of Sciences

2101 Constitution Ave. NW
Washington, DC 20418

URL: http://www4.nas.edu/nas/nashome.nsf

NAS is a private, nonprofit society of distinguished scholars engaged in scientific and engineering research, dedicated to the advancement of science and technology and to their use for the general welfare. Members and foreign associates of the Academy are elected in recognition of their distinguished and continuing achievements in original research. Membership comprises approximately 1,900 members and 300 foreign associates, of whom more than 160 have won Nobel Prizes. The academy includes the National Academy of Engineering (NAE), the Institute of Medicine (IOM), and the National Research Council (NRC).

National Physical Science Consortium

New Mexico State University
Box 30001, Dept. 3 NPS
Las Cruces, NM 88003

Phone: (800) 952-4118
URL: http://www.npsc.org

NPSC, a nonprofit organization, offers a doctoral graduate fellowship program in astronomy, chemistry, computer science, geology, material science, mathematics, and physics, with special emphasis on the recruitment of underrepresented minority and female students in physical sciences. Each fellowship is worth an overall value of $156,000 to $200,000 depending on which university the student attends. This is a full-time study PhD track program open to U.S. citizens who are African American, Hispanic, Native American, and/or female, with an undergraduate GPA of at least 3.0 and admission to a graduate program at a participating university.

National Science Foundation

4201 Wilson Blvd.
Arlington, VI 22230

Phone: (800) 877-8339
URL: http://www.nsf.gov/home/grants.htm

NSF funds research and education in science and engineering through grants, contracts, and cooperative agreements. It accounts for about 20 percent of federal support to academic institutions and is responsible for promoting science and engineering through programs that invest over $3.3 billion per year in almost 20,000 research and education projects in science and engineering. Write or call for scholarship, grant, and graduate research fellowship information.

Women In Technology International

6345 Balboa Blvd., #257
Encino, CA 91316

Phone: (800) 334-9484
Fax: (818) 906-3299
URL: http://www.witi.com/index-c.shtml

WITI, founded in 1989, is dedicated to the advancement of women in technology. It works to increase the number of women in executive roles in technology and technology-based companies. It helps women become more financially independent and technology-literate, and encourages young women to choose careers in science and technology. Membership includes access to online services, discounts to regional chapter meetings and annual conferences, and numerous other discounts. Dues are income-based.

University Organizations

American Association For Higher Education

One Dupont Circle, Suite 360
Washington, DC 20036-1110

Phone: (202) 293-6440
Fax: (202) 293-0073
Email: info@aahe.org
URL: http://www.aahe.org

AAHE is an individual membership organization that promotes changes to ensure the effectiveness in higher education. Membership includes over 9,300 faculty, administrators, and students from all sectors, disciplines, and positions, and policy makers and leaders from foundations, government, accrediting agencies, the media, and business. The association began in the 1870s as the higher education department of the National Education Association (NEA). In 1969, members disassociated themselves from the NEA, forming the independent AAHE.

Association Of American Colleges & Universities

1818 R St. NW
Washington, DC 20009

Email: info@aacu.nw.dc.us
URL: http://www.aacu-edu.org

AACU is committed to making the aims of liberal learning a vigorous and constant influence on institutional purpose and educational practice in higher education. Founded in 1915, its membership consists of accredited public and private colleges and universities of every type and size. It forges links between presidents, academic administrators, and faculty leaders to plan and implement effective educational programs as the means to strengthen their institutions.

Association Of American Medical Colleges

2450 N St. NW
Washington, DC 20037-1126

Phone: (202) 828-0400
Fax: (202) 828-1125
URL: http://www.aamc.org

AAMC, founded in 1876, is a nonprofit association of 125 accredited U.S. medical schools, 16 accredited Canadian medical schools, more than 400 major teaching hospitals and health systems, and the nation's medical students and residents. It works toward the improvement of the nation's health through the advancement of academic medicine. The Association also seeks to strengthen the quality of medical education and training, to enhance the search for biomedical knowledge, to advance research in health services, and to integrate education into the provisions of effective health care.

Association Of Southern Baptist Colleges & Schools

Communications & Operations Office
165A Belle Forest Circle
Nashville, TN 37221-2103

Phone: (615) 673-1896
Fax: (615) 662-1396
Email: info@baptistcolleges.org
URL: http://www.baptistschools.org

ASBCS is owned and operated by its 54 member schools located in 18 states. It serves and promotes its member schools through its website, print materials, and ongoing programs and services. The Directory of Southern Baptist Related Colleges and Schools, with descriptions of programs offered at each school, is available for $3 including postage. Journals and newsletters are also available.

College Board

45 Columbus Ave.
New York, NY 10023-6992

Phone: (212) 713-8000
URL: http://www.collegeboard.org

College Board is an association of schools, colleges, universities, and other educational organizations putting higher education within the reach of all students. For nearly ten years, it has offered programs and services in the areas of teaching and learning, assessment, guidance, placement, financial aid, admissions, and enrollment. It also conducts professional development programs, forums and conferences, policy analysis, and public outreach. Offices across the nation and in Puerto Rico work with students, parents, school and college educators, and policy makers.

Conference Of Southern Graduate Schools

College of Graduate Studies
Jacksonville State University
700 Pelham Rd. N.
Jacksonville, AL 36265-1602

Phone: (256) 782-5329
Fax: (256) 782-5321
Email: bcarr@jsucc.jsu.edu
URL: http://www.csgs.org

This organization consists of over 200 graduate schools in 15 southern states. Since 1969, its purpose has been to consider topics relating to graduate study and research that are of mutual interest and concern to the member institutions. It also serves as a liaison with other national and regional educational bodies on behalf of the institutional members. Associate membership, which carries all privileges other than voting and holding office, may be extended to both profit and nonprofit organizations with a significant commitment to graduate education.

Council For Christian Colleges & Universities

329 Eighth St. NE
Washington, DC 20002

Phone: (202) 546-8713
Fax: (202) 546-8913
URL: http://www.gospelcom.net/cccu

Founded in 1976, CCCU is a professional association of academic institutions that focuses on helping Christian colleges and universities advance the cause of Christian education and effectively integrate biblical faith, scholarship, and service. The Council coordinates professional development opportunities for administrators and faculty, off-campus student programs, public advocacy for Christian higher education, and cooperative efforts among member colleges and universities.

Council Of Graduate Schools

One Dupont Circle NW, Suite 430
Washington, DC 20036-1173

Phone: (202) 223-3791
Fax: (202) 331-7157
URL: http://www.cgsnet.org

CGS members are colleges and universities engaged in research, scholarship, and the preparation of candidates for advanced degrees. The council offers opportunities for deans and graduate school personnel to exchange ideas and share information on major issues in graduate education. Over 400 U.S., Canadian, and International institutions are represented in the CGS membership. CGS also monitors federal legislation and potential legislation affecting graduate education, student fellowships, loans, research support, minority student programs, international studies and students, facilities, libraries, tax policy, and other issues important to the graduate community.

Counseling & Career Planning Organizations

General Advising

National Academic Advising Association

Kansas State University
2323 Anderson Ave., Suite 225
Manhattan, KS 66502-2912

Phone: (785) 532-5717
Fax: (785) 532-7732
Email: nacada@ksu.edu
URL: http://www.ksu.edu/nacada

NAAA has over 4,700 members representing all 50 states, Canada, Puerto Rico, and five other foreign countries. Members represent higher education institutions across the spectrum of Carnegie college classifications and include professional advisors and counselors, faculty, administrators, and students whose responsibilities include academic advising. Membership is open to anyone interested in Academic Advising.

Career Counseling

Eastern Association Of Colleges & Employers

P.O. Box 920484
Needham, MA 02492

Phone: (781) 444-9882
Email: baerwalker@aol.com
URL: http://www.eace.org

This regional organization provides services to its members who are college and university career services and human resources professionals, as well as those who provide services to these members. EACE shares its mission in collaborative agreement with the National Association of Colleges and Employers and other regional associations of colleges and employers.

Midwest Association Of Colleges & Employers

4700 W. Lake Ave.
Glenview, IL 60025-1485

URL: http://www.mwace.org

Since 1949, Midwest ACE has been bringing together professionals in collegiate career services and recruitment staffing to collaborate, communicate, and connect. Through these efforts, college-educated individuals have achieved their career goals and employers add value to their workplace. The mission of Midwest ACE is to maximize the career potential of college educated adults by fostering of employer, college, and university relationships. This geographical region comprises the states of Illinois, Indiana, Iowa, Kansas, Michigan, Minnesota, Missouri, Nebraska, North Dakota, Ohio, South Dakota, and Wisconsin.

National Career Development Association

4700 Reed Road, Suite M
Columbus, Ohio 43220

Phone: (614) 326-1750
Fax: (614) 326-1760
URL: http://www.ncda.org

NCDA is an affiliate of the American Counseling Association. This large association encompasses career and guidance counselors who work in private and public organizations. Its mission is to promote career development of all people over the life span. It provides services to the public and professionals involved with or interested in career development, including professional development activities, publications, research, public information, professional standards, advocacy, and recognition for achievement and service.

National Organization of Career Planners & Employers

62 Highland Avenue
Bethlehem, PA 18017-9085

Phone: (800) 544-5272 or (610) 868-1421, ex.16
Fax: (610) 868-0208
URL: http://www.jobweb.org/nace

NACE is the major association for higher education career planning professionals. It focuses on career development and employment issues and spans three constituencies: 1,700-plus member universities and colleges from across the United States (and their career services professionals); 1,600-plus employer organizations; and 1 million-plus college students and alumni who use their publications and services every year. NACE is an umbrella organization for six distinct regional associations.

Rocky Mountain Association Of Colleges & Employers

Brigham Young University
2446 ELWC
Provo, UT 84602-1227

Phone: (801) 378-6932
Email: lloyd_hawkins@byu.edu
URL: http://www.rmace.org

RMACE, or "ROCKY" as it is known, was organized at the University of Colorado at Boulder. It is a nonprofit professional association providing a link between higher education and the employers of college graduates. Its 200-plus members represent two- and four-year colleges and universities, and employers from business, industry, education, and government who hire from these institutions.

Southeastern Association Of Colleges & Employers

Baldwin-Hunt Associates
SACE Administrative Officer
P. O. Box 4141
Frankfort, KY 40604-4141

Phone: (502) 223-7223
Fax: (502) 223-8223
Email: office@sace.net
URL: http://www.sace.net

SACE is a 600-plus member organization of human resources, college relations, and career service professionals. It works to provide professional development, to promote personal and ethical standards, and to foster relationships among employment and career services professionals. It provides ongoing training and career enhancement through a variety of sources, including workshops, newsletters, awards, networking opportunities and more. This corporation region includes the states of Alabama, Florida, Georgia, Kentucky, Louisiana, Mississippi, North Carolina, South Carolina, Tennessee and Virginia, and the District of Columbia.

Southwest Association Of Colleges & Employers

Box 424388
Denton, Texas 76204-4388

Phone: (817) 898-2972
Fax: (817) 898-2956
Email: s_cook@twu.edu
URL: http://www.swace.org

SWACE is a regional nonprofit professional association comprised of human resource and career service professionals committed to integrating common values in the development and implementation of customer-driven innovative services, strategic financial planning and policies, and use of new and emerging technologies. It supports the career development and employment process of students, recent college graduates and experienced alumni. The SWACE region encompasses six southwestern states: Arkansas, Kansas, Louisiana, New Mexico, Oklahoma, and Texas.

Western Association Of Colleges & Employers

16 Santa Ana Pl.
Walnut Creek, CA 94598

Phone: (925) 934-3877
Fax: (925) 906-0922
Email: d2@dobbsgroup.com
URL: http://www.jobweb.org/wace

WACE was organized in 1951 and now has more than 500 members. It is a professional association of approximately 500 college career planning and placement offices and representatives from business, industry, and government who recruit, employ, and train graduates of colleges and universities in the Western states and Canada. It provides leadership in identifying and responding to issues, changes, and trends affecting career services and college relations. This region includes Alaska, California, Colorado, Guam, Hawaii, Idaho, Montana, Nevada, New Mexico, Oregon, Utah, Washington, and Wyoming.

Prelaw Counseling

Midwest Association Of Pre-Law Advisors

Pre-law Advisor
Career Development Center
Denison University
Granville, OH 43203

Phone: (740) 587-6521
Email: Schillingme@cc.denison.edu
URL: http://www.mapla.org

MAPLA provides a context for the sharing of knowledge and experience among advisors to promote informed advising of students considering a legal career. MAPLA's annual *Law School Admission Profiles* is a compendium of admissions data for all ABA-approved schools in the U.S. The association newsletter is published several times a year with articles on legal education and the profession. MAPLA offers two levels of membership: member and associate. Pre-law advisors at undergraduate institutions are eligible for full membership. Law school admissions representatives and other law-related constituencies (for example, legal assistant programs) are eligible for associate membership.

National Association For Law Placement

1666 Connecticut Ave. NW, Suite 325
Washington, DC 20009-1039

Phone: (202) 667-1666
Fax: (202) 265-6735
Email: info@nalp.org
URL: http://www.nalp.org

Established in 1971, NALP is a nonprofit organization serving as a source of information for legal career planning and recruitment. Its mission is to meet the needs of all participants in the legal employment process for information, coordination, and standards. Members include every ABA-accredited law school and legal employers (law firms, government agencies, corporations, and public interest organizations). NALP publishes videotapes, books, bibliographies, forms, and other materials for its members and for the public. It also designs surveys documenting legal trends.

Northeast Association Of Pre-Law Advisors

Boston College
38 Commonwealth Avenue
Chestnut Hill, MA 02167

Phone: (617) 552-4762
Email: deleo@bc.edu

NAPLA promotes career planning and advising for law school-bound students. It works to enhance the skills of pre-law advisors and to advocate for the interests of undergraduate students and institutions in the counseling and admissions processes leading to law-related careers. It also promotes communication between pre-law advisors, individual law school admissions officers, the Law School Admissions Council, the Educational Testing Service, and other law-related organizations.

Pacific Coast Association Of Pre-Law Advisors

c/o Verity Powell, Advising Consultant
Stanford University
Stanford, CA 94394-3085

Phone: (604) 723-1152
Email: eavkp@leland.stanford.edu

PCAPLA promotes career planning and advising for law school-bound students. It works to enhance the skills of pre-law advisors and to advocate for the interests of undergraduate students and institutions in the counseling and admissions processes leading to law-related careers. It also promotes communication between pre-law advisors, individual law school admissions officers, the Law School Admissions Council, the Educational Testing Service, and other law-related organizations.

Southern Association Of Pre-Law Advisors

2110 Campus Box
Elon College, NC 27244

Phone: (336) 584-2273
Fax: (336) 538-2627
Email: batchelor@elon.edu
URL: http://www.elon.edu/sapla

SAPLA brings together pre-law advisors and admissions staff from various law schools in an effort to provide everyone in the law school admissions process with up-to-date information and expert guidance. SAPLA believes that everyone considering a career in the law can benefit from expert pre-law advising and aims to ensure that it is available.

Southwest Association Of Pre-Law Advisors

Office of Professional School
Texas A&M University
College Stations, TX 77843-4233

Phone: (409) 847-8938
Email: ksevern@tamu.edu

SWAPLA promotes career planning and advising for law school-bound students. It works to enhance the skills of pre-law advisors and to advocate for the interests of undergraduate students and institutions in the counseling and admissions processes leading to law-related careers. It also promotes communication between pre-law advisors, individual law school admissions officers, the Law School Admissions Council, the Educational Testing Service, and other law-related organizations.

Western Association of Pre-Law Advisors

Brigham Young University
P.O. Box 25524
Provo, UT 84602-5524

Phone: (801) 378-2318
Email: cranee@yvax.byu.edu
URL: http://jan.ucc.nau.edu/ ~wapla-p

The purposes of WAPLA is to enhance the skills of pre-law advisors and to advocate for the interests of undergraduate students and institutions in the counseling and admissions processes leading to law-related careers. It also promotes communication between pre-law advisors, individual law school admissions officers, the Law School Admissions Council, the Educational Testing Service, and other law-related organizations. These functions are accomplished through meetings, training of new pre-law advisors, and other means.

Prehealth Counseling

Central Association Of Advisors For The Health Professions

Email: tdkim@cc.ysu.edu
URL: http://www.as.ysu.edu/~tdkim/ CAAHP/

CAAHP works with the National Association Of Advisors For The Health Professions as a clearinghouse for opinions of advisors and news from allied health, allopathic medicine, chiropractic, dentistry, nursing, optometry, osteopathic medicine, pharmacy, podiatric medicine, and veterinary medicine schools. It is committed to the professional development of advisors for the health professions and to sharing information and experiences, debating issues and establishing professional relationships for the benefit of students.

National Association Of Advisors For The Health Professions

P.O. Box 1518
Champaign, IL 61824-1518

Phone: (217) 355-0063
Fax: (217) 355-1287
Email: staff@naahp.org
URL: http://www.naahp.org

NAAHP is an organization of over 800 pre-health professions advisors at colleges and universities throughout the United States. It was established in 1974 to coordinate the activities and efforts of four independent regional associations. It serves as a national clearinghouse for opinions of advisors and news from allied health, allopathic medicine, chiropractic, dentistry, nursing, optometry, osteopathic medicine, pharmacy, podiatric medicine, and veterinary medicine schools. NAAHP is works through its four regional associations Central (CAAHP), Northeast (NEAAHP), Southeast (SAAHP) and West (WAAHP).

Northeast Association Of Advisors For The Health Professions

Email: rip@brown.edu
URL: http://www.netspace.org/ neaahp/

NEAAHP works with the National Association Of Advisors For The Health Professions as a clearinghouse for opinions of advisors and news from allied health, allopathic medicine, chiropractic, dentistry, nursing, optometry, osteopathic medicine, pharmacy, podiatric medicine, and veterinary medicine schools. It is committed to the professional development of advisors for the health professions and to sharing information and experiences, debating issues and establishing professional relationships for the benefit of students.

Southeastern Association Of Advisors For The Health Professions

URL: http://www.millsaps.edu/www/ saahp/

SAAHP is comprised of colleges and universities in the Southeastern U.S. concerned with the preparation of students for further study in health-related professions, including allopathic and osteopathic medicine, dentistry, optometry and podiatry, physician assistants, nursing, pharmacy, medical technology, chiropractic, and others. An arm of the National Association of Advisors for the Health Professions, SAAHP is concerned with effectively sharing information about the preparation of students for entry into the professional programs for the health disciplines. It has also acts as a liaison with these professional groups and provides them with a voice for their concerns about preprofessional preparation.

International Students & Overseas Study

Institute Of International Education

809 United Nations Plaza
New York, NY 10017-3580

Phone: (212) 984-5330
URL: http://www.iie.org

IIE is the largest U.S. higher educational exchange agency. It is a nonprofit organization with other 600 college and university members in the U.S. and abroad. IIE administers 240 programs through which almost 18,000 men and women from 170 nations benefit annually. IIE forges partnerships between the public and private sectors to design and implement international programs and to provide technical assistance in all countries and all fields. IIE also conducts statistical and policy research and provides information on international study to students and prospective students, educators, government officials, and business leaders worldwide.

NAFSA: Association Of International Educators

1307 New York Ave. NW, 8th Floor
Washington, DC 20005-4701

Phone: (800) 836-4994
Fax: (202) 737-365
Email: inbox@nafsa.org
URL: http://www.nafsa.org

This association promotes the exchange of students and scholars to and from the United States. It aims to set and uphold standards of good practice and provides professional education and training to strengthen institutional programs and services related to international educational exchange. Membership includes over 7,000 individuals from the U.S. and 60 countries. The majority are foreign student advisers and admissions officers, study-abroad advisers, directors of international programs, ESL teachers, administrators of intensive English programs, overseas educational advisers, community volunteers, and administrators of sponsored exchange programs.

V

INDICES

TITLE INDEX

AACOMAS Application Kit   224

The Academic Job Search Handbook   26

The Academic's Handbook   19

Accepted.com   303

Access America's Guide To Studying In The USA   293

Access Group   240

The African American Student's Guide To Surviving
  Graduate School   25

The Alliance To Save Student Aid   251

Allyn & Bacon Guide To Master's Programs In Psychology
  & Counseling Psychology   63

AMCAS-E Student & Applicant Information   224

American Association Of Colleges Of Osteopathic
  Medicine   196

American Association Of University Women Educational
  Foundation Fellowships & Grants   289

American Bar Association Approved Law Schools
  (Internet)   172

American Bar Association Guide To Approved Law
  Schools   145

American Chemical Society Minority Affairs   289

American Journalism Review Newslink   273

American Psychological Association: Student Information/
  Education Programs   60

American Universities   315

AmeriCorps Home Page   304

AmeriCorps: Serve Your Country & Pay For College   311

Apply To American Colleges & Universities   296

Applying To Medical School For The Non-Traditional
  Student   208

Arco's Best Graduate Business Schools   109

Arco's Getting Into Graduate Business School Today   100

Arco's Getting Into Law School Today   158

Arco's Getting Into Medical School Today   201

Arco's Law School Survival   162

Arco's Perfect Personal Statements   305

Arco's Ten Minute Guide To Paying For Graduate School   238

Association For Support Of Graduate Students   41

Association Of American Medical Colleges   189

Barron's Essays That Will Get You Into Medical School   193

Barron's Getting Into Medical School   184

Barron's Guide To Distance Learning   20

Barron's Guide To Graduate Business Schools   101

Barron's Guide To Law Schools   146

Barron's Guide To Medical & Dental Schools   197

Barron's How To Succeed In Law School   147

Becoming A Doctor   198

Becoming A Physician   209

Beyond L.A. Law   148

Boston College Online Law School Locator   130

Bschool.com   121

Business Week Online's Business Schools   90

Business Week's Guide To The Best Business Schools   91

Careers In Science And Engineering   70

The College Board Index Of Majors & Graduate Degrees
  2000   298

The College Board International Student Handbook Of
  U.S. Colleges   312

College Board Online   306

The College Board Scholarship Handbook   280

College Financial Aid Made Easy   241

College & University Home Pages   307

CollegeNET   315

CollegeNET MACH25 Scholarship Search   274

The Complete Guide To American Film Schools   68

The Complete Guide To Foreign Medical Schools In Plain
  English   218

The Complete Guide To Graduate School Admission   56

The Complete Law School Companion   149

The Complete MBA Companion   102

The Complete Scholarship Book   281

Completing Graduate School Long Distance   42

Council Of Graduate Schools: Student Page   83

Direct Loan   242

Directory Of Financial Aids For Women 1999–2001   256

Directory Of Private Scholarships & Grants   269

Dollars For College (Series)   287

Don't Miss Out   231

Earn & Learn   243

Educaid Loan Programs: Loans For Graduate Students   251

Education For Action: Undergraduate & Graduate
  Programs That Focus On Social Change   79

Education For The Earth: The College Guide For Careers
  In The Environment   80

eduPASS   297

The Eight Secrets Of Top Exam Performance In Law
  School   163

Embark.com: Going To Business School   95

Embark.com: Going To Graduate School   27

Embark.com: Going To Law School   138

Essays That Worked For Business Schools   98

eStudentLoan.com   232

FastWEB   257

Federal Trade Commission Scholarship Scam Alert   289

Film School Confidential   65

FINAID: Business School Resources   121

FINAID: Graduate School Financial Aid Resources   233

FINAID: Law School Resources   172

FINAID: Medical School Resources   224

The Financial Aid Book   275

Financial Aid For African Americans 1999–2001   258

Financial Aid For Minorities (Series)   284

Financial Aid For Research & Creative Activities Abroad 1999–2001   270

Financial Aid For Study & Training Abroad 1999–2001   259

Financial Aid For The Disabled & Their Families 1998–2000   260

Financial Aid For Veterans, Military Personnel & Their Dependents 1998–2000   271

Financial Resources For International Study   266

Financing Graduate School   234

FindLaw   131

Free Application For Federal Student Aid (FAFSA) Online   235

Free Money For Graduate School   278

From Here To Attorney   132

From Residency To Reality   203

Funding For United States Study   261

The Gay, Lesbian, & Bisexual Students' Guide To Colleges, Universities, And Graduate Schools   35

General Education Online   315

Get Into Medical School!   199

Getting In   57

Getting In: An Applicant's Guide To Graduate School Admissions   48

Getting Into Medical School   190

Getting What You Came For   21

Getting Yours: The Complete Guide To Government Money   249

GMAT Online: MBA Explorer   113

Going To Law School?   164

The Gourman Report   313

The Government Financial Aid Book   245

The Grad School Handbook   28

GradAdvantage   121

GradSchools.Com   43

Graduate Admissions Essays   294

Graduate School   29

The Graduate School Funding Handbook   285

Graduate Student Advice & Research Survival Guide   38

Graduate Student Resources On The Web   30

Graduate Student's Complete Scholarship Book   265

Graduate Study In Psychology 1998–1999   59

GRE Online   39

The Guerrilla Guide To Mastering Student Debt   236

Guide To American Graduate Schools   46

Guide To Completing The 1999–2000 Free Application For Federal Student Aid (FAFSA)   251

Guide To Defaulted Student Loans   239

The Guide To Graduate Environmental Programs   81

Guide To Graduate Management Programs In The USA, 1999   103

Guide To Medical School & The MCAT   185

Guide To Selecting & Applying To Master Of Social Work Programs (1999)   61

How To Cut Tuition   250

How To Get Into Harvard Law School   140

How To Get Into The Right Business School   104

How To Get Into The Right Dental School   210

How To Get Into The Right Law School   133

How To Get Into The Right Medical School   211

How To Get Into The Top MBA Programs   92

How To Write A Winning Personal Statement For Graduate & Professional School   302

Information USA: Education In The USA   316

Inside The Law Schools   155

The Insider's Book Of Law School Lists   171

Insider's Guide To Graduate Programs In Clinical & Counseling Psychology (1998–1999)   58

Insider's Guide To Graduate Programs In Education   54

The Insider's Guide To Medical School Admissions   212

The Interactive Medical Student Lounge   191

International Education Service   314

Internet Legal Resource Guide   139

Kaplan Newsweek Law School Admissions Advisor   160

Kaplan Online: Business   111

Kaplan Online: Financial Aid   246

Kaplan Online: Grad School   37

Kaplan Online: Law   150

Kaplan Online: Medicine   204

Kaplan's Getting Into Business School (1999 Edition)   114

Kaplan's Getting Into Medical School   213

Kaplan's Insider's Book Of Business School Lists   119

Kaplan's Insider's Book Of Medical School Lists   220

Kaplan/Newsweek Graduate School Admissions Adviser 2000   44

Law School Admissions Council Online   156
Law School Basics   151
Law School Without Fear   165
Learning The Law   166
Lifting A Ton Of Feathers   23
Loans & Grants From Uncle Sam   247
Looking At Law School   134

Making A Difference College Guide   82
Marketing Yourself To The Top Ten Business Schools   93
The Mature Medical Student   225
MBA Info   105
The MBA Page   115
MBA Plaza   106
The Medical Education Page   225
Medical School   194
Medical School Admission Requirements   186
Medical School Admissions   187
Medical School Admissions Success!   223
MedicalStudent.net   221
The Minority & Women's Complete Scholarship Book   282
The MLA Guide To The Job Search   55
MOLIS: Minority Online Information Service   283
Money For Graduate Students In The Humanities
    1996–98   272
Money For Graduate Students In The Sciences
    1998–2000   268
Money For Graduate Students In The Social Sciences
    1998–2000   267
Ms. Mentor's Impeccable Advice For Women In Academia   45

National Association For Law Placement   152
National Association Of Graduate-Professional
    Students   301
National Association Of Student Financial Aid
    Administrators: Planning For College   248
National Science Foundation Grad Student Page   252
Nellie Mae   252
NursingNet   214

Office Of Postsecondary Education Home Page   295
The Official GRE/CGS Directory Of Graduate Programs   78
The Official GRE/CGS Directory Of Graduate Programs   120
The Official Guide To U.S. Law Schools 2000   135
On The Market   22
One L   153
ONElist   290
Osteopathic.Com   192

The Penguin Guide To American Law Schools   159
The Penguin Guide To American Medical & Dental
    Schools   215
The Performing Arts Major's College Guide   66
Peterson's 1999 MBA Distance Learning Programs   112
Peterson's Compact Guides: Graduate Studies In
    Education   53
Peterson's Compact Guides: Graduate Studies In Engineering,
    Computer Science & Information Studies 1998   77
Peterson's Computer Science & Electrical Engineering
    Programs   71
Peterson's Graduate & Professional Programs   299
Peterson's Graduate Programs In Business, Education,
    Health, Information Studies, Law & Social Work
    116 (Business), 168 (Law), 216 (Medicine)
Peterson's Graduate Schools In The U.S.   308
Peterson's Graduate Studies In Arts, Humanities, &
    Archaeology 1998   51
Peterson's Graduate Studies In Biology, Health, &
    Agricultural Sciences   72
Peterson's Graduate Studies In Social Sciences & Social
    Work 1998   62
Peterson's Grants For Graduate & Postdoctoral Study   262
Peterson's Guide To Distance Learning Programs 1999   49
Peterson's Guide To MBA Programs 1999   94
Peterson's Guide To Nursing Programs   195
Peterson's Insider's Guide To Medical Schools, 1999   200
Peterson's Professional Degree Programs In The Visual &
    Performing Arts   67
Peterson's U.S. & Canadian Medical Schools   205
Petersons.com: Medical Schools   219
Petersons.com: The Graduate School Channel   31
Petersons.com: The Law Channel   154
Petersons.com: The MBA Channel   96
A Ph.D. Is Not Enough!   69
The Ph.D. Process   73
Planet Law School   169
PowerStudents.com Grad School   310
Premedical Student Forum   225
Preparing For Graduate Study In Psychology   64
Princeton Review Best 75 Business Schools   107
Princeton Review Best Distance Learning Graduate
    Schools   40
Princeton Review Best Graduate Programs: Engineering   74
Princeton Review Best Graduate Programs: Humanities &
    Social Sciences   52
Princeton Review Best Graduate Programs: Physical &
    Biological Sciences   75

Princeton Review Best Law Schools 2000 143

Princeton Review Best Medical Schools 2000 222

The Princeton Review Business School Companion 117

Princeton Review International Students' Guide To The USA 300

The Princeton Review Law School Companion 170

The Princeton Review Medical School Companion 206

Princeton Review Online: Business 110

Princeton Review Online: Graduate 47

Princeton Review Online: Law School 157

Princeton Review Online: Medicine 217

The Princeton Review Prelaw Companion 136

Princeton Review Scholarship Advisor 1999 279

REA's Authoritative Guide To Law Schools 161

REA's Authoritative Guide To Medical & Dental Schools 207

Real Guide To Grad School 50

Sallie Mae: Student Loan Marketing Association 244

Saludos Web Education Center 290

The Scholarship Resource Network 286

Scholarships, Fellowships & Financial Support For Jewish College Students 277

Scholarships & Fellowships For Math & Science Students 263

Scholarships For Women & Minorities 1998 290

Scholarships & Loans For Nursing Education 1997–1998 276

Slaying The Law School Dragon 167

Snapshots From Hell 99

So You Want To Be A Lawyer 141

Study In The USA 309

Surviving Graduate School Part Time 24

Take Control Of Your Student Loans 237

Test Of English As A Foreign Language (TOEFL) 316

Thinking About Law School 137

Tomorrow's Professor 76

Top Ten 122

U.S. Education Journal 316

U.S. News Online: Business 97

U.S. News Online: Graduate School 32

U.S. News Online: Law 144

U.S. News Online: Medicine 188

U.S. News & World Report: Best Graduate Schools 33

UCI Scholarship Opportunities Program 291

The Ultimate Grad School Survival Guide 34

Veterinary Medical School Admission Requirements In The United States And Canada 202

Which MBA? 108

A Woman's Guide To Law School 142

The Women's Guide To Surviving Graduate School 36

Worldwide Graduate Scholarship Directory 288

Yale Daily News Guide To Fellowships & Grants 264

Year One 118

V. Indices

AUTHOR INDEX

Ablow, Keith Russell; *Medical School* 194

Allen, Gregory; *The Medical Education Page* 225

Arnett, J. Robert II; *From Here To Attorney* 132

Asher, Donald; *Graduate Admissions Essays* 294

Association Of American Veterinary Medical Colleges; *Veterinary Medical School Admission Requirements In The United States And Canada* 202

Bachhubr, Thomas; *Arco's Best Graduate Business Schools* 109

Baker, Mark; *The Insider's Book Of Law School Lists* 171

Baker, Mark; *Kaplan's Insider's Book Of Business School Lists* 119

Baker, Mark; *Kaplan's Insider's Book Of Medical School Lists* 220

Baxter, Amy; *Kaplan's Getting Into Medical School* 213

Bellantoni, Patrick L.; *College Financial Aid Made Easy* 241

Bickerstaffe, George; *Which MBA?* 108

Bloom, Dale F.; *The Ph.D. Process* 73

Blum, Laurie; *Free Money For Graduate School* 278

Boufis, Christina; *On The Market* 22

Brennan, Moya; *Apply To American Colleges & Universities* 296

Brooks, Sean; *Education For Action: Undergraduate & Graduate Programs That Focus On Social Change* 79

Brown, Sanford J.; *Barron's Getting Into Medical School* 184

Burrell, David; *Getting In: An Applicant's Guide To Graduate School Admissions* 48

Buskist, William; *Allyn & Bacon Guide To Master's Programs In Psychology & Counseling Psychology* 63

Buskist, William; *Preparing For Graduate Study In Psychology* 64

Byrne, John A.; *Business Week's Guide To The Best Business Schools* 91

Caplan, Paula J.; *Lifting A Ton Of Feathers* 23

Carpenter, Phil; *Marketing Yourself To The Top Ten Business Schools* 93

Cassidy, Dan; *Worldwide Graduate Scholarship Directory* 288

Castleman, Harry; *Going To Law School?* 164

Chu, Larry; *Premedical Student Forum* 225

Clark, Robert; *Real Guide To Grad School* 50

Cohen, Justin; *Yale Daily News Guide To Fellowships & Grants* 264

Coleman, Ron; *The Princeton Review Prelaw Companion* 136

Criscito, Pat; *Barron's Guide To Distance Learning* 20

Curry, Boykin; *Essays That Worked For Business Schools* 98

Danek, Jennifer; *Becoming A Physician* 209

Deaver, Jeff; *The Complete Law School Companion* 149

DeMello, Christina; *College & University Home Pages* 307

DeNeef, A. Leigh; *The Academic's Handbook* 19

Doughty, Harold R.; *Guide To American Graduate Schools* 46

Doughty, Harold R.; *The Penguin Guide To American Law Schools* 159

Doughty, Harold R.; *The Penguin Guide To American Medical & Dental Schools* 215

Drozdowski, Mark J.; *Insider's Guide To Graduate Programs In Education* 54

Epps, Willie J.; *How To Get Into Harvard Law School* 140

Everett, Carole J.; *The Performing Arts Major's College Guide* 66

Falcon, Atticus; *Planet Law School* 169

Feibelman, Peter J.; *A Ph.D. Is Not Enough!* 69

Frank, Steven J.; *Learning The Law* 166

Fung, Ella Y.; *Scholarships For Women & Minorities 1998* 290

Gilbert, Nedda; *Princeton Review Best 75 Business Schools* 107

Gillers, Stephen; *Looking At Law School* 134

Goldfarb, S.F.; *Inside The Law Schools* 155

Goss, Bryan; *Applying To Medical School For The Non-Traditional Student* 208

Gottesman, Greg; *Arco's Law School Survival* 162

Gourman, Jack; *The Gourman Report* 313

Hacker, David A.; *Guide To Medical School & The MCAT* 185

Haft, Tim; *Kaplan/Newsweek Graduate School Admissions Adviser 2000* 160

Hallander, David; *Princeton Review Best Law Schools 2000* 143

Hamadeh, H.S.; *The Princeton Review Business School Companion* 117

Hamel, April Vahle; *The Graduate School Funding Handbook* 285

Hammon, Darrel L.; *Completing Graduate School Long Distance* 42

Heiberger, Mary Morris; *The Academic Job Search Handbook* 26

Hirshman, Linda; *A Woman's Guide To Law School* 142

Hoffmeir, Patricia; *From Residency To Reality* 203

Horn, Dan; *Graduate Student Resources On The Web* 30

Hricik, David; *Law School Basics* 151

Isaac, Alicia; *The African American Student's Guide To Surviving Graduate School*   25

Iserson, Kenneth V.; *Get Into Medical School!*   199

Jacobs, Ian; *Princeton Review International Students' Guide To The USA*   300

James, Edward J.; *Getting Into Medical School*   190

Jerrard, Richard; *The Grad School Handbook*   28

Kantrowitz, Mark; *FINAID: Business School Resources*   121

Kantrowitz, Mark; *FINAID: Graduate School Financial Aid Resources*   233

Kantrowitz, Mark; *FINAID: Law School Resources*   172

Kantrowitz, Mark; *FINAID: Medical School Resources*   224

Kantrowitz, Mark; *Scholarships & Fellowships For Math & Science Students*   263

Kaufman, Daniel; *Barron's Essays That Will Get You Into Medical School*   193

Keith-Spiegel, Patricia; *The Complete Guide To Graduate School Admission*   56

Kelly, Karin; *Film School Confidential*   65

Khlupin, Roman; *The MBA Page*   115

Kirkwood, Hal; *Bschool.com*   121

Konigsberg, Caty; *Scholarships, Fellowships & Financial Support For Jewish College Students*   277

Konner, Melvin; *Becoming A Doctor*   198

Law School Admissions Council; *So You Want To Be A Lawyer*   141

Leider, Anna; *Loans & Grants From Uncle Sam*   247

Leider, Anna & Robert; *Don't Miss Out*   231

Leonard, Robin; *Take Control Of Your Student Loans*   237

Lermack, Paul; *How To Get Into The Right Law School*   133

Lesko, Matthew; *Getting Yours: The Complete Guide To Government Money*   249

Lichtenstein, Ellen; *Arco's Ten Minute Guide To Paying For Graduate School*   238

Lisnek, Paul M.; *The Princeton Review Law School Companion*   170

Martinson, Thomas H.; *Arco's Getting Into Graduate Business School Today*   100

Martinson, Thomas H.; *Arco's Getting Into Law School Today*   158

McWade, Patricia; *Financing Graduate School*   234

Miller, Eugene; *Barron's Guide To Graduate Business Schools*   101

Mitchell, Lesli; *The Ultimate Grad School Survival Guide*   34

Montauk, Richard; *How To Get Into The Top MBA Programs*   92

Mumby, David G.; *Graduate School*   29

Munneke, Gary A.; *Barron's Guide To Law Schools*   146

Munneke, Gary A.; *Barron's How To Succeed In Law School*   147

Murphey, Alice; *Kaplan's Getting Into Business School (1999 Edition)*   114

Nagy, Andrea; *Princeton Review Best Medical Schools 2000*   222

National Association For Law Placement; *Beyond L.A. Law*   148

Oransky, Ivan; *Peterson's Insider's Guide To Medical Schools, 1999*   200

Peters, Robert L.; *Getting What You Came For*   21

Phillips, Vicky; *Princeton Review Best Distance Learning Graduate Schools*   40

Pintoff, Ernest; *The Complete Guide To American Film Schools*   68

Pittman, Von; *Surviving Graduate School Part Time*   24

Plantz, Scott H.; *Arco's Getting Into Medical School Today*   201

Powell, Charles W.; *The Mature Medical Student*   225

Pratt, Wanda; *Graduate Student Advice & Research Survival Guide*   38

Re, Joseph M.; *Earn & Learn*   243

Reeves-Lammert, Ruth; *Kaplan Newsweek Law School Admissions Advisor*   160

Reid, Robert; *Year One*   118

Reis, Richard M.; *Tomorrow's Professor*   76

Reyes, Jesus; *Guide To Selecting & Applying To Master Of Social Work Programs (1999)*   61

Rittner, Barbara; *The Women's Guide To Surviving Graduate School*   36

Robinson, Peter; *Snapshots From Hell*   99

Rogers, Carla S.; *How To Get Into The Right Dental School*   210

Rogers, Carla S.; *How To Get Into The Right Medical School*   211

Ross-Dalen, Mary; *The Princeton Review Medical School Companion*   206

Roth, George; *Slaying The Law School Dragon*   167

Rymniak, Marilyn J.; *Access America's Guide To Studying In The USA*   293

Sayette, Michael A.; *Insider's Guide To Graduate Programs In Clinical & Counseling Psychology* (1998–1999) 58

Schlachter, Gail Ann; *Directory Of Financial Aids For Women 1999–2001* 256

Schlachter, Gail Ann; *Financial Aid For African Americans 1999–2001* 258

Schlachter, Gail Ann; *Financial Aid For Research & Creative Activities Abroad 1999–2001* 270

Schlachter, Gail Ann; *Financial Aid For Study & Training Abroad 1999–2001* 259

Schlachter, Gail Ann; *Financial Aid For The Disabled & Their Families 1998–2000* 260

Schlachter, Gail Ann; *Financial Aid For Veterans, Military Personnel & Their Dependents 1998–2000* 271

Schlachter, Gail Ann; *Money For Graduate Students In The Humanities 1996–98* 272

Schlachter, Gail Ann; *Money For Graduate Students In The Sciences 1998–2000* 268

Schlachter, Gail Ann; *Money For Graduate Students In The Social Sciences 1998–2000* 267

Sen, Nilanjan; *The Complete Guide To Foreign Medical Schools In Plain English* 218

Shapo, Helene; *Law School Without Fear* 165

Sherrill, Jan-Mitchell; *The Gay, Lesbian, & Bisexual Students' Guide To Colleges, Universities, And Graduate Schools* 35

Showalter, English; *The MLA Guide To The Job Search* 55

Spaihts, Jonathan; *Princeton Review Best Graduate Programs: Humanities & Social Sciences* 52

Spaihts, Jonathan; *Princeton Review Best Graduate Programs: Physical & Biological Sciences* 75

Stelzer, Richard J.; *How To Write A Winning Personal Statement For Graduate & Professional School* 302

Stewart, Mark Alan; *Arco's Perfect Personal Statements* 305

Stockwell, Anne; *The Guerrilla Guide To Mastering Student Debt* 236

Strachan, James L.; *How To Get Into The Right Business School* 104

Student Conservation Association; *The Guide To Graduate Environmental Programs* 81

Student Financial Services; *Directory Of Private Scholarships & Grants* 269

Sween, Nancy; *The Interactive Medical Student Lounge* 191

Todd, Daryl F.; *How To Cut Tuition* 250

Toth, Emily; *Ms. Mentor's Impeccable Advice For Women In Academia* 45

Toyos, R. Stephen; *The Insider's Guide To Medical School Admissions* 212

Turow, Scott; *One L* 153

Vuturo, Chris; *Princeton Review Scholarship Advisor 1999* 279

Weinstein, Miriam; *Making A Difference College Guide* 82

Whitebread, Charles H.; *The Eight Secrets Of Top Exam Performance In Law School* 163

Wischnitzer, Saul; *Barron's Guide To Medical & Dental Schools* 197

Zaslau, Stanley; *Medical School Admissions Success!* 223

Zebala, John A.; *Medical School Admissions* 187

PUBLISHER INDEX

Accepted.com; *Accepted.com*   303

Access Group, Inc.; *Access Group*   240

Addison-Wesley; *A Ph.D. Is Not Enough!*   69

Allyn & Bacon; *Allyn & Bacon Guide To Master's Programs In Psychology & Counseling Psychology*   63

Allyn & Bacon; *Insider's Guide To Graduate Programs In Education*   54

Allyn & Bacon; *Preparing For Graduate Study In Psychology*   64

American Association of Colleges of Osteopathic Medicine; *AACOMAS Application Kit*   224

American Association Of Colleges Of Osteopathic Medicine; *American Association Of Colleges Of Osteopathic Medicine*   196

American Association Of University Women; *American Association Of University Women Educational Foundation Fellowships & Grants*   289

American Bar Association; *American Bar Association Approved Law Schools* (Internet)   172

American Chemical Society; *American Chemical Society Minority Affairs*   289

American Collegiate Media; *Directory Of Private Scholarships & Grants*   269

American Journalism Review; *American Journalism Review Newslink*   273

American Psychological Association; *American Psychological Association: Student Information/Education Programs*   60

American Psychological Association; *Getting In*   57

American Psychological Association; *Graduate Study In Psychology 1998–1999*   59

Arco (Macmillan); *Arco's Best Graduate Business Schools*   109

Arco (Macmillan); *Arco's Getting Into Graduate Business School Today*   100

Arco (Macmillan); *Arco's Getting Into Law School Today*   158

Arco (Macmillan); *Arco's Getting Into Medical School Today*   201

Arco (Macmillan); *Arco's Perfect Personal Statements*   305

Arco (Macmillan); *Arco's Ten Minute Guide To Paying For Graduate School*   238

Arco (Simon & Schuster Macmillan); *Arco's Law School Survival*   162

Association For Support Of Graduate Students; *Association For Support Of Graduate Students*   41

Association Of American Medical Colleges; *AMCAS-E Student & Applicant Information*   224

Association Of American Medical Colleges; *Association Of American Medical Colleges*   189

Association Of American Medical Colleges; *Medical School Admission Requirements*   186

Atlantic Educational Publishing; *How To Cut Tuition*   250

Avon (William Morrow); *Year One*   118

Barron's; *Barron's Essays That Will Get You Into Medical School*   193

Barron's Educational Series; *Barron's Getting Into Medical School*   184

Barron's Educational Series; *Barron's Guide To Distance Learning*   20

Barron's Educational Series; *Barron's Guide To Graduate Business Schools*   101

Barron's Educational Series; *Barron's Guide To Law Schools*   146

Barron's Educational Series; *Barron's Guide To Medical & Dental Schools*   197

Barron's Educational Series; *Barron's How To Succeed In Law School*   147

Boston College Board Of Trustees; *Boston College Online Law School Locator*   130

Broadway (Bantam Doubleday Dell); *So You Want To Be A Lawyer*   141

Bschool.com; *Bschool.com*   121

Business Education Commission; *Top Ten*   122

Business Week; *Business Week Online's Business Schools*   90

Career; *The Insider's Guide To Medical School Admissions*   212

Career; *Worldwide Graduate Scholarship Directory*   288

Citadel (Carol); *Learning The Law*   166

College Board; *The College Board Index Of Majors & Graduate Degrees 2000*   298

College Board; *The College Board International Student Handbook Of U.S. Colleges*   312

College Board; *College Board Online*   306

College Board; *The College Board Scholarship Handbook*   280

College of Liberal Arts and Sciences, University of Florida; *American Universities*   315

Contemporary Books (Tribune New Media/Education); *How To Get Into Harvard Law School*   140

Conway Greene; *AmeriCorps: Serve Your Country & Pay For College*   311

Corporation For National Service; *AmeriCorps Home Page*   304

Council Of Graduate Schools; *Council Of Graduate Schools: Student Page*   83

Dan Horn; *Graduate Student Resources On The Web*   30

Duke University; *The Academic's Handbook*   19

Educational Testing Service; *GRE Online*   39

Educational Testing Service; *The Official GRE/CGS Directory Of Graduate Programs*   78

Educational Testing Service; *The Official GRE/CGS Directory Of Graduate Programs*   120

Educational Testing Service; *Test Of English As A Foreign Language (TOEFL)*   316

EI Education International; *Guide To Graduate Management Programs In The USA, 1999*   103

Embark.com; *Embark.com: Going To Business School*   95

Embark.com; *Embark.com: Going To Graduate School*   27

Embark.com; *Embark.com: Going To Law School*   138

eStudentLoan.com, L.L.C.; *eStudentLoan.com*   232

ETS and Peterson's; *GradAdvantage*   121

Facts on File; *Free Money For Graduate School*   278

FastWEB; *FastWEB*   257

Fawcett Columbine (Ballantine); *Essays That Worked For Business Schools*   98

Federal Trade Commission; *Federal Trade Commission Scholarship Scam Alert*   289

FinAid Page, L.L.C.; *FINAID: Business School Resources*   121

FinAid Page, L.L.C.; *FINAID: Graduate School Financial Aid Resources*   233

FinAid Page, L.L.C.; *FINAID: Law School Resources*   172

FinAid Page, L.L.C.; *FINAID: Medical School Resources*   224

Financial Times Management; *The Complete MBA Companion*   102

Financial Times Management/Economist Intelligence Unit; *Which MBA?*   108

Find Law; *FindLaw*   131

Fine Print; *Planet Law School*   169

First Union; *Educaid Loan Programs: Loans For Graduate Students*   251

FMSG Publishing; *Medical School Admissions Success!*   223

Food First; *Education For Action: Undergraduate & Graduate Programs That Focus On Social Change*   79

Foundation; *Law School Without Fear*   165

Galen; *Get Into Medical School!*   199

Garrett Park; *Dollars for College* (Series)   287

Garrett Park; *Financial Aid For Minorities* (Series)   284

GMAC; *GMAT Online: MBA Explorer*   113

Guilford; *Insider's Guide To Graduate Programs In Clinical & Counseling Psychology (1998–1999)*   58

Harcourt Brace Legal & Professional Publications; *The Eight Secrets Of Top Exam Performance In Law School*   163

Harcourt Brace Legal & Professional Publications, Inc.; *Beyond L.A. Law*   148

HarperCollins; *The Guerrilla Guide To Mastering Student Debt*   236

IDG Books Worldwide; *American Bar Association Guide To Approved Law Schools*   145

IDG Books Worldwide; *The Performing Arts Major's College Guide*   66

IEEE; *Tomorrow's Professor*   76

Indus; *The Complete Guide To Foreign Medical Schools In Plain English*   218

Institute of International Education; *Financial Resources For International Study*   266

Institute of International Education; *Funding For United States Study*   261

International Education Service; *International Education Service*   314

Internet Legal Resource Guide; *Internet Legal Resource Guide*   139

Island; *The Guide To Graduate Environmental Programs*   81

John Wiley & Sons; *Becoming A Physician*   209

John Wiley & Sons; *The Complete Law School Companion*   149

John Wiley & Sons; *Going To Law School?*   164

John Wiley & Sons; *Marketing Yourself To The Top Ten Business Schools*   93

John Wiley & Sons; *Slaying The Law School Dragon*   167

Kantrowitz, Mark; *eduPASS*   297

Kaplan Educational Centers; *Kaplan Online: Business*   111

Kaplan Educational Centers; *Kaplan Online: Financial Aid*   246

Kaplan Educational Centers; *Kaplan Online: Grad School*   37

Kaplan Educational Centers; *Kaplan Online: Law*   150

Kaplan Educational Centers; *Kaplan Online: Medicine*   204

Kaplan Educational Centers and Simon & Schuster; *Kaplan/Newsweek Graduate School Admissions Adviser 2000*   44

Kaplan Educational Centers and Simon & Schuster; *Yale Daily News Guide To Fellowships & Grants*   264

Kaplan (Simon & Schuster); *Kaplan Newsweek Law School Admissions Advisor*   160

Kaplan (Simon & Schuster); *Kaplan's Getting Into Business School (1999 Edition)* 114

Kaplan (Simon & Schuster); *Kaplan's Getting Into Medical School* 213

Kaplan (Simon & Schuster); *Kaplan's Insider's Book Of Business School Lists* 119

Kaplan (Simon & Schuster); *Kaplan's Insider's Book Of Medical School Lists* 220

Lakeshore-Pearson; *Applying To Medical School For The Non-Traditional Student* 208

Law School Admissions Council; *Law School Admissions Council Online* 156

Law School Admissions Council; *Thinking About Law School* 137

Lawrence Erlbaum Associates; *The Complete Guide To Graduate School Admission* 56

Liberty City Promotions, Inc.; *GradSchools.Com* 43

Linguafranca; *Real Guide To Grad School* 50

Los Angeles Hillel Council/ FACETS; *Scholarships, Fellowships & Financial Support For Jewish College Students* 277

McGraw-Hill; *Business Week's Guide To The Best Business Schools* 91

McGraw-Hill; *From Residency To Reality* 203

Medical World; *Premedical Student Forum* 225

MedicalStudent.net; *MedicalStudent.net* 221

Meridian (Penguin); *Looking At Law School* 134

Modern Language Association Of America; *The MLA Guide To The Job Search* 55

Mustang; *Medical School Admissions* 187

Nancy Sween; *The Interactive Medical Student Lounge* 191

National Academy Press; *Careers In Science And Engineering* 70

National Association for Law Placement; *National Association For Law Placement* 152

National Association Of Graduate-Professional Students; *National Association Of Graduate-Professional Students* 301

National Association Of Student Financial Aid Administrators; *National Association Of Student Financial Aid Administrators: Planning For College* 248

National Education Standards; *The Gourman Report* 313

National League for Nursing; *Scholarships & Loans For Nursing Education 1997–1998* 276

National Science Foundation; *National Science Foundation Grad Student Page* 252

Nellie Mae; *Nellie Mae* 252

New York University; *The Gay, Lesbian, & Bisexual Students' Guide To Colleges, Universities, And Graduate Schools* 35

Nolo; *Take Control Of Your Student Loans* 237

Noonday; *Getting What You Came For* 21

Nova; *Law School Basics* 151

NTC LearningWorks; *Apply To American Colleges & Universities* 296

NursingNet; *NursingNet* 214

Octameron Associates; *Don't Miss Out* 231

Octameron Associates; *Earn & Learn* 243

Octameron Associates; *Loans & Grants From Uncle Sam* 247

Ohio State University; *The MBA Page* 115

OMEGA; *Osteopathic.Com* 192

ONElist, Inc.; *ONElist* 290

Oxford University; *The Ph.D. Process* 73

Penguin; *Becoming A Doctor* 198

Penguin; *The Complete Guide To American Film Schools* 68

Penguin; *Getting Yours: The Complete Guide To Government Money* 249

Penguin; *Guide To American Graduate Schools* 46

Penguin; *The Penguin Guide To American Law Schools* 159

Penguin; *The Penguin Guide To American Medical & Dental Schools* 215

Penguin; *A Woman's Guide To Law School* 142

Perigee (Berkley); *Film School Confidential* 65

Perigee (Berkley); *The Grad School Handbook* 28

Peterson's; *Education For The Earth: The College Guide For Careers In The Environment* 80

Peterson's; *Financing Graduate School* 234

Peterson's; *How To Write A Winning Personal Statement For Graduate & Professional School* 302

Peterson's; *Peterson's 1999 MBA Distance Learning Programs* 112

Peterson's; *Peterson's Compact Guides: Graduate Studies In Education* 53

Peterson's; *Peterson's Compact Guides: Graduate Studies In Engineering, Computer Science & Information Studies 1998* 77

Peterson's; *Peterson's Computer Science & Electrical Engineering Programs* 71

Peterson's; *Peterson's Graduate & Professional Programs* 299

Peterson's Graduate Programs In Business, Education, Health, Information Studies, Law & Social Work 116 (Business), 168 (Law), 216 (Medicine)

Peterson's; *Peterson's Graduate Schools In The U.S.* 308

Peterson's; *Peterson's Graduate Studies In Arts, Humanities, & Archaeology 1998* 51

Peterson's; *Peterson's Graduate Studies In Biology, Health, & Agricultural Sciences* 72

Peterson's; *Peterson's Graduate Studies In Social Sciences & Social Work 1998* 62

Peterson's; *Peterson's Grants For Graduate & Postdoctoral Study* 262

Peterson's; *Peterson's Guide To Distance Learning Programs 1999* 49

Peterson's; *Peterson's Guide To MBA Programs 1999* 94

Peterson's; *Peterson's Guide To Nursing Programs* 195

Peterson's; *Peterson's Insider's Guide To Medical Schools, 1999* 200

Peterson's; *Peterson's Professional Degree Programs In The Visual & Performing Arts* 67

Peterson's; *Peterson's U.S. & Canadian Medical Schools* 205

Peterson's; *Petersons.com: Medical Schools* 219

Peterson's; *Petersons.com: The Graduate School Channel* 31

Peterson's; *Petersons.com: The Law Channel* 154

Peterson's; *Petersons.com: The MBA Channel* 96

Peterson's; *The Ultimate Grad School Survival Guide* 34

Plume (Penguin); *Inside The Law Schools* 155

PowerStudents.com; *PowerStudents.com Grad School* 310

Prentice Hall; *How To Get Into The Top MBA Programs* 92

Prentice Hall; *Scholarships & Fellowships For Math & Science Students* 263

Princeton Review; *Princeton Review Online: Business* 110

Princeton Review; *Princeton Review Online: Graduate* 47

Princeton Review; *Princeton Review Online: Law School* 157

Princeton Review; *Princeton Review Online: Medicine* 217

Princeton Review (Random House); *Princeton Review Best 75 Business Schools* 107

Princeton Review (Random House); *Princeton Review Best Distance Learning Graduate Schools* 40

Princeton Review (Random House); *Princeton Review Best Graduate Programs: Engineering* 74

Princeton Review (Random House); *Princeton Review Best Graduate Programs: Humanities & Social Sciences* 52

Princeton Review (Random House); *Princeton Review Best Graduate Programs: Physical & Biological Sciences* 75

Princeton Review (Random House); *Princeton Review Best Law Schools 2000* 143

Princeton Review (Random House); *Princeton Review Best Medical Schools 2000* 222

Princeton Review (Random House); *The Princeton Review Business School Companion* 117

Princeton Review (Random House); *Princeton Review International Students' Guide To The USA* 300

Princeton Review (Random House); *The Princeton Review Law School Companion* 170

Princeton Review (Random House); *The Princeton Review Medical School Companion* 206

Princeton Review (Random House); *The Princeton Review Prelaw Companion* 136

Princeton Review (Random House); *Princeton Review Scholarship Advisor 1999* 279

Professional Publications; *From Here To Attorney* 132

Proto Press; *Graduate School* 29

Purdue University; *Veterinary Medical School Admission Requirements In The United States And Canada* 202

RAMS-FIE; *MOLIS: Minority Online Information Service* 283

Reference Service Press; *Directory Of Financial Aids For Women 1999–2001* 256

Reference Service Press; *Financial Aid For African Americans 1999–2001* 258

Reference Service Press; *Financial Aid For Research & Creative Activities Abroad 1999–2001* 270

Reference Service Press; *Financial Aid For Study & Training Abroad 1999–2001* 259

Reference Service Press; *Financial Aid For The Disabled & Their Families 1998–2000* 260

Reference Service Press; *Financial Aid For Veterans, Military Personnel & Their Dependents 1998–2000* 271

Reference Service Press; *Money For Graduate Students In The Humanities 1996–98* 272

Reference Service Press; *Money For Graduate Students In The Sciences 1998–2000* 268

Reference Service Press; *Money For Graduate Students In The Social Sciences 1998–2000* 267

Research & Education Association; *REA's Authoritative Guide To Law Schools* 161

Research & Education Association; *REA's Authoritative Guide To Medical & Dental Schools* 207

Riverhead; *On The Market* 22

Sage; *The African American Student's Guide To Surviving Graduate School* 25

Sage; *Completing Graduate School Long Distance* 42

Sage; *Surviving Graduate School Part Time* 24

Sage; *The Women's Guide To Surviving Graduate School* 36

Sageworks; *Making A Difference College Guide* 82

Sallie Mae; *Sallie Mae: Student Loan Marketing Association* 244

Saludos Hispanos Magazine; *Saludos Web Education Center*   290

Scholarship Resource Network; *The Scholarship Resource Network*   286

Simon & Schuster; *Access America's Guide To Studying In The USA*   293

Simon & Schuster; *The Insider's Book Of Law School Lists*   171

Sourcebooks; *Graduate Student's Complete Scholarship Book*   265

Sourcebooks; *The Minority & Women's Complete Scholarship Book*   282

St. Martin's; *Medical School*   194

Student Aid Alliance; *The Alliance To Save Student Aid*   251

Student Financial Services /Perpetual; *The Financial Aid Book*   275

Student Financial Services/Perpetual; *The Government Financial Aid Book*   245

Student Services, Inc.; *The Complete Scholarship Book*   281

Study in the USA, Inc.; *Study In The USA*   309

Ten Speed; *College Financial Aid Made Easy*   241

Ten Speed; *Graduate Admissions Essays*   294

Time (Random); *The Official Guide To U.S. Law Schools 2000*   135

U.S. Department Of Education; *Guide To Completing The 1999–2000 Free Application For Federal Student Aid (FAFSA)*   251

U.S. Department Of Education, Debt Collection Service; *Guide To Defaulted Student Loans*   239

U.S. Department Of Education, Office Of Postsecondary Education; *Direct Loan*   242

U.S. Department Of Education, Office Of Postsecondary Education; *Free Application For Federal Student Aid (FAFSA) Online*   235

U.S. Department Of Education, Office Of Postsecondary Education; *Office Of Postsecondary Education Home Page*   295

U.S. Education Journal; *U.S. Education Journal*   316

U.S. News and World Report; *U.S. News Online: Business*   97

U.S. News and World Report; *U.S. News Online: Graduate School*   32

U.S. News and World Report; *U.S. News Online: Law*   144

U.S. News and World Report; *U.S. News Online: Medicine*   188

U.S. News and World Report; *U.S. News & World Report: Best Graduate Schools*   33

United States Information Agency; *Information USA: Education In The USA*   316

Universal Algorithms, Inc.; *CollegeNET*   315

Universal Algorithms, Inc.; *CollegeNET MACH25 Scholarship Search*   274

University of California, Irvine; *UCI Scholarship Opportunities Program*   291

University of Pennsylvania; *The Academic Job Search Handbook*   26

University of Pennsylvania; *The Graduate School Funding Handbook*   285

University of Pennsylvania; *Ms. Mentor's Impeccable Advice For Women In Academia*   45

University of Toronto; *Lifting A Ton Of Feathers*   23

VGM Career Horizons; *How To Get Into The Right Dental School*   210

VGM Career Horizons (NTC Publishing Group); *How To Get Into The Right Business School*   104

VGM Career Horizons (NTC Publishing Group); *How To Get Into The Right Law School*   133

VGM Career Horizons (NTC Publishing Group); *How To Get Into The Right Medical School*   211

VNU Business Publications; *MBA Plaza*   106

Warner; *One L*   153

Warner; *Snapshots From Hell*   99

WebInfoCo; *MBA Info*   105

White Hat Communications; *Guide To Selecting & Applying To Master Of Social Work Programs (1999)*   61

Williams & Wilkins; *Getting Into Medical School*   190

Williams & Wilkins; *Guide To Medical School & The MCAT*   185

MEDIA INDEX:

Note: This media index is created using the media **reviewed**. In some cases, resources are also available in other media formats (audiotape, videotape, etc.); the availability of these other formats is noted in the "Where To Find/Buy" section found in the full-page reviews of such resources.

Book

★★★★ *The Academic's Handbook* 19

★★★★ *Access America's Guide To Studying In The USA* 293

★★★★ *Barron's Getting Into Medical School* 184

★★★★ *Barron's Guide To Distance Learning* 20

★★★★ *Business Week's Guide To The Best Business Schools* 91

★★★★ *The Complete Guide To Graduate School Admission* 56

★★★★ *Directory Of Financial Aids For Women 1999–2001* 256

★★★★ *Don't Miss Out* 231

★★★★ *Education For Action: Undergraduate & Graduate Programs That Focus On Social Change* 79

★★★★ *Education For The Earth: The College Guide For Careers In The Environment* 80

★★★★ *Film School Confidential* 65

★★★★ *Financial Aid For African Americans 1999–2001* 258

★★★★ *Financial Aid For Study & Training Abroad 1999–2001* 259

★★★★ *Financial Aid For The Disabled & Their Families 1998–2000* 260

★★★★ *Financing Graduate School* 234

★★★★ *From Here To Attorney* 132

★★★★ *Funding For United States Study* 261

★★★★ *Getting In* 57

★★★★ *Getting Into Medical School* 190

★★★★ *Getting What You Came For* 21

★★★★ *Graduate Student's Complete Scholarship Book* 265

★★★★ *Graduate Study In Psychology 1998–1999* 59

★★★★ *The Guerrilla Guide To Mastering Student Debt* 236

★★★★ *Guide To Medical School & The MCAT* 185

★★★★ *How To Get Into The Right Law School* 133

★★★★ *How To Get Into The Top MBA Programs* 92

★★★★ *Insider's Guide To Graduate Programs In Clinical & Counseling Psychology (1998–1999)* 58

★★★★ *Lifting A Ton Of Feathers* 23

★★★★ *Looking At Law School* 134

★★★★ *Marketing Yourself To The Top Ten Business Schools* 93

★★★★ *Medical School Admission Requirements* 186

★★★★ *Medical School Admissions* 187

★★★★ *The MLA Guide To The Job Search* 55

★★★★ *The Official Guide To U.S. Law Schools 2000* 135

★★★★ *On The Market* 22

★★★★ *The Performing Arts Major's College Guide* 66

★★★★ *Peterson's Grants For Graduate & Postdoctoral Study* 262

★★★★ *Peterson's Guide To MBA Programs 1999* 94

★★★★ *Princeton Review Best Law Schools 2000* 143

★★★★ *The Princeton Review Prelaw Companion* 136

★★★★ *Real Guide To Grad School* 50

★★★★ *Scholarships & Fellowships For Math & Science Students* 263

★★★★ *Surviving Graduate School Part Time* 24

★★★★ *Take Control Of Your Student Loans* 237

★★★★ *Thinking About Law School* 137

★★★★ *A Woman's Guide To Law School* 142

★★★★ *Yale Daily News Guide To Fellowships & Grants* 264

★★★ *The Academic Job Search Handbook* 26

★★★ *The African American Student's Guide To Surviving Graduate School* 25

★★★ *American Bar Association Guide To Approved Law Schools* 145

★★★ *Apply To American Colleges & Universities* 296

★★★ *Arco's Best Graduate Business Schools* 109

★★★ *Arco's Getting Into Graduate Business School Today* 100

★★★ *Arco's Getting Into Medical School Today* 201

★★★ *Arco's Ten Minute Guide To Paying For Graduate School* 238

★★★ *Barron's Essays That Will Get You Into Medical School* 193

★★★ *Barron's Guide To Graduate Business Schools* 101

★★★ *Barron's Guide To Law Schools* 146

★★★ *Barron's Guide To Medical & Dental Schools* 197

★★★ *Barron's How To Succeed In Law School* 147

★★★ *Becoming A Doctor* 198

★★★ *Beyond L.A. Law* 148

★★★ *Careers In Science And Engineering* 70

★★★ *The College Board Index Of Majors & Graduate Degrees 2000* 298

★★★ *College Financial Aid Made Easy* 241

★★★ *The Complete Law School Companion* 149

★★★ *The Complete MBA Companion* 102

★★★ *Directory Of Private Scholarships & Grants* 269

★★★ *Earn & Learn* 243

★★★ *Essays That Worked For Business Schools* 98

★★★ *The Financial Aid Book* 275

★★★ *Financial Aid For Research & Creative Activities Abroad 1999–2001* 270

★★★ *Financial Aid For Veterans, Military Personnel & Their Dependents 1998–2000* 271

★★★ Financial Resources For International Study   266

★★★ The Gay, Lesbian, & Bisexual Students' Guide To Colleges, Universities, And Graduate Schools   35

★★★ Get Into Medical School!   199

★★★ The Grad School Handbook   28

★★★ Graduate Admissions Essays   294

★★★ Graduate School   29

★★★ The Guide To Graduate Environmental Programs   81

★★★ Guide To Graduate Management Programs In The USA, 1999   103

★★★ How To Get Into Harvard Law School   140

★★★ How To Get Into The Right Business School   104

★★★ Inside The Law Schools   155

★★★ Law School Basics   151

★★★ Medical School   194

★★★ Money For Graduate Students In The Humanities 1996–98   272

★★★ Money For Graduate Students In The Sciences 1998–2000   268

★★★ Money For Graduate Students In The Social Sciences 1998–2000   267

★★★ One L   153

★★★ Peterson's Computer Science & Electrical Engineering Programs   71

★★★ Peterson's Graduate & Professional Programs   299

★★★ Peterson's Guide To Nursing Programs   195

★★★ Peterson's Insider's Guide To Medical Schools, 1999   200

★★★ A Ph.D. Is Not Enough!   69

★★★ The Ph.D. Process   73

★★★ Princeton Review Best 75 Business Schools   107

★★★ Princeton Review Best Graduate Programs: Engineering   74

★★★ Princeton Review Best Graduate Programs: Physical & Biological Sciences   75

★★★ Princeton Review International Students' Guide To The USA   300

★★★ Scholarships, Fellowships & Financial Support For Jewish College Students   277

★★★ Scholarships & Loans For Nursing Education 1997–1998   276

★★★ Snapshots From Hell   99

★★★ So You Want To Be A Lawyer   141

★★★ Tomorrow's Professor   76

★★★ The Ultimate Grad School Survival Guide   34

★★★ Veterinary Medical School Admission Requirements In The United States And Canada   202

★★★ Which MBA?   108

★★★ The Women's Guide To Surviving Graduate School   36

★★ Allyn & Bacon Guide To Master's Programs In Psychology & Counseling Psychology   63

★★ Applying To Medical School For The Non-Traditional Student   208

★★ Arco's Getting Into Law School Today   158

★★ Arco's Law School Survival   162

★★ Arco's Perfect Personal Statements   305

★★ Becoming A Physician   209

★★ The College Board Scholarship Handbook   280

★★ The Complete Scholarship Book   281

★★ Completing Graduate School Long Distance   42

★★ The Eight Secrets Of Top Exam Performance In Law School   163

★★ Financial Aid For Minorities (Series)   284

★★ Free Money For Graduate School   278

★★ From Residency To Reality   203

★★ Getting Yours: The Complete Guide To Government Money   249

★★ Going To Law School?   164

★★ The Government Financial Aid Book   245

★★ The Graduate School Funding Handbook   285

★★ Guide To American Graduate Schools   46

★★ Guide To Selecting & Applying To Master Of Social Work Programs (1999)   61

★★ How To Cut Tuition   250

★★ How To Get Into The Right Dental School   210

★★ How To Get Into The Right Medical School   211

★★ How To Write A Winning Personal Statement For Graduate & Professional School   302

★★ The Insider's Guide To Medical School Admissions   212

★★ Kaplan Newsweek Law School Admissions Advisor   160

★★ Kaplan's Getting Into Business School (1999 Edition)   114

★★ Kaplan's Getting Into Medical School   213

★★ Kaplan/Newsweek Graduate School Admissions Adviser 2000   44

★★ Law School Without Fear   165

★★ Learning The Law   166

★★ Loans & Grants From Uncle Sam   247

★★ Making A Difference College Guide   82

★★ The Minority & Women's Complete Scholarship Book   282

★★ Ms. Mentor's Impeccable Advice For Women In Academia   45

★★ *The Penguin Guide To American Law Schools* 159

★★ *The Penguin Guide To American Medical & Dental Schools* 215

★★ *Peterson's 1999 MBA Distance Learning Programs* 112

★★ *Peterson's Graduate Programs In Business, Education, Health, Information Studies, Law & Social Work (Business)* 116

★★ *Peterson's Graduate Programs In Business, Education, Health, Information Studies, Law & Social Work (Health Sciences)* 216

★★ *Peterson's Professional Degree Programs In The Visual & Performing Arts* 67

★★ *Peterson's U.S. & Canadian Medical Schools* 205

★★ *Princeton Review Best Distance Learning Graduate Schools* 40

★★ *Princeton Review Best Graduate Programs: Humanities & Social Sciences* 52

★★ *The Princeton Review Business School Companion* 117

★★ *The Princeton Review Medical School Companion* 206

★★ *Princeton Review Scholarship Advisor 1999* 279

★★ *REA's Authoritative Guide To Law Schools* 161

★★ *REA's Authoritative Guide To Medical & Dental Schools* 207

★★ *Slaying The Law School Dragon* 167

★★ *Year One* 118

★ *AmeriCorps: Serve Your Country & Pay For College* 311

★ *The College Board International Student Handbook Of U.S. Colleges* 312

★ *The Complete Guide To American Film Schools* 68

★ *The Complete Guide To Foreign Medical Schools In Plain English* 218

★ *Dollars For College (Series)* 287

★ *The Gourman Report* 313

★ *The Insider's Book Of Law School Lists* 171

★ *Insider's Guide To Graduate Programs In Education* 54

★ *Kaplan's Insider's Book Of Business School Lists* 119

★ *Kaplan's Insider's Book Of Medical School Lists* 220

★ *Medical School Admissions Success!* 223

★ *The Official GRE/CGS Directory Of Graduate Programs* 78

★ *The Official GRE/CGS Directory Of Graduate Programs* 120

★ *Peterson's Graduate Programs In Business, Education, Health, Information Studies, Law & Social Work (Law)* 168

★ *Peterson's Guide To Distance Learning Programs 1999* 49

★ *Planet Law School* 169

★ *Preparing For Graduate Study In Psychology* 64

★ *Princeton Review Best Medical Schools 2000* 222

★ *The Princeton Review Law School Companion* 170

★ *Worldwide Graduate Scholarship Directory* 288

Internet

★★★★ *Association Of American Medical Colleges* 189

★★★★ *Boston College Online Law School Locator* 130

★★★★ *Business Week Online's Business Schools* 90

★★★★ *Embark.com: Going To Business School* 95

★★★★ *Embark.com: Going To Law School* 138

★★★★ *eStudentLoan.com* 232

★★★★ *FastWEB* 257

★★★★ *FINAID: Graduate School Financial Aid Resources* 233

★★★★ *FindLaw* 131

★★★★ *Free Application For Federal Student Aid (FAFSA) Online* 235

★★★★ *The Interactive Medical Student Lounge* 191

★★★★ *Internet Legal Resource Guide* 139

★★★★ *Osteopathic.Com* 192

★★★★ *Petersons.com: The MBA Channel* 96

★★★★ *U.S. News Online: Medicine* 188

★★★ *Access Group* 240

★★★ *American Association Of Colleges Of Osteopathic Medicine* 196

★★★ *American Journalism Review Newslink* 273

★★★ *American Psychological Association: Student Information/Education Programs* 60

★★★ *CollegeNET MACH25 Scholarship Search* 274

★★★ *Direct Loan* 242

★★★ *eduPASS* 297

★★★ *Embark.com: Going To Graduate School* 27

★★★ *Graduate Student Resources On The Web* 30

★★★ *Guide To Defaulted Student Loans* 239

★★★ *Kaplan Online: Law* 150

★★★ *Law School Admissions Council Online* 156

★★★ *MBA Info* 105

★★★ *MBA Plaza* 106

★★★ *National Association For Law Placement* 152

★★★ *National Association Of Graduate-Professional Students* 301

★★★ *Office Of Postsecondary Education Home Page* 295

★★★ *Petersons.com: The Graduate School Channel* 31

★★★ *Petersons.com: The Law Channel* 154

★★★ Princeton Review Online: Business 110
★★★ Princeton Review Online: Law School 157
★★★ Sallie Mae: Student Loan Marketing Association 244
★★★ U.S. News Online: Business 97
★★★ U.S. News Online: Graduate School 32
★★★ U.S. News Online: Law 144
★★ Accepted.com 303
★★ AmeriCorps Home Page 304
★★ Association For Support Of Graduate Students 41
★★ College Board Online 306
★★ College & University Home Pages 307
★★ GMAT Online: MBA Explorer 113
★★ GradSchools.Com 43
★★ Graduate Student Advice & Research Survival Guide 38
★★ GRE Online 39
★★ Kaplan Online: Business 111
★★ Kaplan Online: Financial Aid 246
★★ Kaplan Online: Grad School 37
★★ Kaplan Online: Medicine 204
★★ The MBA Page 115
★★ MOLIS: Minority Online Information Service 283
★★ National Association Of Student Financial Aid Administrators: Planning For College 248
★★ NursingNet 214
★★ Princeton Review Online: Medicine 217
★★ The Scholarship Resource Network 286
★★ Study In The USA 309
★ Getting In: An Applicant's Guide To Graduate School Admissions 48
★ International Education Service 314
★ MedicalStudent.net 221
★ Petersons.com: Medical Schools 219
★ PowerStudents.com Grad School 310
★ Princeton Review Online: Graduate 47
N/R AACOMAS Application Kit 224
N/R The Alliance To Save Student Aid 251
N/R AMCAS-E Student & Applicant Information 224
N/R American Association Of University Women Educational Foundation Fellowships & Grants 289
N/R American Bar Association Approved Law Schools (Internet) 145
N/R American Chemical Society Minority Affairs 289
N/R American Universities 315
N/R Bschool.com 121

N/R CollegeNET 315
N/R Council Of Graduate Schools: Student Page 83
N/R Educaid Loan Programs: Loans For Graduate Students 251
N/R Federal Trade Commission Scholarship Scam Alert 289
N/R FINAID: Business School Resources 121
N/R FINAID: Law School Resources 172
N/R FINAID: Medical School Resources 224
N/R General Education Online 315
N/R GradAdvantage 121
N/R Guide To Completing The 1999–2000 Free Application For Federal Student Aid (FAFSA) 251
N/R Information USA: Education In The USA 316
N/R The Mature Medical Student 225
N/R The Medical Education Page 225
N/R National Science Foundation Grad Student Page 252
N/R Nellie Mae 252
N/R ONElist 290
N/R Premedical Student Forum 225
N/R Saludos Web Education Center 290
N/R Scholarships For Women & Minorities 1998 290
N/R Test Of English As A Foreign Language (TOEFL) 316
N/R Top Ten 122
N/R U.S. Education Journal 316
N/R UCI Scholarship Opportunities Program 291

Book & CD-ROM

★★★ Peterson's Graduate Studies In Biology, Health, & Agricultural Sciences 72
★★ Peterson's Compact Guides: Graduate Studies In Education 53
★★ Peterson's Compact Guides: Graduate Studies In Engineering, Computer Science & Information Studies 1998 77
★★ Peterson's Graduate Schools In The U.S. 308
★★ Peterson's Graduate Studies In Arts, Humanities, & Archaeology 1998 51
★★ Peterson's Graduate Studies In Social Sciences & Social Work 1998 62

Magazine

★★★ U.S. News & World Report: Best Graduate Schools 33

SUBJECT INDEX
1–4 Stars (4 = Best)

Obtaining A Master's Or PhD

★★★★ *The Academic's Handbook*   19

★★★★ *Barron's Guide To Distance Learning*   20

★★★★ *The Complete Guide To Graduate School Admission*   56

★★★★ *Education For Action: Undergraduate & Graduate Programs That Focus On Social Change*   79

★★★★ *Education For The Earth: The College Guide For Careers In The Environment*   80

★★★★ *Film School Confidential*   65

★★★★ *Getting In*   57

★★★★ *Getting What You Came For*   21

★★★★ *Graduate Study In Psychology 1998–1999*   59

★★★★ *Insider's Guide To Graduate Programs In Clinical & Counseling Psychology (1998–1999)*   58

★★★★ *Lifting A Ton Of Feathers*   23

★★★★ *The MLA Guide To The Job Search*   55

★★★★ *On The Market*   22

★★★★ *The Performing Arts Major's College Guide*   66

★★★★ *Real Guide To Grad School*   50

★★★★ *Surviving Graduate School Part Time*   24

★★★ *The Academic Job Search Handbook*   26

★★★ *The African American Student's Guide To Surviving Graduate School*   25

★★★ *American Psychological Association: Student Information/Education Programs*   60

★★★ *Careers In Science And Engineering*   70

★★★ *Embark.com: Going To Graduate School*   27

★★★ *The Gay, Lesbian, & Bisexual Students' Guide To Colleges, Universities, And Graduate Schools*   35

★★★ *The Grad School Handbook*   28

★★★ *Graduate School*   29

★★★ *Graduate Student Resources On The Web*   30

★★★ *The Guide To Graduate Environmental Programs*   81

★★★ *Peterson's Computer Science & Electrical Engineering Programs*   71

★★★ *Peterson's Graduate Studies In Biology, Health, & Agricultural Sciences*   72

★★★ *Petersons.com: The Graduate School Channel*   31

★★★ *A Ph.D. Is Not Enough!*   69

★★★ *The Ph.D. Process*   73

★★★ *Princeton Review Best Graduate Programs: Engineering*   74

★★★ *Princeton Review Best Graduate Programs: Physical & Biological Sciences*   75

★★★ *Tomorrow's Professor*   76

★★★ *U.S. News Online: Graduate School*   32

★★★ *U.S. News & World Report: Best Graduate Schools*   33

★★★ *The Ultimate Grad School Survival Guide*   34

★★★ *The Women's Guide To Surviving Graduate School*   36

★★ *Allyn & Bacon Guide To Master's Programs In Psychology & Counseling Psychology*   63

★★ *Association For Support Of Graduate Students*   41

★★ *Completing Graduate School Long Distance*   42

★★ *GradSchools.Com*   43

★★ *Graduate Student Advice & Research Survival Guide*   38

★★ *GRE Online*   39

★★ *Guide To American Graduate Schools*   46

★★ *Guide To Selecting & Applying To Master Of Social Work Programs (1999)*   61

★★ *Kaplan Online: Grad School*   37

★★ *Kaplan/Newsweek Graduate School Admissions Adviser 2000*   44

★★ *Making A Difference College Guide*   82

★★ *Ms. Mentor's Impeccable Advice For Women In Academia*   45

★★ *Peterson's Compact Guides: Graduate Studies In Education*   53

★★ *Peterson's Compact Guides: Graduate Studies In Engineering, Computer Science & Information Studies 1998*   77

★★ *Peterson's Graduate Studies In Arts, Humanities, & Archaeology 1998*   51

★★ *Peterson's Graduate Studies In Social Sciences & Social Work 1998*   62

★★ *Peterson's Professional Degree Programs In The Visual & Performing Arts*   67

★★ *Princeton Review Best Distance Learning Graduate Schools*   40

★★ *Princeton Review Best Graduate Programs: Humanities & Social Sciences*   52

★ *The Complete Guide To American Film Schools*   68

★ *Getting In: An Applicant's Guide To Graduate School Admissions*   48

★ *Insider's Guide To Graduate Programs In Education*   54

★ *The Official GRE/CGS Directory Of Graduate Programs*   78

★ *Peterson's Guide To Distance Learning Programs 1999*   49

★ *Preparing For Graduate Study In Psychology*   64

★ *Princeton Review Online: Graduate*   47

N/R *Council Of Graduate Schools: Student Page*   83

Business School

★★★★ Business Week Online's Business Schools   90

★★★★ Business Week's Guide To The Best Business Schools   91

★★★★ Embark.com: Going To Business School   95

★★★★ How To Get Into The Top MBA Programs   92

★★★★ Marketing Yourself To The Top Ten Business Schools   93

★★★★ Peterson's Guide To MBA Programs 1999   94

★★★★ Petersons.com: The MBA Channel   96

★★★ Arco's Best Graduate Business Schools   109

★★★ Arco's Getting Into Graduate Business School Today   100

★★★ Barron's Guide To Graduate Business Schools   101

★★★ The Complete MBA Companion   102

★★★ Essays That Worked For Business Schools   98

★★★ Guide To Graduate Management Programs In The USA, 1999   103

★★★ How To Get Into The Right Business School   104

★★★ MBA Info   105

★★★ MBA Plaza   106

★★★ Princeton Review Best 75 Business Schools   107

★★★ Princeton Review Online: Business   110

★★★ Snapshots From Hell   99

★★★ U.S. News Online: Business   97

★★★ Which MBA?   108

★★ GMAT Online: MBA Explorer   113

★★ Kaplan Online: Business   111

★★ Kaplan's Getting Into Business School (1999 Edition)   114

★★ The MBA Page   115

★★ Peterson's 1999 MBA Distance Learning Programs   112

★★ Peterson's Graduate Programs In Business, Education, Health, Information Studies, Law & Social Work   116

★★ The Princeton Review Business School Companion   117

★★ Year One   118

★ Kaplan's Insider's Book Of Business School Lists   119

★ The Official GRE/CGS Directory Of Graduate Programs   120

N/R Bschool.com   121

N/R FINAID: Business School Resources   121

N/R GradAdvantage   121

N/R Top Ten   122

Law School

★★★★ Boston College Online Law School Locator   130

★★★★ Embark.com: Going To Law School   138

★★★★ FindLaw   131

★★★★ From Here To Attorney   132

★★★★ How To Get Into The Right Law School   133

★★★★ Internet Legal Resource Guide   139

★★★★ Looking At Law School   134

★★★★ The Official Guide To U.S. Law Schools 2000   135

★★★★ Princeton Review Best Law Schools 2000   143

★★★★ The Princeton Review Prelaw Companion   136

★★★★ Thinking About Law School   137

★★★★ A Woman's Guide To Law School   142

★★★ American Bar Association Guide To Approved Law Schools   145

★★★ Barron's Guide To Law Schools   146

★★★ Barron's How To Succeed In Law School   147

★★★ Beyond L.A. Law   148

★★★ The Complete Law School Companion   149

★★★ How To Get Into Harvard Law School   140

★★★ Inside The Law Schools   155

★★★ Kaplan Online: Law   150

★★★ Law School Admissions Council Online   156

★★★ Law School Basics   151

★★★ National Association For Law Placement   152

★★★ One L   153

★★★ Petersons.com: The Law Channel   154

★★★ Princeton Review Online: Law School   157

★★★ So You Want To Be A Lawyer   141

★★★ U.S. News Online: Law   144

★★ Arco's Getting Into Law School Today   158

★★ Arco's Law School Survival   162

★★ The Eight Secrets Of Top Exam Performance In Law School   163

★★ Going To Law School?   164

★★ Kaplan Newsweek Law School Admissions Advisor   160

★★ Law School Without Fear   165

★★ Learning The Law   166

★★ The Penguin Guide To American Law Schools   159

★★ REA's Authoritative Guide To Law Schools   161

★★ Slaying The Law School Dragon   167

★ The Insider's Book Of Law School Lists   171

★ Peterson's Graduate Programs In Business, Education, Health, Information Studies, Law & Social Work   168

★ Planet Law School   169

V. Indices

★ *The Princeton Review Law School Companion* 170

N/R *American Bar Association Approved Law Schools (Internet)* 172

N/R *FINAID: Law School Resources* 172

Medical School & Health Science Programs

★★★★ *Association Of American Medical Colleges* 189

★★★★ *Barron's Getting Into Medical School* 184

★★★★ *Getting Into Medical School* 190

★★★★ *Guide To Medical School & The MCAT* 185

★★★★ *The Interactive Medical Student Lounge* 191

★★★★ *Medical School Admission Requirements* 186

★★★★ *Medical School Admissions* 187

★★★★ *Osteopathic.Com* 192

★★★★ *U.S. News Online: Medicine* 188

★★★ *American Association Of Colleges Of Osteopathic Medicine* 196

★★★ *Arco's Getting Into Medical School Today* 158

★★★ *Barron's Essays That Will Get You Into Medical School* 193

★★★ *Barron's Guide To Medical & Dental Schools* 197

★★★ *Becoming A Doctor* 198

★★★ *Get Into Medical School!* 199

★★★ *Medical School* 194

★★★ *Peterson's Guide To Nursing Programs* 195

★★★ *Peterson's Insider's Guide To Medical Schools, 1999* 200

★★★ *Veterinary Medical School Admission Requirements In The United States And Canada* 202

★★ *Applying To Medical School For The Non-Traditional Student* 208

★★ *Becoming A Physician* 209

★★ *From Residency To Reality* 203

★★ *How To Get Into The Right Dental School* 210

★★ *How To Get Into The Right Medical School* 211

★★ *The Insider's Guide To Medical School Admissions* 212

★★ *Kaplan Online: Medicine* 204

★★ *Kaplan's Getting Into Medical School* 213

★★ *NursingNet* 214

★★ *The Penguin Guide To American Medical & Dental Schools* 215

★★ *Peterson's Graduate Programs In Business, Education, Health, Information Studies, Law & Social Work* 216

★★ *Peterson's U.S. & Canadian Medical Schools* 205

★★ *The Princeton Review Medical School Companion* 206

★★ *Princeton Review Online: Medicine* 217

★★ *REA's Authoritative Guide To Medical & Dental Schools* 207

★ *The Complete Guide To Foreign Medical Schools In Plain English* 218

★ *Kaplan's Insider's Book Of Medical School Lists* 220

★ *Medical School Admissions Success!* 223

★ *MedicalStudent.net* 221

★ *Petersons.com: Medical Schools* 219

★ *Princeton Review Best Medical Schools 2000* 222

N/R *AACOMAS Application Kit* 224

N/R *AMCAS-E Student & Applicant Information* 224

N/R *FINAID: Medical School Resources* 224

N/R *The Mature Medical Student* 225

N/R *The Medical Education Page* 225

N/R *Premedical Student Forum* 225

Financing A Graduate Or Professional Degree

★★★★ *Don't Miss Out* 231

★★★★ *eStudentLoan.com* 232

★★★★ *FINAID: Graduate School Financial Aid Resources* 233

★★★★ *Financing Graduate School* 234

★★★★ *Free Application For Federal Student Aid (FAFSA) Online* 235

★★★★ *The Guerrilla Guide To Mastering Student Debt* 236

★★★★ *Take Control Of Your Student Loans* 237

★★★ *Access Group* 240

★★★ *Arco's Ten Minute Guide To Paying For Graduate School* 238

★★★ *College Financial Aid Made Easy* 241

★★★ *Direct Loan* 242

★★★ *Earn & Learn* 243

★★★ *Guide To Defaulted Student Loans* 239

★★★ *Sallie Mae: Student Loan Marketing Association* 244

★★ *Getting Yours: The Complete Guide To Government Money* 249

★★ *The Government Financial Aid Book* 245

★★ *How To Cut Tuition* 250

★★ *Kaplan Online: Financial Aid* 246

★★ *Loans & Grants From Uncle Sam* 247

★★ *National Association Of Student Financial Aid Administrators: Planning For College* 248

N/R *The Alliance To Save Student Aid* 251

N/R *Educaid Loan Programs: Loans For Graduate Students* 251

N/R *Guide To Completing The 1999–2000 Free Application For Federal Student Aid (FAFSA)* 251

N/R *National Science Foundation Grad Student Page* 252
N/R *Nellie Mae* 252

Scholarship Directories & Search Services

★★★★ *Directory Of Financial Aids For Women 1999–2001* 256
★★★★ *FastWEB* 257
★★★★ *Financial Aid For African Americans 1999–2001* 258
★★★★ *Financial Aid For Study & Training Abroad 1999–2001* 259
★★★★ *Financial Aid For The Disabled & Their Families 1998–2000* 260
★★★★ *Funding For United States Study* 261
★★★★ *Graduate Student's Complete Scholarship Book* 265
★★★★ *Peterson's Grants For Graduate & Postdoctoral Study* 262
★★★★ *Scholarships & Fellowships For Math & Science Students* 263
★★★★ *Yale Daily News Guide To Fellowships & Grants* 264
★★★ *American Journalism Review Newslink* 273
★★★ *CollegeNET MACH25 Scholarship Search* 274
★★★ *Directory Of Private Scholarships & Grants* 269
★★★ *The Financial Aid Book* 275
★★★ *Financial Aid For Research & Creative Activities Abroad 1999–2001* 270
★★★ *Financial Aid For Veterans, Military Personnel & Their Dependents 1998–2000* 271
★★★ *Financial Resources For International Study* 266
★★★ *Money For Graduate Students In The Humanities 1996–98* 272
★★★ *Money For Graduate Students In The Sciences 1998–2000* 268
★★★ *Money For Graduate Students In The Social Sciences 1998–2000* 267
★★★ *Scholarships, Fellowships & Financial Support For Jewish College Students* 277
★★★ *Scholarships & Loans For Nursing Education 1997–1998* 276
★★ *The College Board Scholarship Handbook* 280
★★ *The Complete Scholarship Book* 281
★★ *Financial Aid For Minorities (Series)* 284
★★ *Free Money For Graduate School* 278
★★ *The Graduate School Funding Handbook* 285
★★ *The Minority & Women's Complete Scholarship Book* 282
★★ *MOLIS: Minority Online Information Service* 283
★★ *Princeton Review Scholarship Advisor 1999* 279
★★ *The Scholarship Resource Network* 286

★ *Dollars for College (Series)* 287
★ *Worldwide Graduate Scholarship Directory* 288
N/R *American Association Of University Women Educational Foundation Fellowships & Grants* 289
N/R *American Chemical Society Minority Affairs* 289
N/R *Federal Trade Commission Scholarship Scam Alert* 289
N/R *ONElist* 290
N/R *Saludos Web Education Center* 290
N/R *Scholarships For Women & Minorities 1998* 290
N/R *UCI Scholarship Opportunities Program* 291

Of General Interest

★★★★ *Access America's Guide To Studying In The USA* 293
★★★ *Apply To American Colleges & Universities* 296
★★★ *The College Board Index Of Majors & Graduate Degrees 2000* 298
★★★ *eduPASS* 297
★★★ *Graduate Admissions Essays* 294
★★★ *National Association Of Graduate-Professional Students* 301
★★★ *Office Of Postsecondary Education Home Page* 295
★★★ *Peterson's Graduate & Professional Programs* 299
★★★ *Princeton Review International Students' Guide To The USA* 300
★★ *Accepted.com* 303
★★ *AmeriCorps Home Page* 304
★★ *Arco's Perfect Personal Statements* 305
★★ *College Board Online* 306
★★ *College & University Home Pages* 307
★★ *How To Write A Winning Personal Statement For Graduate & Professional School* 302
★★ *Peterson's Graduate Schools In The U.S.* 308
★★ *Study In The USA* 309
★ *AmeriCorps: Serve Your Country & Pay For College* 311
★ *The College Board International Student Handbook Of U.S. Colleges* 312
★ *The Gourman Report* 313
★ *International Education Service* 314
★ *PowerStudents.com Grad School* 310
N/R *American Universities* 315
N/R *CollegeNET* 315
N/R *General Education Online* 315
N/R *Information USA: Education In The USA* 316
N/R *Test Of English As A Foreign Language (TOEFL)* 316
N/R *U.S. Education Journal* 316

V. Indices

INDEX OF RESOURCES OF INTEREST TO SPECIFIC AUDIENCES

Of Interest To Persons Of Color

Obtaining A Master's Or PhD

★★★★ Getting What You Came For   21

★★★ The African American Student's Guide To Surviving Graduate School   25

★★ Kaplan/Newsweek Graduate School Admissions Adviser 2000   44

Law School

★★★★ How To Get Into The Right Law School   133

★★★★ Looking At Law School   134

★★★★ The Official Guide To U.S. Law Schools 2000   315

★★★★ Princeton Review Best Law Schools 2000   143

★★★★ Thinking About Law School   137

★★★ Beyond L.A. Law   148

★★★ How To Get Into Harvard Law School   140

★★★ Law School Admissions Council Online   156

★★★ National Association For Law Placement   152

★★ Arco's Law School Survival   162

Medical School & Health Sciences

★★★★ Association Of American Medical Colleges   189

★★★★ Getting Into Medical School   190

★★★ Arco's Getting Into Medical School Today   158

★★★ Barron's Guide To Medical & Dental Schools   197

★★★ Get Into Medical School!   199

★★ How To Get Into The Right Medical School   211

Financing A Graduate Or Professional Degree

★★★★ Don't Miss Out   231

★★★★ Financing Graduate School   234

★★★ Arco's Ten Minute Guide To Paying For Graduate School   238

N/R National Science Foundation Grad Student Page   252

Scholarship Directories & Search Services

★★★★ Financial Aid For African Americans 1999–2001   258

★★ Financial Aid For Minorities (Series)   284

★★ The Minority & Women's Complete Scholarship Book   282

★★ MOLIS: Minority Online Information Service   283

N/R American Chemical Society Minority Affairs   289

N/R Saludos Web Education Center   290

N/R Scholarships For Women & Minorities 1998   290

N/R UCI Scholarship Opportunities Program   291

Of Interest To Women

Obtaining A Master's Or PhD

★★★★ Getting What You Came For   21

★★★★ Lifting A Ton Of Feathers   23

★★★ The Women's Guide To Surviving Graduate School   36

★★ Kaplan/Newsweek Graduate School Admissions Adviser 2000   44

★★ Ms. Mentor's Impeccable Advice For Women In Academia   45

Law School

★★★★ How To Get Into The Right Law School   133

★★★★ Looking At Law School   134

★★★★ Princeton Review Best Law Schools 2000   143

★★★★ A Woman's Guide To Law School   142

★★★ Beyond L.A. Law   148

★★★ National Association For Law Placement   152

Medical School & Health Sciences

★★★★ Association Of American Medical Colleges   189

★★★ Arco's Getting Into Medical School Today   201

★★★ Barron's Guide To Medical & Dental Schools   197

★★★ Get Into Medical School!   199

★★ Applying To Medical School For The Non-Traditional Student   208

★★ How To Get Into The Right Medical School   211

Financing A Graduate Or Professional Degree

★★★★ Don't Miss Out   231

★★★★ FINAID: Graduate School Financial Aid Resources   233

★★★★ Financing Graduate School   234

★★★ Arco's Ten Minute Guide To Paying For Graduate School   238

Scholarship Directories & Search Services

★★★★ Directory Of Financial Aids For Women 1999–2001   256

★★ The Minority & Women's Complete Scholarship Book   282

★ Dollars for College (Series)   287

N/R American Association Of University Women Educational Foundation Fellowships & Grants   289

N/R Scholarships For Women & Minorities 1998   290

Of Interest To International Students

Obtaining A Master's Or PhD

★★★★ Getting What You Came For   21

★★★ Petersons.com: The Graduate School Channel   31

★★★ The Ph.D. Process   73

★★ Kaplan/Newsweek Graduate School Admissions Adviser 2000   44

Business School

★★★★ Petersons.com: The MBA Channel   96

★★★ Guide To Graduate Management Programs In The USA, 1999   103

★★★ Which MBA?   108

★★ GMAT Online: MBA Explorer   113

Medical School & Health Sciences

★★★ Get Into Medical School!   199

★★ Kaplan's Getting Into Medical School   213

Financing A Graduate Or Professional Degree

★★★★ eStudentLoan.com   232

★★★★ Financing Graduate School   234

★★★ Arco's Ten Minute Guide To Paying For Graduate School   238

Scholarship Directories & Search Services

★★★★ Funding For United States Study   261

General Interest

★★★★ Access America's Guide To Studying In The USA   293

★★★ Apply To American Colleges & Universities   296

★★★ eduPASS   297

★★★ Princeton Review International Students' Guide To The USA   300

★★ Study In The USA   309

★ The College Board International Student Handbook Of U.S. Colleges   312

★ International Education Service   314

N/R Information USA: Education In The USA   316

N/R Test Of English As A Foreign Language (TOEFL)   316

N/R U.S. Education Journal   316

Of Interest To Disabled Students

Obtaining A Master's Or PhD

★★ Kaplan/Newsweek Graduate School Admissions Adviser 2000   44

Law School

★★★★ How To Get Into The Right Law School   133

Medical School & Health Sciences

★★★ Get Into Medical School!   199

Financing A Graduate Or Professional Degree

★★★ Arco's Ten Minute Guide To Paying For Graduate School   238

Scholarship Directories & Search Services

★★★★ Financial Aid For The Disabled & Their Families 1998–2000   260

★ Dollars for College (Series)   287

V. Indices

ABOUT THE EDITOR

Jane Finkle, MS, is the Associate Director of Career Services at the University of Pennsylvania. She is an advisor for *U.S. News and World Report*'s "Answer Zone" on the World Wide Web and served as member of the Executive Board of the Northeast Association of Pre-Law Advisors (NAPLA) in 1997–98. The focus of her counseling (13-plus years) has been in higher education. For the past nine years, she has advised both students and alumni applying to graduate programs in a wide variety of fields and disciplines. Jane is currently an adjunct faculty at Chestnut Hill College and, since 1989, has taught a Career Evaluation Course at the University of Pennsylvania's College of General Studies for professionals at all stages of their career development. Before coming to Penn, she was a Program Coordinator at the Rochester Institute of Technology's Office of Cooperative Education where she counseled students in the School of Photographic Arts and Imaging Science on career-related issues.

ABOUT THE ADVISORY COUNCIL

Martina J. Bryant, EdD, is Associate Dean at Duke University and Adjunct Associate Professor in the University's Program in Education. She is also director of the Early Childhood Education Studies Program, a certificate program offered through the Program in Education. Prior to coming to Duke in 1977, she was on the faculty at Delaware State University. She received a BS from Hampton University, a MEd from Florida A&M University, and an EdD from the University of Georgia. Among her responsibilities at Duke is serving as prebusiness advisor. In this capacity, she provides Duke students and alumni information and materials relating to graduate business schools. She also works with students as they plan their course of study for a career in business.

Linda Cades, PhD, is the Director of Career Development at Washington College in Chestertown, Maryland, where she has assisted students with career planning since 1984. She has also served as a Prelaw Advisor and as a member of the Premedical committee and assists students with graduate school planning. She holds a BA from Washington College in French Literature and Masters and PhD degrees from the University of Maryland in English and American Literature.

Mary Hanneman, PhD, earned her doctorate in Japanese history at the University of Washington in 1991 and is a visiting assistant professor at the University of Washington, Tacoma, where she teaches Asian history. She is the co-founder and assistant director of the Pacific Rim Center at UW-Tacoma, which sponsors a variety of activities associated with East Asia. The author of several articles and numerous book reviews, she recently completed a textbook on modern Japan for Addison-Wesley-Longman. She is now working on a book about Vietnamese immigrants in Washington State. Mary holds a BA in East Asian Studies from Western Washington University and an MA in East Asian Studies from Yale University.

Larry Knopp, PhD, is Professor and Head of Geography at the University of Minnesota-Duluth, where he is also Director of the Center for Community and Regional Research and Coordinator of Urban and Regional Studies. In addition, Larry is a University of Minnesota McKnight Land-Grant Professor, Adjunct Professor of Geography at the University of Minnesota-Twin Cities. He also serves as North American Book Review Editor for *Gender, Place and Culture: A Journal of Feminist Geography.* Larry earned a BA in Political Science from the University of Washington in 1983, and MA and PhD degrees in Geography from the University of Iowa in 1985 and 1989, respectively.

Lauren Pound Somers is a part-time graduate student and the owner of Communications Support, a service designed to assist communications professionals with writing, editing, research and project management needs. A board member of the Philadelphia Public Relations Association, Somers has ten years of experience in communications with a background in professional services marketing and public relations for trade associations and government. She holds a bachelor's degree in journalism/public relations from Temple University, where she has served as an adjunct professor and is completing her Master of Journalism degree.

Heather Struck, JD, has been the Pre-Law Advisor at Binghamton University since 1995. She is responsible for advising students and graduates who plan to attend law school. She also serves on the Academic Honesty Committee. A member of the Executive Board of Northeast Association of Pre-Law Advisors, Heather has been an active participant in the planning of the annual NAPLA conferences and has chaired various conference programs. A graduate of the University of Michigan (BA), and George Washington University Law School (JD), she also worked as a staff attorney for the National Oceanic and Atmospheric Administration and for the Environmental Protection Agency in Washington, DC.

GUIDEBOOKS FOR LIFE'S BIG DECISIONS

For every important issue we face, there are resources that offer suggestions and help. Unfortunately, we don't always know much about the issue we've enountered and we don't know:

- Where to find these sources of information

- Much about their quality, value, or relevance

Resource Pathways guidebooks help those facing an important decision or challenging life-event by directing them to the information they need to understand the issues they face and make decisions with confidence. In every Resource Pathways guidebook:

- We **describe and evaluate virtually all quality resources** available in any media (books, the Internet, CD-ROMs, videotape, audiotape, and more).

- We **explain the issues** that are typically encountered in dealing with each subject, and **classify each resource** reviewed according to its primary focus.

- We **make a reasoned judgment** about the quality of each resource, give it a **rating**, and decide whether it should be **recommended**. We select only the best as "Recommended" (roughly 1 in 4).

- We **provide information on where to buy or how to access** each resource, including ISBN numbers for books and URL "addresses" for Internet websites.

- We **publish a new edition of each guidebook frequently**, with updated reviews and recommendations.

Those who turn to Resource Pathways guidebooks will be able to locate the resource they need, saving time, money, and frustration as they begin their research and learning process.

LIFECYCLES SERIES

- *"...a calm and hope-filled guide..."*

  Anxiety & Depression: The Best Resources To Help You Cope

  Editor: Rich Wemhoff, PhD
  ISBN: 1-892148-09-9 (2nd Ed); 292 Pages

- *"...an invaluable tool for couples and therapists..."*

  Marriage: The Best Resources To Help Yours Thrive

  Editor: Rich Wemhoff, PhD
  ISBN: 1-892148-05-6; 244 Pages

- *"...positive, user-friendly guidebook..."*

  Divorce: The Best Resources To Help You Survive

  Editor: Rich Wemhoff, PhD
  ISBN: 1-892148-00-5 (2nd Ed); 324 Pages

- *"...like advice from a wise and caring friend..."*

  Eldercare: The Best Resources To Help You Help Your Aging Relatives

  Editor: Marty Richards, MSW, ACSW
  ISBN: 1-892148-07-2; 256 Pages

PARENTING SERIES

- *"...well-organized, easy-to-read, and to-the-point."*

  Having Children: The Best Resources To Help You Prepare

  Editor: Anne Montgomery, MD, IBCLC, FAAFP
  ISBN: 1-892148-06-4 (2nd Ed); 312 Pages

- *"...a practical guide through the often dense forest of parenting information..."*

  Infants & Toddlers: The Best Resources To Help You Parent

  Editor: Julie Soto, MS
  ISBN: 1-892148-10-2 (2nd Ed); 372 Pages

- *"...an incredible resource guide..."*

  Raising Teenagers: The Best Resources To Help Yours Succeed

  Editor: John Ganz, MC, EdD
  ISBN: 1-892148-04-8; 262 Pages

- Stepparenting: The Best Resources To Help Blend Your Family

  Editor: Patricia W. Stephens, PhD
  ISBN: 1-892148-13-7; 256 Pages
  Available: March 2000

HIGHER EDUCATION & CAREERS SERIES

■ *". . . quintessential guide to the guides . . ."*

College Choice & Admissions: The Best Resources To Help You Get In

Editor: Dodge Johnson, PhD
ISBN: 0-9653424-9-2 (3rd Ed); 336 Pages

■ *". . . comprehensive . . . a real time and money saver . . ."*

College Financial Aid: The Best Resources To Help You Find The Money

Editor: David Hoy
ISBN: 1-892148-01-3 (3rd Ed); 222 Pages

■ *". . . thorough, honest, and complete . . ."*

Graduate School: The Best Resources To Help You Choose, Get In, & Pay

Editor: Jane Finkle, MS
ISBN: 1-892148-11-0 (2nd Ed); 278 Pages
Available: February 2000

■ *". . . a clear and concise roadmap . . ."*

Starting Your Career: The Best Resources To Help You Find The Right Job

Editor: Laura Praglin, PhD
ISBN: 1-892148-03-X; 248 Pages

■ *"Great resources gathered with an eye for the practical . . ."*

Career Transitions: The Best Resources To Help You Advance

Editor: David Goodenough, MS, CMHS
ISBN: 1-892148-08-0; 268 Pages

■ *". . . a tremendous time saver . . . a must read."*

Going Solo: The Best Resources For Entrepreneurs & Freelancers

Editor: Stanley I. Mason, Jr.
ISBN: 1-892148-12-9; 268 Pages

Your favorite bookstore or library may order any of these guidebooks for you, or you can order direct, using the pre-paid postcards on the following pages.

ORDERING INFORMATION

Order by phone: 888-702-8882 (Toll-free 24/7)
Order by fax: 425-557-4366
Order by mail: Resource Pathways, Inc.
22525 SE 64th Place, Suite 253
Issaquah, WA 98027-5387

ORDER FORM

Order by phone: 888-702-8882 (Toll-free 24/7)
Order by fax: 425-557-4366

Order by mail: Resource Pathways, Inc.
22525 SE 64th Place, Suite 253
Issaquah, WA 98027-5387

☐ *Anxiety & Depression:* The Best Resources To Help You Cope
☐ *Marriage:* The Best Resources To Help Yours Thrive
☐ *Divorce:* The Best Resources To Help You Survive
☐ *Eldercare:* The Best Resources To Help You Help Your Aging Relatives

☐ *Having Children:* The Best Resources To Help You Prepare
☐ *Infants & Toddlers:* The Best Resources To Help You Parent
☐ *Raising Teenagers:* The Best Resources To Help Yours Succeed
☐ *Stepparenting:* The Best Resources To Help Blend Your Family

☐ *College Choice & Admissions:* The Best Resources To Help You Get In
☐ *College Financial Aid:* The Best Resources To Help You Find The Money
☐ *Graduate School:* The Best Resources To Help You Choose, Get In, & Pay
☐ *Starting Your Career:* The Best Resources To Help You Find The Right Job
☐ *Career Transitions:* The Best Resources To Help You Advance
☐ *Going Solo:* The Best Resources For Entrepreneurs & Freelancers

Shipping (USPS Priority Mail): $3.95 for first copy; $2.00/copy for additional copies
We will include an invoice with your shipment

_____ copies at $24.95 = _____
\+ Shipping & Handling = _____
Total = _____

Name (please print) _____

Organization _____ Title _____

Address _____

City _____ State _____ Zip _____

Phone _____ Email _____

ORDER FORM

Order by phone: 888-702-8882 (Toll-free 24/7)
Order by fax: 425-557-4366

Order by mail: Resource Pathways, Inc.
22525 SE 64th Place, Suite 253
Issaquah, WA 98027-5387

☐ *Anxiety & Depression:* The Best Resources To Help You Cope
☐ *Marriage:* The Best Resources To Help Yours Thrive
☐ *Divorce:* The Best Resources To Help You Survive
☐ *Eldercare:* The Best Resources To Help You Help Your Aging Relatives

☐ *Having Children:* The Best Resources To Help You Prepare
☐ *Infants & Toddlers:* The Best Resources To Help You Parent
☐ *Raising Teenagers:* The Best Resources To Help Yours Succeed
☐ *Stepparenting:* The Best Resources To Help Blend Your Family

☐ *College Choice & Admissions:* The Best Resources To Help You Get In
☐ *College Financial Aid:* The Best Resources To Help You Find The Money
☐ *Graduate School:* The Best Resources To Help You Choose, Get In, & Pay
☐ *Starting Your Career:* The Best Resources To Help You Find The Right Job
☐ *Career Transitions:* The Best Resources To Help You Advance
☐ *Going Solo:* The Best Resources For Entrepreneurs & Freelancers

Shipping (USPS Priority Mail): $3.95 for first copy; $2.00/copy for additional copies
We will include an invoice with your shipment

_____ copies at $24.95 = _____
\+ Shipping & Handling = _____
Total = _____

Name (please print) _____

Organization _____ Title _____

Address _____

City _____ State _____ Zip _____

Phone _____ Email _____

BUSINESS REPLY MAIL

FIRST-CLASS MAIL   PERMIT NO. 176   ISSAQUAH, WA

POSTAGE WILL BE PAID BY ADDRESSEE

RESOURCE PATHWAYS INC.

22525 SE 64TH PL STE 253

ISSAQUAH WA 98027-9939

NO POSTAGE
NECESSARY
IF MAILED
IN THE
UNITED STATES

BUSINESS REPLY MAIL

FIRST-CLASS MAIL   PERMIT NO. 176   ISSAQUAH, WA

POSTAGE WILL BE PAID BY ADDRESSEE

RESOURCE PATHWAYS INC.

22525 SE 64TH PL STE 253

ISSAQUAH WA 98027-9939

DISCOUNTS AND SUBSCRIPTIONS FOR PROFESSIONALS

Do you provide professional services to adults or families affected by one of the life-events outlined in a Resource Pathways' guidebook?

If so, you should know that Resource Pathways offers very attractive discounts to professionals for subscriptions to current and new editions of any title.

To obtain additional information or place an order, complete and return this postcard, or call 425-557-4382 (8-6 PST), or 888-702-8882 (Toll-free 24/7).

Name (please print) _____

Organization _____ Title _____

Address _____

City _____ State _____ Zip _____

Phone _____ Email _____

DISCOUNTS AND STANDING ORDERS FOR LIBRARIES

Resource Pathways' titles are distributed to libraries throughout North America by the National Book Network, through Ingram, Baker & Taylor, and many other regional wholesalers.

You can order any of our titles through your usual wholesaler or distributor, or direct from the National Book Network:

**National Book Network, Inc., 15200 NBN Way, Blue Ridge Summit, PA 17214
800-462-6420 / 800-338-4550 (fax)**

You can order directly from Resource Pathways at very attractive discounts, for both individual and standing orders.

To obtain additional information or place an order, complete and return this postcard, or call 425-557-4382 (8-6 PST), or 888-702-8882 (Toll-free 24/7).

Name (please print) _____

Organization _____ Title _____

Address _____

City _____ State _____ Zip _____

Phone _____ Email _____

NO POSTAGE
NECESSARY
IF MAILED
IN THE
UNITED STATES

BUSINESS REPLY MAIL

FIRST-CLASS MAIL   PERMIT NO. 176   ISSAQUAH, WA

POSTAGE WILL BE PAID BY ADDRESSEE

RESOURCE PATHWAYS INC.

22525 SE 64TH PL STE 253

ISSAQUAH WA 98027-9811

NO POSTAGE
NECESSARY
IF MAILED
IN THE
UNITED STATES

BUSINESS REPLY MAIL

FIRST-CLASS MAIL   PERMIT NO. 176   ISSAQUAH, WA

POSTAGE WILL BE PAID BY ADDRESSEE

RESOURCE PATHWAYS INC.

22525 SE 64TH PL STE 253

ISSAQUAH WA 98027-9811